PREACHER™
Dixie Fried

Featuring
CASSIDY: BLOOD & WHISKEY
A Tale from the Good Ol' Days

GARTH ENNIS
Writer

STEVE DILLON
Artist

MATT HOLLINGSWORTH
PAMELA RAMBO
JAMES SINCLAIR
Colorists

CLEM ROBINS
Letterer

GLENN FABRY
Original Covers

PREACHER
created by
Garth Ennis and Steve Dillon

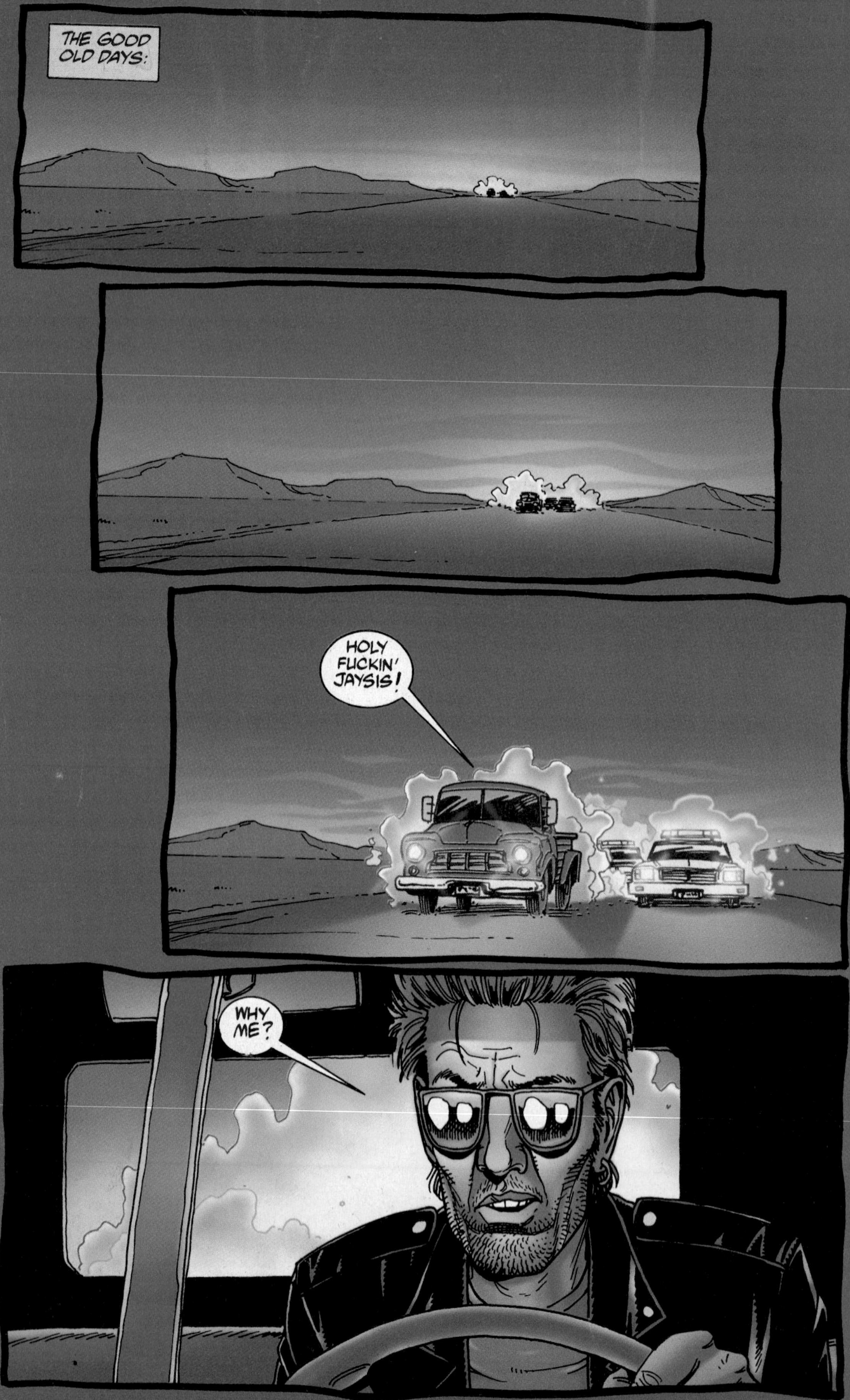
THE GOOD OLD DAYS:
HOLY FUCKIN' JAYSIS!
WHY ME?

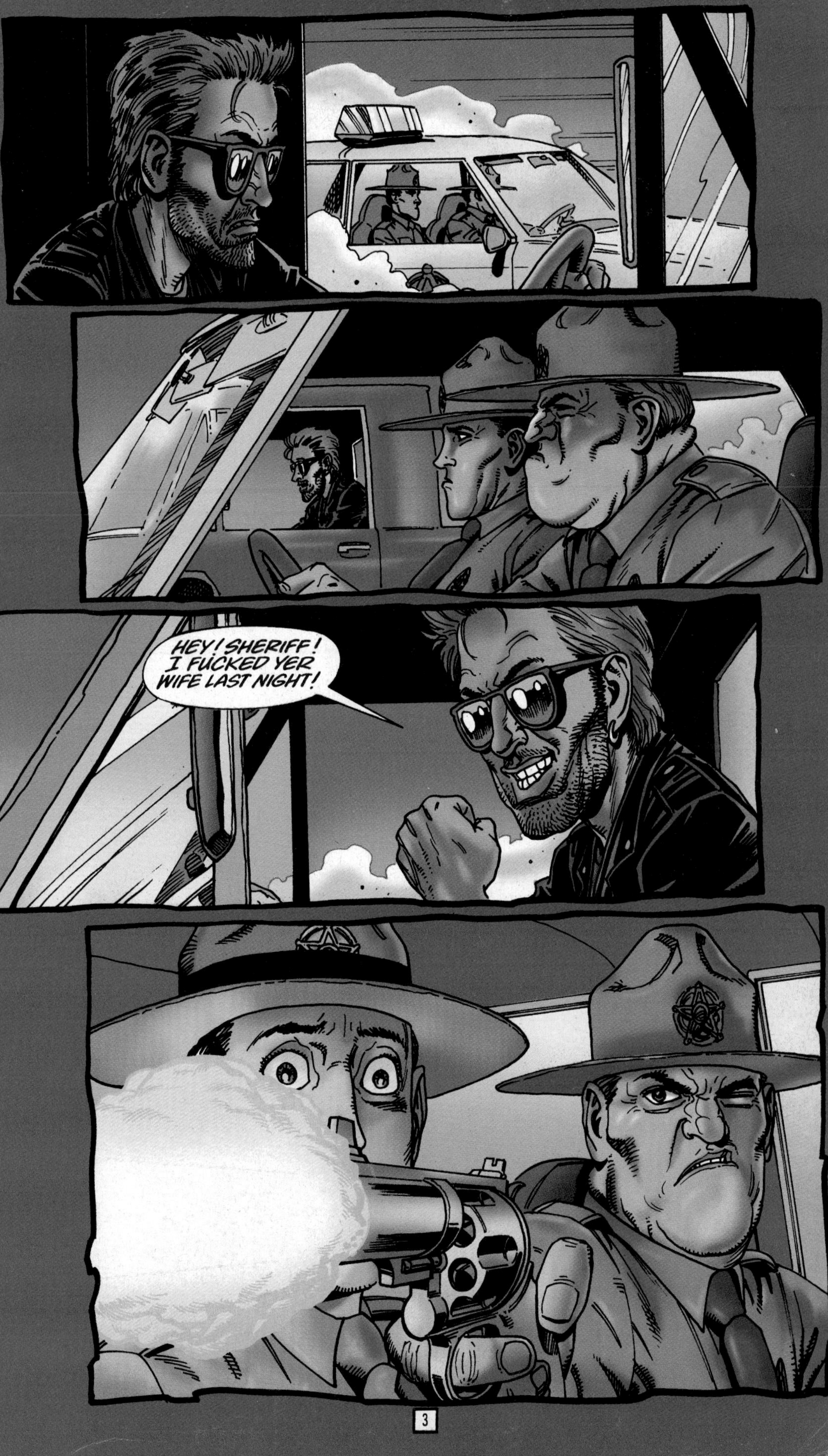
HEY! SHERIFF! I FUCKED YER WIFE LAST NIGHT!

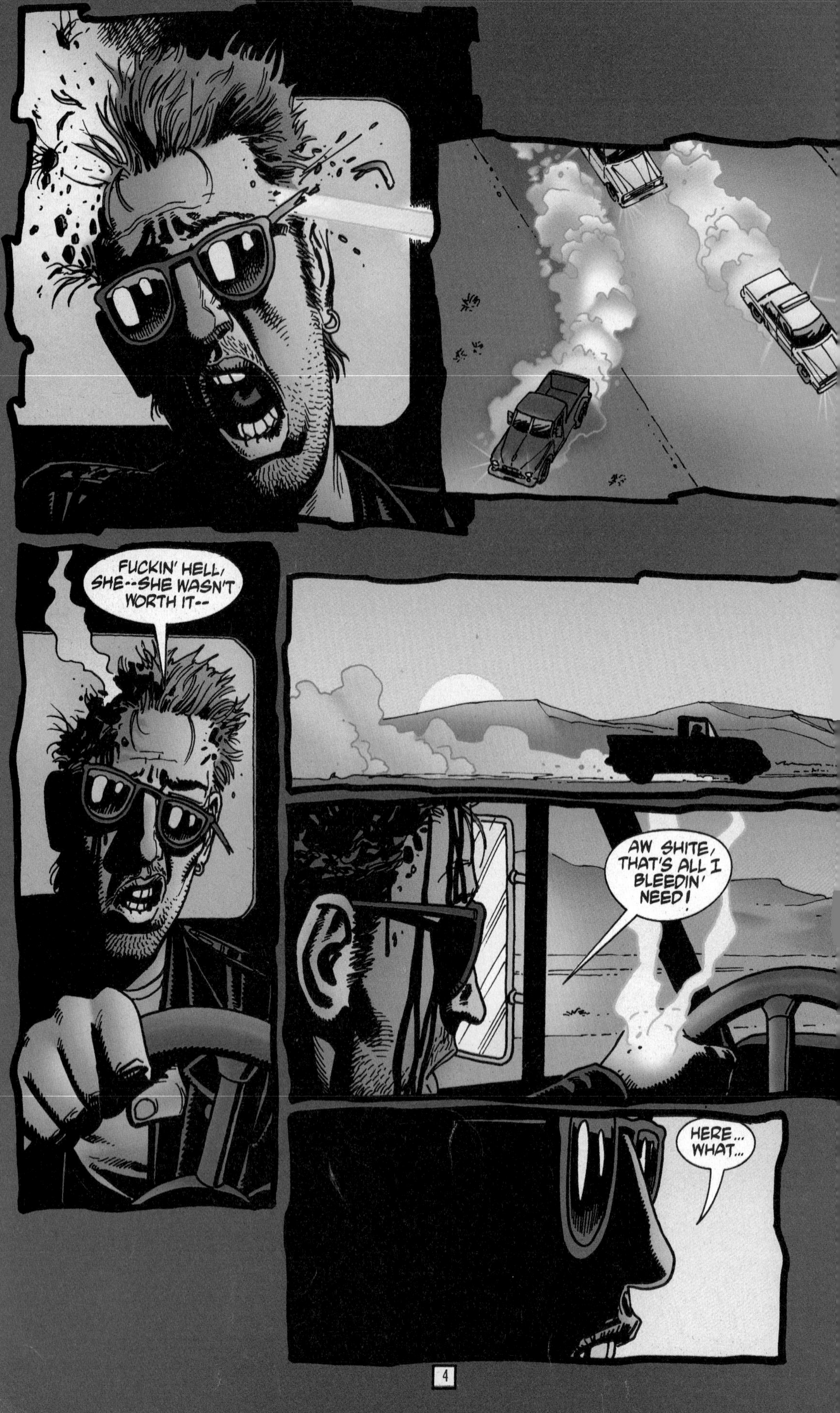
FUCKIN' HELL, SHE--SHE WASN'T WORTH IT--
AW SHITE, THAT'S ALL I BLEEDIN' NEED!
HERE... WHAT...

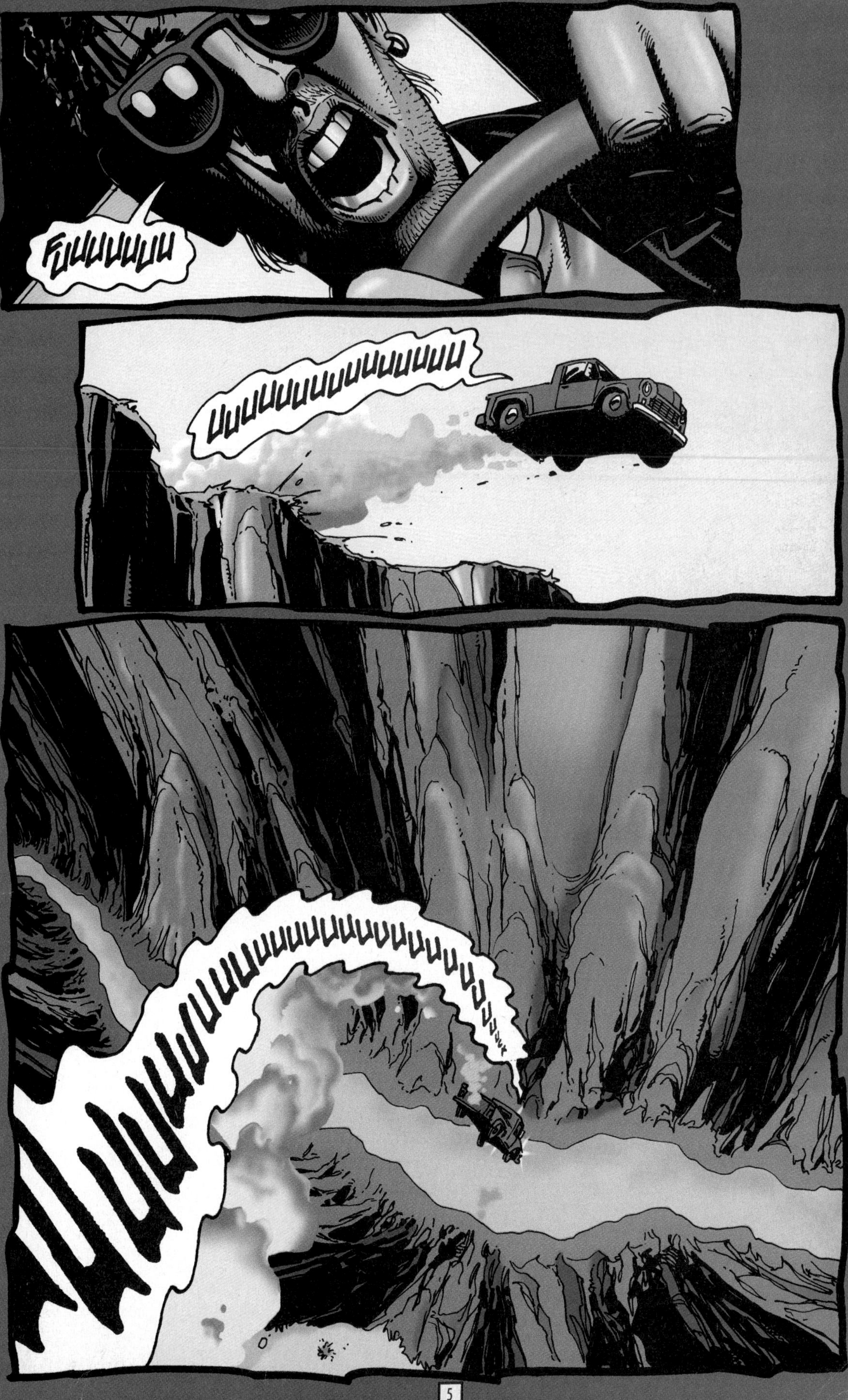
FUUUUUUU
UUUUUUUUUUUUUUU
UUUUUUUUUUUUUUUUUUUUUUUUUUUUUUR

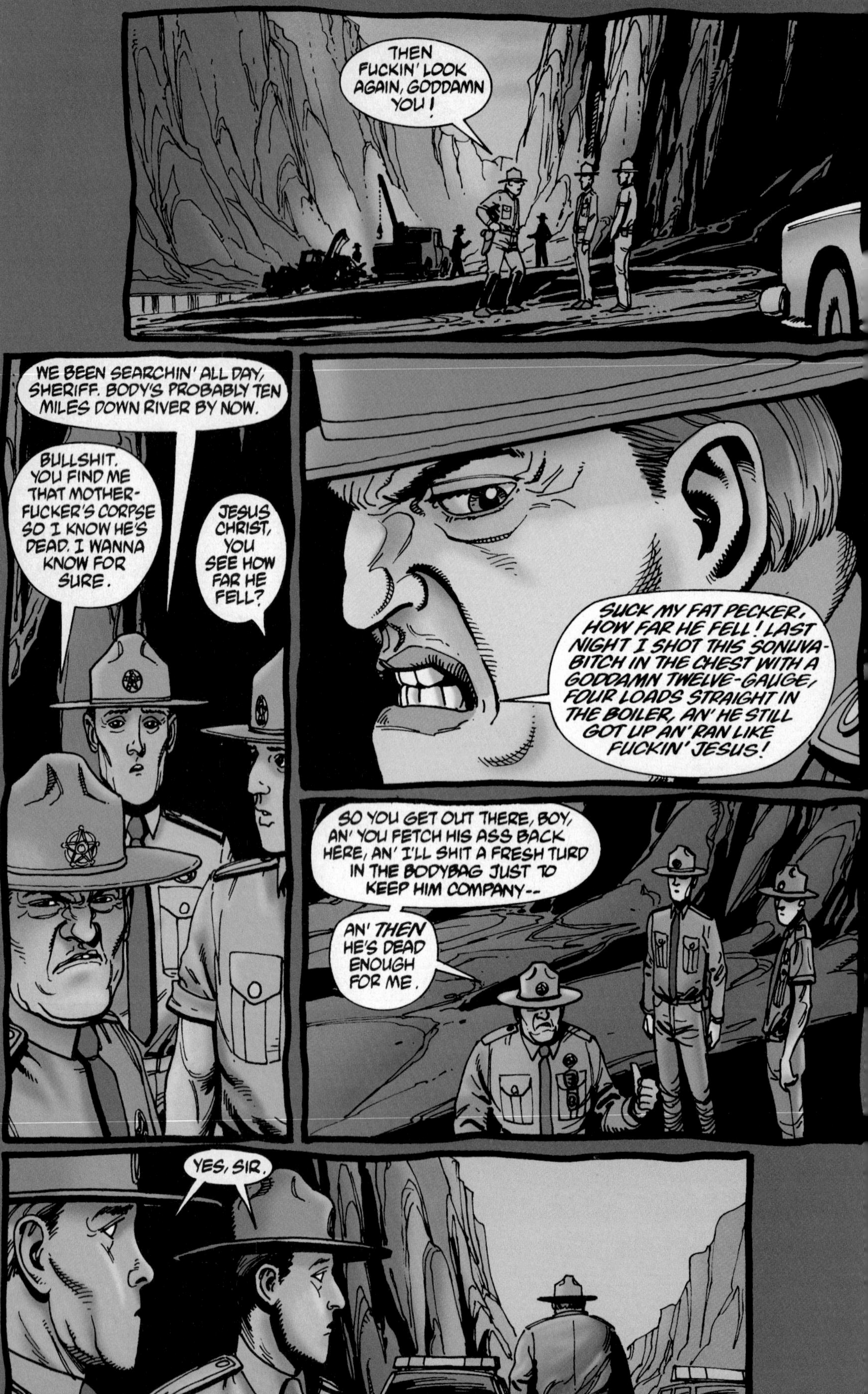
THEN FUCKIN' LOOK AGAIN, GODDAMN YOU!
WE BEEN SEARCHIN' ALL DAY, SHERIFF. BODY'S PROBABLY TEN MILES DOWN RIVER BY NOW.
BULLSHIT. YOU FIND ME THAT MOTHER-FUCKER'S CORPSE SO I KNOW HE'S DEAD. I WANNA KNOW FOR SURE.
JESUS CHRIST, YOU SEE HOW FAR HE FELL?
SUCK MY FAT PECKER, HOW FAR HE FELL! LAST NIGHT I SHOT THIS SONUVA-BITCH IN THE CHEST WITH A GODDAMN TWELVE-GAUGE, FOUR LOADS STRAIGHT IN THE BOILER, AN' HE STILL GOT UP AN' RAN LIKE FUCKIN' JESUS!
SO YOU GET OUT THERE, BOY, AN' YOU FETCH HIS ASS BACK HERE, AN' I'LL SHIT A FRESH TURD IN THE BODYBAG JUST TO KEEP HIM COMPANY--
AN' *THEN* HE'S DEAD ENOUGH FOR ME.
YES, SIR.

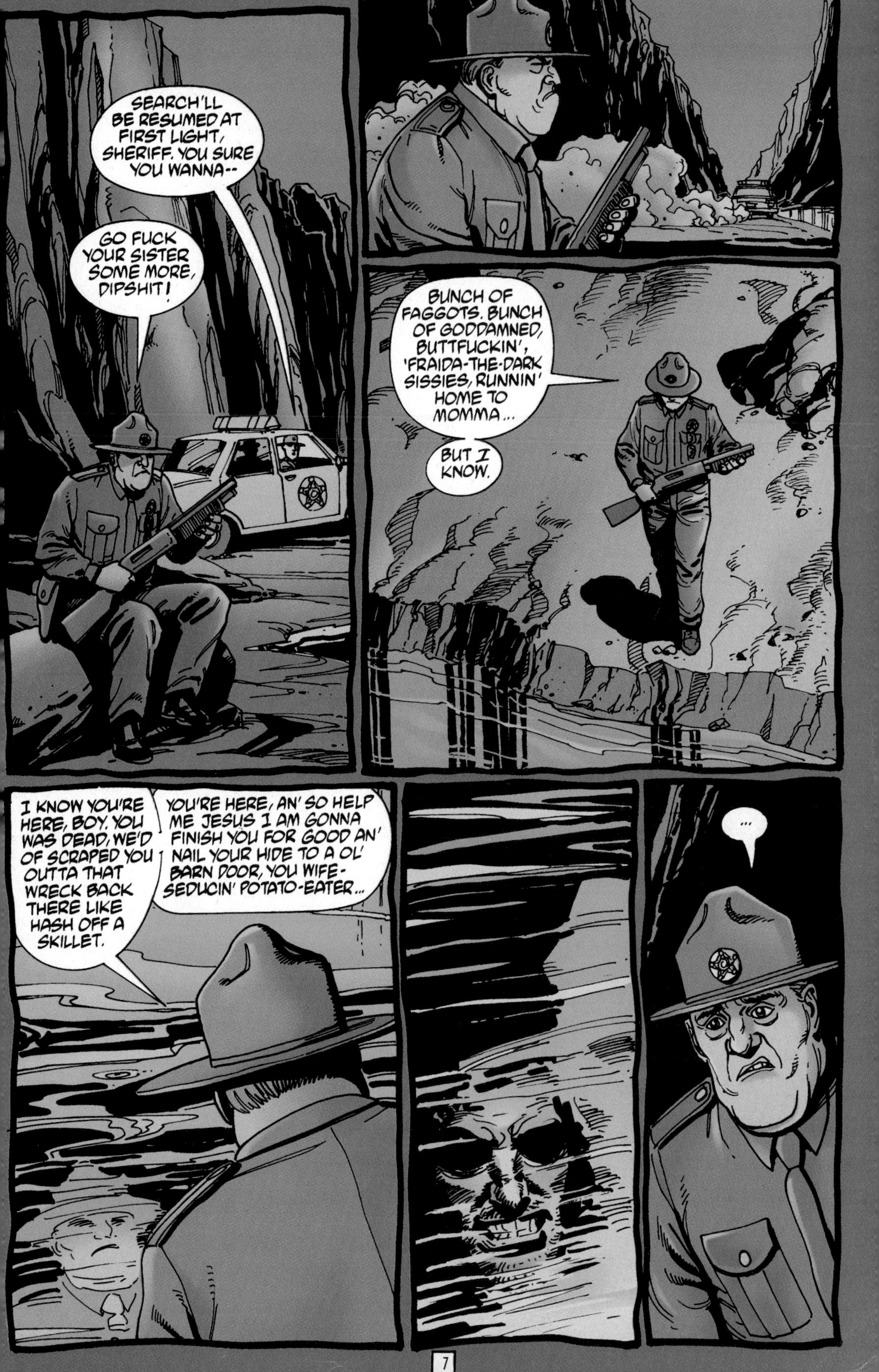
SEARCH'LL BE RESUMED AT FIRST LIGHT, SHERIFF. YOU SURE YOU WANNA--
GO FUCK YOUR SISTER SOME MORE, DIPSHIT!
BUNCH OF FAGGOTS. BUNCH OF GODDAMNED, BUTTFUCKIN', 'FRAIDA-THE-DARK SISSIES, RUNNIN' HOME TO MOMMA...
BUT I KNOW.
I KNOW YOU'RE HERE, BOY. YOU WAS DEAD, WE'D OF SCRAPED YOU OUTTA THAT WRECK BACK THERE LIKE HASH OFF A SKILLET.
YOU'RE HERE, AN' SO HELP ME JESUS I AM GONNA FINISH YOU FOR GOOD AN' NAIL YOUR HIDE TO A OL' BARN DOOR, YOU WIFE-SEDUCIN' POTATO-EATER...
...

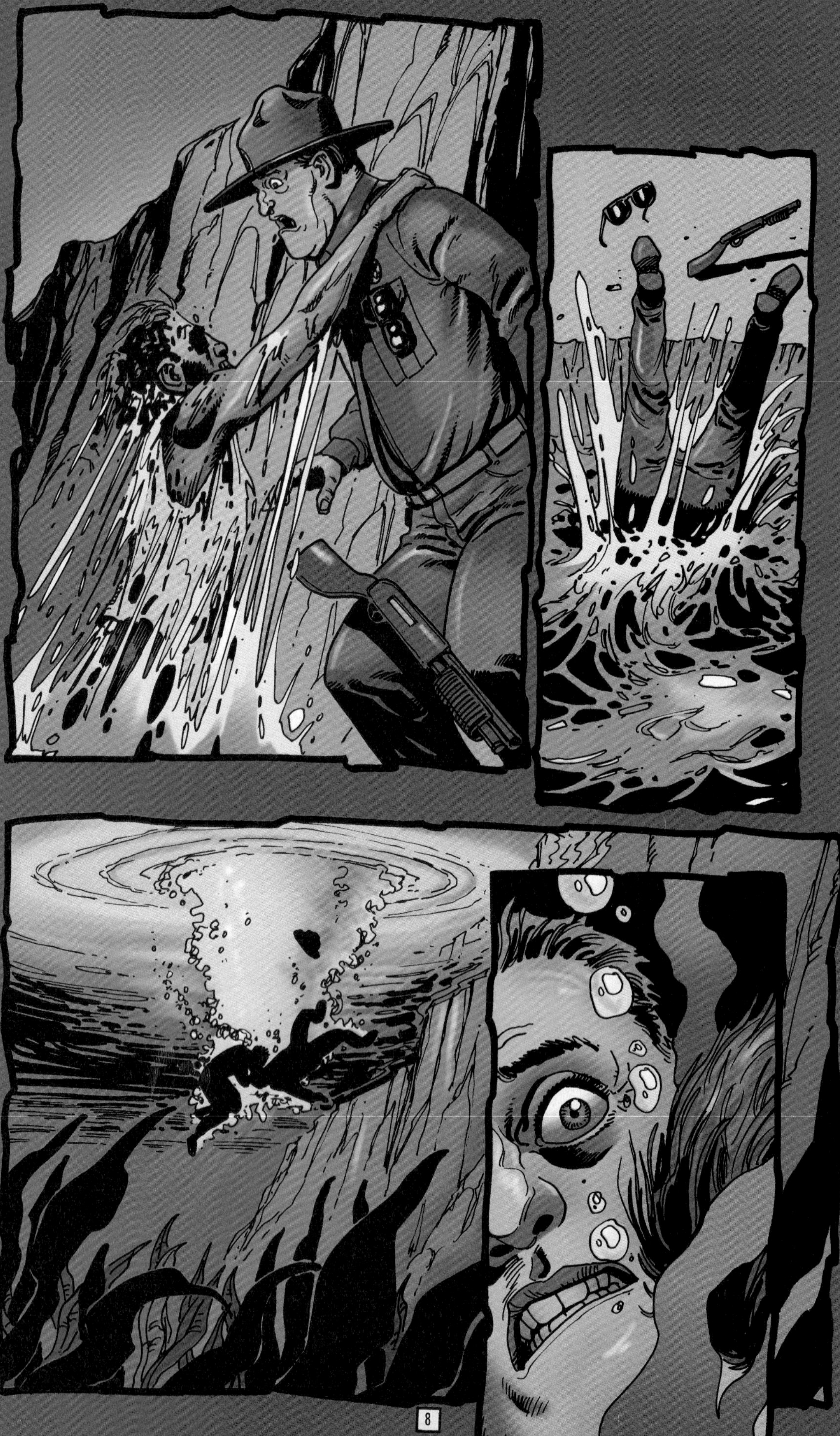

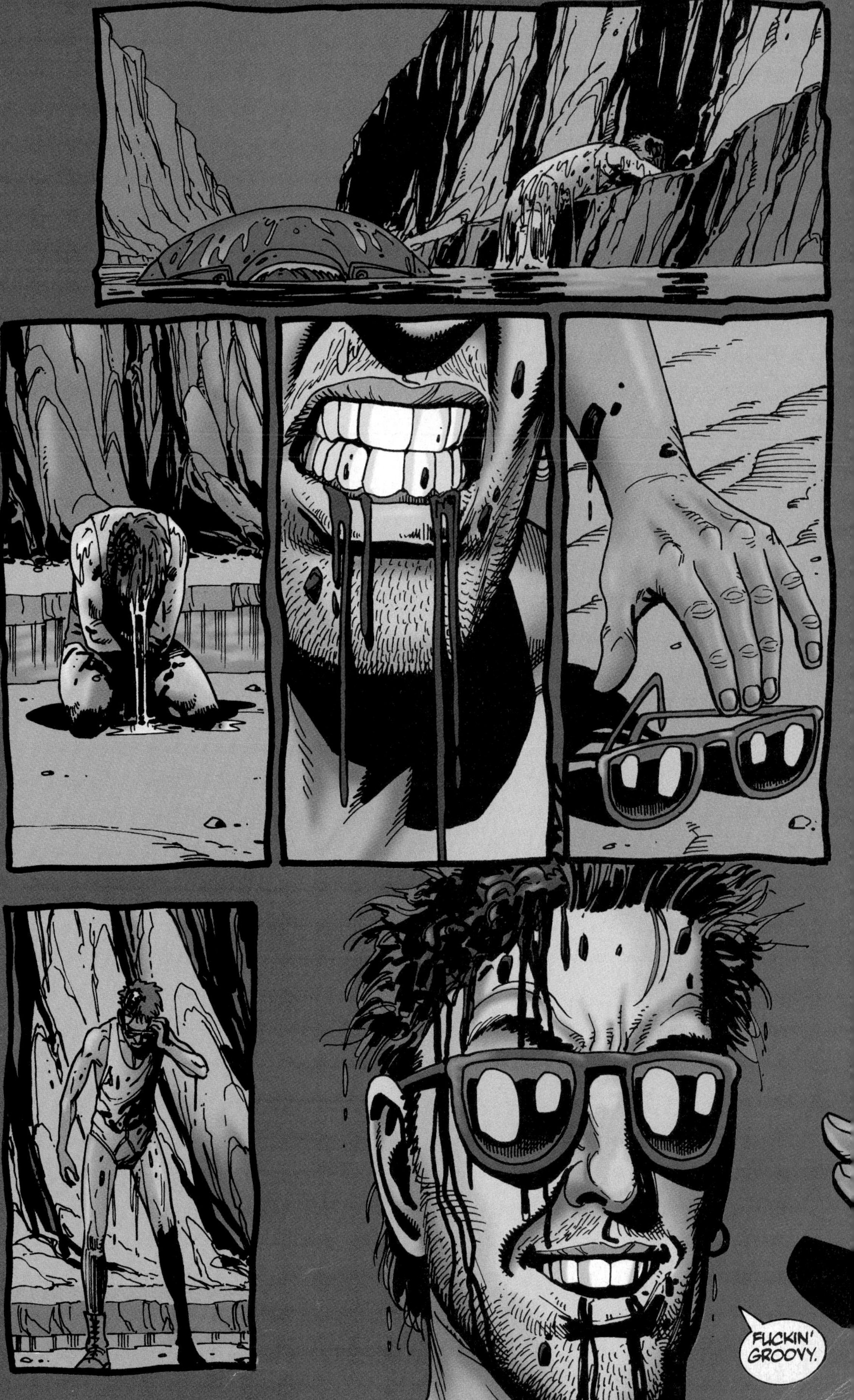
FUCKIN' GROOVY.

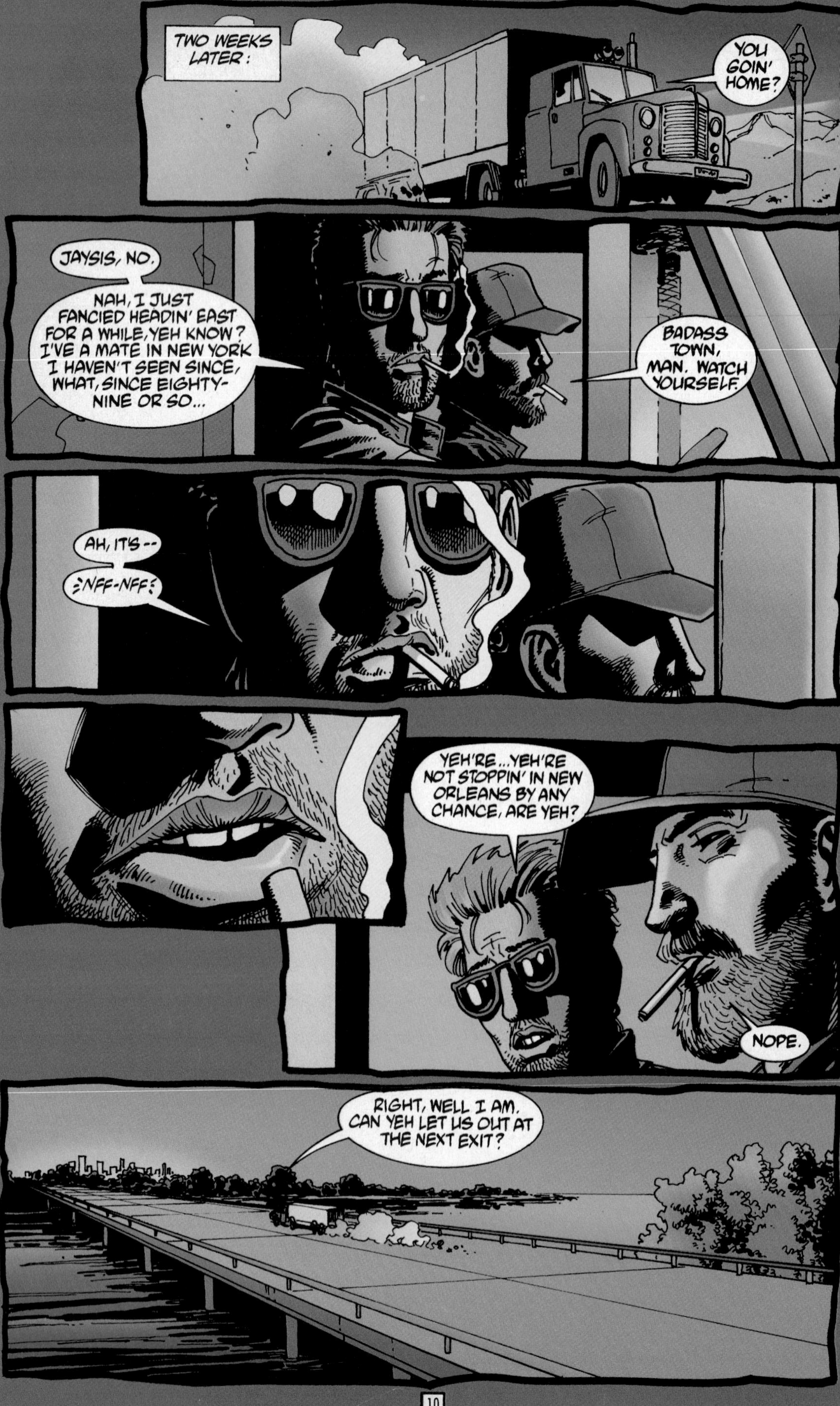

TWO WEEKS LATER:
YOU GOIN' HOME?
JAYSIS, NO.
NAH, I JUST FANCIED HEADIN' EAST FOR A WHILE, YEH KNOW? I'VE A MATE IN NEW YORK I HAVEN'T SEEN SINCE, WHAT, SINCE EIGHTY-NINE OR SO...
BADASS TOWN, MAN. WATCH YOURSELF.
AH, IT'S --
NFF-NFF
YEH'RE... YEH'RE NOT STOPPIN' IN NEW ORLEANS BY ANY CHANCE, ARE YEH?
NOPE.
RIGHT, WELL I AM. CAN YEH LET US OUT AT THE NEXT EXIT?

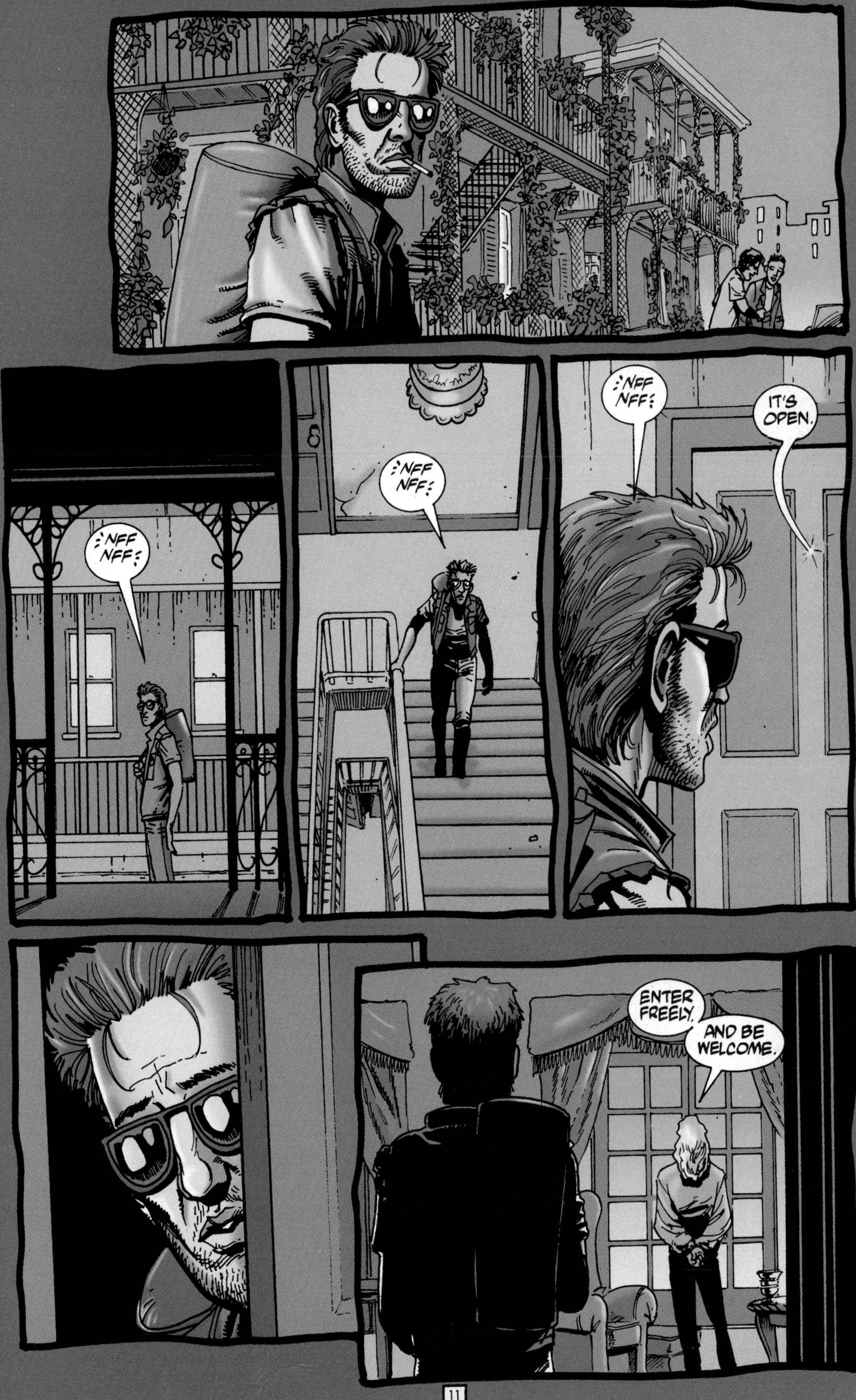
NFF NFF
NFF NFF
NFF NFF
IT'S OPEN.
ENTER FREELY.
AND BE WELCOME.

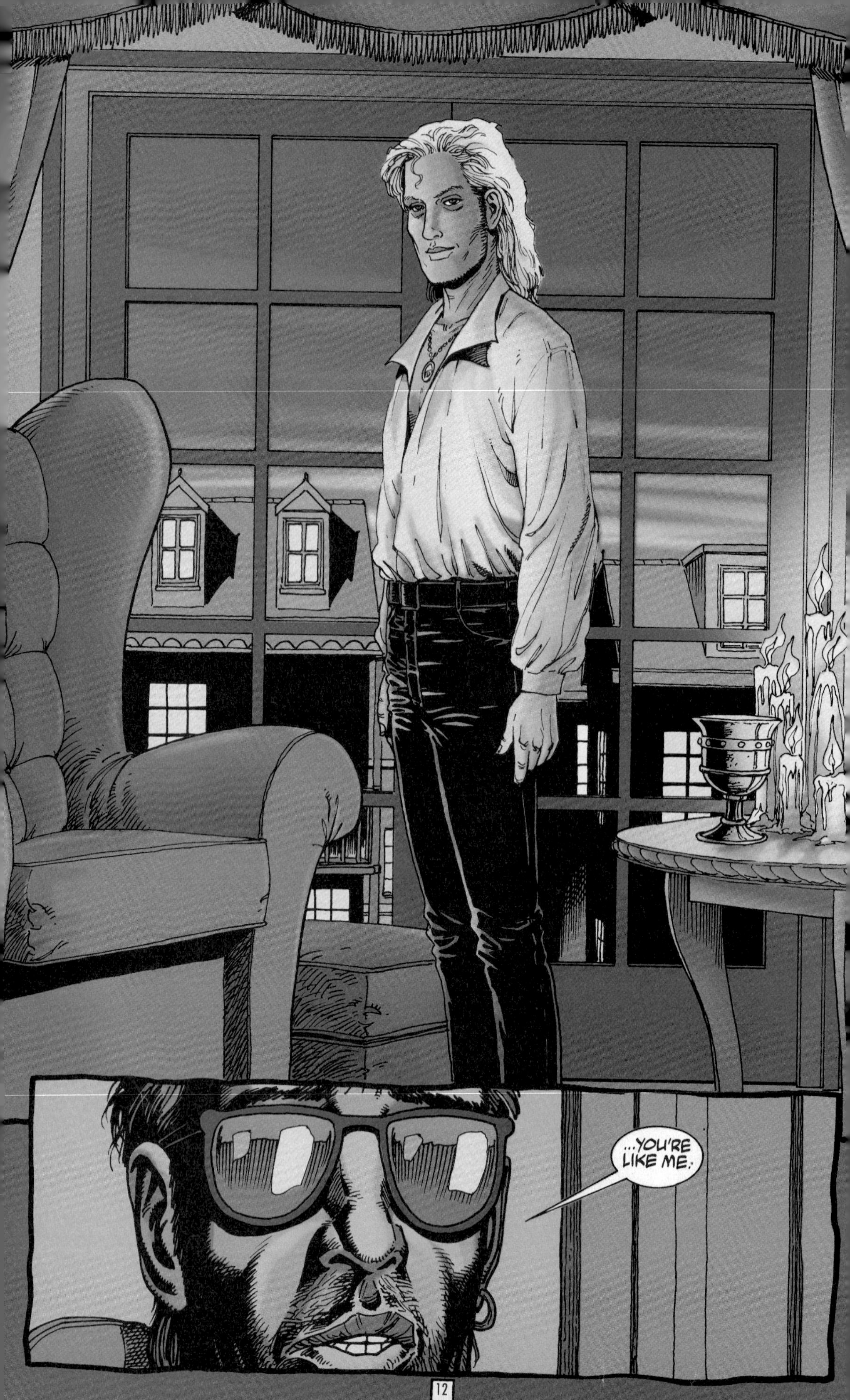
...YOU'RE LIKE ME.

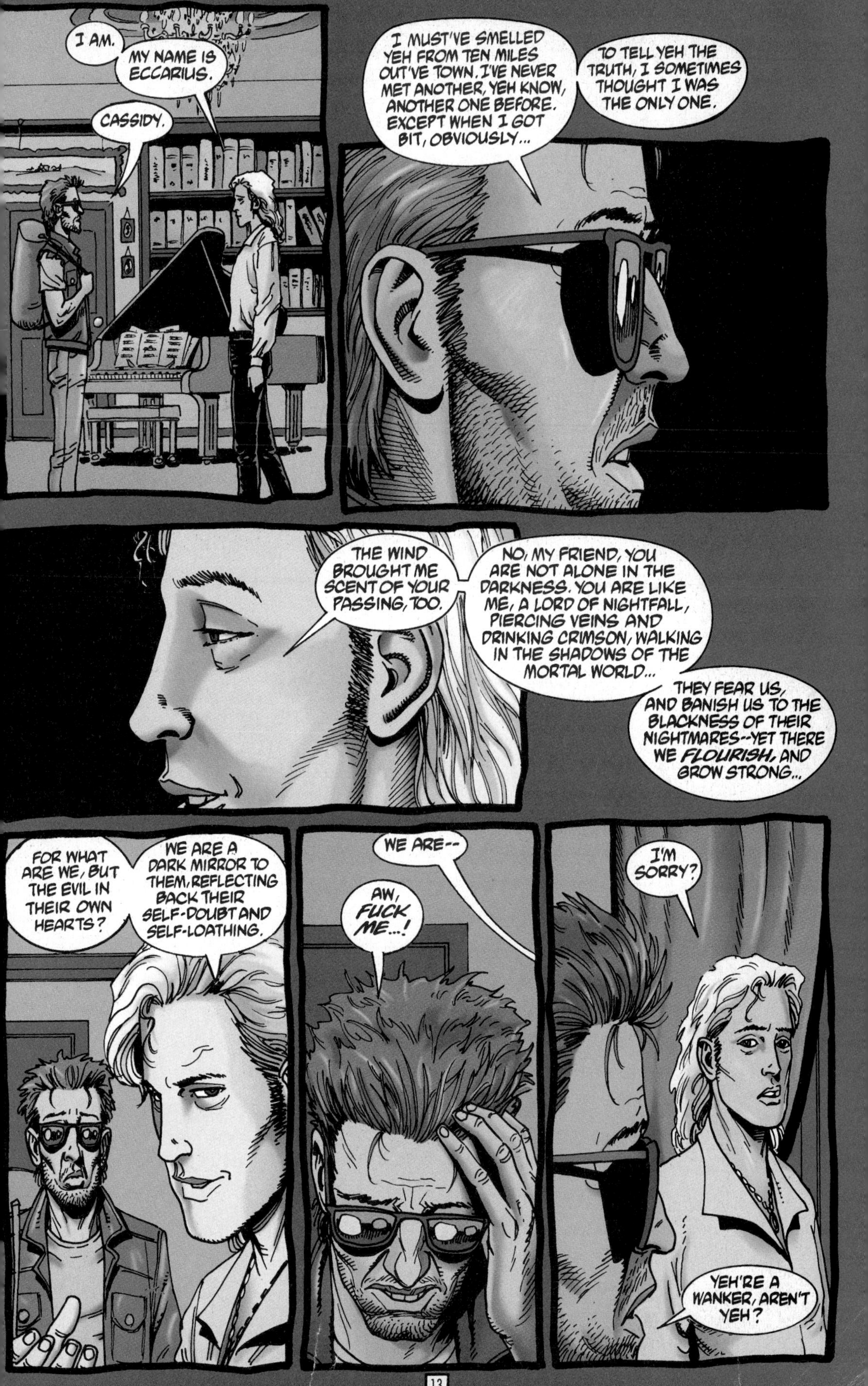
I AM.
MY NAME IS ECCARIUS.
CASSIDY.
I MUST'VE SMELLED YEH FROM TEN MILES OUT'VE TOWN. I'VE NEVER MET ANOTHER, YEH KNOW, ANOTHER ONE BEFORE. EXCEPT WHEN I GOT BIT, OBVIOUSLY...
TO TELL YEH THE TRUTH, I SOMETIMES THOUGHT I WAS THE ONLY ONE.
THE WIND BROUGHT ME SCENT OF YOUR PASSING, TOO.
NO, MY FRIEND, YOU ARE NOT ALONE IN THE DARKNESS. YOU ARE LIKE ME, A LORD OF NIGHTFALL, PIERCING VEINS AND DRINKING CRIMSON, WALKING IN THE SHADOWS OF THE MORTAL WORLD...
THEY FEAR US, AND BANISH US TO THE BLACKNESS OF THEIR NIGHTMARES--YET THERE WE *FLOURISH,* AND GROW STRONG...
FOR WHAT ARE WE, BUT THE EVIL IN THEIR OWN HEARTS?
WE ARE A DARK MIRROR TO THEM, REFLECTING BACK THEIR SELF-DOUBT AND SELF-LOATHING.
WE ARE--
AW, *FUCK ME...!*
I'M SORRY?
YEH'RE A WANKER, AREN'T YEH?

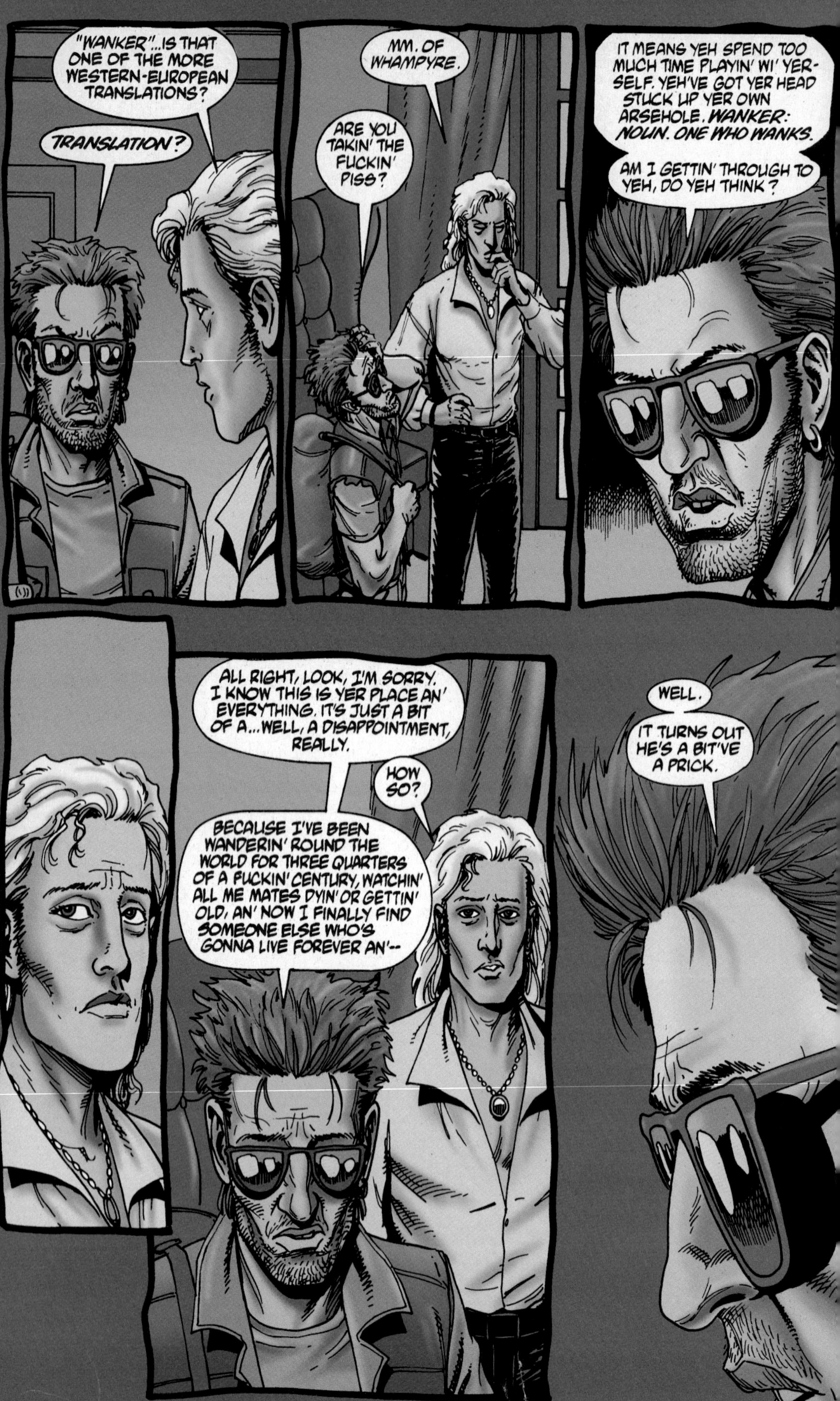
"WANKER"...IS THAT ONE OF THE MORE WESTERN-EUROPEAN TRANSLATIONS?
TRANSLATION?
MM. OF WHAMPYRE.
ARE YOU TAKIN' THE FUCKIN' PISS?
IT MEANS YEH SPEND TOO MUCH TIME PLAYIN' WI' YERSELF. YEH'VE GOT YER HEAD STUCK UP YER OWN ARSEHOLE. WANKER: NOUN. ONE WHO WANKS.
AM I GETTIN' THROUGH TO YEH, DO YEH THINK?
ALL RIGHT, LOOK, I'M SORRY. I KNOW THIS IS YER PLACE AN' EVERYTHING. IT'S JUST A BIT OF A...WELL, A DISAPPOINTMENT, REALLY.
HOW SO?
BECAUSE I'VE BEEN WANDERIN' ROUND THE WORLD FOR THREE QUARTERS OF A FUCKIN' CENTURY, WATCHIN' ALL ME MATES DYIN' OR GETTIN' OLD, AN' NOW I FINALLY FIND SOMEONE ELSE WHO'S GONNA LIVE FOREVER AN'--
WELL.
IT TURNS OUT HE'S A BIT'VE A PRICK.

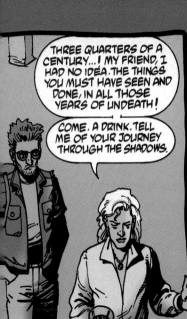

THREE QUARTERS OF A CENTURY...! MY FRIEND, I HAD NO IDEA. THE THINGS YOU MUST HAVE SEEN AND DONE, IN ALL THOSE YEARS OF UNDEATH!

COME. A DRINK. TELL ME OF YOUR JOURNEY THROUGH THE SHADOWS.

WHY, HOW LONG IS IT SINCE YEH WERE BIT YERSELF?

TEN YEARS.

TEN YEARS SINCE I PASSED OVER, EXPECTING AT LAST TO EXPLORE THE GREAT MYSTERY--ONLY TO FIND A MYRIAD OF GREATER MYSTERIES AWAITING ME IN THIS ETERNAL NIGHT...

PWUUUSHH

THIS IS FUCKIN' BLOOD!

DON'T YOU LIKE IT?

ABOUT AS MUCH AS I LIKE EATIN' RAW STEAK! JESUS FUCKIN' CHRIST!

WHAT I'M SAYIN' IS, THERE'S A TIME AN' A PLACE, YEH KNOW? HAVE YEH BEER?

I HAVE WINE...

DRY WHITE.

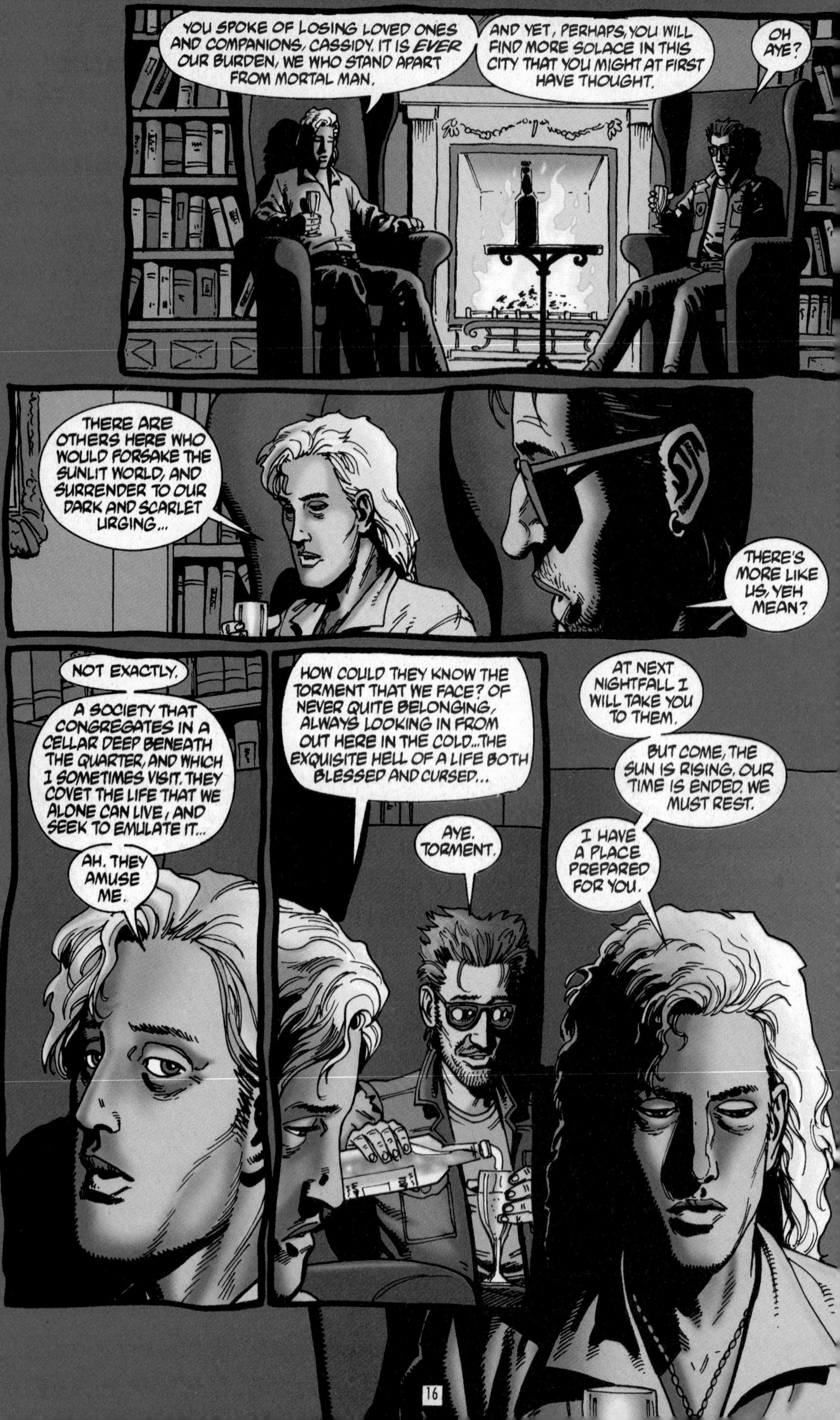

YOU SPOKE OF LOSING LOVED ONES AND COMPANIONS, CASSIDY. IT IS *EVER* OUR BURDEN, WE WHO STAND APART FROM MORTAL MAN.
AND YET, PERHAPS, YOU WILL FIND MORE SOLACE IN THIS CITY THAT YOU MIGHT AT FIRST HAVE THOUGHT.
OH AYE?
THERE ARE OTHERS HERE WHO WOULD FORSAKE THE SUNLIT WORLD, AND SURRENDER TO OUR DARK AND SCARLET URGING...
THERE'S MORE LIKE US, YEH MEAN?
NOT EXACTLY.
A SOCIETY THAT CONGREGATES IN A CELLAR DEEP BENEATH THE QUARTER, AND WHICH I SOMETIMES VISIT. THEY COVET THE LIFE THAT WE ALONE CAN LIVE, AND SEEK TO EMULATE IT...
AH. THEY AMUSE ME.
HOW COULD THEY KNOW THE TORMENT THAT WE FACE? OF NEVER QUITE BELONGING, ALWAYS LOOKING IN FROM OUT HERE IN THE COLD...THE EXQUISITE HELL OF A LIFE BOTH BLESSED AND CURSED...
AYE. TORMENT.
AT NEXT NIGHTFALL I WILL TAKE YOU TO THEM.
BUT COME, THE SUN IS RISING. OUR TIME IS ENDED. WE MUST REST.
I HAVE A PLACE PREPARED FOR YOU.

I'M NOT SLEEPIN' IN A FUCKIN' COFFIN!

WHY NOT...?

IT'S FUCKIN' UNNATURAL, THAT'S WHY? I MEAN, DO YOU?

YES, OF COURSE YEH FUCKIN' DO. STUPID QUESTION, CASS.

BUT IT IS OUR ACCEPTED WAY. IT HAS BEEN SO FOR CENTURIES.

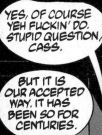

WHAT YEH MEAN IS, THAT'S WHAT THEY DO IN ALL THE FUCKIN' MOVIES--AW, FORGET IT. WE'LL TALK ABOUT THIS TOMORROW.

GIVE US A SLEEPIN' BAG AN' I'LL SLEEP ON YER BLEEDIN' COUCH.

NO ELMORE LEONARD, I SUPPOSE.

BOLLICKS.

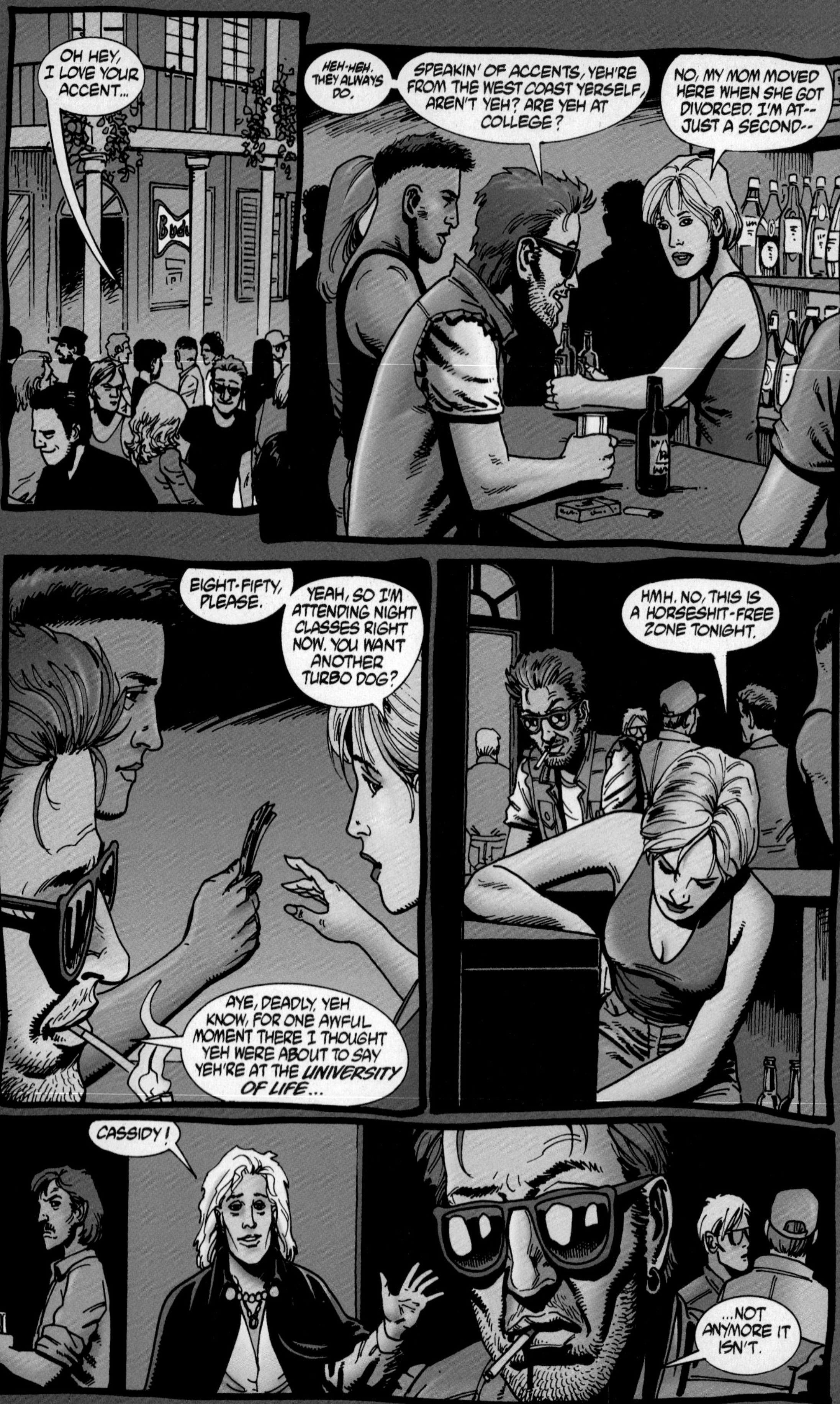
OH HEY, I LOVE YOUR ACCENT...
HEH-HEH. THEY ALWAYS DO.
SPEAKIN' OF ACCENTS, YEH'RE FROM THE WEST COAST YERSELF, AREN'T YEH? ARE YEH AT COLLEGE?
NO, MY MOM MOVED HERE WHEN SHE GOT DIVORCED. I'M AT-- JUST A SECOND--
EIGHT-FIFTY, PLEASE.
YEAH, SO I'M ATTENDING NIGHT CLASSES RIGHT NOW. YOU WANT ANOTHER TURBO DOG?
AYE, DEADLY. YEH KNOW, FOR ONE AWFUL MOMENT THERE I THOUGHT YEH WERE ABOUT TO SAY YEH'RE AT THE *UNIVERSITY OF LIFE*...
HMH. NO, THIS IS A HORSESHIT-FREE ZONE TONIGHT.
CASSIDY!
...NOT ANYMORE IT ISN'T.

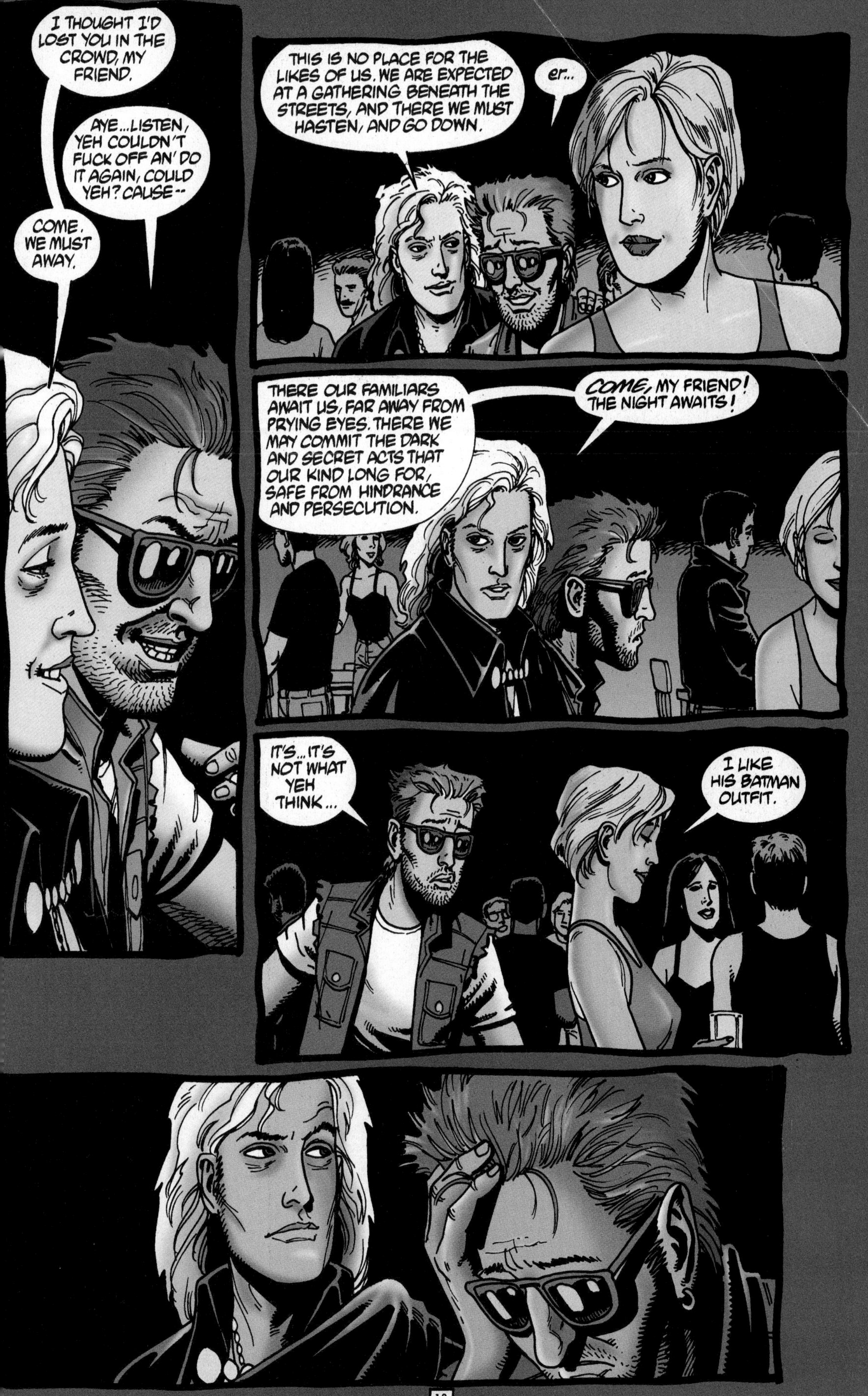

I THOUGHT I'D LOST YOU IN THE CROWD, MY FRIEND.
AYE...LISTEN, YEH COULDN'T FUCK OFF AN' DO IT AGAIN, COULD YEH? CAUSE--
COME. WE MUST AWAY.
THIS IS NO PLACE FOR THE LIKES OF US. WE ARE EXPECTED AT A GATHERING BENEATH THE STREETS, AND THERE WE MUST HASTEN, AND GO DOWN.
er...
THERE OUR FAMILIARS AWAIT US, FAR AWAY FROM PRYING EYES. THERE WE MAY COMMIT THE DARK AND SECRET ACTS THAT OUR KIND LONG FOR, SAFE FROM HINDRANCE AND PERSECUTION.
COME, MY FRIEND! THE NIGHT AWAITS!
IT'S...IT'S NOT WHAT YEH THINK...
I LIKE HIS BATMAN OUTFIT.

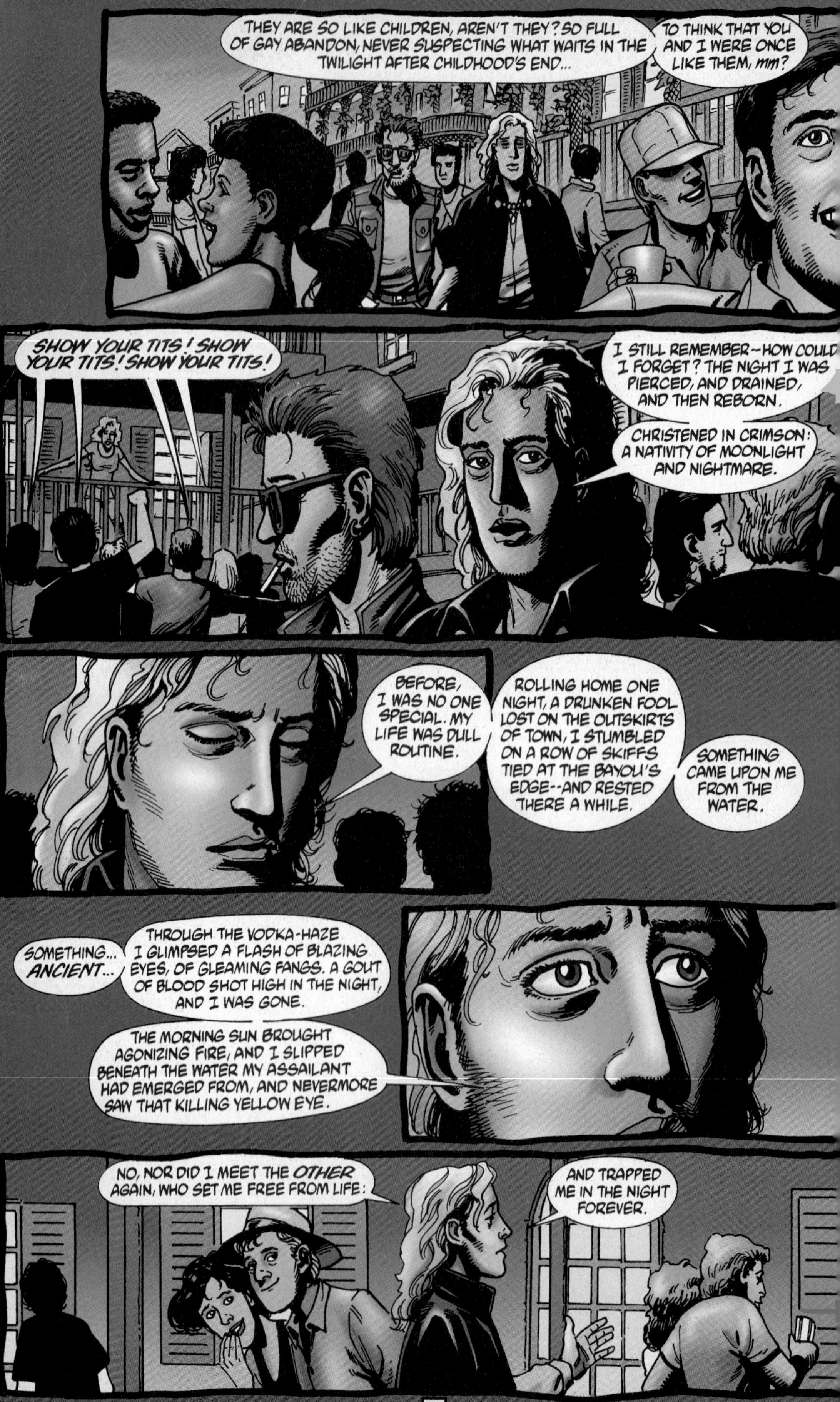
THEY ARE SO LIKE CHILDREN, AREN'T THEY? SO FULL OF GAY ABANDON, NEVER SUSPECTING WHAT WAITS IN THE TWILIGHT AFTER CHILDHOOD'S END...
TO THINK THAT YOU AND I WERE ONCE LIKE THEM, *mm*?
SHOW YOUR TITS! SHOW YOUR TITS! SHOW YOUR TITS!
I STILL REMEMBER--HOW COULD I FORGET? THE NIGHT I WAS PIERCED, AND DRAINED, AND THEN REBORN.
CHRISTENED IN CRIMSON: A NATIVITY OF MOONLIGHT AND NIGHTMARE.
BEFORE, I WAS NO ONE SPECIAL. MY LIFE WAS DULL ROUTINE.
ROLLING HOME ONE NIGHT, A DRUNKEN FOOL LOST ON THE OUTSKIRTS OF TOWN, I STUMBLED ON A ROW OF SKIFFS TIED AT THE BAYOU'S EDGE--AND RESTED THERE A WHILE.
SOMETHING CAME UPON ME FROM THE WATER.
SOMETHING... *ANCIENT*...
THROUGH THE VODKA-HAZE I GLIMPSED A FLASH OF BLAZING EYES, OF GLEAMING FANGS. A GOUT OF BLOOD SHOT HIGH IN THE NIGHT, AND I WAS GONE.
THE MORNING SUN BROUGHT AGONIZING FIRE, AND I SLIPPED BENEATH THE WATER MY ASSAILANT HAD EMERGED FROM, AND NEVERMORE SAW THAT KILLING YELLOW EYE.
NO, NOR DID I MEET THE *OTHER* AGAIN, WHO SET ME FREE FROM LIFE:
AND TRAPPED ME IN THE NIGHT FOREVER.

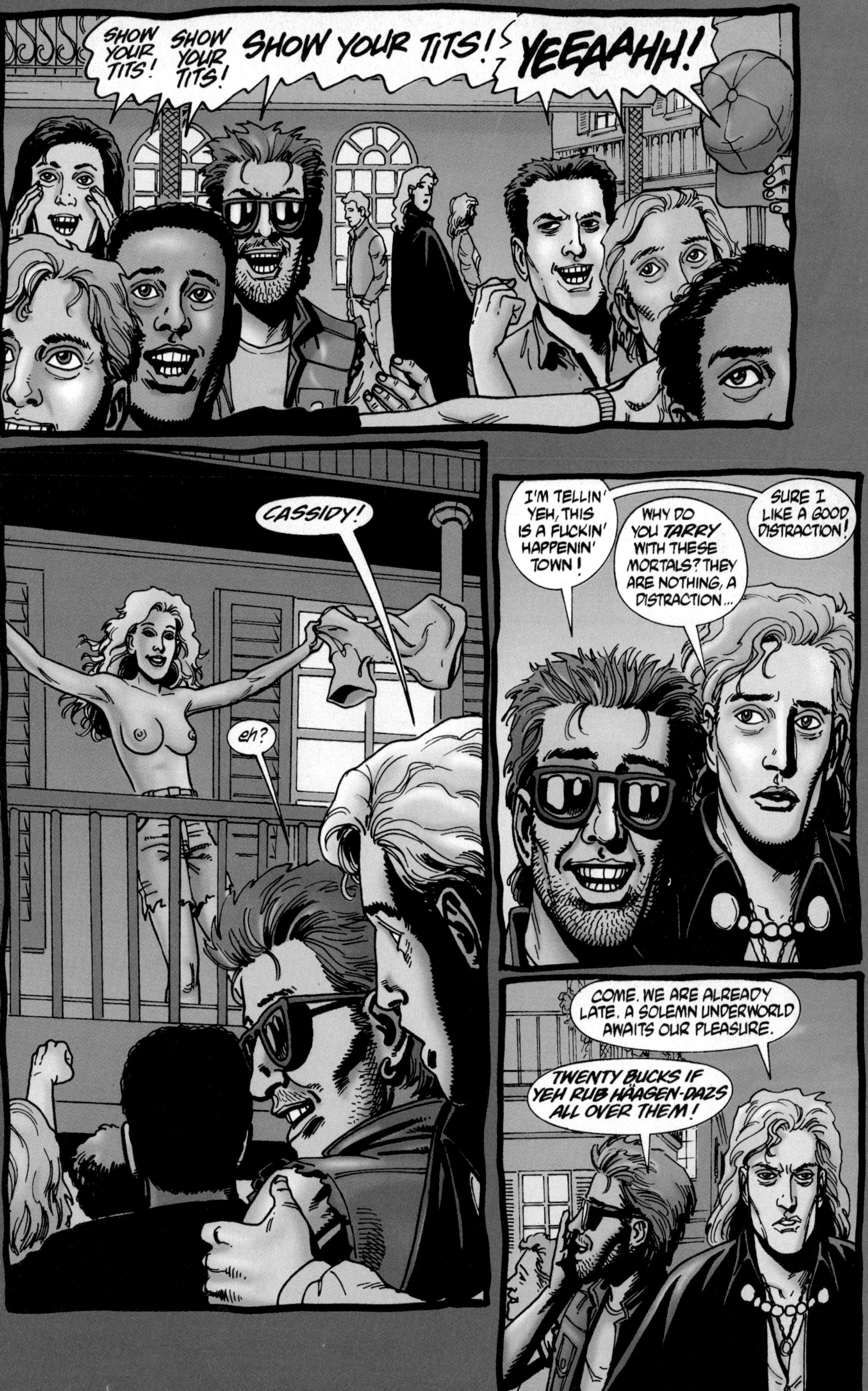
SHOW YOUR TITS!
SHOW YOUR TITS!
SHOW YOUR TITS!
YEEAAHH!
CASSIDY!
eh?
I'M TELLIN' YEH, THIS IS A FUCKIN' HAPPENIN' TOWN!
WHY DO YOU TARRY WITH THESE MORTALS? THEY ARE NOTHING, A DISTRACTION...
SURE I LIKE A GOOD DISTRACTION!
COME. WE ARE ALREADY LATE. A SOLEMN UNDERWORLD AWAITS OUR PLEASURE.
TWENTY BUCKS IF YEH RUB HÄAGEN-DAZS ALL OVER THEM!

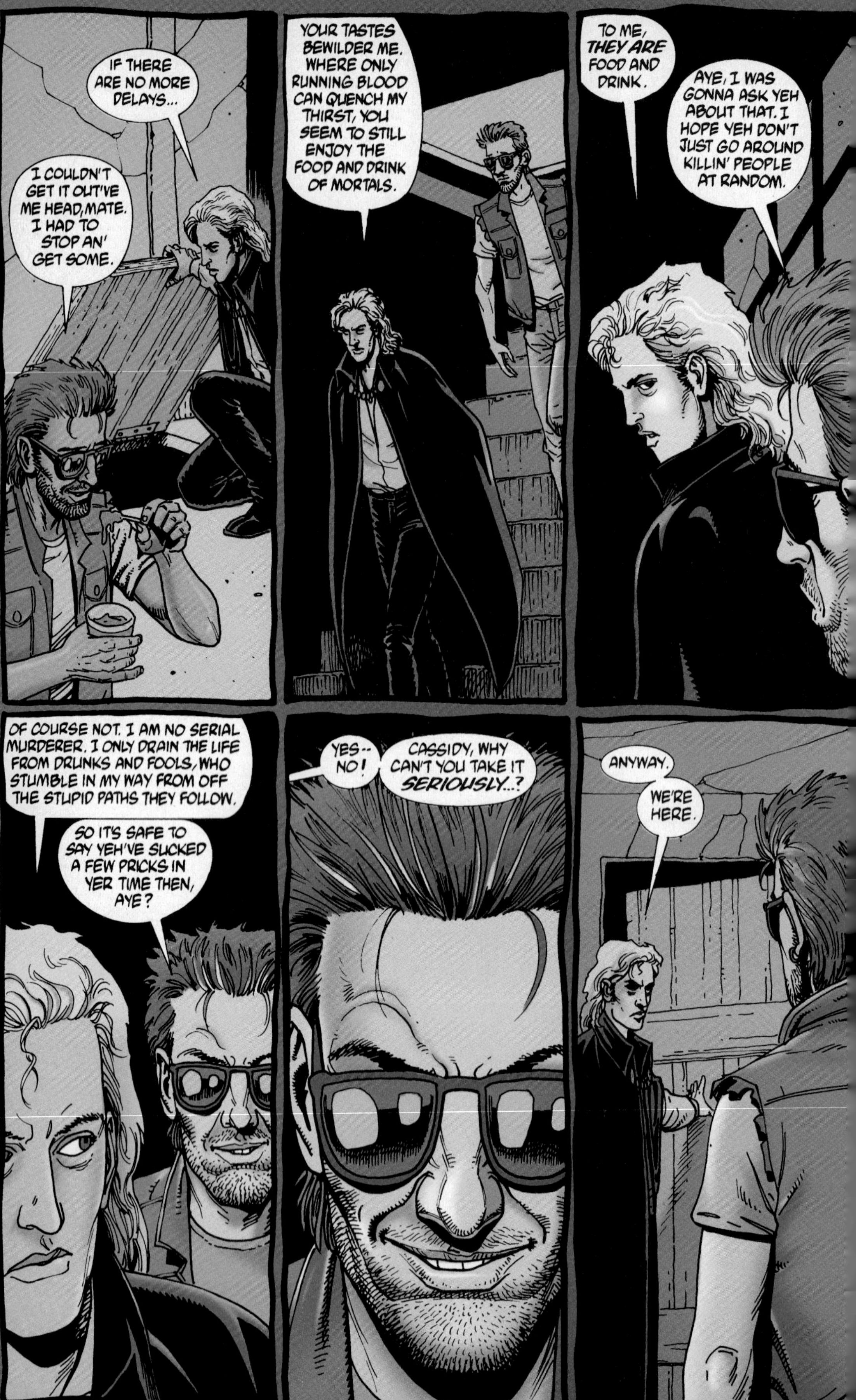

IF THERE ARE NO MORE DELAYS...
I COULDN'T GET IT OUT'VE ME HEAD, MATE. I HAD TO STOP AN' GET SOME.
YOUR TASTES BEWILDER ME. WHERE ONLY RUNNING BLOOD CAN QUENCH MY THIRST, YOU SEEM TO STILL ENJOY THE FOOD AND DRINK OF MORTALS.
TO ME, THEY ARE FOOD AND DRINK.
AYE, I WAS GONNA ASK YEH ABOUT THAT. I HOPE YEH DON'T JUST GO AROUND KILLIN' PEOPLE AT RANDOM.
OF COURSE NOT. I AM NO SERIAL MURDERER. I ONLY DRAIN THE LIFE FROM DRUNKS AND FOOLS, WHO STUMBLE IN MY WAY FROM OFF THE STUPID PATHS THEY FOLLOW.
SO IT'S SAFE TO SAY YEH'VE SUCKED A FEW PRICKS IN YER TIME THEN, AYE?
YES-- NO!
CASSIDY, WHY CAN'T YOU TAKE IT SERIOUSLY...?
ANYWAY.
WE'RE HERE.

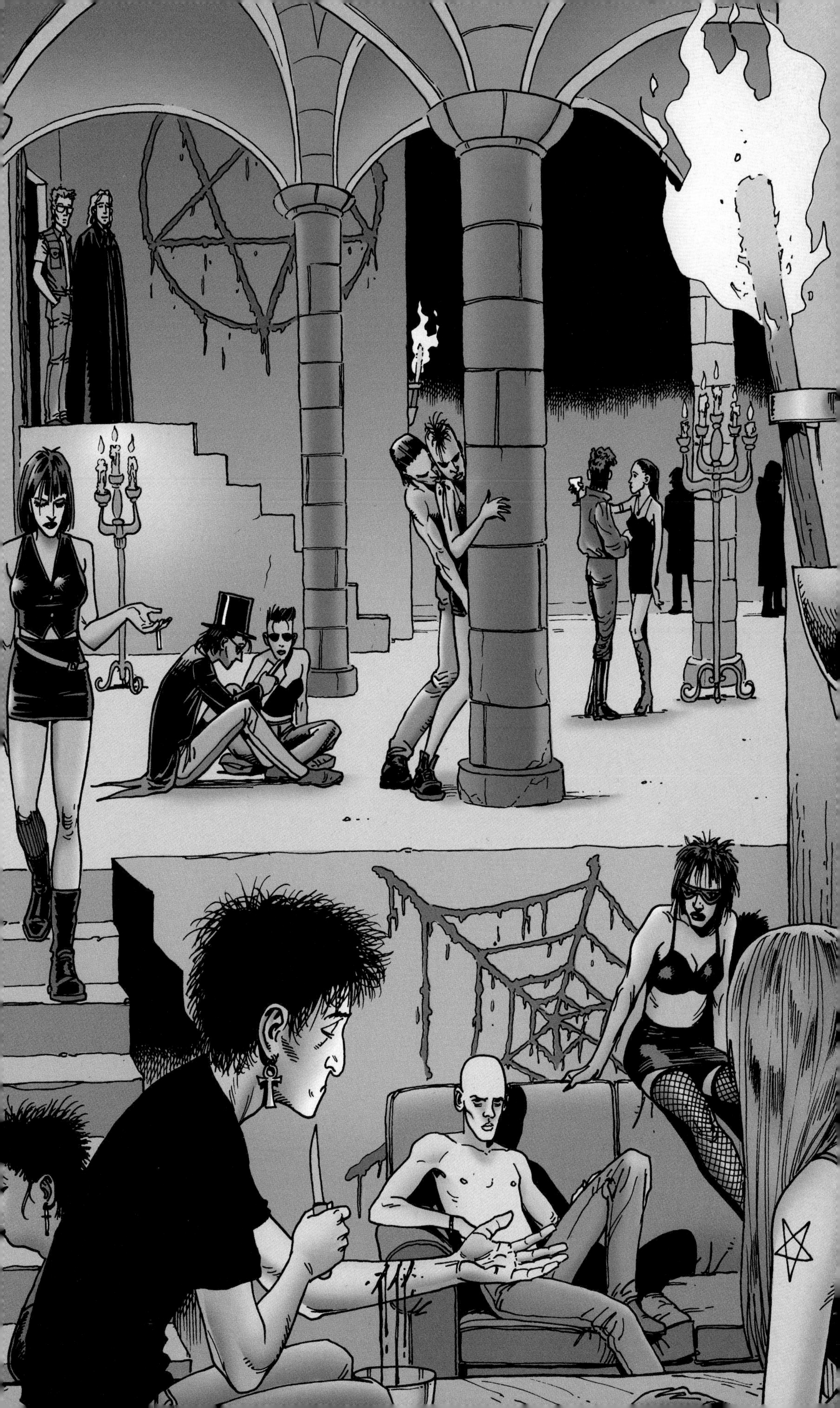

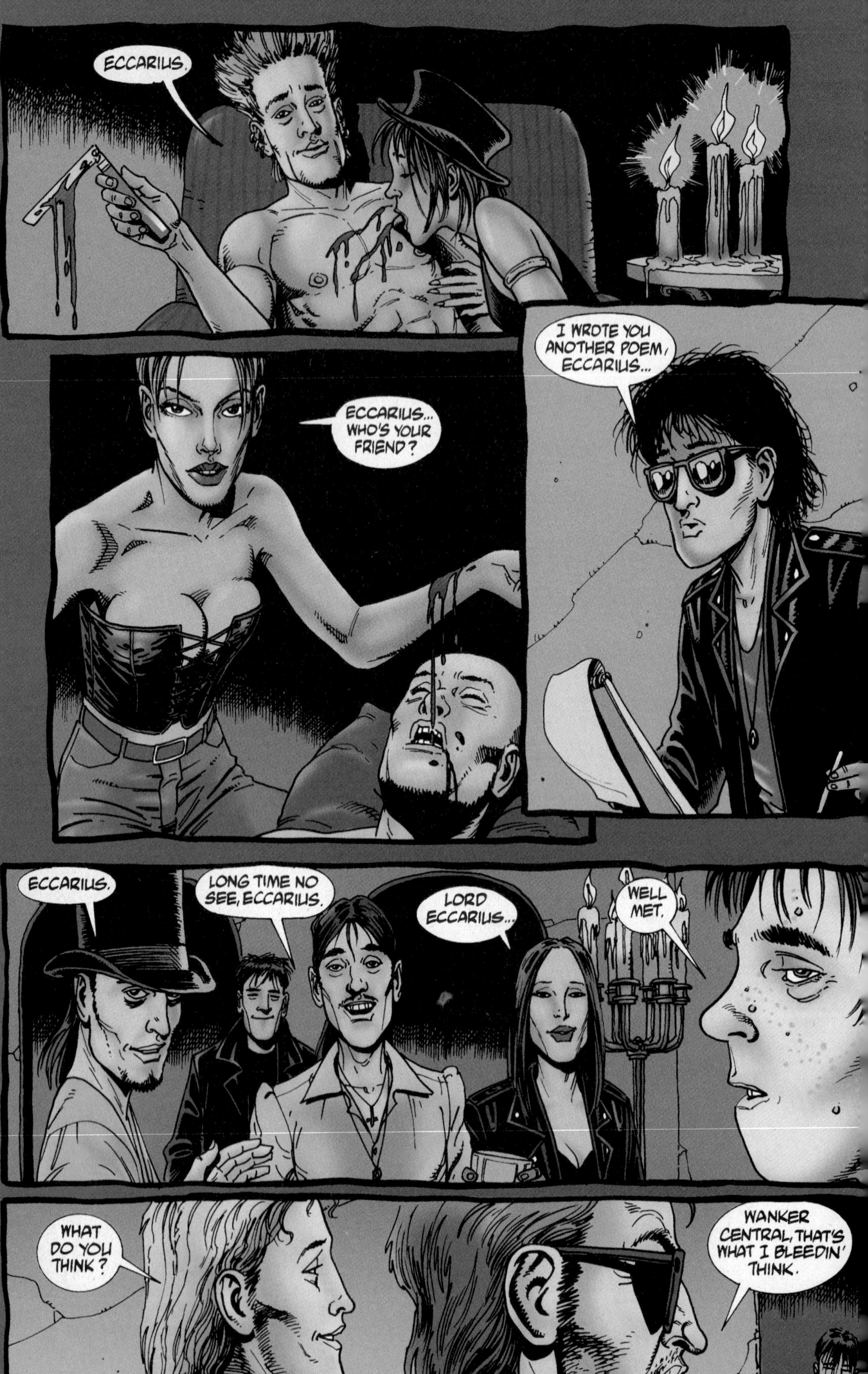
ECCARIUS.
ECCARIUS... WHO'S YOUR FRIEND?
I WROTE YOU ANOTHER POEM, ECCARIUS...
ECCARIUS.
LONG TIME NO SEE, ECCARIUS.
LORD ECCARIUS...
WELL MET.
WHAT DO YOU THINK?
WANKER CENTRAL, THAT'S WHAT I BLEEDIN' THINK.

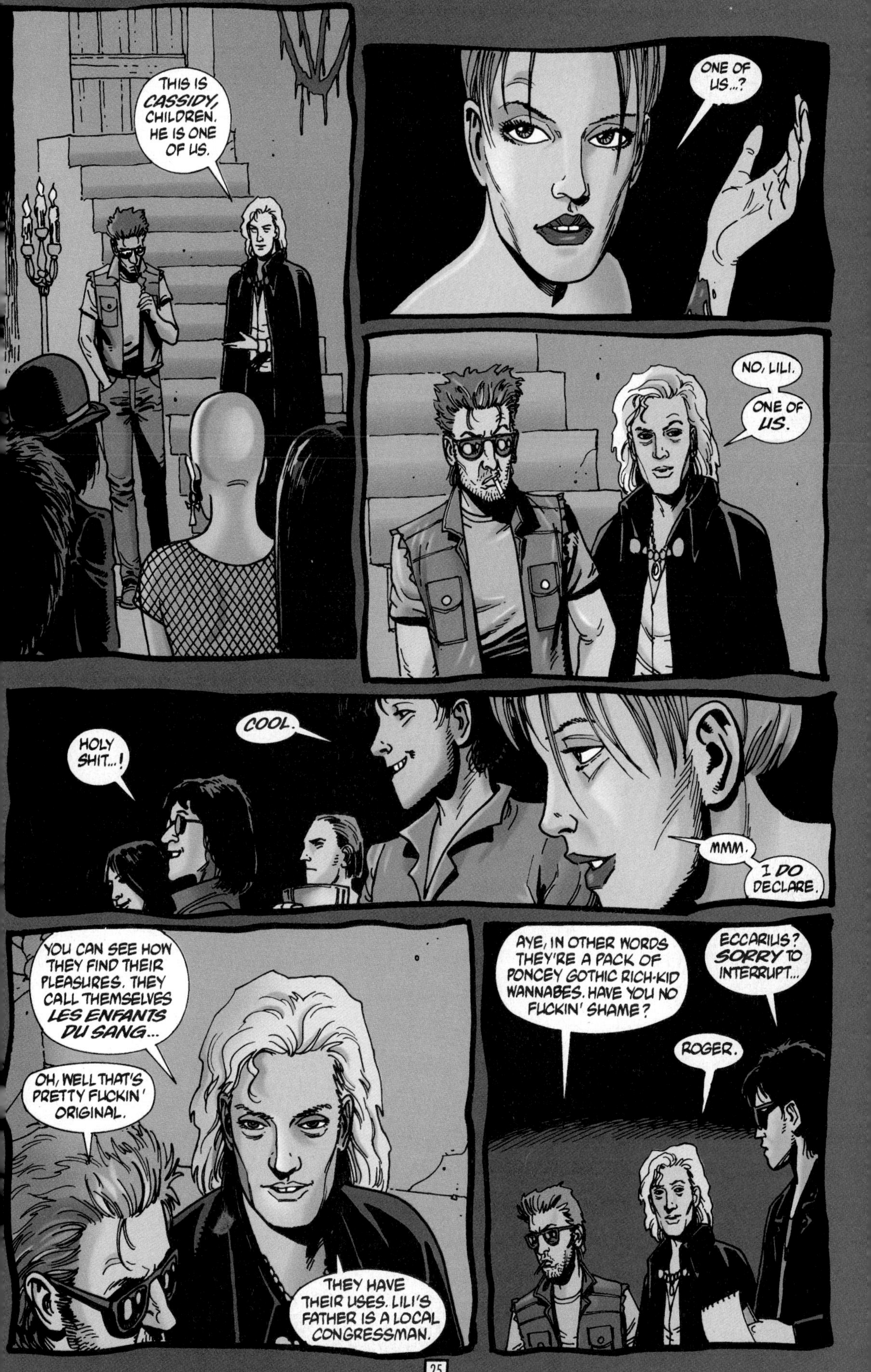

THIS IS *CASSIDY*, CHILDREN. HE IS ONE OF US.
ONE OF US...?
NO, LILI.
ONE OF *US*.
HOLY SHIT...!
COOL.
MMM.
I DO DECLARE.
YOU CAN SEE HOW THEY FIND THEIR PLEASURES. THEY CALL THEMSELVES *LES ENFANTS DU SANG*...
OH, WELL THAT'S PRETTY FUCKIN' ORIGINAL.
THEY HAVE THEIR USES. LILI'S FATHER IS A LOCAL CONGRESSMAN.
AYE, IN OTHER WORDS THEY'RE A PACK OF PONCEY GOTHIC RICH-KID WANNABES. HAVE YOU NO FUCKIN' SHAME?
ECCARIUS? *SORRY* TO INTERRUPT...
ROGER.

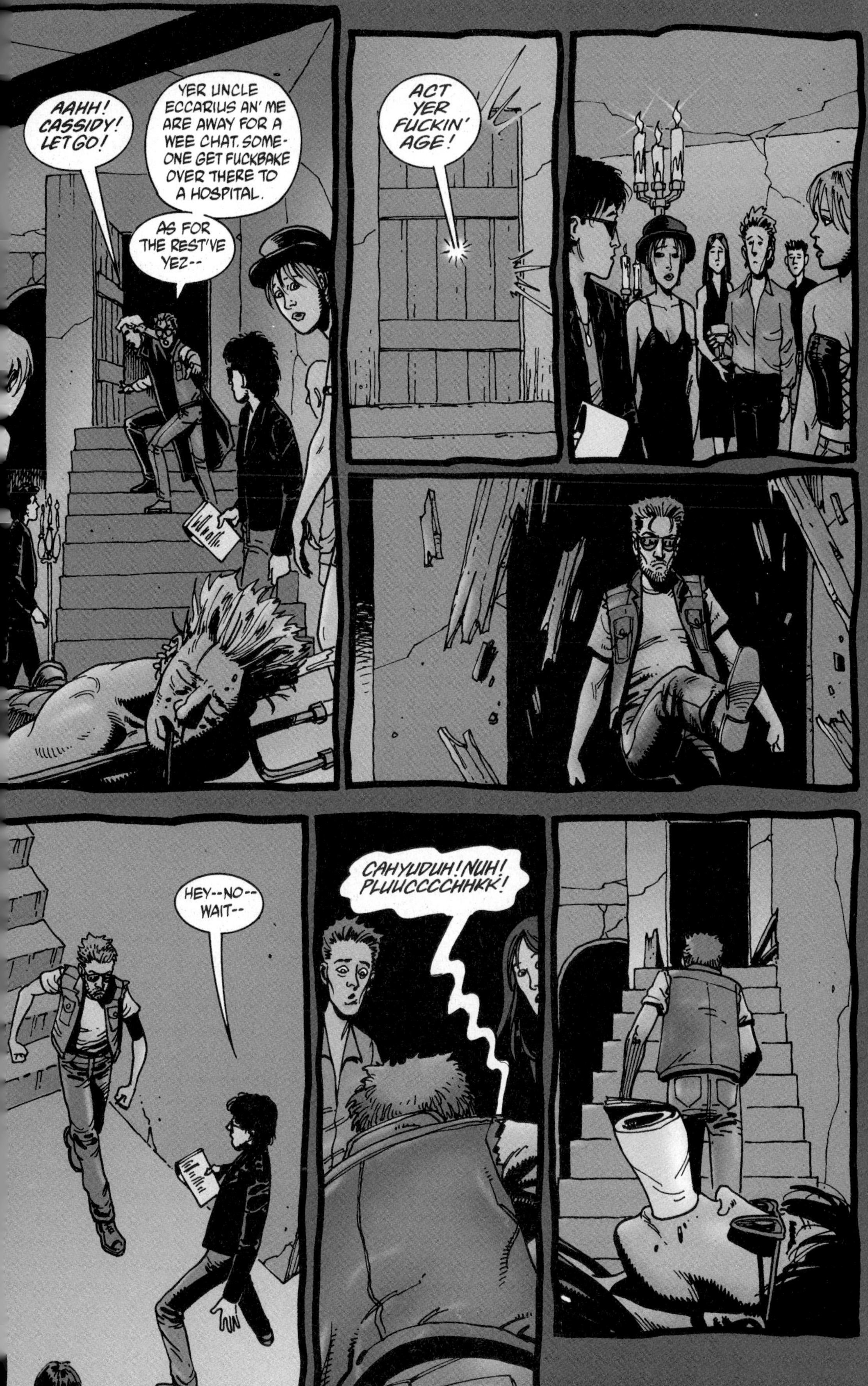
AAHH! CASSIDY! LETGO!
YER UNCLE ECCARIUS AN' ME ARE AWAY FOR A WEE CHAT. SOME-ONE GET FUCKBAKE OVER THERE TO A HOSPITAL.
AS FOR THE REST'VE YEZ--
ACT YER FUCKIN' AGE!
HEY--NO--WAIT--
CAHYUDUH! NUH! PLUUCCCCHHKK!

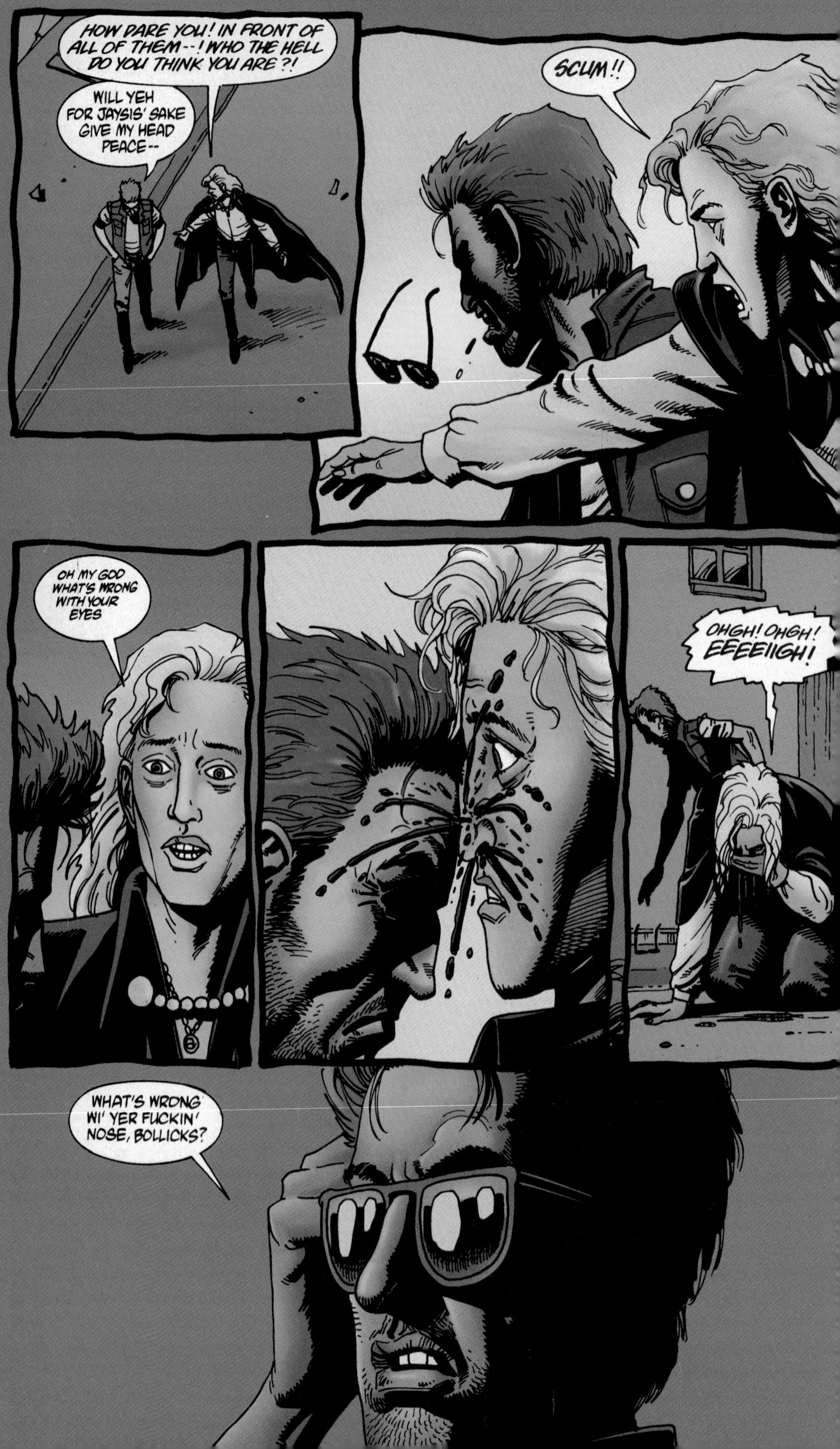
HOW DARE YOU! IN FRONT OF ALL OF THEM--! WHO THE HELL DO YOU THINK YOU ARE?!
WILL YEH FOR JAYSIS' SAKE GIVE MY HEAD PEACE--
SCUM!!
OH MY GOD WHAT'S WRONG WITH YOUR EYES
OHGH! OHGH! EEEEIIGH!
WHAT'S WRONG WI' YER FUCKIN' NOSE, BOLLICKS?

HHHH.
WHAT'S THE MATTER NOW?

CAND FIND BY CONTACND LENDS.

SHIT, YEH MEAN TO SAY YER EYES AREN'T REALLY THAT COLOR?

DO YEH SMOKE?

DNO.

...YES.

HAIR DYED TOO, WHA'?

WHAT PART?

MM. THOD I-- HNFF--THOUGHT I OUGHT TO TRY AND LOOK THE PART.

YOU KNOW. A NIGHTWALKER. A LORD OF THE UNDEAD.

AAOW!

WHAT WAS THAT FOR?

FOR TALKIN' SHITE. FROM NOW ON YEH GET A CLIP ROUND THE EAR EVERY TIME YEH ACT THE PRICK, RIGHT?

YEH'VE BEEN GOIN' ABOUT THIS COMPLETELY THE WRONG WAY. YEH NEED SORTIN' OUT, SON.

AN' I'M JUST THE BOY TO DO THE SORTIN'.

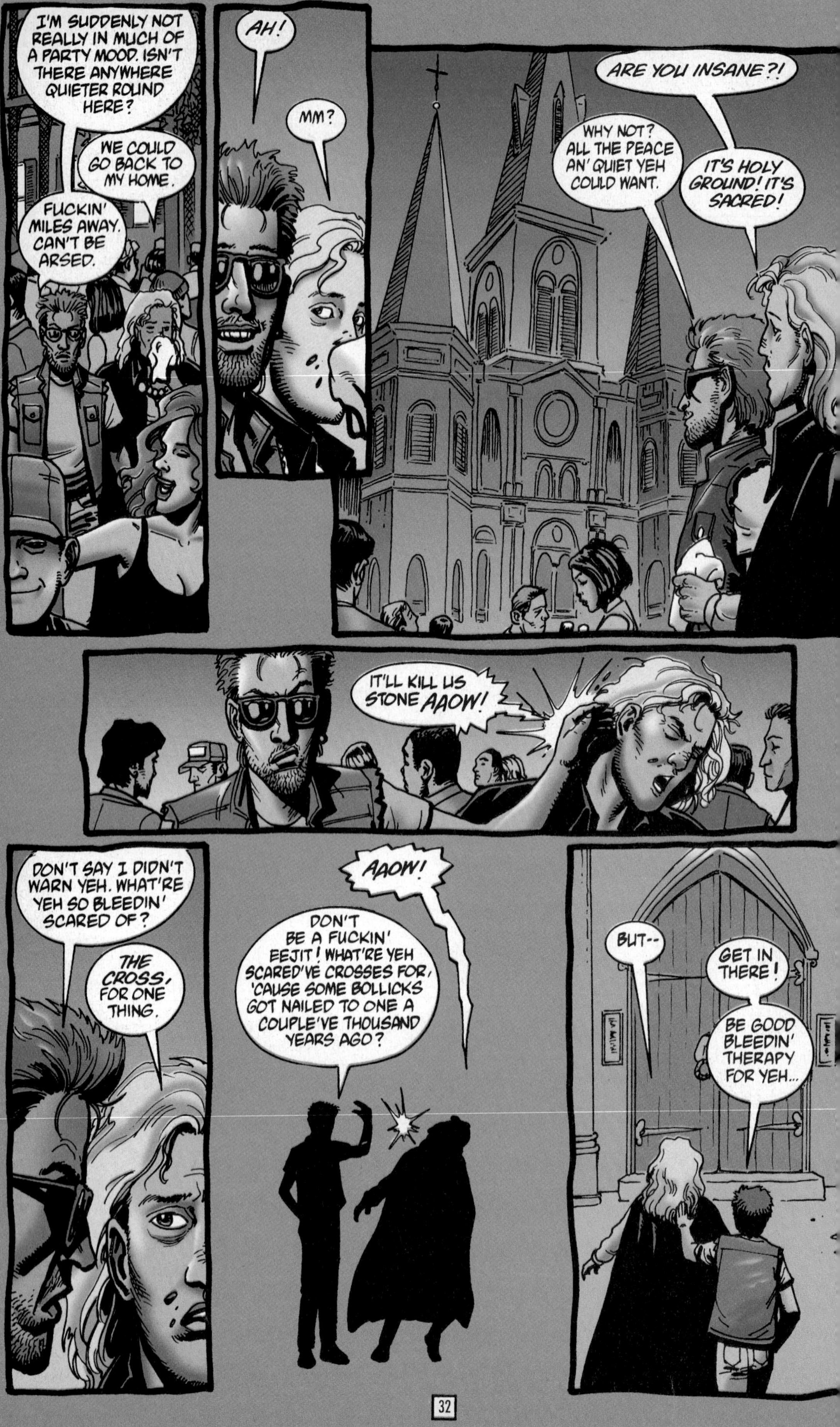
I'M SUDDENLY NOT REALLY IN MUCH OF A PARTY MOOD. ISN'T THERE ANYWHERE QUIETER ROUND HERE?
WE COULD GO BACK TO MY HOME.
FUCKIN' MILES AWAY. CAN'T BE ARSED.
AH!
MM?
ARE YOU INSANE?!
WHY NOT? ALL THE PEACE AN' QUIET YEH COULD WANT.
IT'S HOLY GROUND! IT'S SACRED!
IT'LL KILL US STONE AAOW!
DON'T SAY I DIDN'T WARN YEH. WHAT'RE YEH SO BLEEDIN' SCARED OF?
THE CROSS, FOR ONE THING.
AAOW!
DON'T BE A FUCKIN' EEJIT! WHAT'RE YEH SCARED'VE CROSSES FOR, 'CAUSE SOME BOLLICKS GOT NAILED TO ONE A COUPLE'VE THOUSAND YEARS AGO?
BUT--
GET IN THERE!
BE GOOD BLEEDIN' THERAPY FOR YEH...

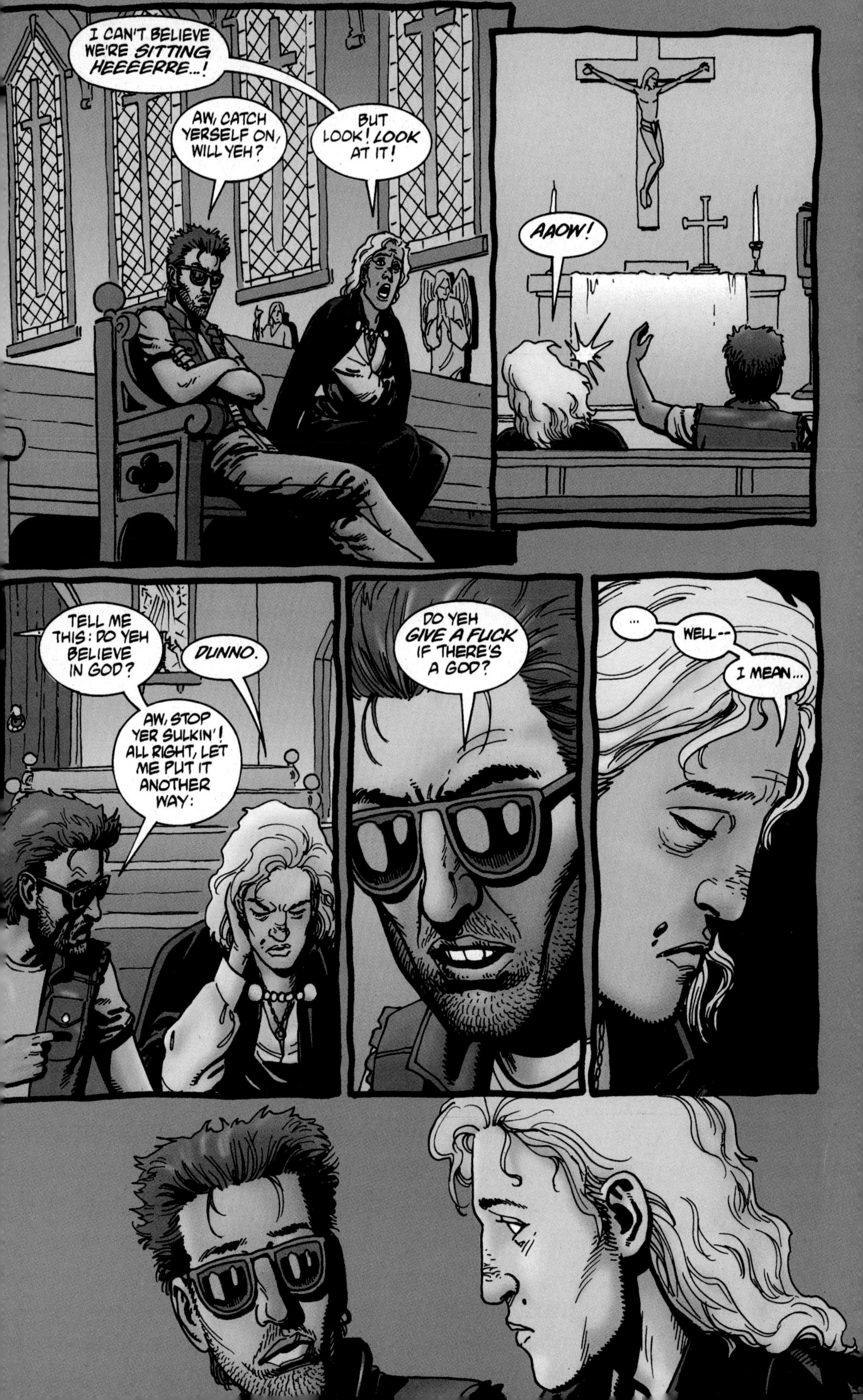
I CAN'T BELIEVE WE'RE SITTING HEEEERRE...!
AW, CATCH YERSELF ON, WILL YEH?
BUT LOOK! LOOK AT IT!
AAOW!
TELL ME THIS: DO YEH BELIEVE IN GOD?
DUNNO.
AW, STOP YER SULKIN'! ALL RIGHT, LET ME PUT IT ANOTHER WAY:
DO YEH GIVE A FUCK IF THERE'S A GOD?
...
WELL--
I MEAN...

SO WHY'RE YEH AFRAID'VE THAT THING?

WELL...I REALLY DON'T WANT TO GET HIT AGAIN, BUT I SORT OF THOUGHT IT WENT WITH THE TERRITORY...

WHY?

BECAUSE--YOU KNOW. BECAUSE IT ALWAYS DOES.

ALWAYS MEANIN' IN NOVELS AN' MOVIES AN' SPOOKY OUL' STORIES, AYE?

JUST AS A MATTER'VE INTEREST, WHAT'D YEH DO, ONCE YEH TWIGGED ON WHAT'D HAPPENED TO YEH?

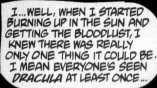

I...WELL, WHEN I STARTED BURNING UP IN THE SUN AND GETTING THE BLOODLUST, I KNEW THERE WAS REALLY ONLY ONE THING IT COULD BE. I MEAN EVERYONE'S SEEN DRACULA AT LEAST ONCE...

SO I SORT OF READ UP ON IT. OBVIOUSLY THERE'S NO ACTUAL TEXTBOOK ON THE BEHAVIOR OF OUR KIND, SO--

SO YEH WENT BY WHAT ALL THE TOSSY FUCKIN' NOVELS SAID.

UM...YES. THE LIFESTYLE SORT'VE APPEALED TO ME, I SUPPOSE.

YOU KNOW.

THE GOTHIC THING.

HAVE YEH EVER HAD A STAKE THROUGH THE HEART?

NO!

I HAVE. IT FUCKIN' HURTS. D'YEH EAT GARLIC?

NO...

I LOVE THE STUFF. THERE'S A PLACE IN SAN FRANCISCO, *THE STINKING ROSE*, THEY COOK EVERYTHING WITH IT. WHAT ABOUT HOLY WATER?

WHAT ABOUT IT?

EXACTLY.

WHY THE FUCK *SHOULD* ANY'VE THAT STUFF HURT US? IT'S FAIRY TALES. IT'S LIKE EXPECTIN' TO HAVE A BAD DAY 'CAUSE YEH'VE WALKED UNDER A LADDER. IT'S *BOLLICKS*...

DID YEH EVER TRY JUMPIN' OFF A ROOF AN' TURNIN' INTO A BAT? OR RIDIN' MOONBEAMS AS A CLOUD OF DUST?

I TRIED THE BAT THING ONCE.

BROKE BOTH MY FUCKING LEGS.

SUPPOSE YEH'RE AN ORDINARY FELLA, NOT LIKE US, AN' YEH'RE IN A PLANE CRASH IN THE FUCKIN' JUNGLE. NO OTHER SURVIVORS. NO SIGNS'VE CIVILIZATION. YEH'RE STRANDED.

BY SOME MIRACLE, YEH STUMBLE ACROSS A COPY OF *TARZAN OF THE APES*. YEH READ IT.

DO YEH GO AN' LIVE IN THE TREETOPS AN' TALK TO MONKEYS?

POINT.

DON'T GET ME WRONG, I FUCKIN' LOVE *DRACULA*. READ IT LOADS'VE TIMES. BUT EVERY TIME I GET TO THE END I THINK-- WHAT AN ARSEHOLE!

NO FUCKIN' WAY ARE THEY GONNA GET ME LIKE THAT!

AH, JAYSIS.

YEH KNOW...WHEN I THINK OF THE STUFF I'VE GOT UP TO IN ME TIME--AN' YEH SHOULD FUCKIN' SEE SOME'VE IT, I'M TELLIN' YEH--IT JUST MAKES ME THINK HOW LUCKY WE ARE BEIN' LIKE THIS, YEH KNOW?

WE'VE THE WHOLE WIDE WORLD OUT THERE WAITIN' FOR US, AN' WE'VE FOREVER TO MAKE THE MOST'VE IT. AN' THAT'S THE THING, MATE: ENJOYIN' LIFE.

NOT LIVIN' DEATH, OR ANYTHIN' STUPID LIKE THAT.

AN' SURE WHAT'VE WE GOT TO FEAR EXCEPT THE SUN?

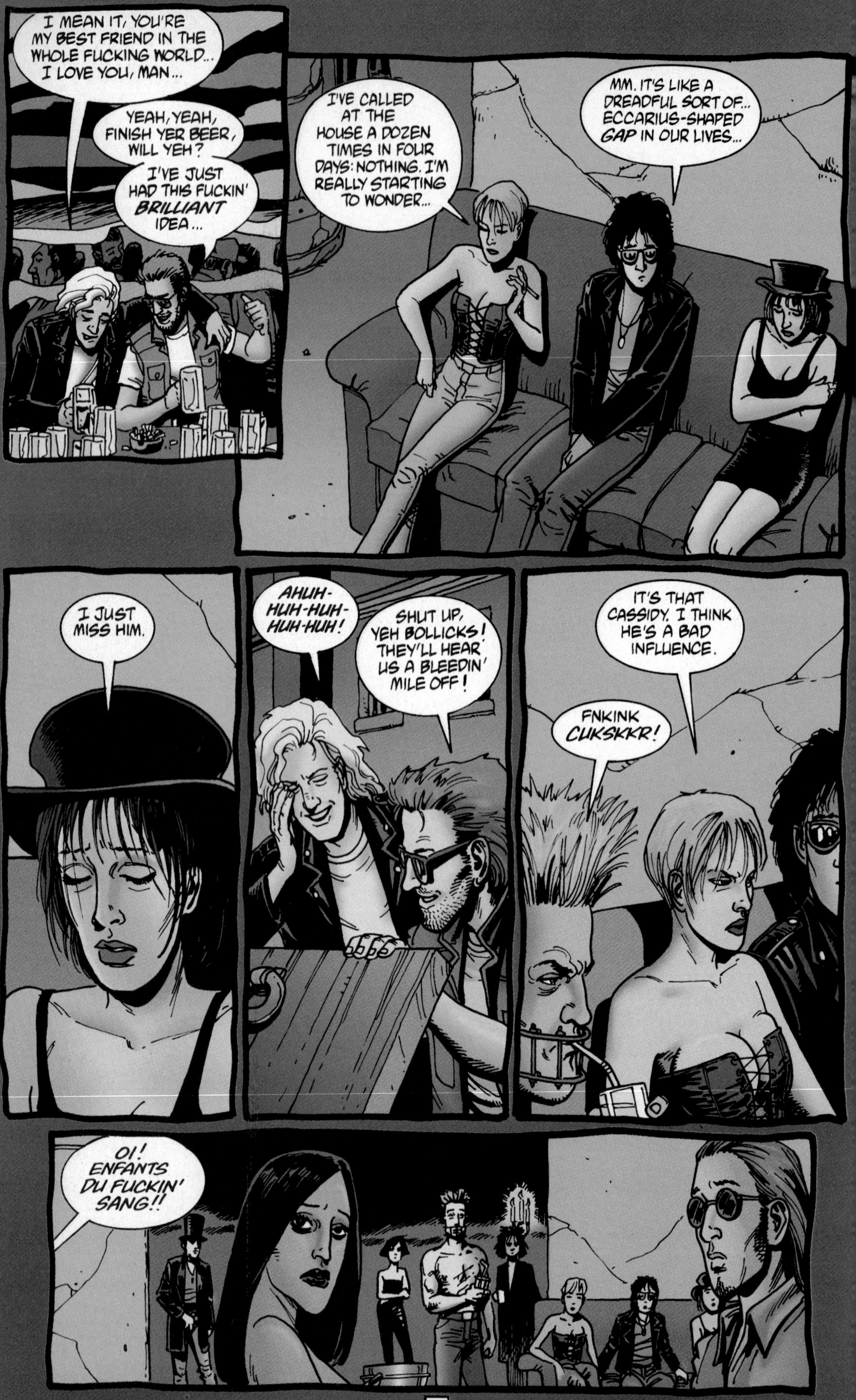
I MEAN IT, YOU'RE MY BEST FRIEND IN THE WHOLE FUCKING WORLD... I LOVE YOU, MAN...
YEAH, YEAH, FINISH YER BEER, WILL YEH?
I'VE JUST HAD THIS FUCKIN' BRILLIANT IDEA...
I'VE CALLED AT THE HOUSE A DOZEN TIMES IN FOUR DAYS: NOTHING. I'M REALLY STARTING TO WONDER...
MM. IT'S LIKE A DREADFUL SORT OF... ECCARIUS-SHAPED GAP IN OUR LIVES...
I JUST MISS HIM.
AHUH-HUH-HUH-HUH-HUH!
SHUT UP, YEH BOLLICKS! THEY'LL HEAR US A BLEEDIN' MILE OFF!
IT'S THAT CASSIDY. I THINK HE'S A BAD INFLUENCE.
FNKINK CUKSKKR!
OI! ENFANTS DU FUCKIN' SANG!!

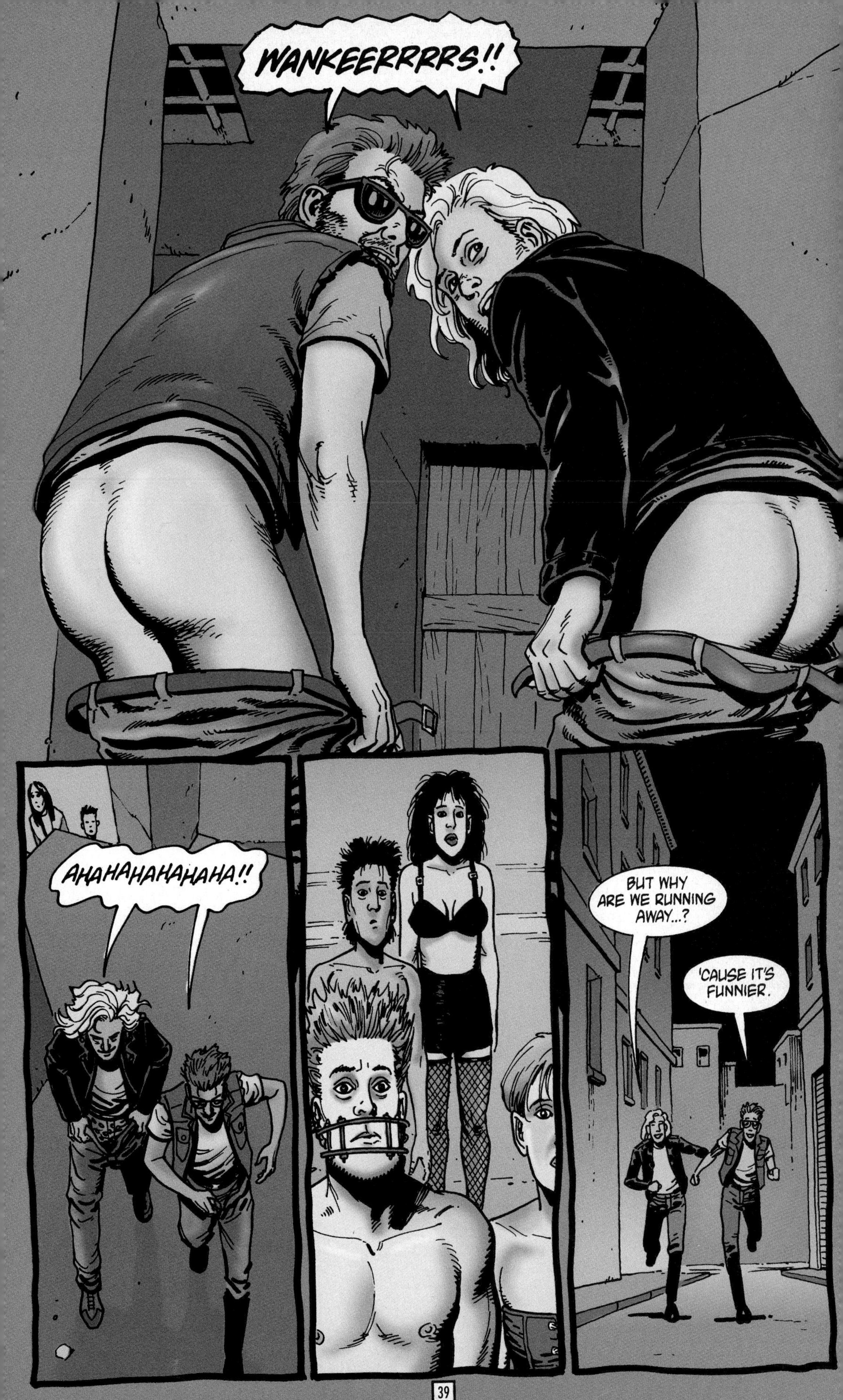
WANKEERRRRS!!
AHAHAHAHAHAHAHA!!
BUT WHY ARE WE RUNNING AWAY...?
'CAUSE IT'S FUNNIER.

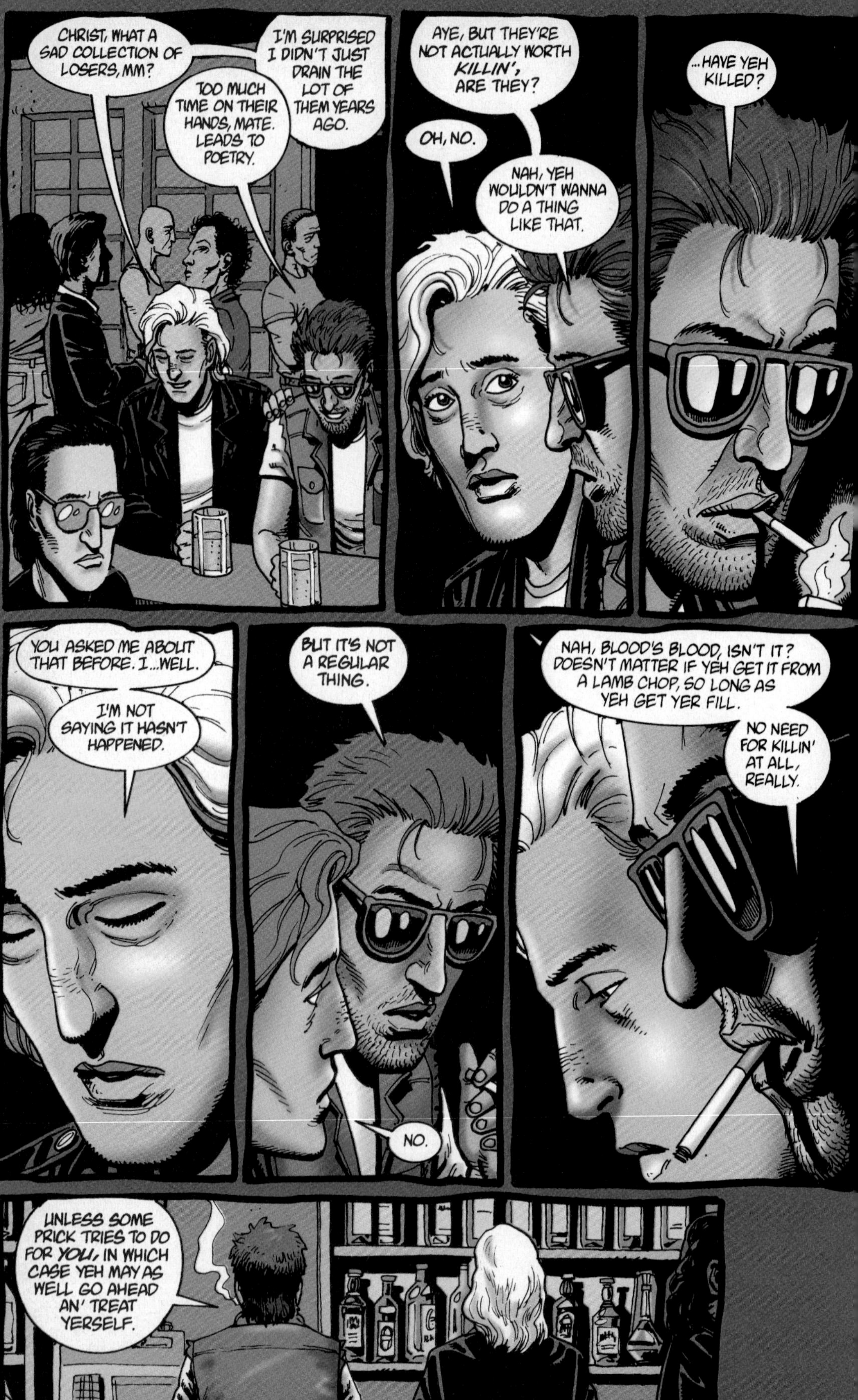
CHRIST, WHAT A SAD COLLECTION OF LOSERS, MM?
TOO MUCH TIME ON THEIR HANDS, MATE. LEADS TO POETRY.
I'M SURPRISED I DIDN'T JUST DRAIN THE LOT OF THEM YEARS AGO.
AYE, BUT THEY'RE NOT ACTUALLY WORTH KILLIN', ARE THEY?
OH, NO.
NAH, YEH WOULDN'T WANNA DO A THING LIKE THAT.
...HAVE YEH KILLED?
YOU ASKED ME ABOUT THAT BEFORE. I...WELL.
I'M NOT SAYING IT HASN'T HAPPENED.
BUT IT'S NOT A REGULAR THING.
NO.
NAH, BLOOD'S BLOOD, ISN'T IT? DOESN'T MATTER IF YEH GET IT FROM A LAMB CHOP, SO LONG AS YEH GET YER FILL.
NO NEED FOR KILLIN' AT ALL, REALLY.
UNLESS SOME PRICK TRIES TO DO FOR YOU, IN WHICH CASE YEH MAY AS WELL GO AHEAD AN' TREAT YERSELF.

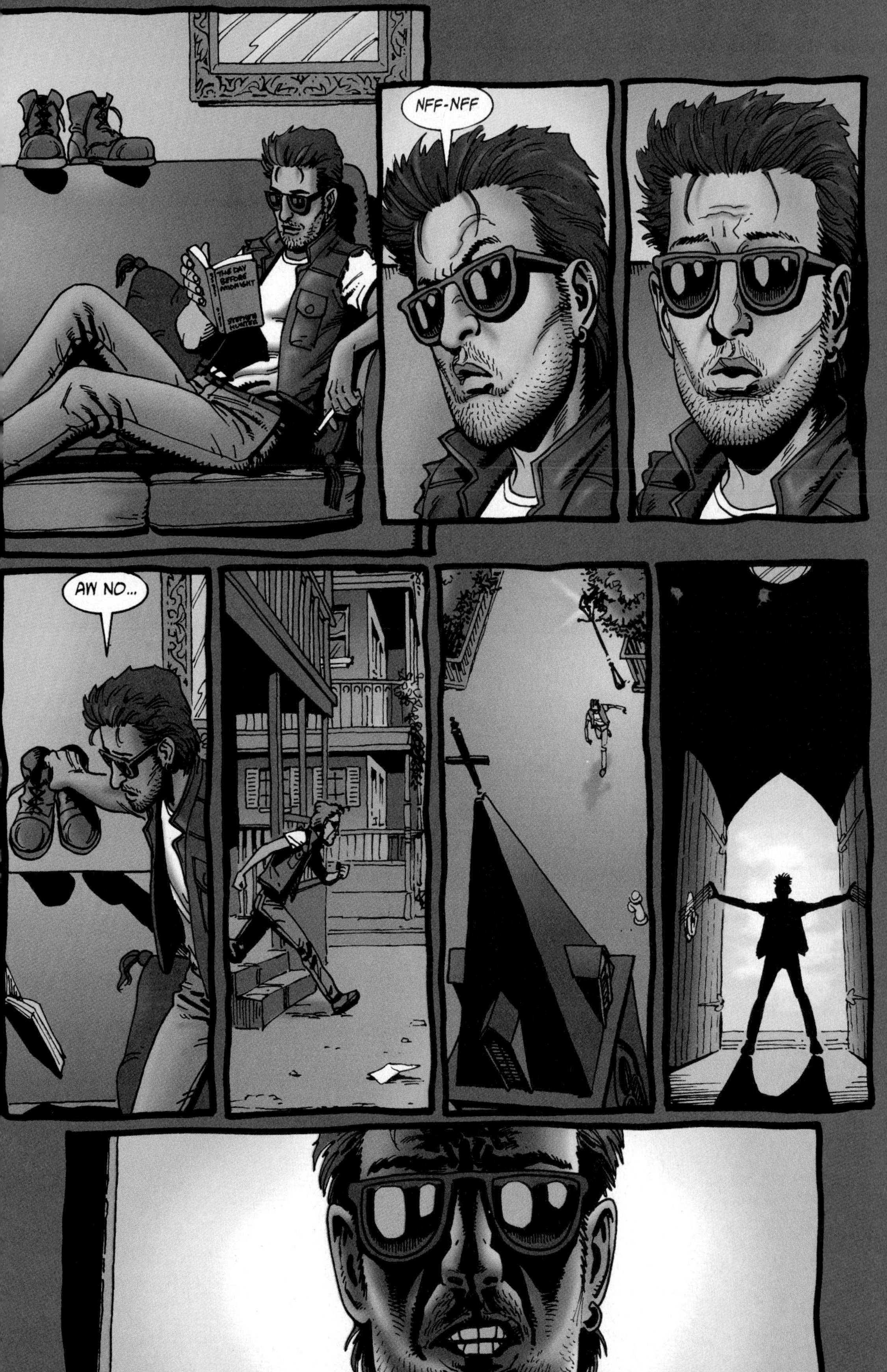
THE DAY BEFORE MIDNIGHT
STEPHEN HUNTER
NFF-NFF
AW NO...

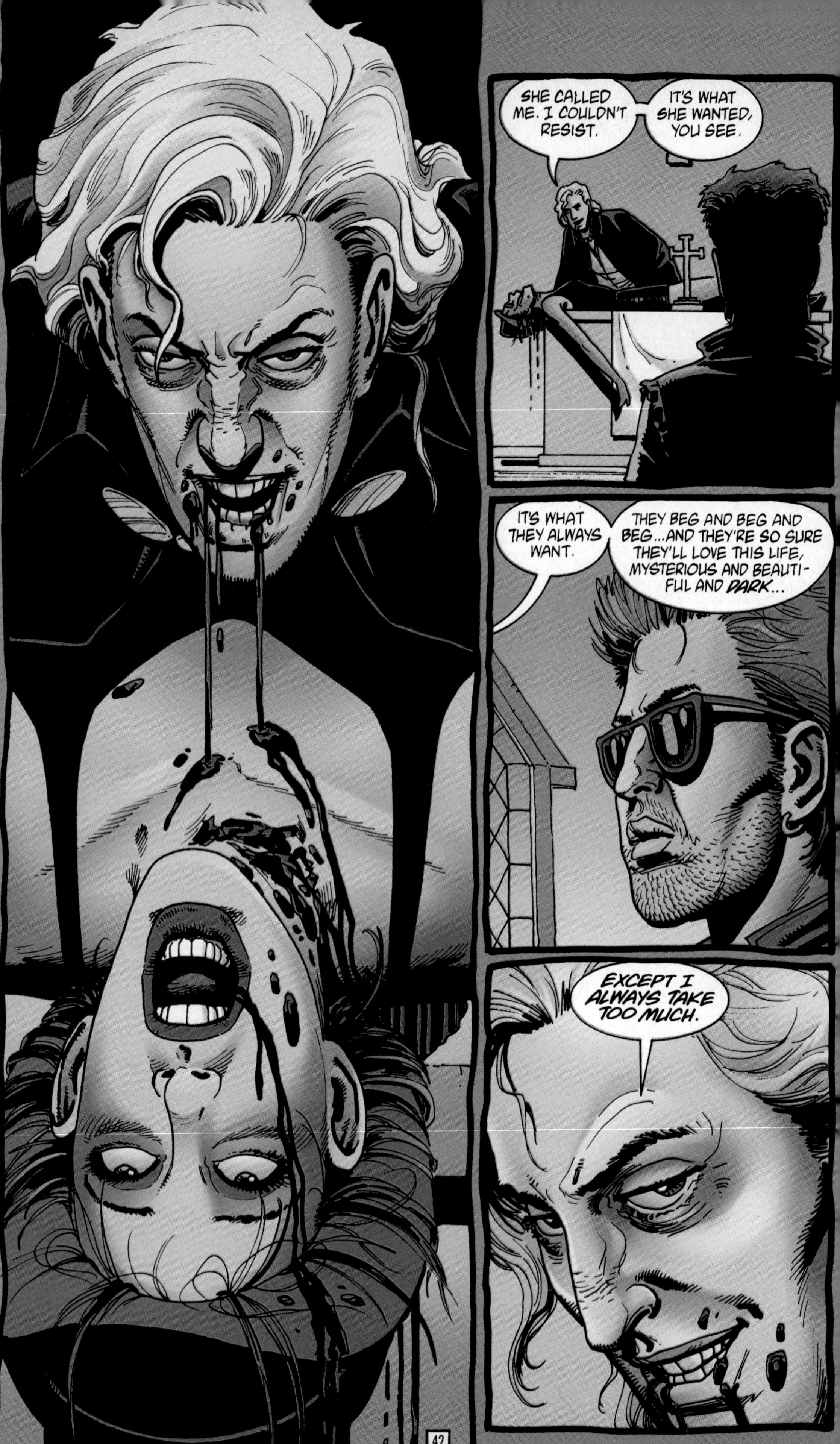
SHE CALLED ME. I COULDN'T RESIST.
IT'S WHAT SHE WANTED, YOU SEE.
IT'S WHAT THEY ALWAYS WANT.
THEY BEG AND BEG AND BEG...AND THEY'RE SO SURE THEY'LL LOVE THIS LIFE, MYSTERIOUS AND BEAUTIFUL AND DARK...
EXCEPT I ALWAYS TAKE TOO MUCH.

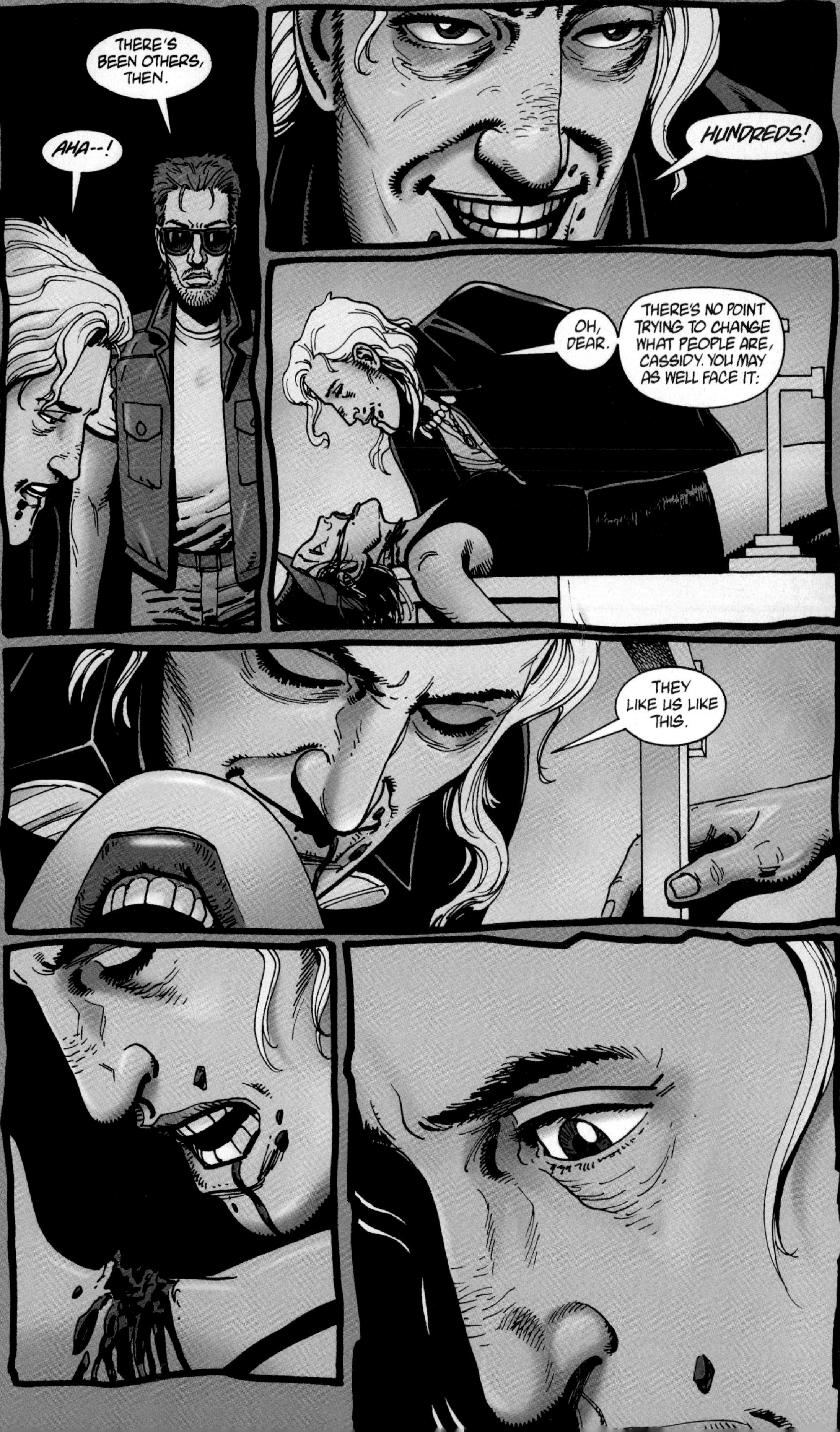
THERE'S BEEN OTHERS, THEN.
AHA--!
HUNDREDS!
OH, DEAR.
THERE'S NO POINT TRYING TO CHANGE WHAT PEOPLE ARE, CASSIDY. YOU MAY AS WELL FACE IT:
THEY LIKE US LIKE THIS.

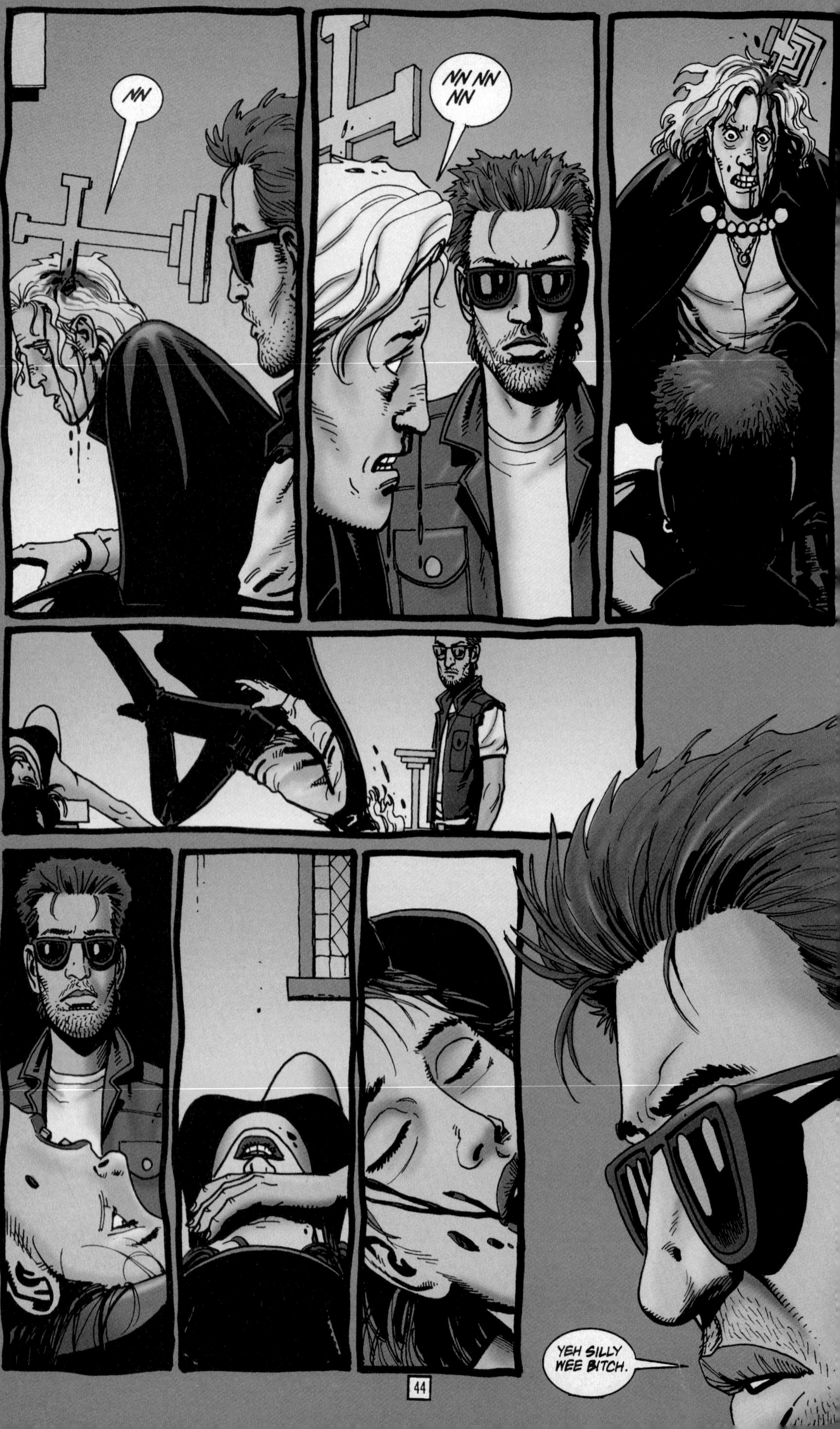
NN
NN NN NN
YEH SILLY WEE BITCH.

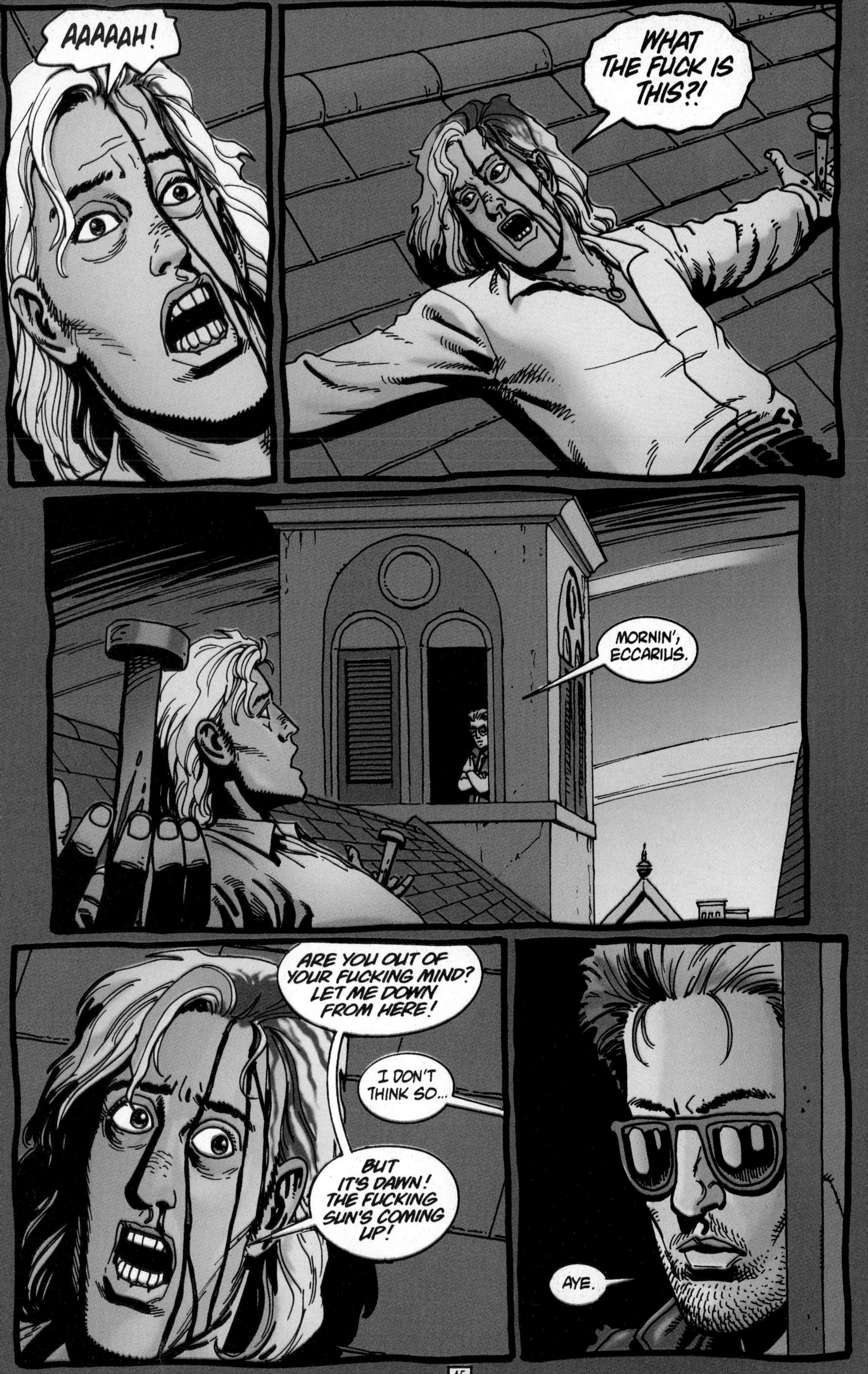
AAAAAH!
WHAT THE FUCK IS THIS?!
MORNIN', ECCARIUS.
ARE YOU OUT OF YOUR FUCKING MIND? LET ME DOWN FROM HERE!
I DON'T THINK SO...
BUT IT'S DAWN! THE FUCKING SUN'S COMING UP!
AYE.

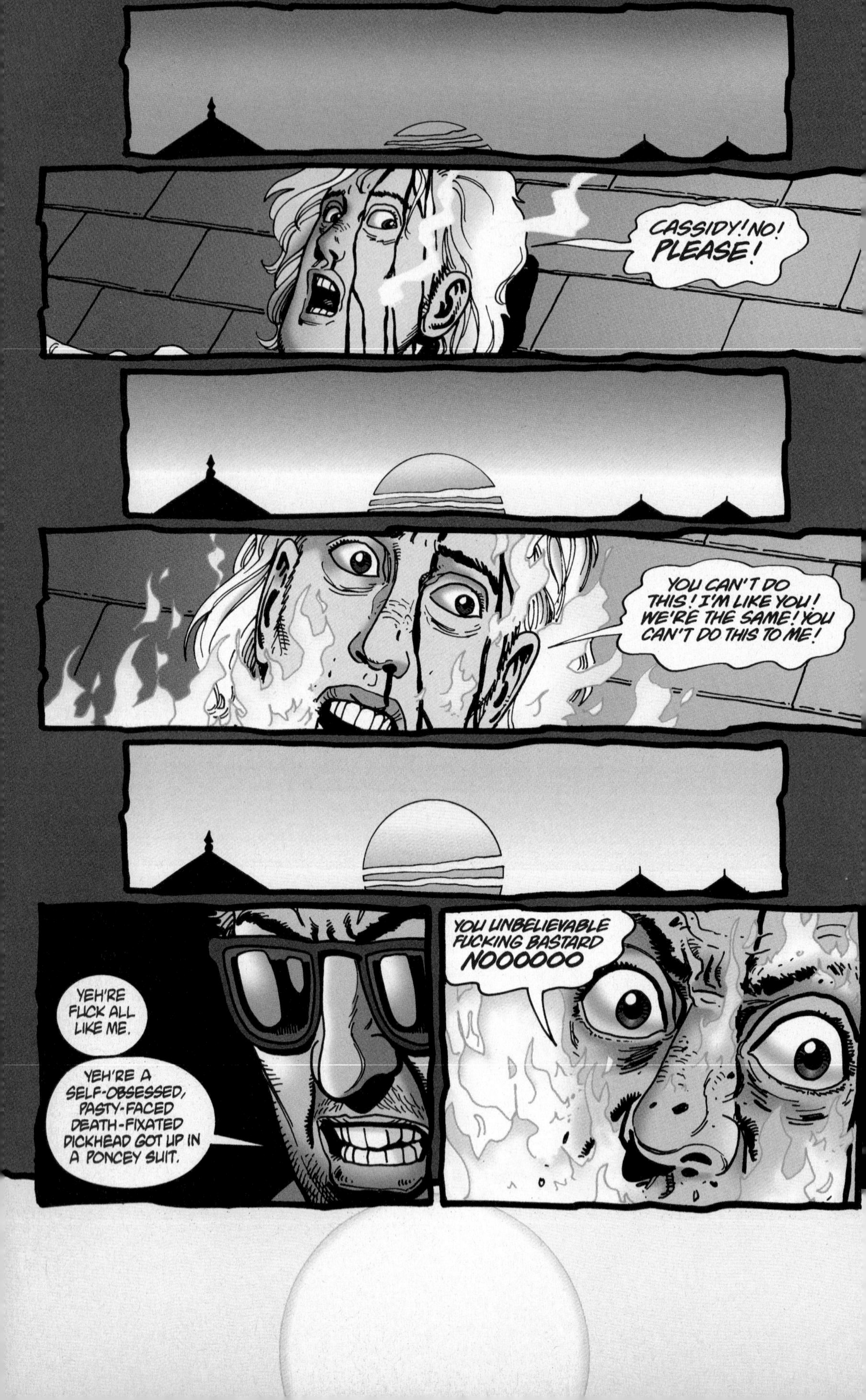
CASSIDY! NO! PLEASE!
YOU CAN'T DO THIS! I'M LIKE YOU! WE'RE THE SAME! YOU CAN'T DO THIS TO ME!
YEH'RE FUCK ALL LIKE ME.
YEH'RE A SELF-OBSESSED, PASTY-FACED DEATH-FIXATED DICKHEAD GOT UP IN A PONCEY SUIT.
YOU UNBELIEVABLE FUCKING BASTARD NOOOOOO

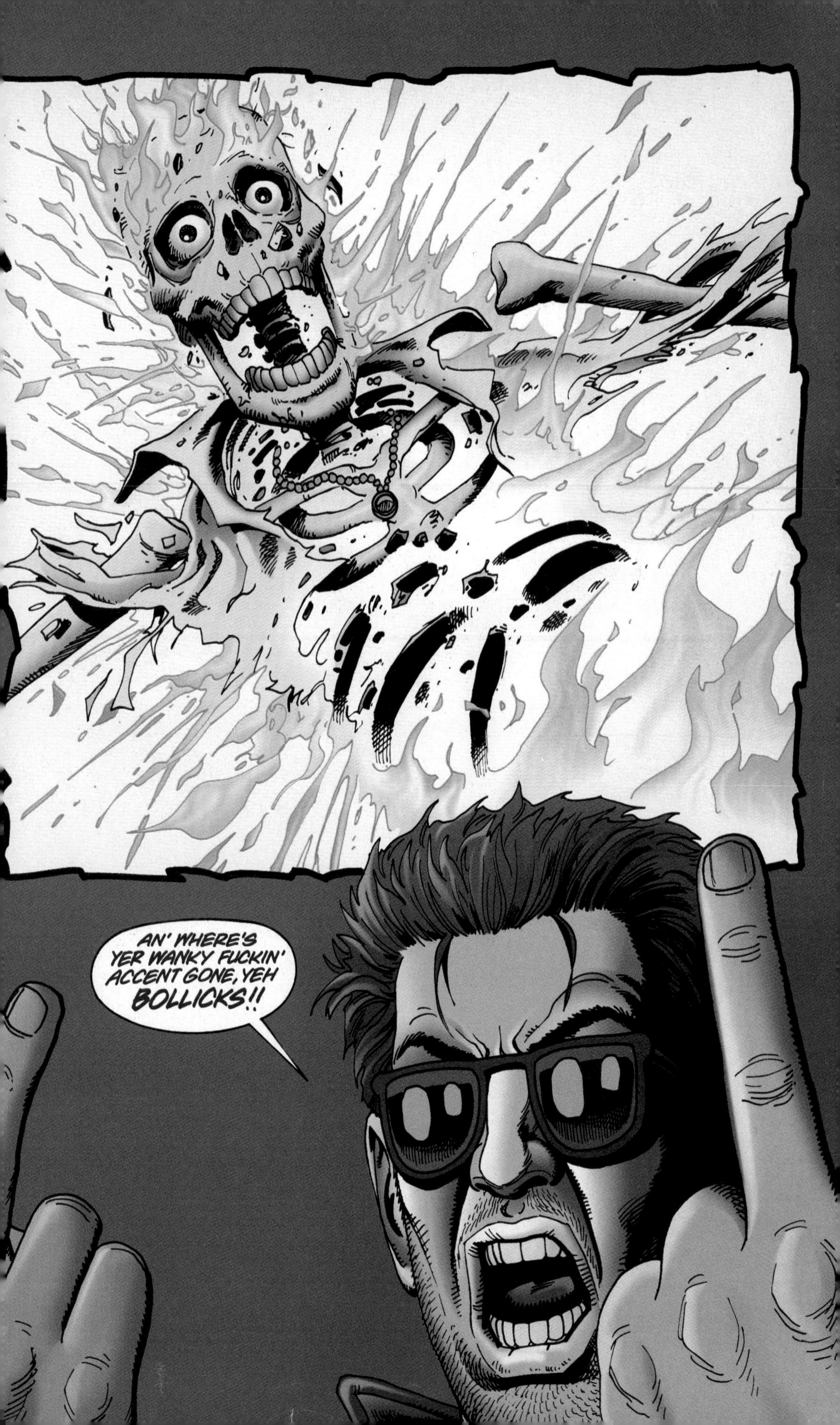
AN' WHERE'S YER WANKY FUCKIN' ACCENT GONE, YEH BOLLICKS!!

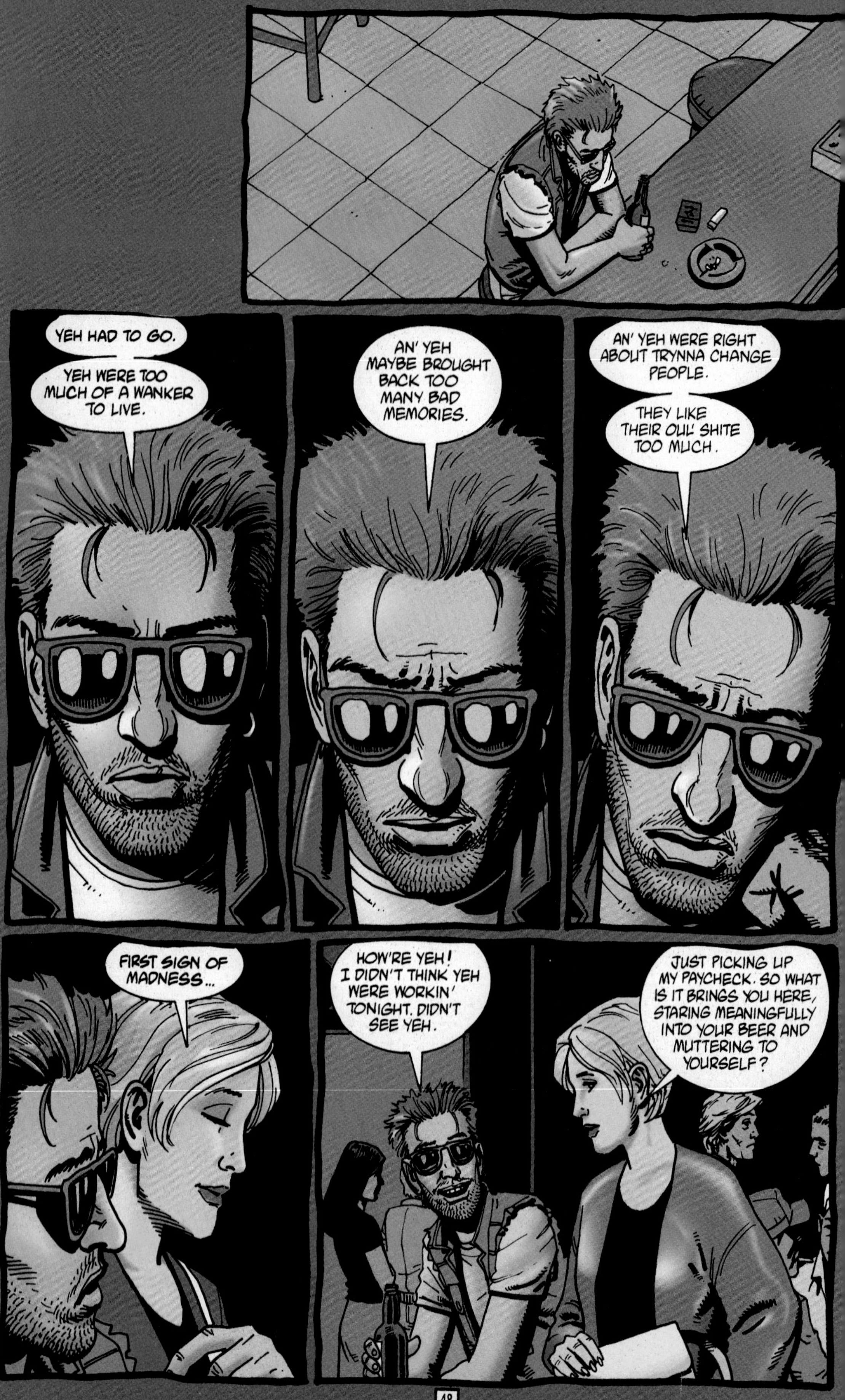
YEH HAD TO GO.
YEH WERE TOO MUCH OF A WANKER TO LIVE.
AN' YEH MAYBE BROUGHT BACK TOO MANY BAD MEMORIES.
AN' YEH WERE RIGHT ABOUT TRYNNA CHANGE PEOPLE.
THEY LIKE THEIR OUL' SHITE TOO MUCH.
FIRST SIGN OF MADNESS...
HOW'RE YEH! I DIDN'T THINK YEH WERE WORKIN' TONIGHT. DIDN'T SEE YEH.
JUST PICKING UP MY PAYCHECK. SO WHAT IS IT BRINGS YOU HERE, STARING MEANINGFULLY INTO YOUR BEER AND MUTTERING TO YOURSELF?

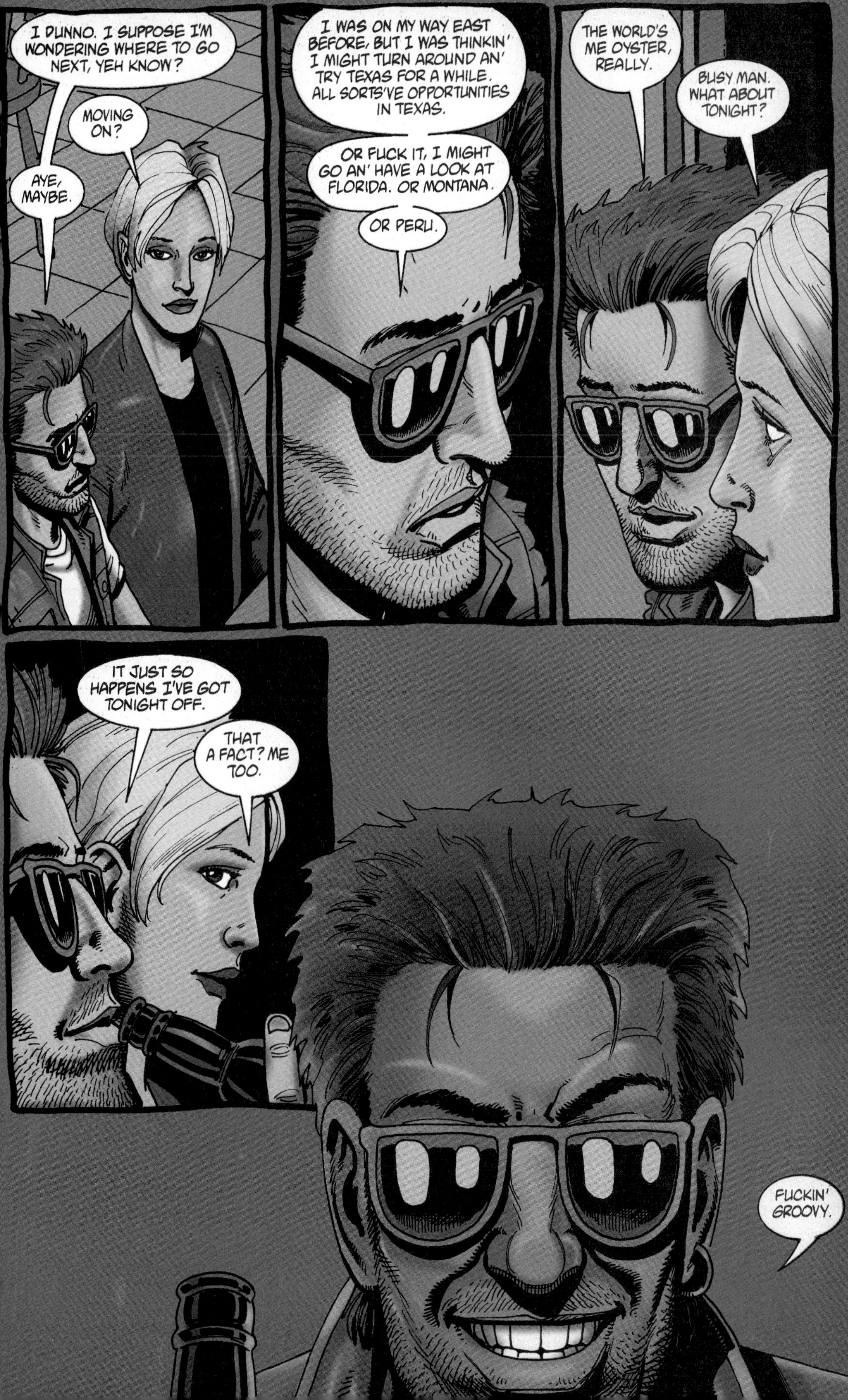
I DUNNO. I SUPPOSE I'M WONDERING WHERE TO GO NEXT, YEH KNOW?
MOVING ON?
AYE, MAYBE.
I WAS ON MY WAY EAST BEFORE, BUT I WAS THINKIN' I MIGHT TURN AROUND AN' TRY TEXAS FOR A WHILE. ALL SORTS'VE OPPORTUNITIES IN TEXAS.
OR FUCK IT, I MIGHT GO AN' HAVE A LOOK AT FLORIDA. OR MONTANA.
OR PERU.
THE WORLD'S ME OYSTER, REALLY.
BUSY MAN. WHAT ABOUT TONIGHT?
IT JUST SO HAPPENS I'VE GOT TONIGHT OFF.
THAT A FACT? ME TOO.
FUCKIN' GROOVY.

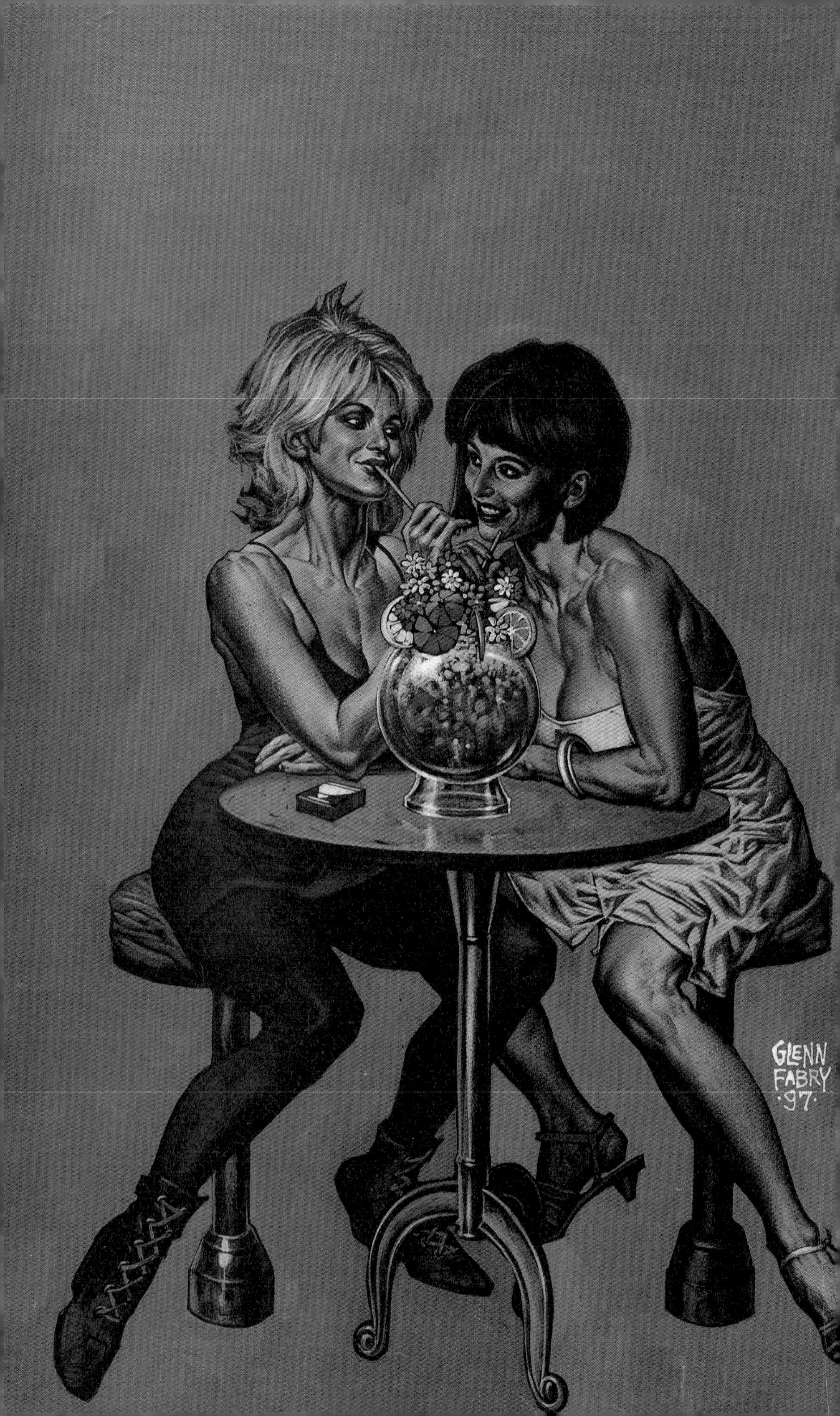
GLENN
FABRY
·97·

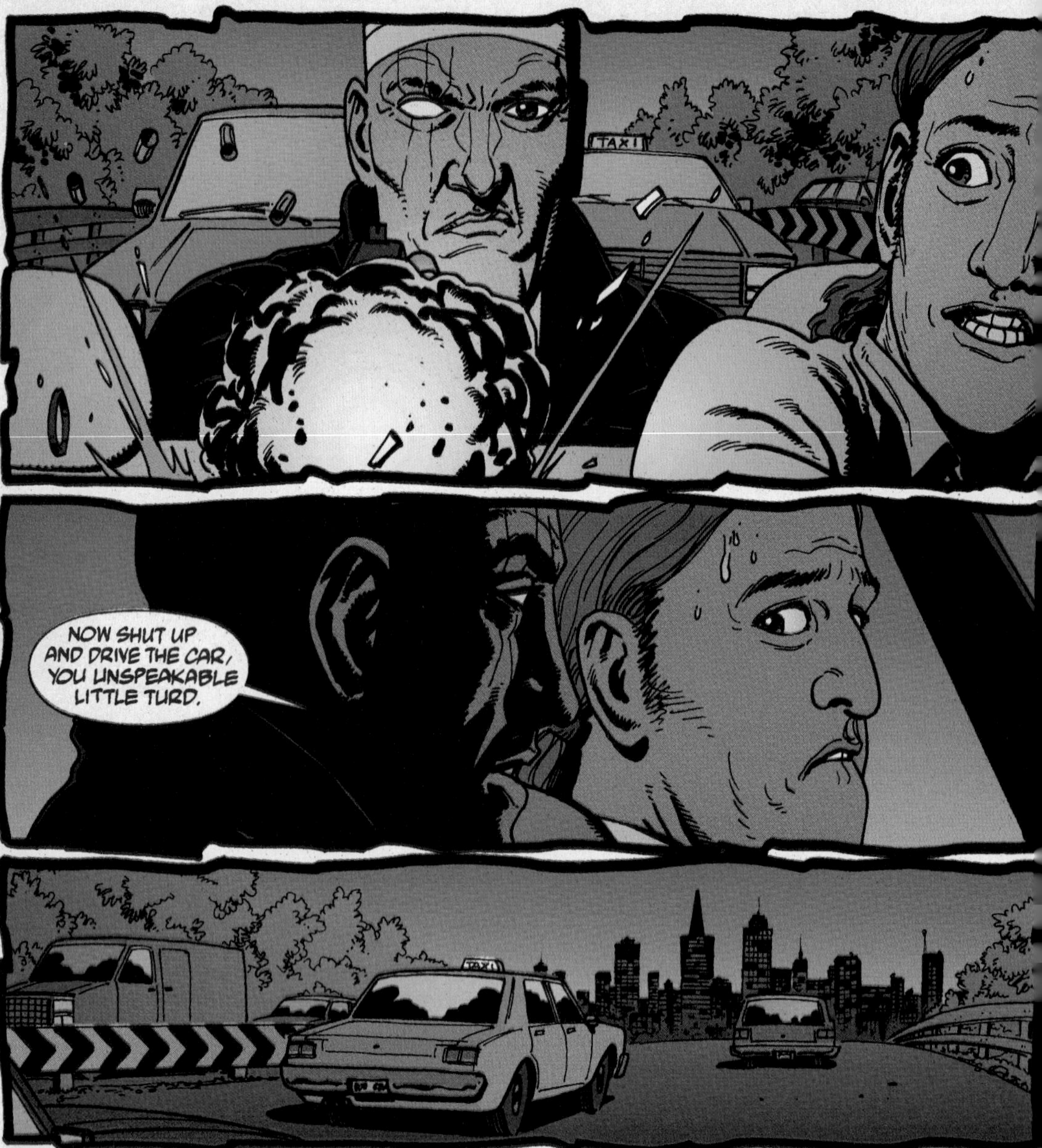
TAXI
NOW SHUT UP AND DRIVE THE CAR, YOU UNSPEAKABLE LITTLE TURD.
TAXI

GUNCHICKS

GARTH ENNIS - Writer STEVE DILLON - Artist
PAMELA RAMBO & MATT HOLLINGSWORTH - Color
CLEM ROBINS - Letterer AXEL ALONSO - Editor

PREACHER created by GARTH ENNIS and STEVE DILLON

N.Y.C.:

WELL, BEEN NICE KNOWIN' YOU...

GET ON IN THERE AN' STOP BEIN' SUCH A BIG DRAMA QUEEN. SHE'S BOUND TO'VE CALMED DOWN BY NOW.

SURE, ALL I DID WAS STRAND HER IN THE MIDDLE OF GODDAMN FRANCE. SHE'S PROBABLY FORGOTTEN ALL ABOUT IT.

I'M SURE SHE'LL LET YEH OFF WI' JUST A LIGHT MAIMIN'...

AHA HA HA. GUESS I'LL BE SEEIN' YOU.

OR NOT.

BABY!

MMMMWAHH!

MMMMMM LIKE THE NEW SLEEENKY THEENGS...?

uh-- YEAH--

BOUGHT 'EM SPECIALLY MMMMM

I WAS SURE YOU'D BE-- PISSED AT ME--

DON'T BE SILLY...I'M JUST SO RELIEVED YOU'RE OKAY...

WHAT HAPPENED TO YOUR POOR CHEEK...?

uh? HELL, YOU SHOULD SEE THE OTHER GUY--

SWEET JESUS...

heh heh heh...

WANNA SEE WHAT ELSE I BOUGHT...?

MM?

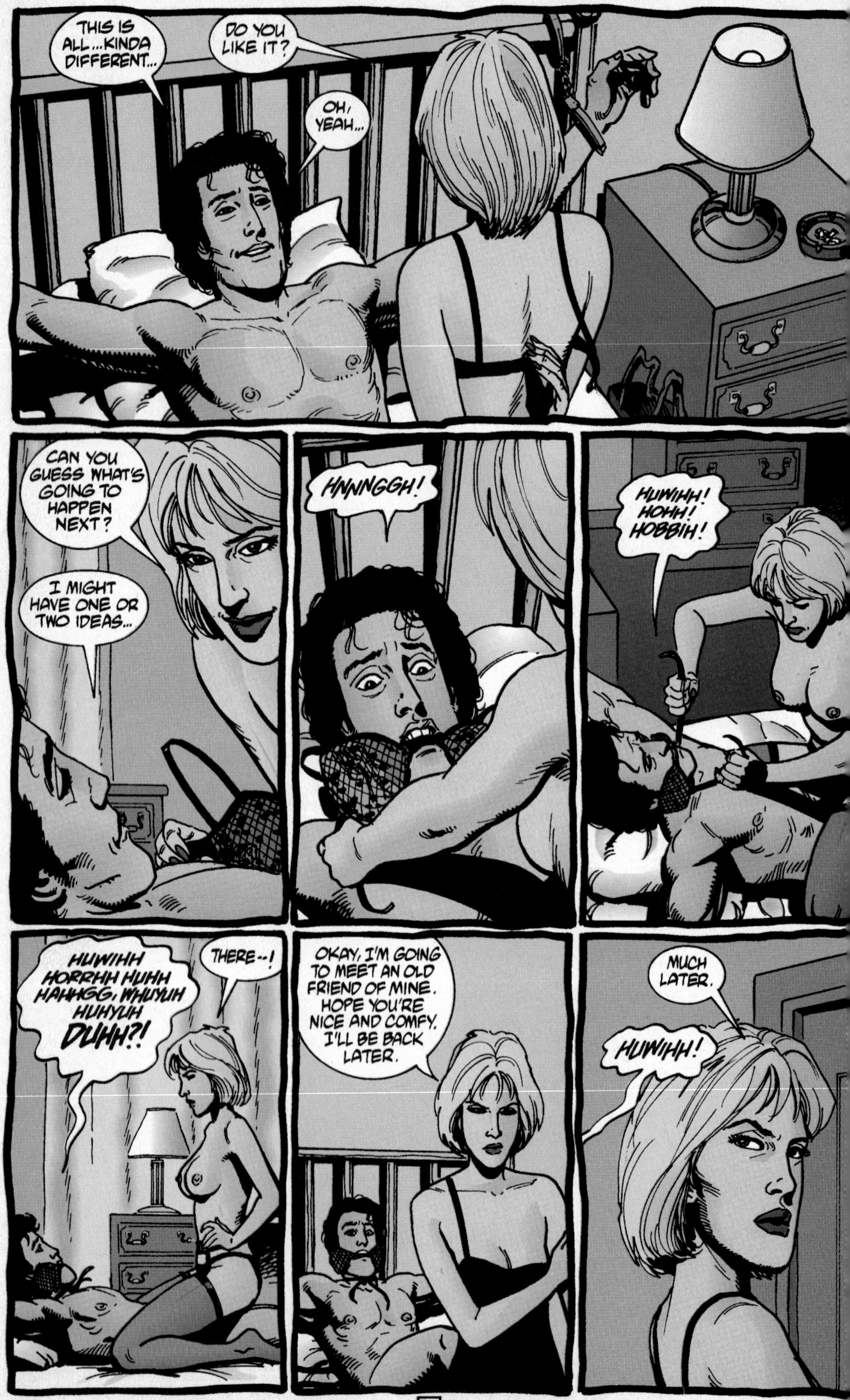
THIS IS ALL...KINDA DIFFERENT...
DO YOU LIKE IT?
OH, YEAH...
CAN YOU GUESS WHAT'S GOING TO HAPPEN NEXT?
I MIGHT HAVE ONE OR TWO IDEAS...
HNNNGGH!
HUWIHH! HOHH! HOBBIH!
HUWIHH HORRHH HUHH HAHHGG, WHUYUH HUHYUH DUHH?!
THERE--!
OKAY, I'M GOING TO MEET AN OLD FRIEND OF MINE. HOPE YOU'RE NICE AND COMFY. I'LL BE BACK LATER.
MUCH LATER.
HUWIHH!

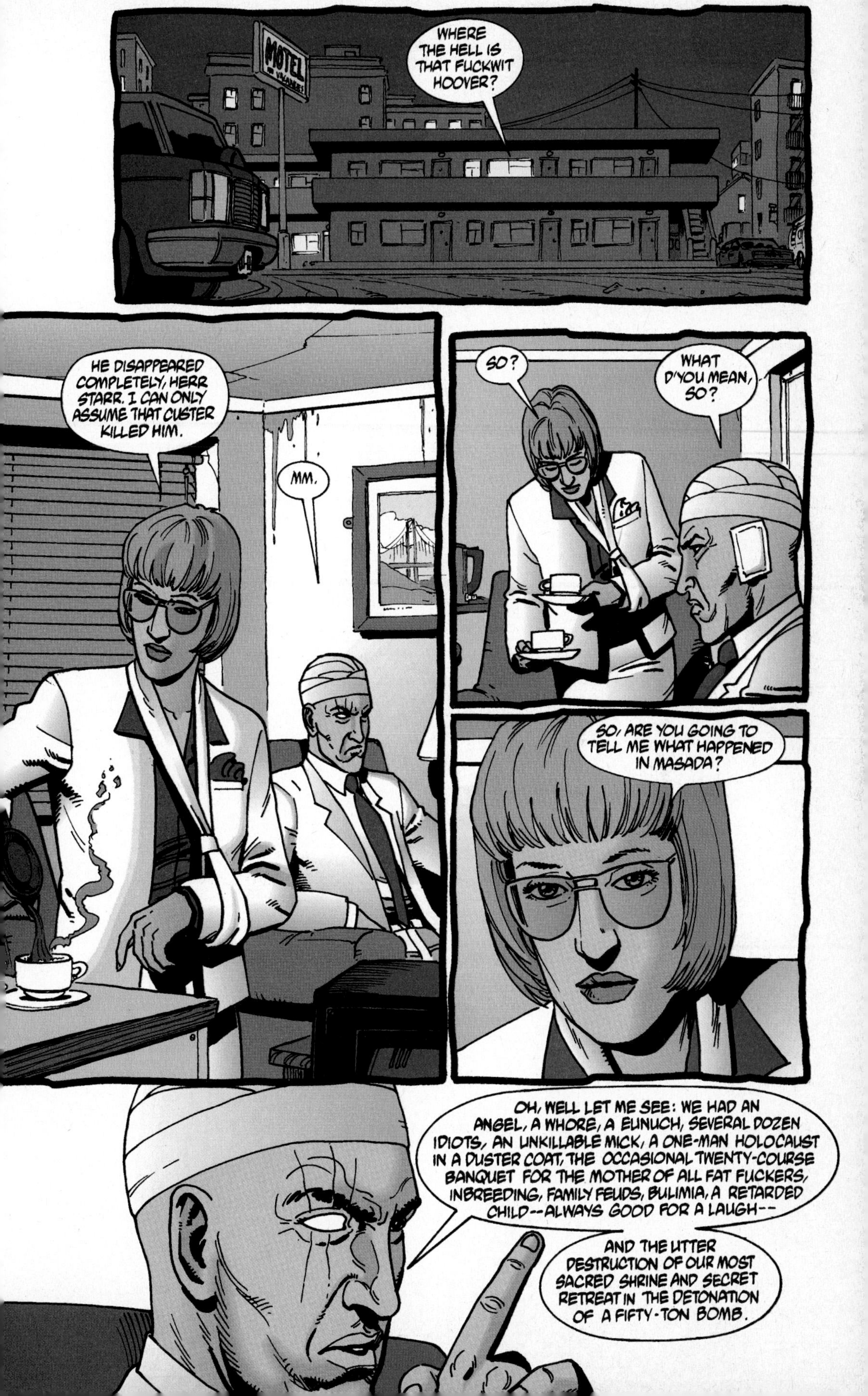
MOTEL
WHERE THE HELL IS THAT FUCKWIT HOOVER?
HE DISAPPEARED COMPLETELY, HERR STARR. I CAN ONLY ASSUME THAT CUSTER KILLED HIM.
MM.
SO?
WHAT D'YOU MEAN, SO?
SO, ARE YOU GOING TO TELL ME WHAT HAPPENED IN MASADA?
OH, WELL LET ME SEE: WE HAD AN ANGEL, A WHORE, A EUNUCH, SEVERAL DOZEN IDIOTS, AN UNKILLABLE MICK, A ONE-MAN HOLOCAUST IN A DUSTER COAT, THE OCCASIONAL TWENTY-COURSE BANQUET FOR THE MOTHER OF ALL FAT FUCKERS, INBREEDING, FAMILY FEUDS, BULIMIA, A RETARDED CHILD--ALWAYS GOOD FOR A LAUGH--
AND THE UTTER DESTRUCTION OF OUR MOST SACRED SHRINE AND SECRET RETREAT IN THE DETONATION OF A FIFTY-TON BOMB.

AND WE ALSO HAD JESSE CUSTER...

ANYWAY, IF I REMEMBER ANY MORE, I'LL BE SURE TO LET YOU KNOW.

THERE'S NO NEED TO BE SARCASTIC.

ACTUALLY, FEATHERSTONE, THERE IS EVERY NEED TO BE SARCASTIC.

AND WHAT ARE WE DOING IN THIS WRETCHED LITTLE SHITHOLE? DON'T TELL ME THE BUDGET'S FUCKED AS WELL...

NOT AT ALL. I SIMPLY FELT THAT AFTER THE GUNFIGHT AT THE DeSADE MANSION, IT MIGHT BE BEST TO MAINTAIN A LOW PROFILE FOR A WHILE.

HORSESHIT, I WANT THE RITZ. AND IF ANYONE COMPLAINS ABOUT OUR PROFILE I'LL PHONE BILL CLINTON AND HAVE THE FUCKERS SHIPPED TO SOME GULAG IN ALASKA.

YOU CAN DO THAT KIND OF THING WHEN YOU'RE ALL-FATHER OF THE GRAIL.

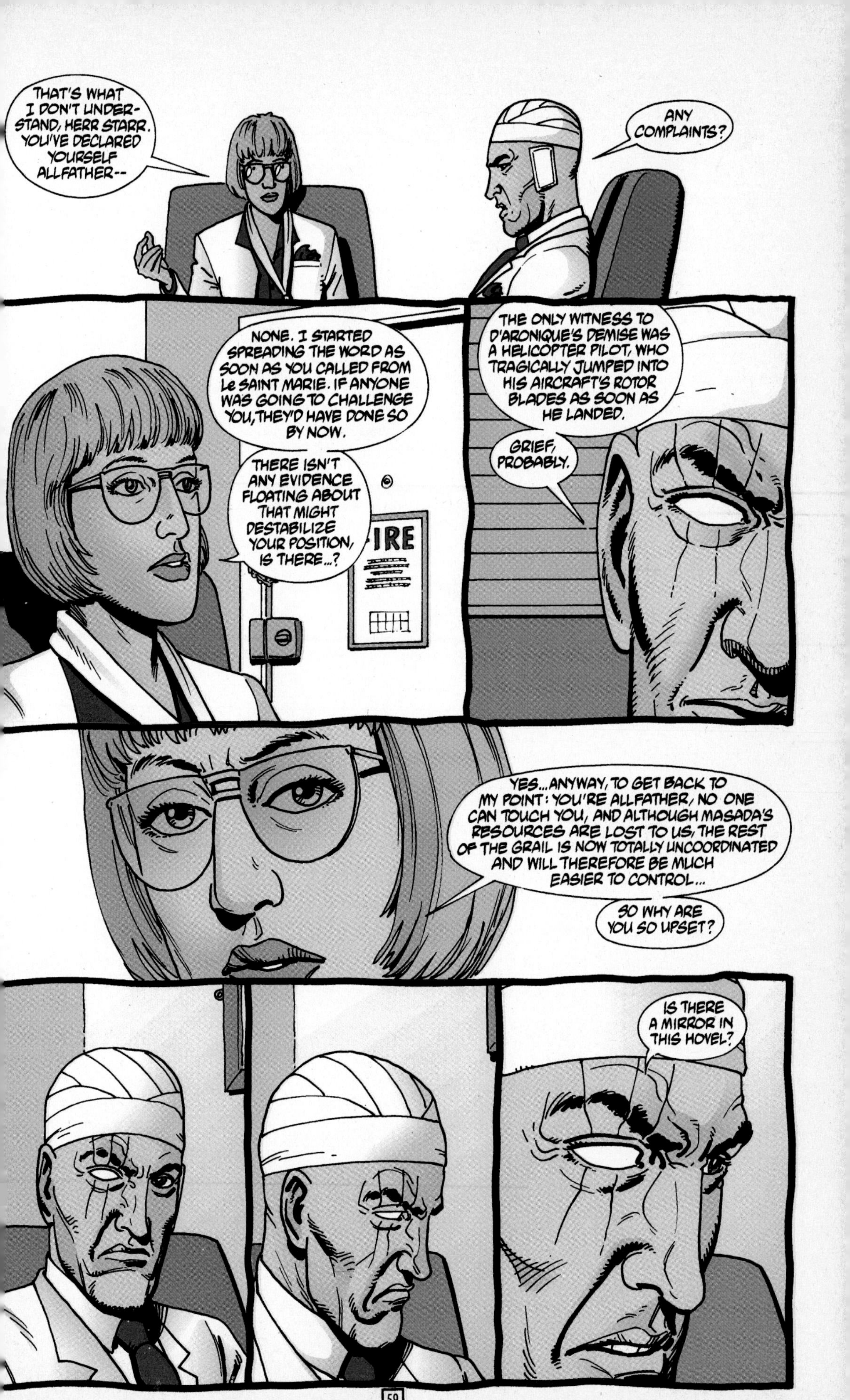
THAT'S WHAT I DON'T UNDER-STAND, HERR STARR. YOU'VE DECLARED YOURSELF ALLFATHER--
ANY COMPLAINTS?
NONE. I STARTED SPREADING THE WORD AS SOON AS YOU CALLED FROM Le SAINT MARIE. IF ANYONE WAS GOING TO CHALLENGE YOU, THEY'D HAVE DONE SO BY NOW.
THERE ISN'T ANY EVIDENCE FLOATING ABOUT THAT MIGHT DESTABILIZE YOUR POSITION, IS THERE...?
IRE
THE ONLY WITNESS TO D'ARONIQUE'S DEMISE WAS A HELICOPTER PILOT, WHO TRAGICALLY JUMPED INTO HIS AIRCRAFT'S ROTOR BLADES AS SOON AS HE LANDED.
GRIEF, PROBABLY.
YES...ANYWAY, TO GET BACK TO MY POINT: YOU'RE ALLFATHER, NO ONE CAN TOUCH YOU, AND ALTHOUGH MASADA'S RESOURCES ARE LOST TO US, THE REST OF THE GRAIL IS NOW TOTALLY UNCOORDINATED AND WILL THEREFORE BE MUCH EASIER TO CONTROL...
SO WHY ARE YOU SO UPSET?
IS THERE A MIRROR IN THIS HOVEL?

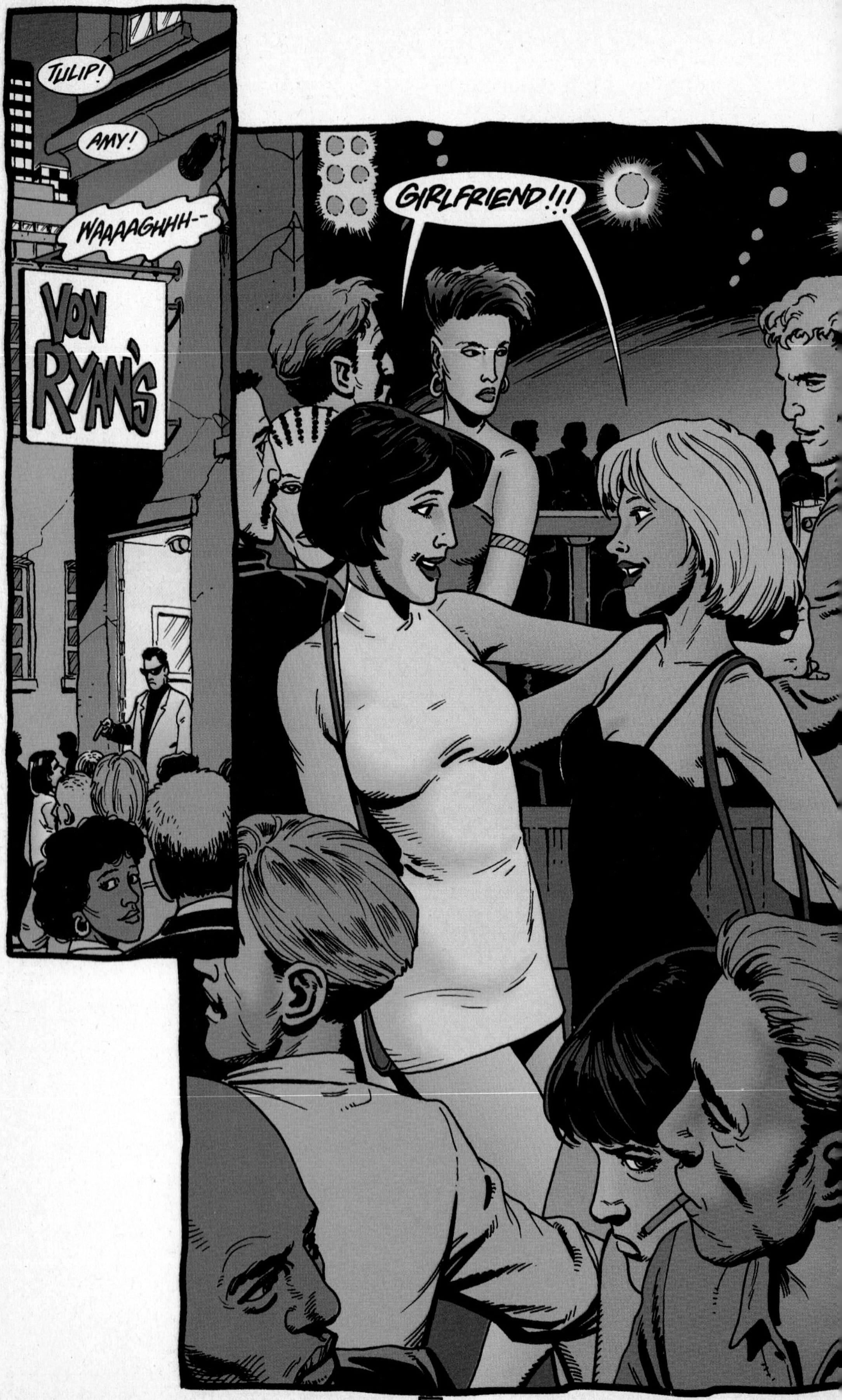
TULIP!
AMY!
WAAAAGHHH--
VON RYAN'S
GIRLFRIEND!!!

OH MY GOD OH MY GOD--

I CAN'T BELIEVE IT--

OH STOP IT--

OH YOU ARE *SUCH* A LIAR, I AM LIKE A TOTAL BLIMP--

OH LOOK AT YOUR HAIR, I *KNEW* YOU'D BE GREAT WITH LONG HAIR--

TWO YEARS--

OH YOU LOOK SO GOOD--

NO YOU DO, YOU DO. YOU'VE LOST SO MUCH WEIGHT--

OH BULL-SHIT--

BARMAN!

WHAT'LL IT BE?

TWO NAGASAKI AIRBURSTS, PLENTY OF FALLOUT.

COMING UP.

SO: I JUST CAN'T BELIEVE IT: I GET YOUR MESSAGE AND I'M THINKING, ISN'T SHE IN VEGAS OR DALLAS OR FLAGSTAFF OR SOMEWHERE?

SHE'S HERE?

I KNOW, I KNOW. THINGS HAVE BEEN CRAZY.

OH. TELL ME. DID YOU FIND HIM?

I FOUND HIM.

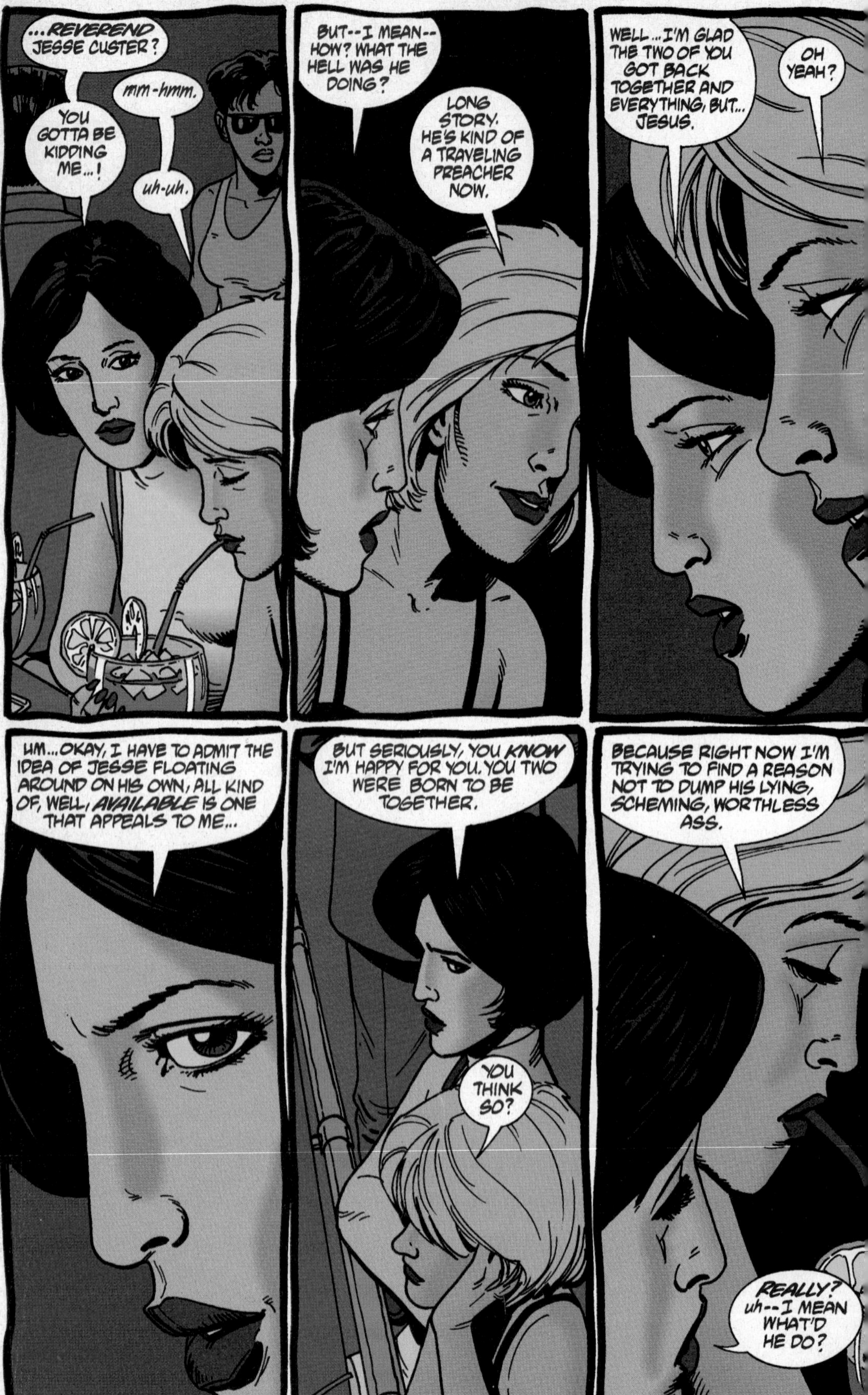
...REVEREND JESSE CUSTER?
YOU GOTTA BE KIDDING ME...!
mm-hmm.
uh-uh.
BUT--I MEAN--HOW? WHAT THE HELL WAS HE DOING?
LONG STORY. HE'S KIND OF A TRAVELING PREACHER NOW.
WELL...I'M GLAD THE TWO OF YOU GOT BACK TOGETHER AND EVERYTHING, BUT... JESUS.
OH YEAH?
UM...OKAY, I HAVE TO ADMIT THE IDEA OF JESSE FLOATING AROUND ON HIS OWN, ALL KIND OF, WELL, AVAILABLE IS ONE THAT APPEALS TO ME...
BUT SERIOUSLY, YOU KNOW I'M HAPPY FOR YOU. YOU TWO WERE BORN TO BE TOGETHER.
YOU THINK SO?
BECAUSE RIGHT NOW I'M TRYING TO FIND A REASON NOT TO DUMP HIS LYING, SCHEMING, WORTHLESS ASS.
REALLY? uh--I MEAN WHAT'D HE DO?

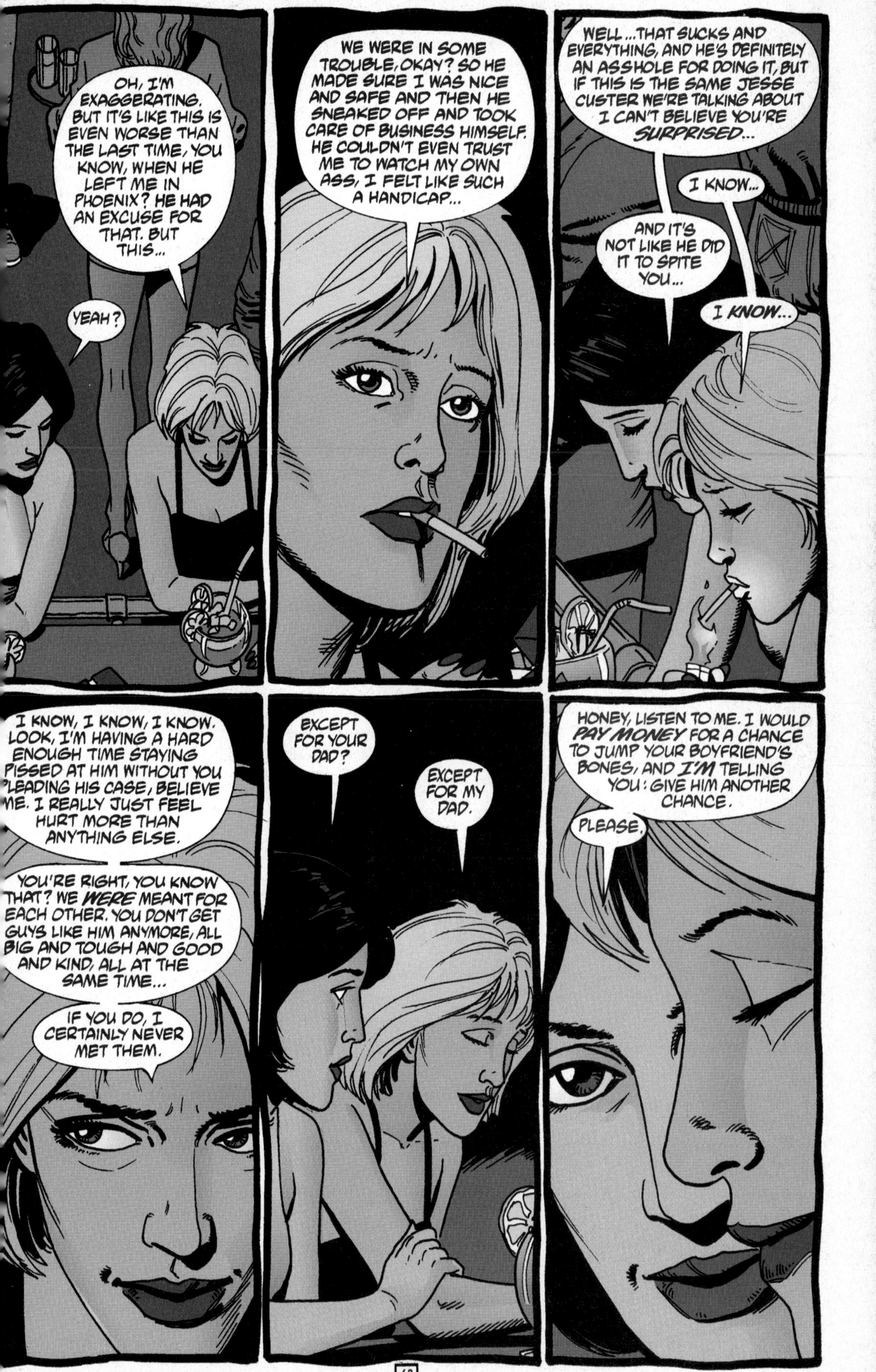
OH, I'M EXAGGERATING. BUT IT'S LIKE THIS IS EVEN WORSE THAN THE LAST TIME, YOU KNOW, WHEN HE LEFT ME IN PHOENIX? HE HAD AN EXCUSE FOR THAT. BUT THIS...
YEAH?
WE WERE IN SOME TROUBLE, OKAY? SO HE MADE SURE I WAS NICE AND SAFE AND THEN HE SNEAKED OFF AND TOOK CARE OF BUSINESS HIMSELF. HE COULDN'T EVEN TRUST ME TO WATCH MY OWN ASS, I FELT LIKE SUCH A HANDICAP...
WELL ...THAT SUCKS AND EVERYTHING, AND HE'S DEFINITELY AN ASSHOLE FOR DOING IT, BUT IF THIS IS THE SAME JESSE CUSTER WE'RE TALKING ABOUT I CAN'T BELIEVE YOU'RE SURPRISED...
I KNOW...
AND IT'S NOT LIKE HE DID IT TO SPITE YOU...
I KNOW...
I KNOW, I KNOW, I KNOW. LOOK, I'M HAVING A HARD ENOUGH TIME STAYING PISSED AT HIM WITHOUT YOU PLEADING HIS CASE, BELIEVE ME. I REALLY JUST FEEL HURT MORE THAN ANYTHING ELSE.
YOU'RE RIGHT, YOU KNOW THAT? WE WERE MEANT FOR EACH OTHER. YOU DON'T GET GUYS LIKE HIM ANYMORE, ALL BIG AND TOUGH AND GOOD AND KIND, ALL AT THE SAME TIME...
IF YOU DO, I CERTAINLY NEVER MET THEM.
EXCEPT FOR YOUR DAD?
EXCEPT FOR MY DAD.
HONEY, LISTEN TO ME. I WOULD PAY MONEY FOR A CHANCE TO JUMP YOUR BOYFRIEND'S BONES, AND I'M TELLING YOU: GIVE HIM ANOTHER CHANCE.
PLEASE.

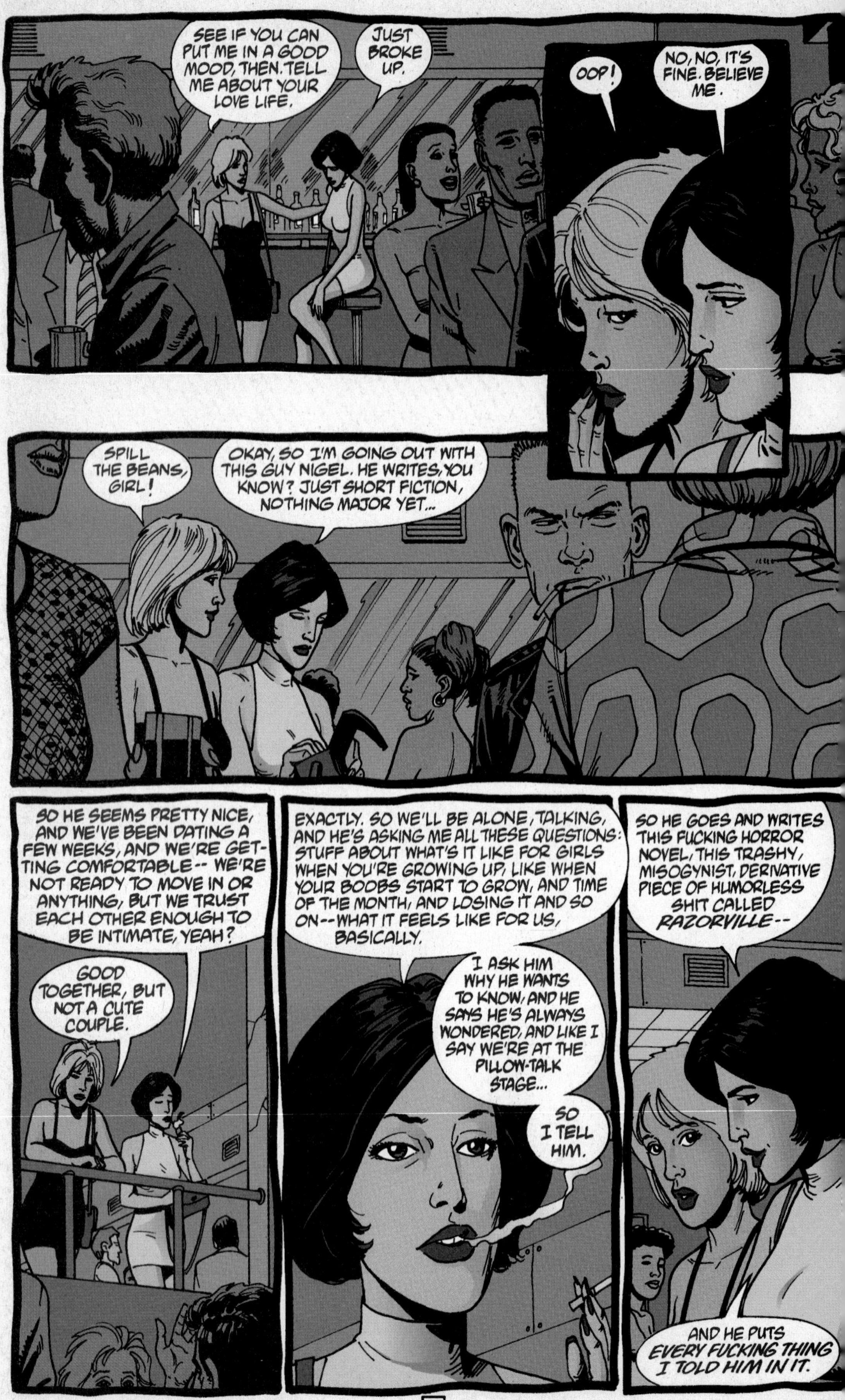
SEE IF YOU CAN PUT ME IN A GOOD MOOD, THEN. TELL ME ABOUT YOUR LOVE LIFE.
JUST BROKE UP.
OOP!
NO, NO, IT'S FINE. BELIEVE ME.
SPILL THE BEANS, GIRL!
OKAY, SO I'M GOING OUT WITH THIS GUY NIGEL. HE WRITES, YOU KNOW? JUST SHORT FICTION, NOTHING MAJOR YET...
SO HE SEEMS PRETTY NICE, AND WE'VE BEEN DATING A FEW WEEKS, AND WE'RE GETTING COMFORTABLE-- WE'RE NOT READY TO MOVE IN OR ANYTHING, BUT WE TRUST EACH OTHER ENOUGH TO BE INTIMATE, YEAH?
GOOD TOGETHER, BUT NOT A CUTE COUPLE.
EXACTLY. SO WE'LL BE ALONE, TALKING, AND HE'S ASKING ME ALL THESE QUESTIONS: STUFF ABOUT WHAT'S IT LIKE FOR GIRLS WHEN YOU'RE GROWING UP, LIKE WHEN YOUR BOOBS START TO GROW, AND TIME OF THE MONTH, AND LOSING IT AND SO ON--WHAT IT FEELS LIKE FOR US, BASICALLY.
I ASK HIM WHY HE WANTS TO KNOW, AND HE SAYS HE'S ALWAYS WONDERED, AND LIKE I SAY WE'RE AT THE PILLOW-TALK STAGE...
SO I TELL HIM.
SO HE GOES AND WRITES THIS FUCKING HORROR NOVEL, THIS TRASHY, MISOGYNIST, DERIVATIVE PIECE OF HUMORLESS SHIT CALLED *RAZORVILLE*--
AND HE PUTS *EVERY FUCKING THING I TOLD HIM IN IT.*

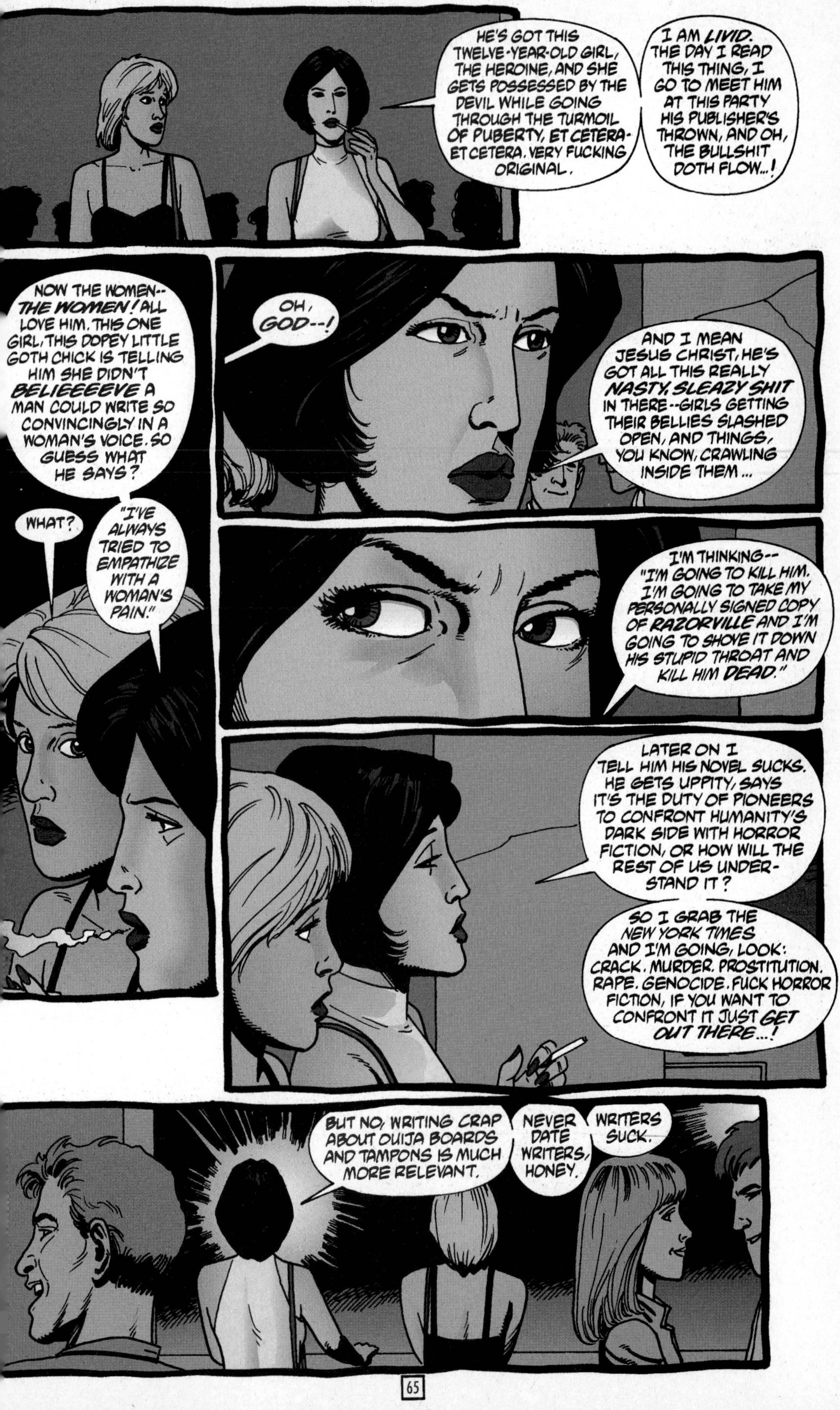
HE'S GOT THIS TWELVE-YEAR-OLD GIRL, THE HEROINE, AND SHE GETS POSSESSED BY THE DEVIL WHILE GOING THROUGH THE TURMOIL OF PUBERTY, ET CETERA-ET CETERA. VERY FUCKING ORIGINAL.
I AM LIVID. THE DAY I READ THIS THING, I GO TO MEET HIM AT THIS PARTY HIS PUBLISHER'S THROWN, AND OH, THE BULLSHIT DOTH FLOW...!
NOW THE WOMEN-- THE WOMEN! ALL LOVE HIM. THIS ONE GIRL, THIS DOPEY LITTLE GOTH CHICK IS TELLING HIM SHE DIDN'T BELIEEEEVE A MAN COULD WRITE SO CONVINCINGLY IN A WOMAN'S VOICE. SO GUESS WHAT HE SAYS?
OH, GOD--!
AND I MEAN JESUS CHRIST, HE'S GOT ALL THIS REALLY NASTY, SLEAZY SHIT IN THERE--GIRLS GETTING THEIR BELLIES SLASHED OPEN, AND THINGS, YOU KNOW, CRAWLING INSIDE THEM...
WHAT?
"I'VE ALWAYS TRIED TO EMPATHIZE WITH A WOMAN'S PAIN."
I'M THINKING-- "I'M GOING TO KILL HIM. I'M GOING TO TAKE MY PERSONALLY SIGNED COPY OF RAZORVILLE AND I'M GOING TO SHOVE IT DOWN HIS STUPID THROAT AND KILL HIM DEAD."
LATER ON I TELL HIM HIS NOVEL SUCKS. HE GETS UPPITY, SAYS IT'S THE DUTY OF PIONEERS TO CONFRONT HUMANITY'S DARK SIDE WITH HORROR FICTION, OR HOW WILL THE REST OF US UNDER-STAND IT?
SO I GRAB THE NEW YORK TIMES AND I'M GOING, LOOK: CRACK. MURDER. PROSTITUTION. RAPE. GENOCIDE. FUCK HORROR FICTION, IF YOU WANT TO CONFRONT IT JUST GET OUT THERE...!
BUT NO, WRITING CRAP ABOUT OUIJA BOARDS AND TAMPONS IS MUCH MORE RELEVANT.
NEVER DATE WRITERS, HONEY.
WRITERS SUCK.

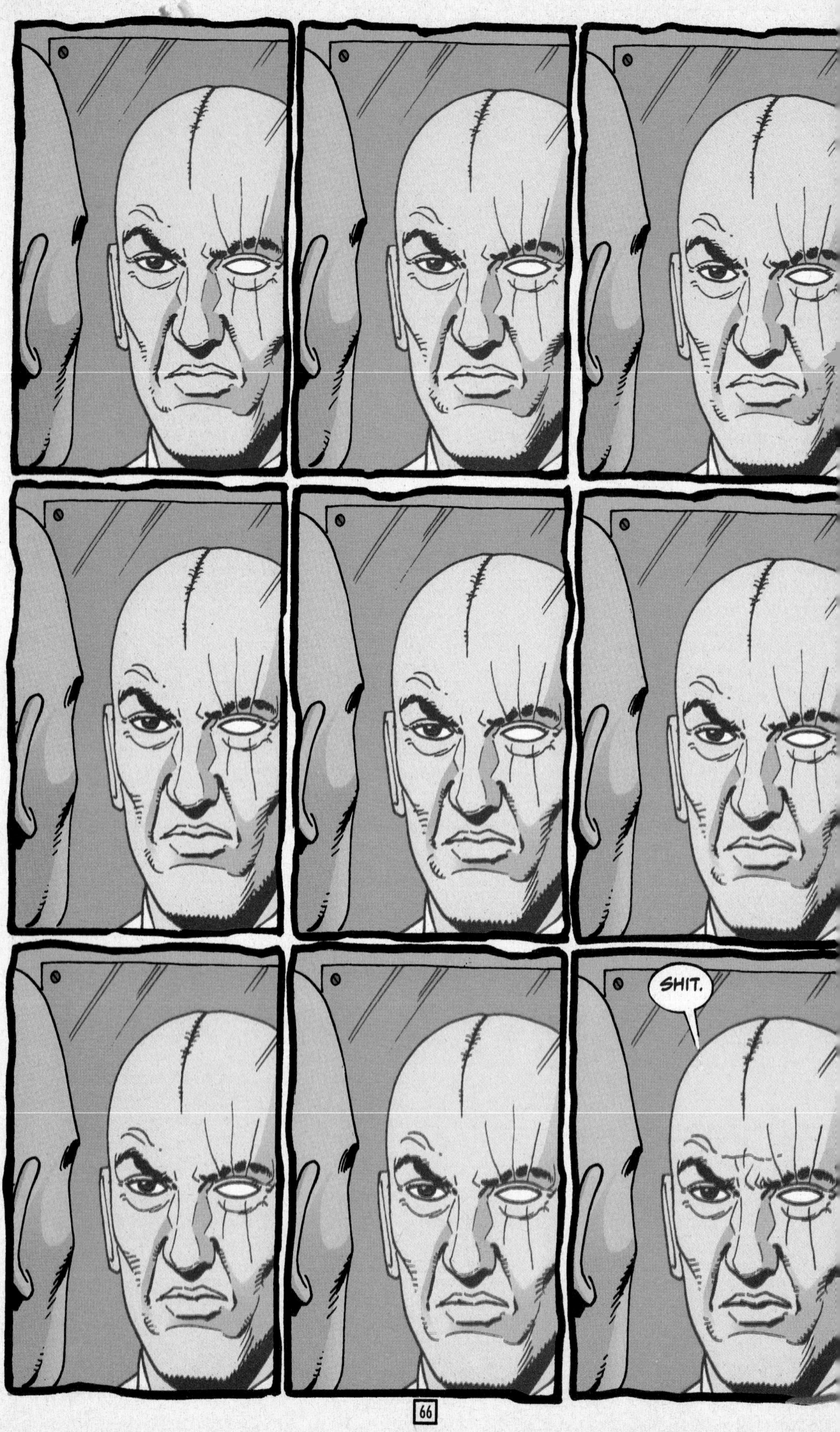
SHIT.

ARE YOU STILL TEACHING?

YEAH, AT PILCHER HIGH. IT ISN'T IDEAL, BUT IT'S NOT *DANGEROUS MINDS* JUST YET.

SEE ANYTHING YOU LIKE?

MM...WHO ARE YOU DEALING WITH, THE GUY YOU HAD IN MEMPHIS?

YOU MEAN ROY? NO, THIS IS A LOCAL GUY, PRETTY REPUTABLE, MOSTLY DEALS WITH COUPLES OR OLD FOLKS--YOU KNOW, PEOPLE WHO WANT SOMETHING FOR THE APARTMENT, JUST IN CASE?

HE TRUSTS ME WITH MONEY, SO HE WAS COOL ABOUT LEAVING THESE FOR YOU TO LOOK AT. HE'S CUTE, ACTUALLY, BUT HE'S IN A LITTLE TOO DEEP FOR ME...

AH, FROM THE COUNTRY THAT BROUGHT YOU THE UZI. YOU WANT IT IN THREE FIFTY-SEVEN OR FORTY-FOUR?

I READ YOU CAN GET 'EM IN FIFTY.

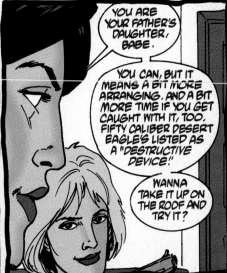

YOU ARE YOUR FATHER'S DAUGHTER, BABE.

YOU CAN, BUT IT MEANS A BIT MORE ARRANGING. AND A BIT MORE TIME IF YOU GET CAUGHT WITH IT, TOO. FIFTY CALIBER DESERT EAGLE'S LISTED AS A "DESTRUCTIVE DEVICE."

WANNA TAKE IT UP ON THE ROOF AND TRY IT?

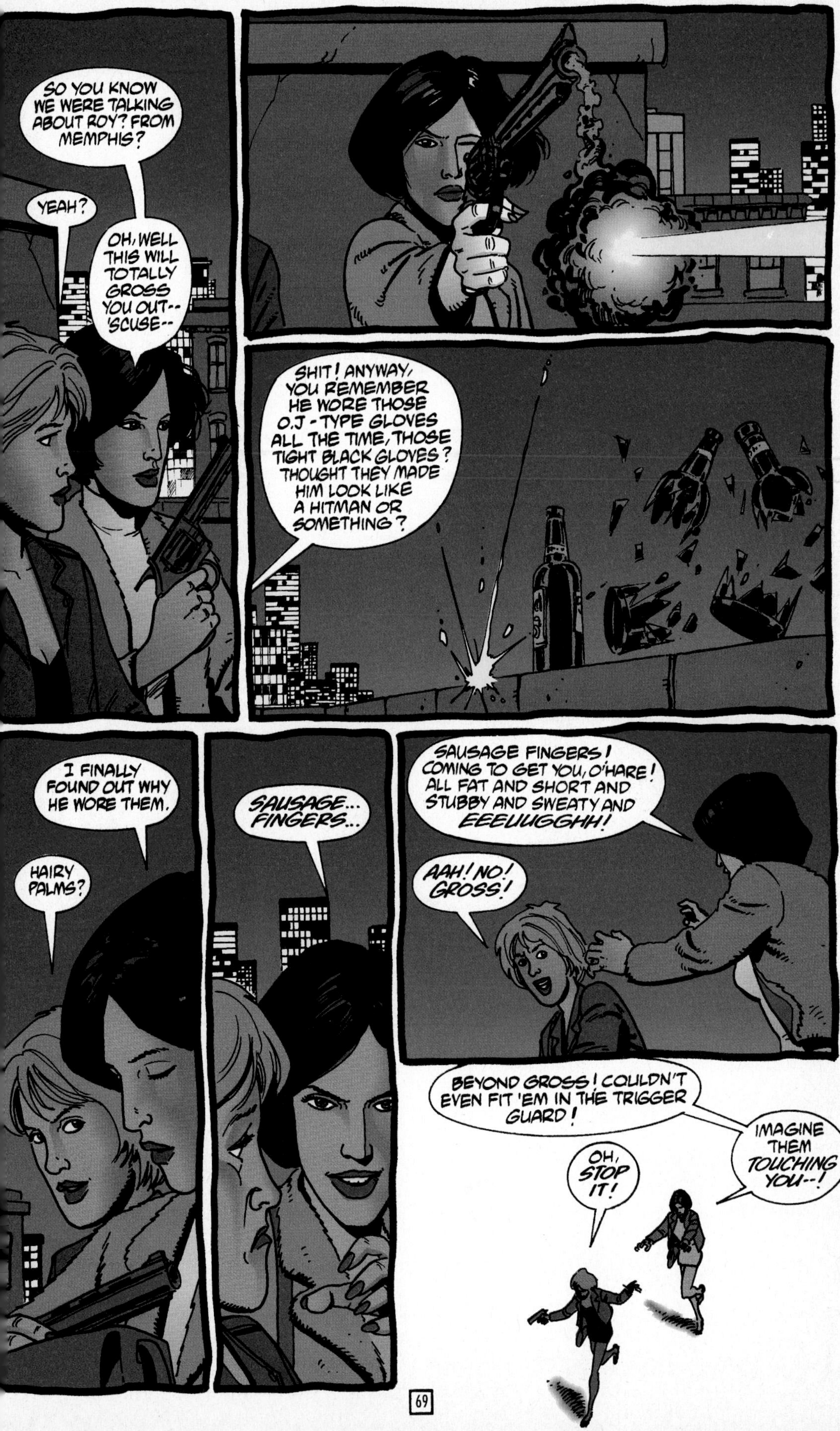
SO YOU KNOW WE WERE TALKING ABOUT ROY? FROM MEMPHIS?
YEAH?
OH, WELL THIS WILL TOTALLY GROSS YOU OUT-- 'SCUSE--
SHIT! ANYWAY, YOU REMEMBER HE WORE THOSE O.J-TYPE GLOVES ALL THE TIME, THOSE TIGHT BLACK GLOVES? THOUGHT THEY MADE HIM LOOK LIKE A HITMAN OR SOMETHING?
I FINALLY FOUND OUT WHY HE WORE THEM.
HAIRY PALMS?
SAUSAGE... FINGERS...
SAUSAGE FINGERS! COMING TO GET YOU, O'HARE! ALL FAT AND SHORT AND STUBBY AND SWEATY AND EEEUUGGHH!
AAH! NO! GROSS!
BEYOND GROSS! COULDN'T EVEN FIT 'EM IN THE TRIGGER GUARD!
IMAGINE THEM TOUCHING YOU--!
OH, STOP IT!

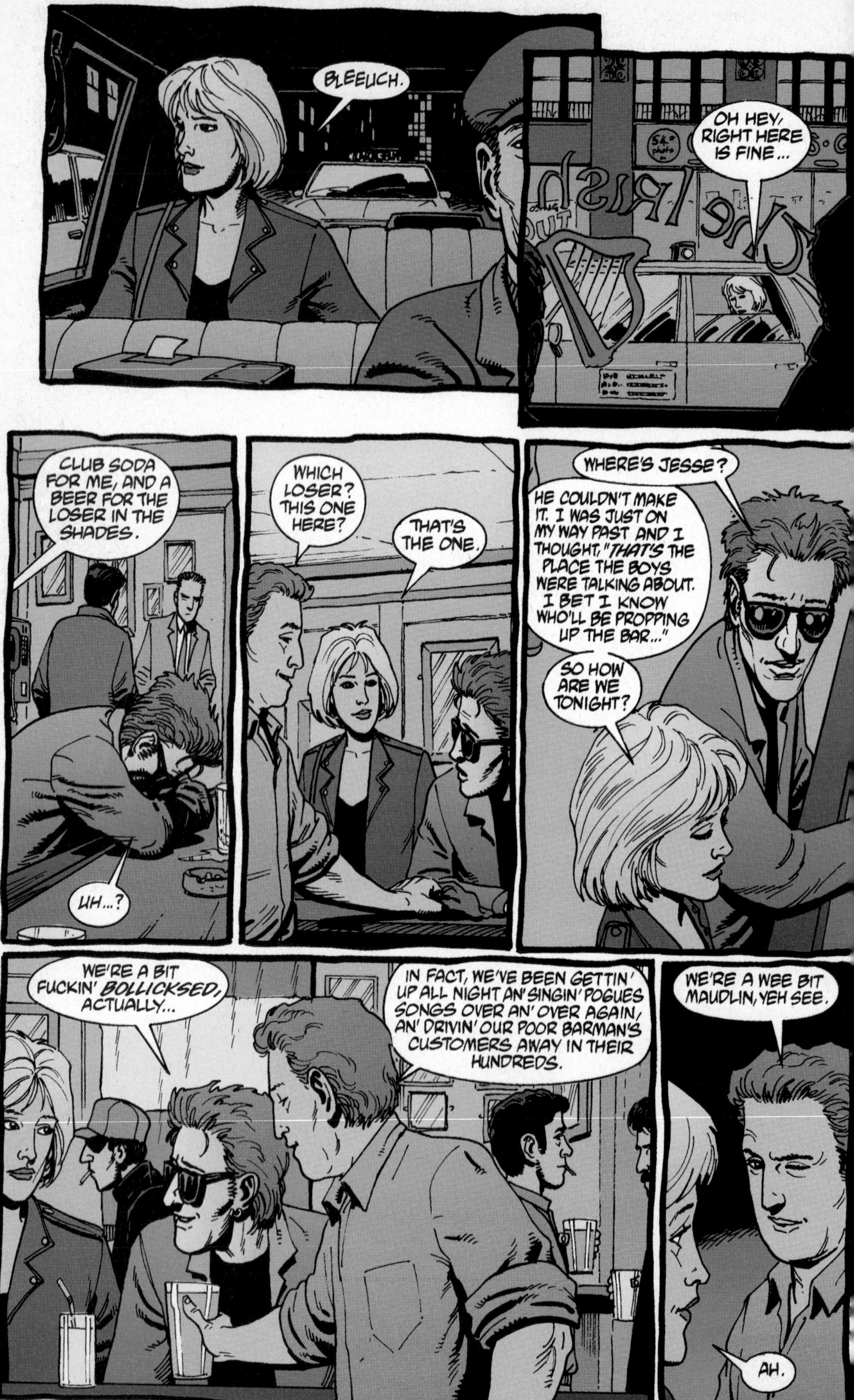
BLEEUCH.
OH HEY, RIGHT HERE IS FINE...
The Irish
CLUB SODA FOR ME, AND A BEER FOR THE LOSER IN THE SHADES.
UH...?
WHICH LOSER? THIS ONE HERE?
THAT'S THE ONE.
WHERE'S JESSE?
HE COULDN'T MAKE IT. I WAS JUST ON MY WAY PAST AND I THOUGHT, "THAT'S THE PLACE THE BOYS WERE TALKING ABOUT. I BET I KNOW WHO'LL BE PROPPING UP THE BAR..."
SO HOW ARE WE TONIGHT?
WE'RE A BIT FUCKIN' BOLLICKSED, ACTUALLY...
IN FACT, WE'VE BEEN GETTIN' UP ALL NIGHT AN' SINGIN' POGUES SONGS OVER AN' OVER AGAIN, AN' DRIVIN' OUR POOR BARMAN'S CUSTOMERS AWAY IN THEIR HUNDREDS.
WE'RE A WEE BIT MAUDLIN, YEH SEE.
AH.

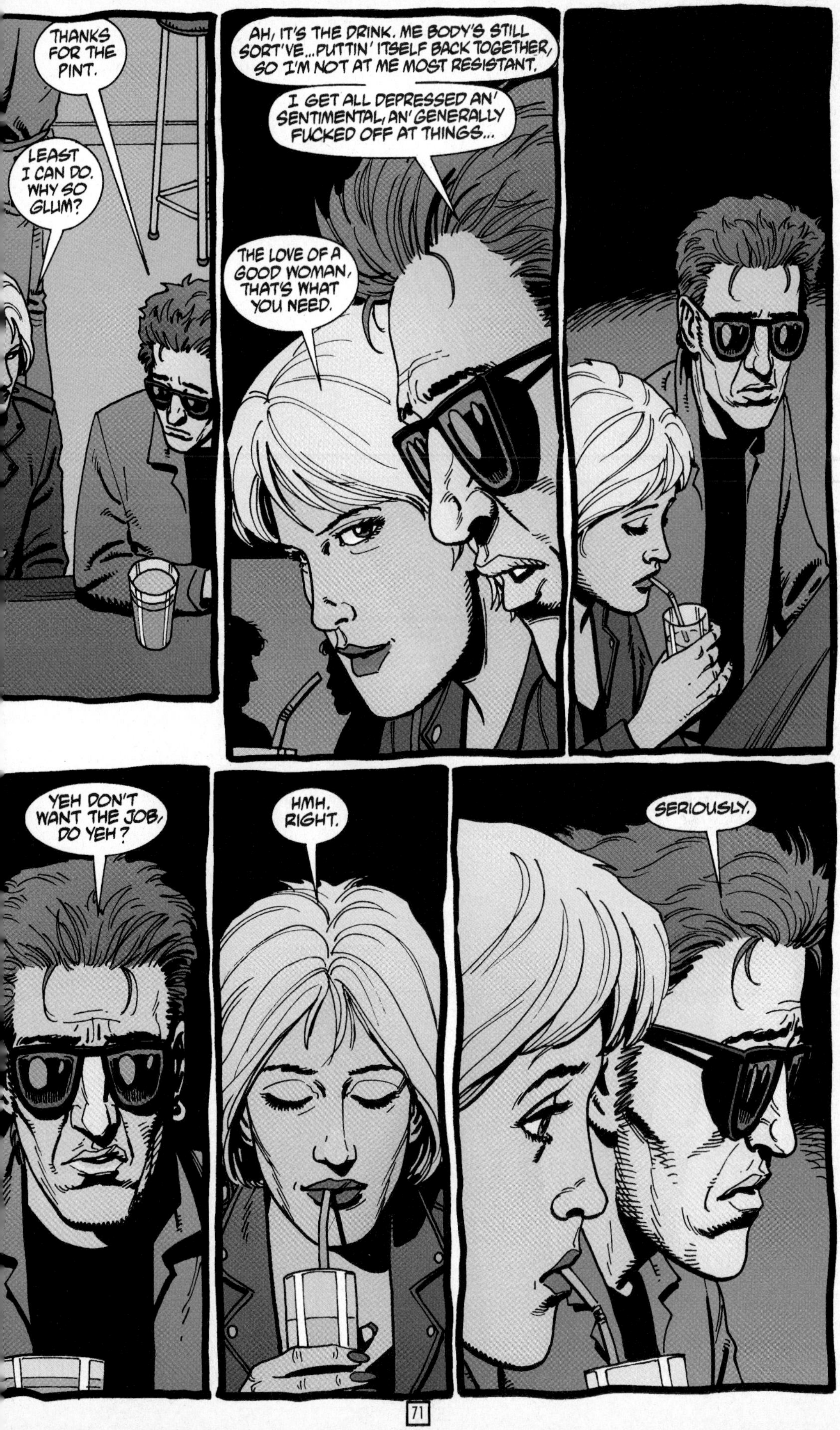
THANKS FOR THE PINT.
LEAST I CAN DO. WHY SO GLUM?
AH, IT'S THE DRINK. ME BODY'S STILL SORT'VE...PUTTIN' ITSELF BACK TOGETHER, SO I'M NOT AT ME MOST RESISTANT.
I GET ALL DEPRESSED AN' SENTIMENTAL, AN' GENERALLY FUCKED OFF AT THINGS...
THE LOVE OF A GOOD WOMAN, THAT'S WHAT YOU NEED.
YEH DON'T WANT THE JOB, DO YEH?
HMH. RIGHT.
SERIOUSLY.

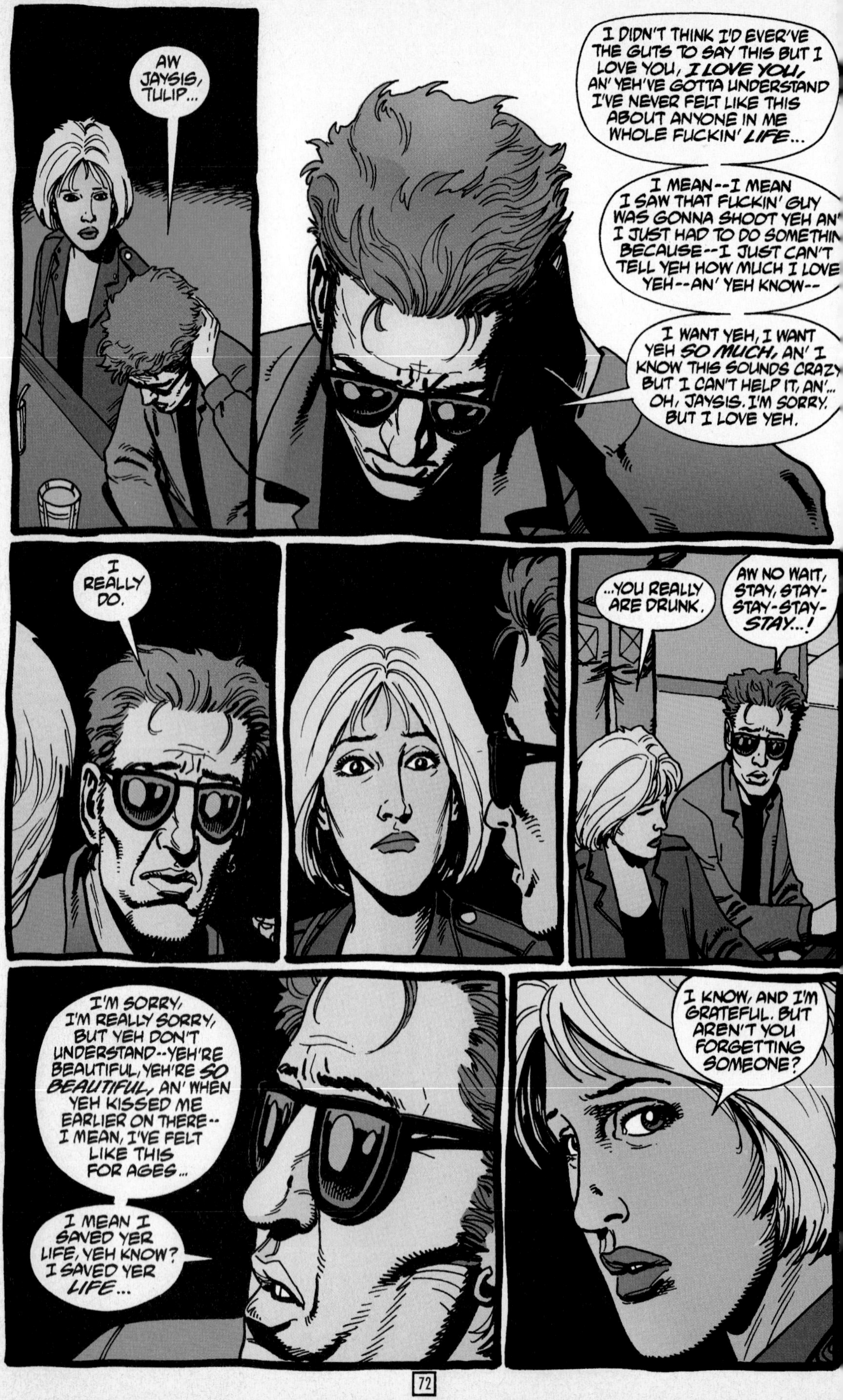
AW JAYSIS, TULIP...
I DIDN'T THINK I'D EVER'VE THE GUTS TO SAY THIS BUT I LOVE YOU, I LOVE YOU, AN' YEH'VE GOTTA UNDERSTAND I'VE NEVER FELT LIKE THIS ABOUT ANYONE IN ME WHOLE FUCKIN' LIFE...
I MEAN--I MEAN I SAW THAT FUCKIN' GUY WAS GONNA SHOOT YEH AN' I JUST HAD TO DO SOMETHIN BECAUSE--I JUST CAN'T TELL YEH HOW MUCH I LOVE YEH--AN' YEH KNOW--
I WANT YEH, I WANT YEH SO MUCH, AN' I KNOW THIS SOUNDS CRAZY BUT I CAN'T HELP IT, AN'... OH, JAYSIS. I'M SORRY. BUT I LOVE YEH.
I REALLY DO.
...YOU REALLY ARE DRUNK.
AW NO WAIT, STAY, STAY-STAY-STAY-STAY...!
I'M SORRY, I'M REALLY SORRY, BUT YEH DON'T UNDERSTAND--YEH'RE BEAUTIFUL, YEH'RE SO BEAUTIFUL, AN' WHEN YEH KISSED ME EARLIER ON THERE--I MEAN, I'VE FELT LIKE THIS FOR AGES...
I MEAN I SAVED YER LIFE, YEH KNOW? I SAVED YER LIFE...
I KNOW, AND I'M GRATEFUL. BUT AREN'T YOU FORGETTING SOMEONE?

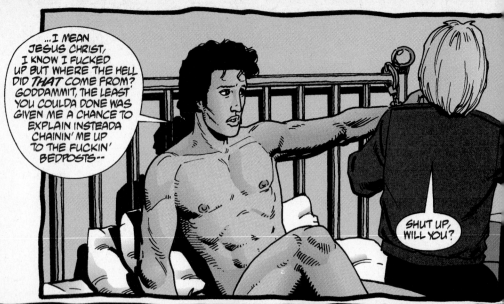

...I MEAN JESUS CHRIST, I KNOW I FUCKED UP BUT WHERE THE HELL DID *THAT* COME FROM? GODDAMMIT, THE LEAST YOU COULDA DONE WAS GIVEN ME A CHANCE TO EXPLAIN INSTEADA CHAININ' ME UP TO THE FUCKIN' BEDPOSTS--

SHUT UP, WILL YOU?

SHUT UP AND HOLD ME.

I GUESS THAT SOUNDS LIKE A PLAN.

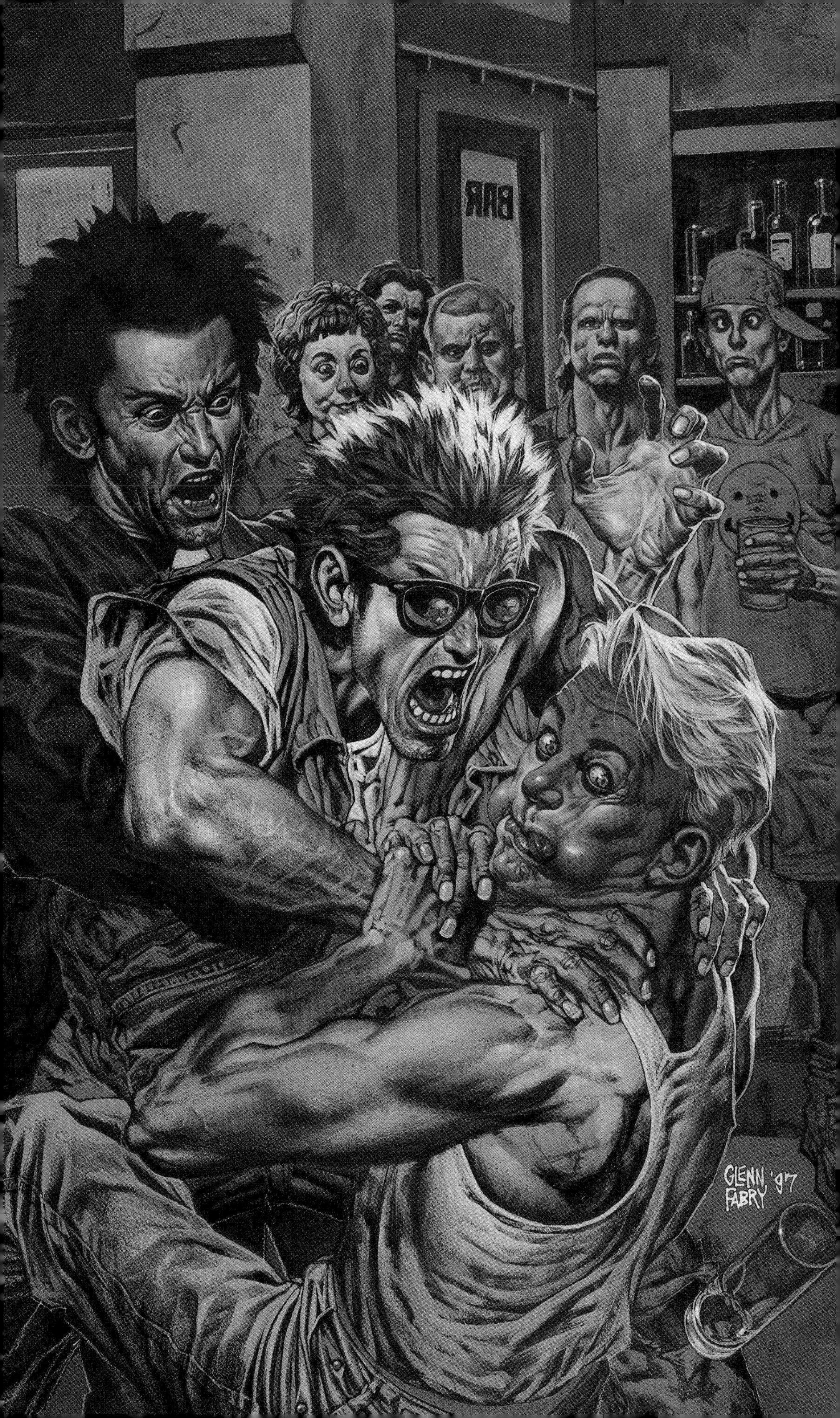
BAR
GLENN '97
FABRY

RUMORS OF WAR

GARTH ENNIS - Writer   STEVE DILLON - Artist

MATT HOLLINGSWORTH - Colorist

CLEM ROBINS - Letterer   AXEL ALONSO - Editor

PREACHER created by GARTH ENNIS and STEVE DILLON

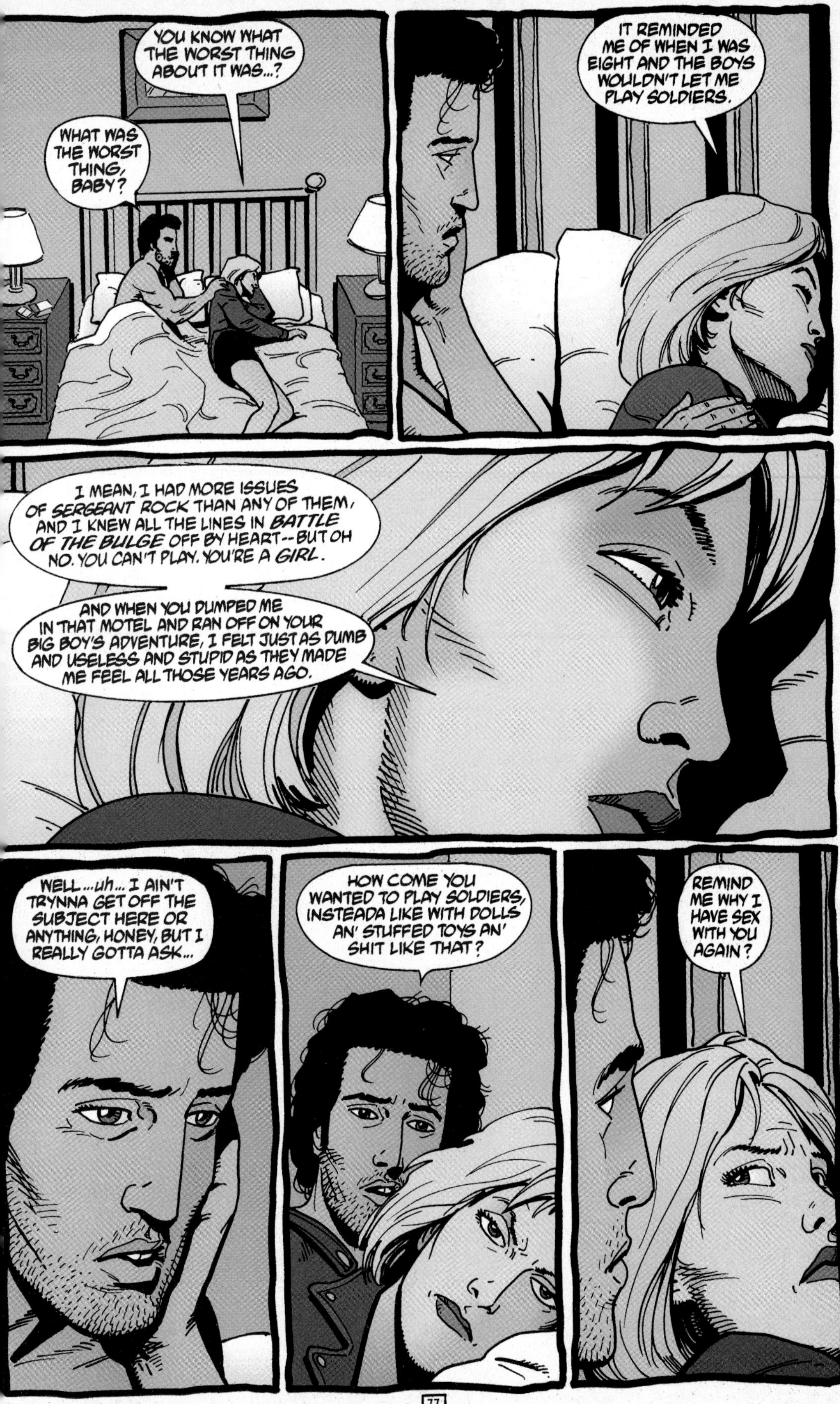
YOU KNOW WHAT THE WORST THING ABOUT IT WAS...?
WHAT WAS THE WORST THING, BABY?
IT REMINDED ME OF WHEN I WAS EIGHT AND THE BOYS WOULDN'T LET ME PLAY SOLDIERS.
I MEAN, I HAD MORE ISSUES OF SERGEANT ROCK THAN ANY OF THEM, AND I KNEW ALL THE LINES IN BATTLE OF THE BULGE OFF BY HEART--BUT OH NO. YOU CAN'T PLAY. YOU'RE A GIRL.
AND WHEN YOU DUMPED ME IN THAT MOTEL AND RAN OFF ON YOUR BIG BOY'S ADVENTURE, I FELT JUST AS DUMB AND USELESS AND STUPID AS THEY MADE ME FEEL ALL THOSE YEARS AGO.
WELL...uh... I AIN'T TRYNNA GET OFF THE SUBJECT HERE OR ANYTHING, HONEY, BUT I REALLY GOTTA ASK...
HOW COME YOU WANTED TO PLAY SOLDIERS, INSTEADA LIKE WITH DOLLS AN' STUFFED TOYS AN' SHIT LIKE THAT?
REMIND ME WHY I HAVE SEX WITH YOU AGAIN?

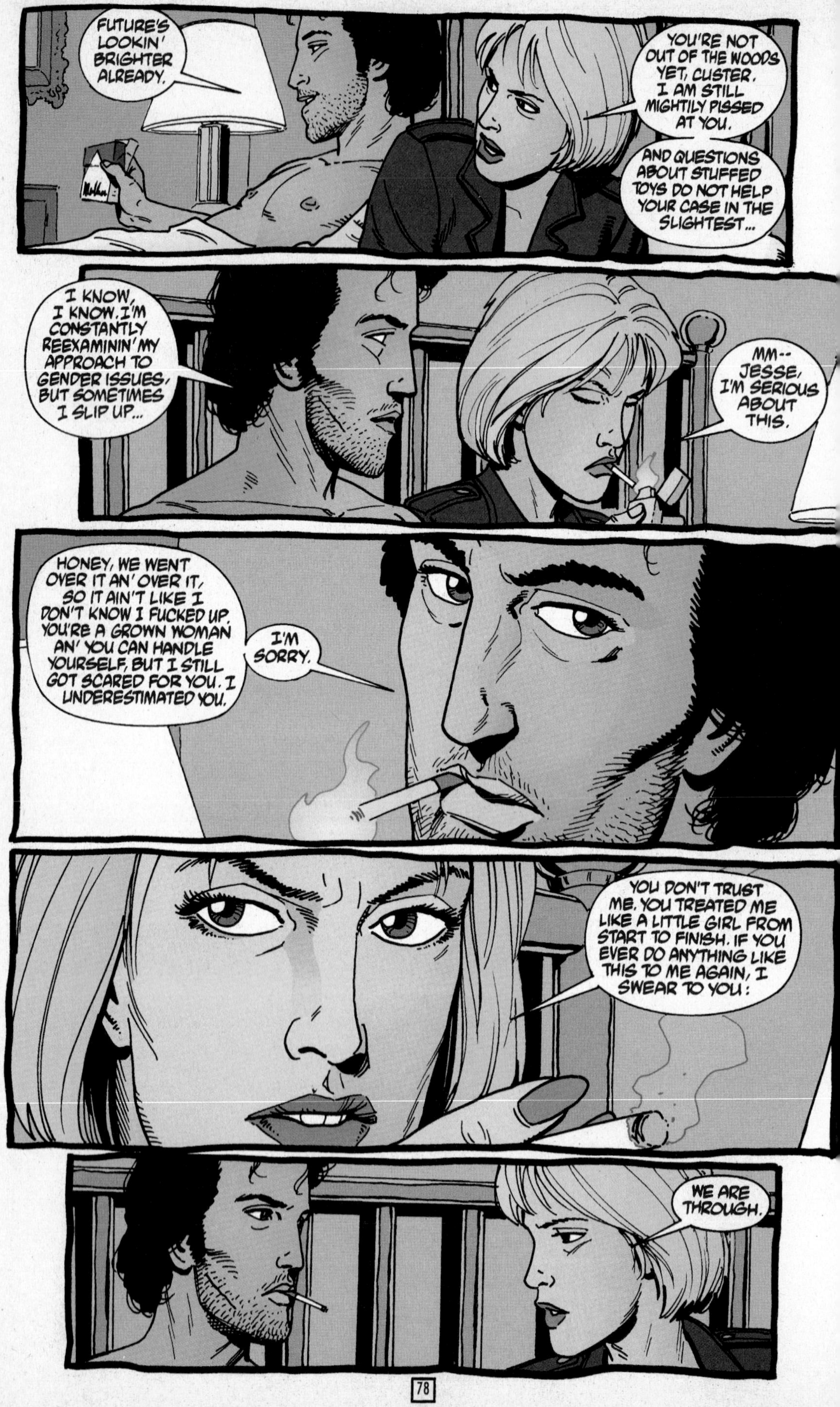
FUTURE'S LOOKIN' BRIGHTER ALREADY.
YOU'RE NOT OUT OF THE WOODS YET, CUSTER. I AM STILL MIGHTILY PISSED AT YOU.
AND QUESTIONS ABOUT STUFFED TOYS DO NOT HELP YOUR CASE IN THE SLIGHTEST...
I KNOW, I KNOW. I'M CONSTANTLY REEXAMININ' MY APPROACH TO GENDER ISSUES, BUT SOMETIMES I SLIP UP...
MM-- JESSE, I'M SERIOUS ABOUT THIS.
HONEY, WE WENT OVER IT AN' OVER IT, SO IT AIN'T LIKE I DON'T KNOW I FUCKED UP. YOU'RE A GROWN WOMAN AN' YOU CAN HANDLE YOURSELF, BUT I STILL GOT SCARED FOR YOU. I UNDERESTIMATED YOU.
I'M SORRY.
YOU DON'T TRUST ME. YOU TREATED ME LIKE A LITTLE GIRL FROM START TO FINISH. IF YOU EVER DO ANYTHING LIKE THIS TO ME AGAIN, I SWEAR TO YOU:
WE ARE THROUGH.

TULIP, LEMME TELL YOU SOMETHIN'. YOU MEAN MORE TO ME THAN ANYTHIN'. MORE'N THIS CRAZY PATH I'M ON, OR LIFE ITSELF, OR EVEN MY DAMN HONOR. I'M GONNA MAKE YOU A PROMISE, RIGHT HERE AN' NOW: I WILL NEVER FAIL YOU LIKE THIS AGAIN.

I WILL *ALWAYS* TRUST YOU.

YEAH?

YOU GOT MY WORD.

THAT'S ALL I NEEDED TO HEAR.

HOW LONG AM I GONNA LOVE YOU, GIRL?

UNTIL THE END OF THE WORLD?

BABY?

MM?

WHAT WERE YOU SO UPSET ABOUT WHEN YOU GOT BACK THIS MORNIN'?

... IT WAS JUST, YOU KNOW, I GUESS I THOUGHT ENOUGH WAS ENOUGH. LIKE CUFFING YOU TO THE BED AND LEAVING YOU WAS A GREAT IDEA, BUT ACTUALLY GOING THROUGH WITH IT GOT HARDER AND HARDER TO DO...

WE'LL SEE. SO WHAT HAVE YOU BEEN UP TO SINCE YOU GOT INTO TOWN?

HANGIN' OUT WITH CASS, MOSTLY.

NO SHIT. NEXT TIME, DON'T WAIT SIX OR SEVEN HOURS BEFORE GIVIN' IN TO YOUR CONSCIENCE, OKAY?

I TELL YOU, SEEIN' HIM KINDA GROWIN' BACK TOGETHER, THAT WAS SOME CRAZY SHIT, AN' HE TOLD ME HIS LIFE STORY, WHICH WAS SORTA LIKE IF BRENDAN BEHAN FUCKED BRAM STOKER AN' THEY LET THE BABY DO CRACK ALL THE TIME...

HE DID A REAL NICE THING, TOO. YOU KNOW WHAT HE SAID TO ME?

WHAT?

SAID HE WAS GONNA STICK BY ME.

HE'S GONNA STAY AROUND UNTIL THIS THING GETS DONE.

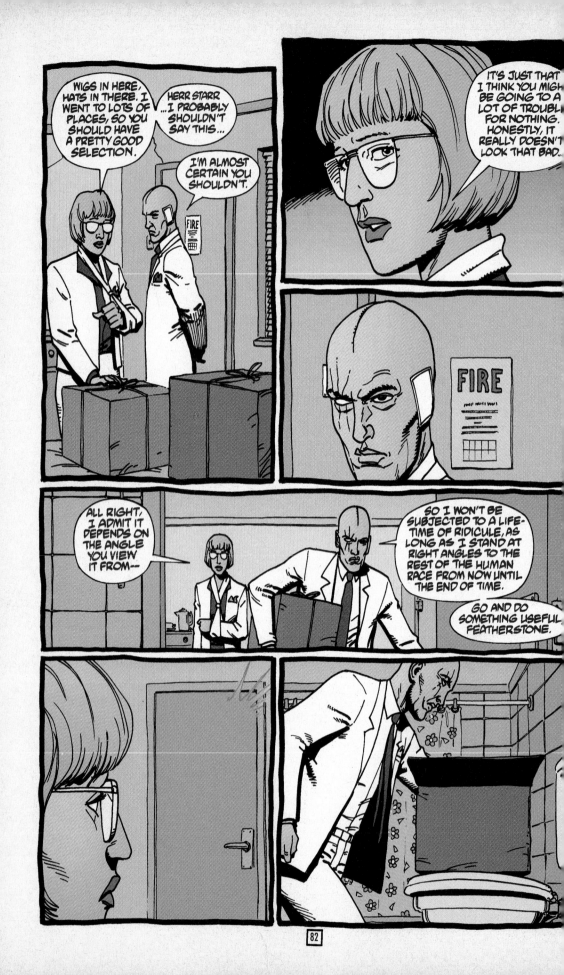

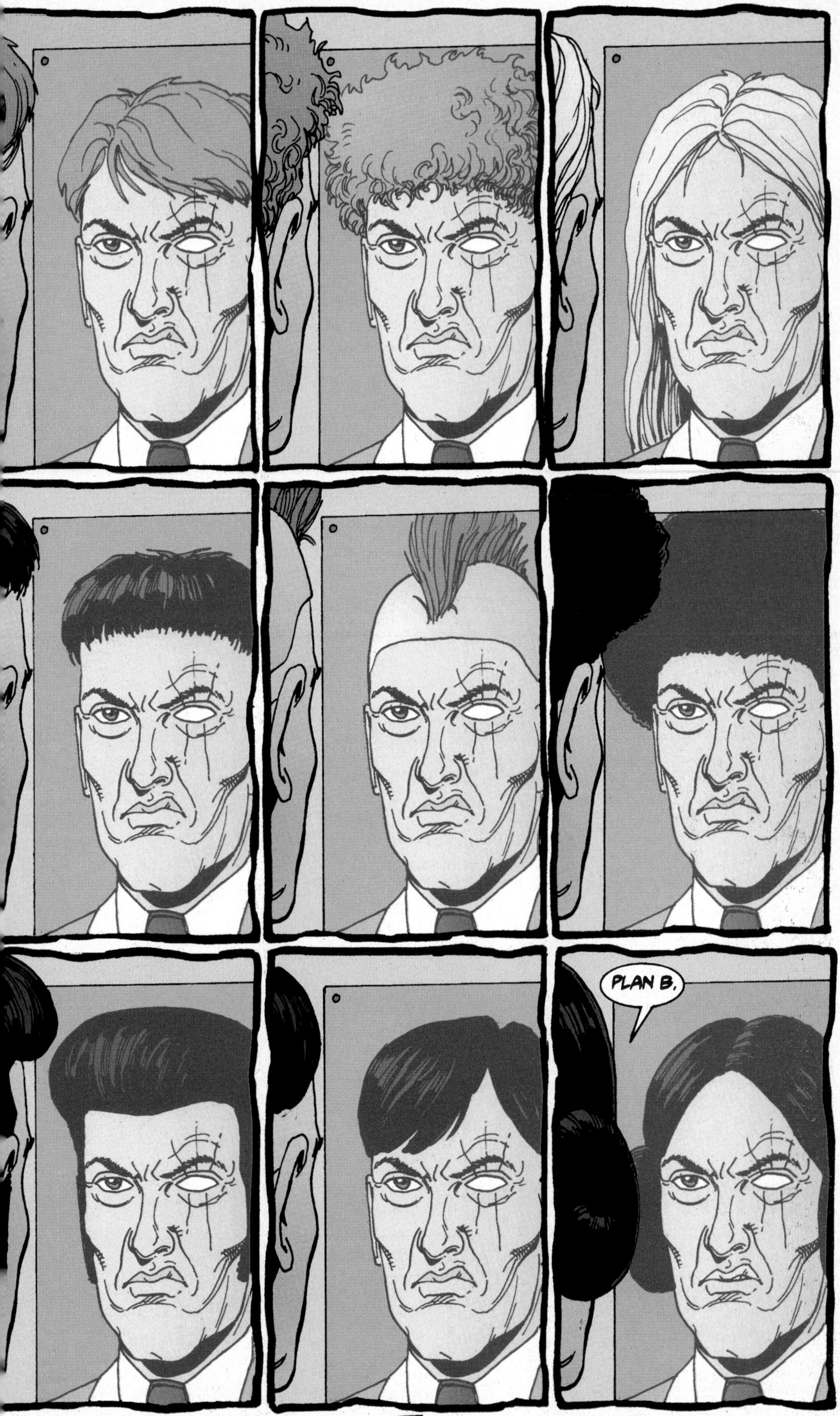
PLAN B.

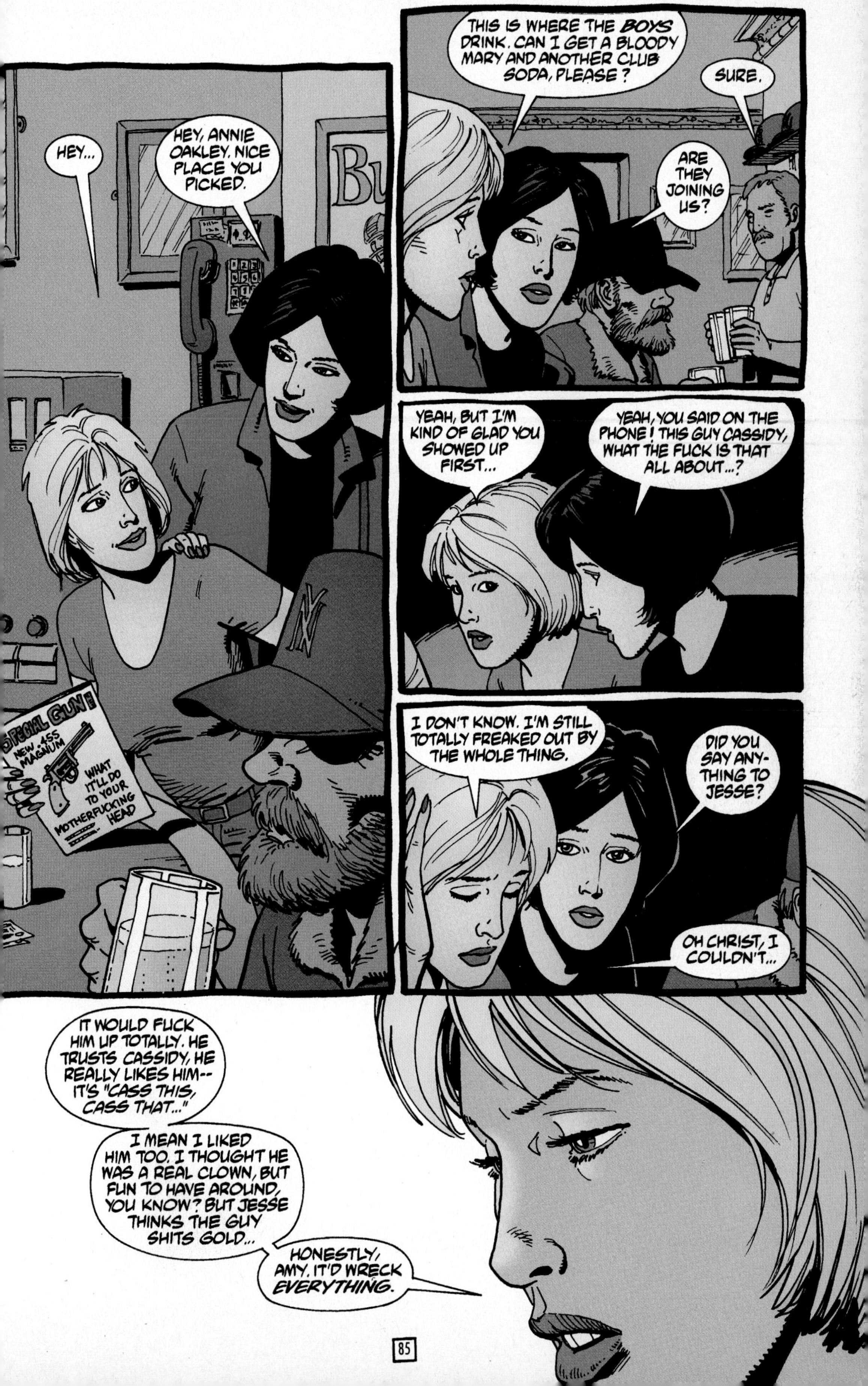
HEY...
HEY, ANNIE OAKLEY. NICE PLACE YOU PICKED.
SPECIAL GUN! NEW .455 MAGNUM WHAT IT'LL DO TO YOUR MOTHERFUCKING HEAD
THIS IS WHERE THE *BOYS* DRINK. CAN I GET A BLOODY MARY AND ANOTHER CLUB SODA, PLEASE?
SURE.
ARE THEY JOINING US?
YEAH, BUT I'M KIND OF GLAD YOU SHOWED UP FIRST...
YEAH, YOU SAID ON THE PHONE! THIS GUY CASSIDY, WHAT THE FUCK IS THAT ALL ABOUT...?
I DON'T KNOW. I'M STILL TOTALLY FREAKED OUT BY THE WHOLE THING.
DID YOU SAY ANYTHING TO JESSE?
OH CHRIST, I COULDN'T...
IT WOULD FUCK HIM UP TOTALLY. HE TRUSTS CASSIDY, HE REALLY LIKES HIM-- IT'S "CASS THIS, CASS THAT..."
I MEAN I LIKED HIM TOO. I THOUGHT HE WAS A REAL CLOWN, BUT FUN TO HAVE AROUND, YOU KNOW? BUT JESSE THINKS THE GUY SHITS GOLD...
HONESTLY, AMY. IT'D WRECK *EVERYTHING*.

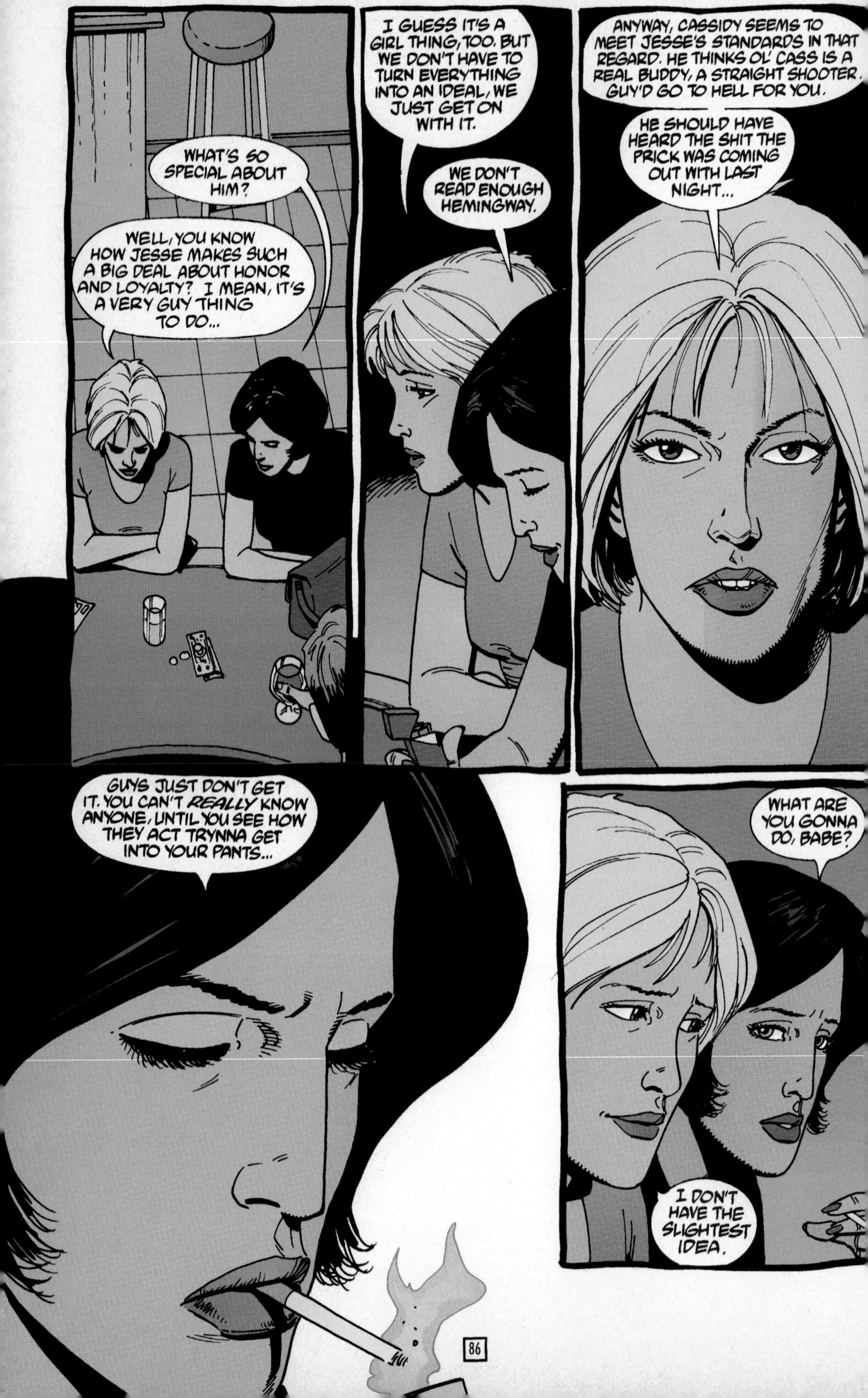
WHAT'S SO SPECIAL ABOUT HIM?
WELL, YOU KNOW HOW JESSE MAKES SUCH A BIG DEAL ABOUT HONOR AND LOYALTY? I MEAN, IT'S A VERY GUY THING TO DO...
I GUESS IT'S A GIRL THING, TOO. BUT WE DON'T HAVE TO TURN EVERYTHING INTO AN IDEAL, WE JUST GET ON WITH IT.
WE DON'T READ ENOUGH HEMINGWAY.
ANYWAY, CASSIDY SEEMS TO MEET JESSE'S STANDARDS IN THAT REGARD. HE THINKS OL' CASS IS A REAL BUDDY, A STRAIGHT SHOOTER. GUY'D GO TO HELL FOR YOU.
HE SHOULD HAVE HEARD THE SHIT THE PRICK WAS COMING OUT WITH LAST NIGHT...
GUYS JUST DON'T GET IT. YOU CAN'T *REALLY* KNOW ANYONE, UNTIL YOU SEE HOW THEY ACT TRYNNA GET INTO YOUR PANTS...
WHAT ARE YOU GONNA DO, BABE?
I DON'T HAVE THE SLIGHTEST IDEA.

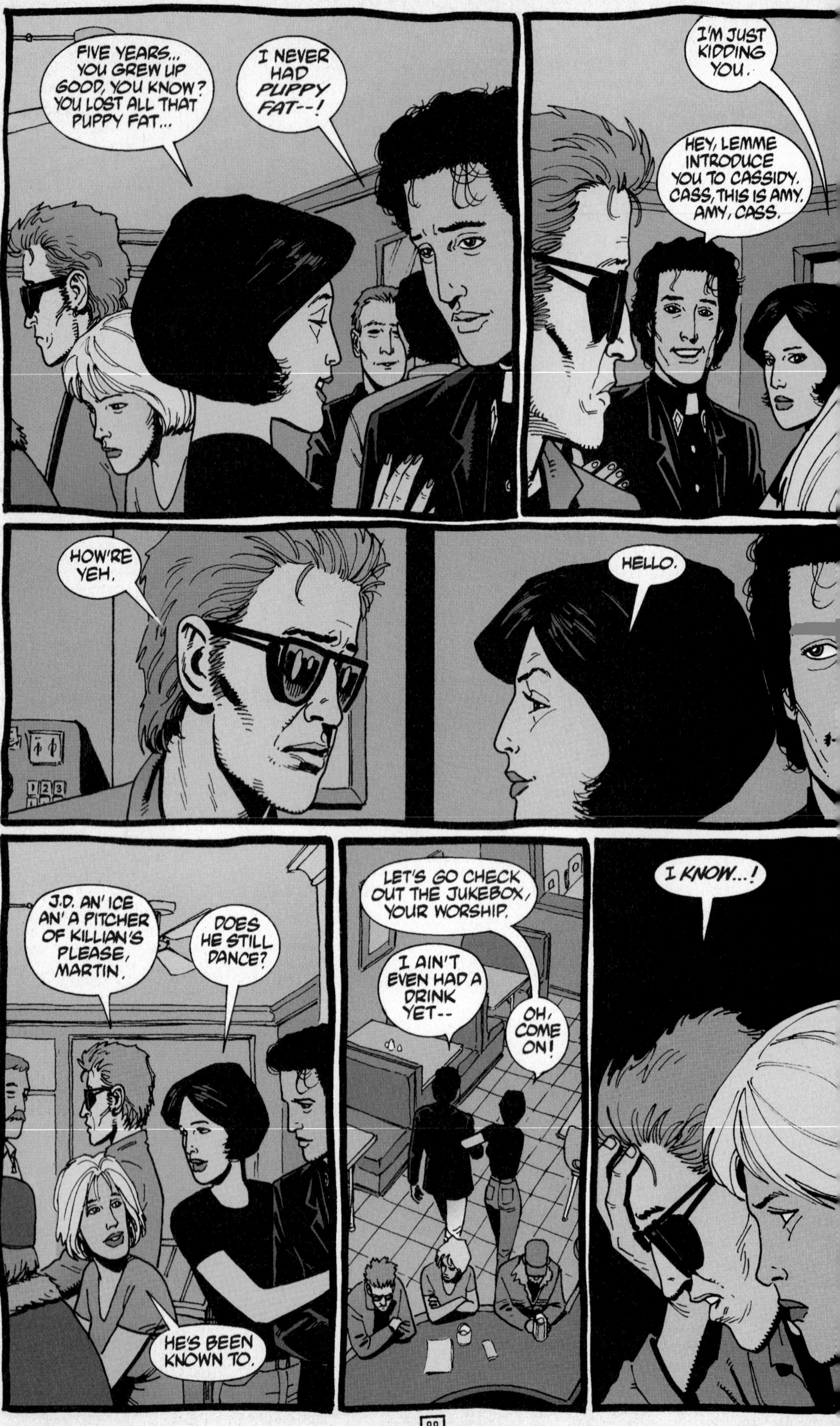
FIVE YEARS... YOU GREW UP GOOD, YOU KNOW? YOU LOST ALL THAT PUPPY FAT...
I NEVER HAD *PUPPY FAT*--!
I'M JUST KIDDING YOU.
HEY, LEMME INTRODUCE YOU TO CASSIDY. CASS, THIS IS AMY. AMY, CASS.
HOW'RE YEH.
HELLO.
J.D. AN' ICE AN' A PITCHER OF KILLIAN'S PLEASE, MARTIN.
DOES HE STILL DANCE?
HE'S BEEN KNOWN TO.
LET'S GO CHECK OUT THE JUKEBOX, YOUR WORSHIP.
I AIN'T EVEN HAD A DRINK YET--
OH, COME ON!
I *KNOW*...!

♪ ARMORED CARS AND TRUCKS AND GUNS; COME TO TAKE AWAY OUR SONS-- ♪

WHAT THE FUCK IS THIS?

I THINK IT'S THIS OR THE MACARENA...

♪ EVERY MAN MUST STAND BEHIND THE MEN BEHIND THE WY-ERR! ♪

YOU CONVINCED ME!

D'YEH NOT THINK THE TWO'VE THEM LOOK A WEE BIT COZY...?

I KNOW THEM. I TRUST THEM. DON'T EVEN TRY TO CHANGE THE SUBJECT, OKAY?

YEH TOLD HER ABOUT IT, DIDN'T YEH?

SO?

SHE HAD THAT YOU'RE-THE-ASSHOLE-TRYNNA-WRECK-MY-MATE'S-RELATIONSHIP LOOK ON HER FACE. I FELT ABOUT TWO INCHES TALL.

SHE'S MY FRIEND. I'LL TELL HER WHATEVER THE FUCK I WANT TO, THANKS.

BESIDES, NEVER MIND ABOUT AMY. WHAT YOU SHOULD BE WORRYING ABOUT--

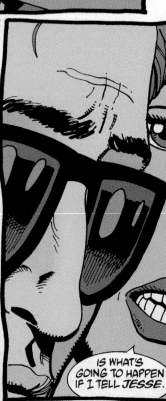

IS WHAT'S GOING TO HAPPEN IF I TELL JESSE.

AW NO--I NO, DON'T, NOW! IT'D FUCKIN' DESTROY HIM!

YEAH, I KNOW. IT WOULD ABSOLUTELY BREAK HIM IN TWO. AND THAT'S THE ONLY THING STOPPING ME FROM TELLING HIM.

HE'S DEVOTED TO YOU, YOU KNOW THAT? I'VE NEVER REALLY KNOWN HIM TO HAVE A CLOSE FRIEND BEFORE. WITH THE LIFE HE'S HAD, HE'S GOT *VERY* HIGH STANDARDS OF WHAT HE CONSIDERS A GOOD GUY--

BUT YOU *KNEW* HOW TO PUSH ALL THE RIGHT BUTTONS WITH HIM RIGHT FROM THE BEGINNING, *DIDN'T YOU?*

AW, TULIP... I MEAN... YEH'RE MAKIN' IT SOUND LIKE I PLANNED THIS, LIKE IT WAS ALL CALCULATED...

I *MEANT IT* WHEN I MADE HIM THAT PROMISE, BECAUSE HE SAVED ME FUCKIN' LIFE AN' I'LL NEVER FORGET IT. AN' WI' YOU, JAYSIS, I JUST GOT ARSEHOLED AN' MADE A DICK'VE MESELF. THERE WAS NOTHIN' MORE TO IT THAN THAT.

I MEAN IT.

I LOVE HIM LIKE A BROTHER, TULIP.

YOU'D FUCKING BETTER.

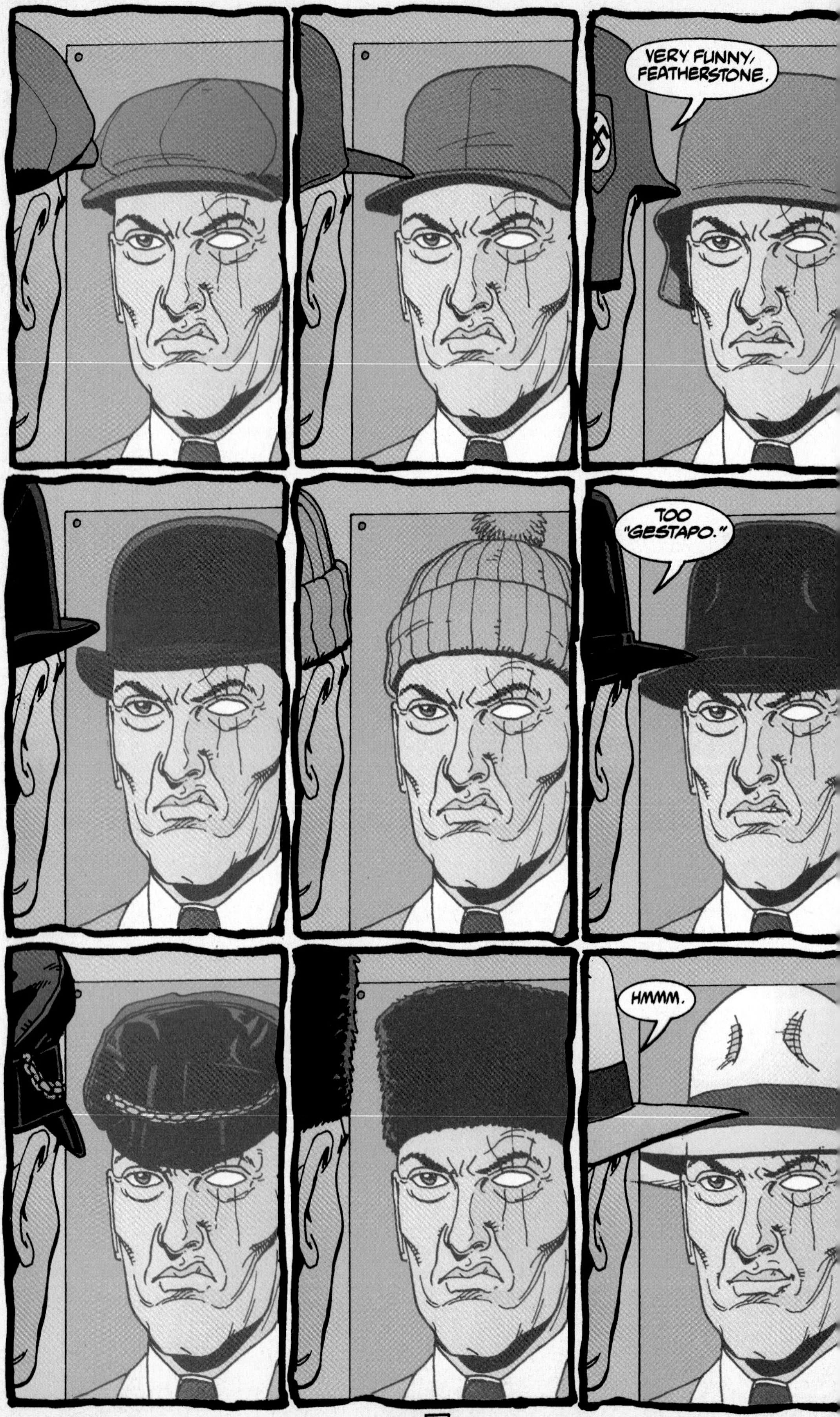
VERY FUNNY, FEATHERSTONE.
TOO "GESTAPO."
HMMM.

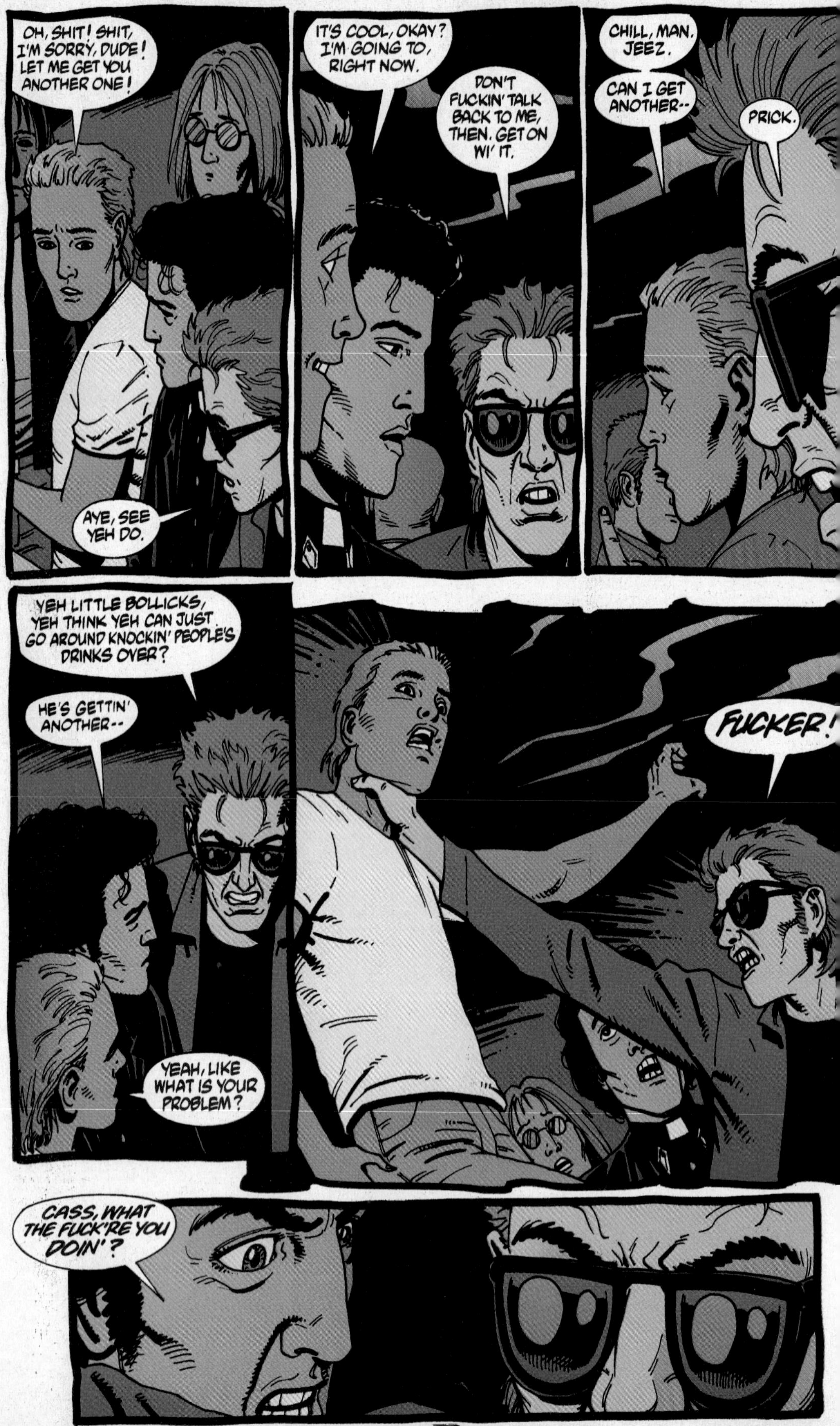

OH, SHIT! SHIT, I'M SORRY, DUDE! LET ME GET YOU ANOTHER ONE!
AYE, SEE YEH DO.
IT'S COOL, OKAY? I'M GOING TO, RIGHT NOW.
DON'T FUCKIN' TALK BACK TO ME, THEN. GET ON WI' IT.
CHILL, MAN. JEEZ.
CAN I GET ANOTHER--
PRICK.
YEH LITTLE BOLLICKS, YEH THINK YEH CAN JUST GO AROUND KNOCKIN' PEOPLE'S DRINKS OVER?
HE'S GETTIN' ANOTHER--
YEAH, LIKE WHAT IS YOUR PROBLEM?
FUCKER!
CASS, WHAT THE FUCK'RE YOU DOIN'?

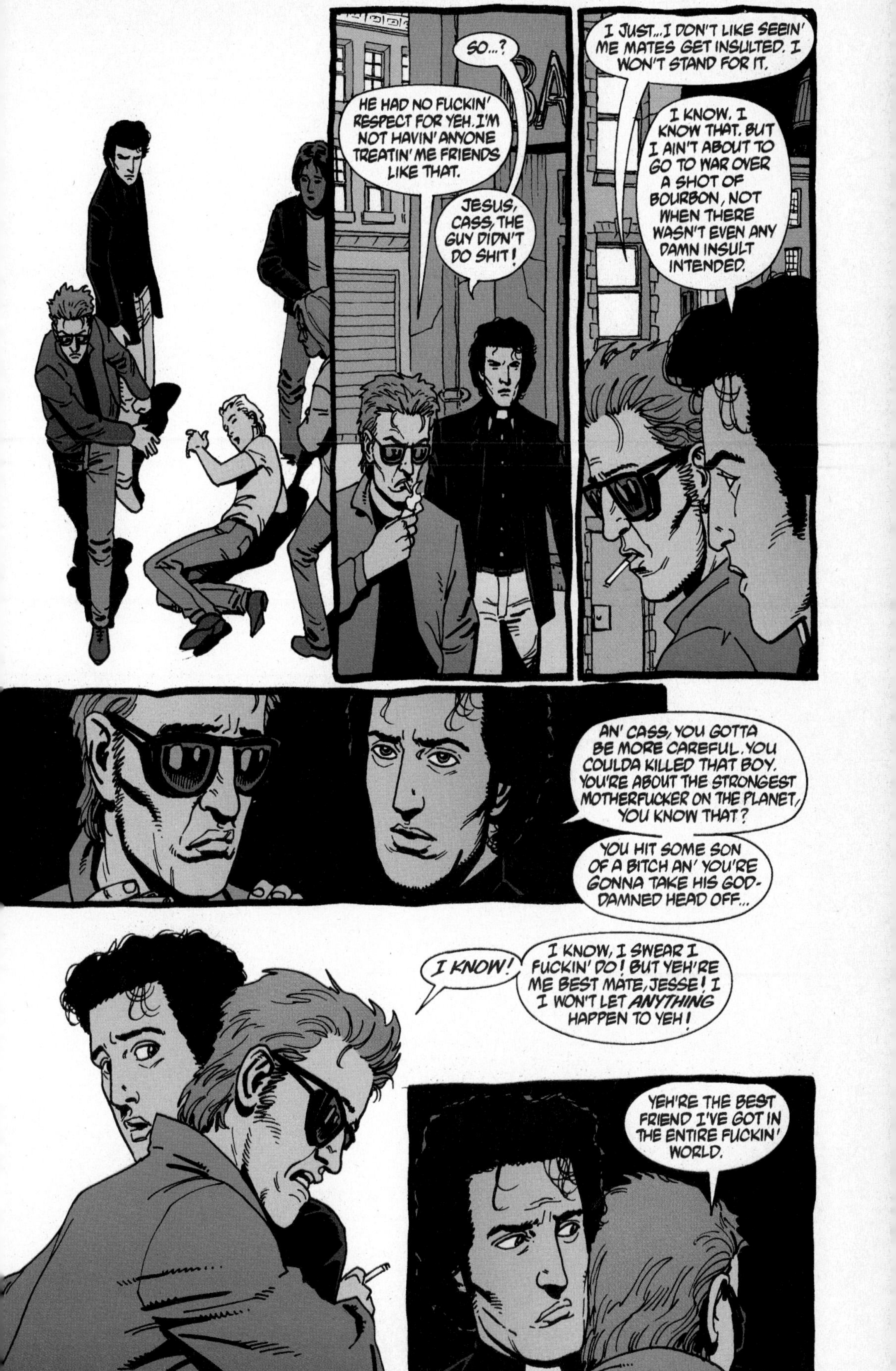
SO...?
HE HAD NO FUCKIN' RESPECT FOR YEH. I'M NOT HAVIN' ANYONE TREATIN' ME FRIENDS LIKE THAT.
JESUS, CASS, THE GUY DIDN'T DO SHIT!
I JUST...I DON'T LIKE SEEIN' ME MATES GET INSULTED. I WON'T STAND FOR IT.
I KNOW. I KNOW THAT. BUT I AIN'T ABOUT TO GO TO WAR OVER A SHOT OF BOURBON, NOT WHEN THERE WASN'T EVEN ANY DAMN INSULT INTENDED.
AN' CASS, YOU GOTTA BE MORE CAREFUL. YOU COULDA KILLED THAT BOY. YOU'RE ABOUT THE STRONGEST MOTHERFUCKER ON THE PLANET, YOU KNOW THAT?
YOU HIT SOME SON OF A BITCH AN' YOU'RE GONNA TAKE HIS GOD-DAMNED HEAD OFF...
I KNOW!
I KNOW, I SWEAR I FUCKIN' DO! BUT YEH'RE ME BEST MATE, JESSE! I I WON'T LET ANYTHING HAPPEN TO YEH!
YEH'RE THE BEST FRIEND I'VE GOT IN THE ENTIRE FUCKIN' WORLD.

I WANTED A CHANCE TO YELL AT THE IDIOT. LAST THING I NEEDED WAS JESSE OVERHEARING.

YOU THINK IT WORKED?

I WASN'T SURE IF I DID THE RIGHT THING, LEAVING YOU ALONE WITH HIM...

NO, YOU WERE GREAT.

I HOPE SO. HE SEEMED GENUINELY HURT WHEN I SAID HE HAD ULTERIOR MOTIVES. HE CAN BE SO SINCERE, YOU KNOW?

BUT I SOMETIMES WONDER ABOUT CASSIDY...

I DUNNO.

SO WHERE NEXT?

JESSE SAID SOMETHING ABOUT GOING WEST. HE MENTIONED ARIZONA, UTAH, LIKE THAT.

WELL, YOU'VE GOT MY NUMBER.

YOU REMEMBER, GIRLFRIEND-- IF THE SHIT EVER HITS THE FAN, NO MATTER WHERE YOU ARE OR WHAT KIND OF TROUBLE YOU'RE IN, YOU CALL ME...

I'LL COME RUNNING.

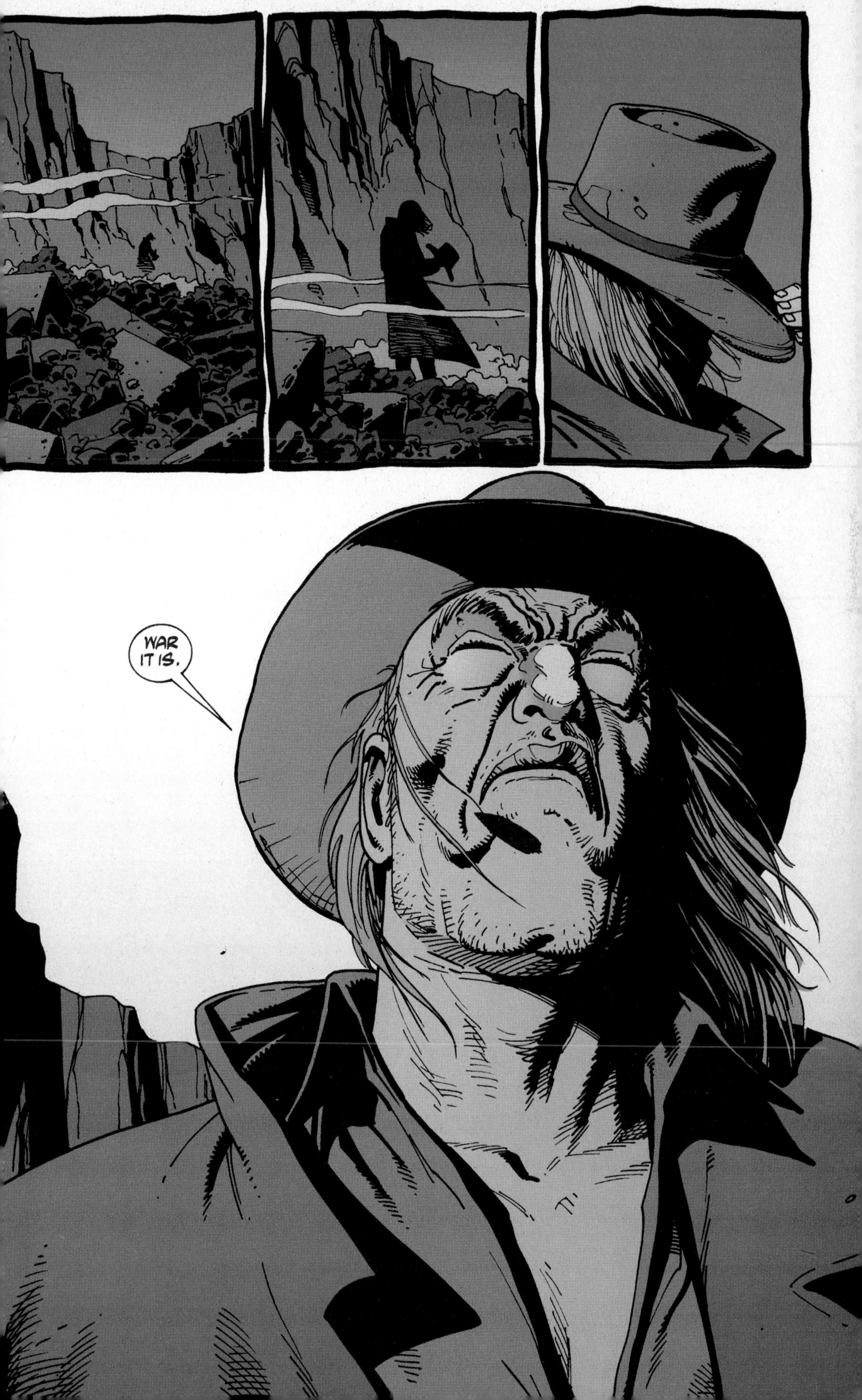
WAR IT IS.

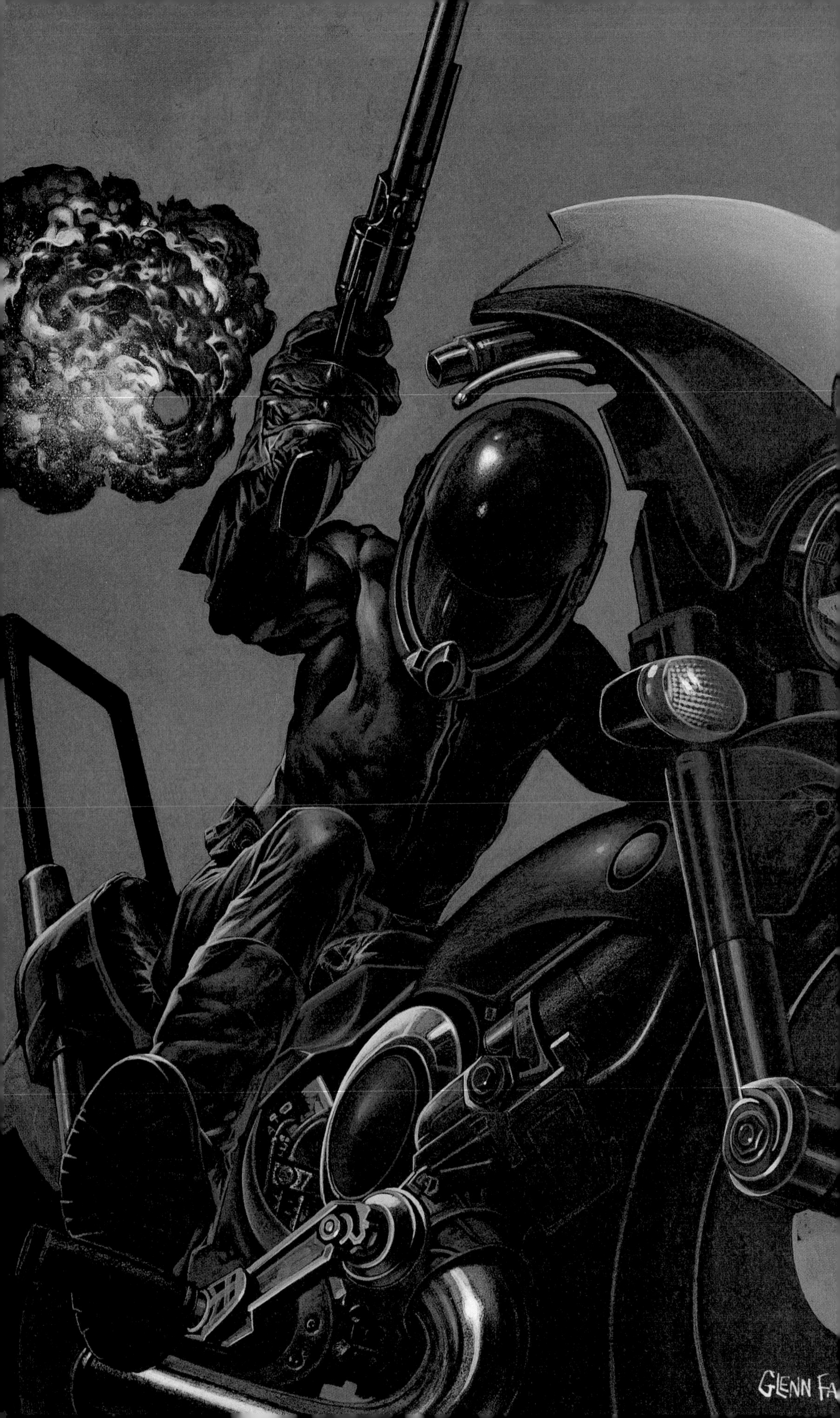
GLENN FA

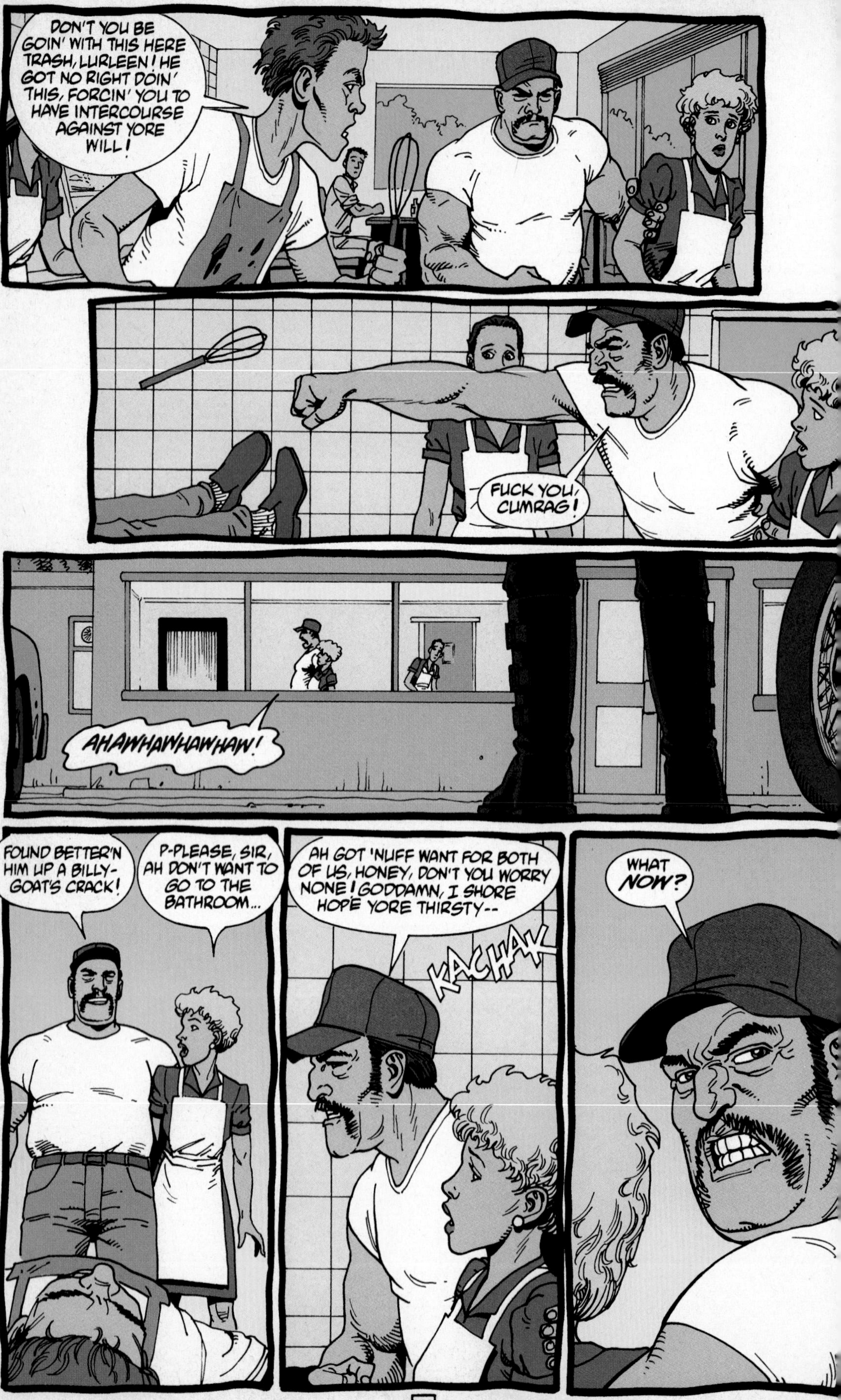
DON'T YOU BE GOIN' WITH THIS HERE TRASH, LURLEEN! HE GOT NO RIGHT DOIN' THIS, FORCIN' YOU TO HAVE INTERCOURSE AGAINST YORE WILL!
FUCK YOU, CUMRAG!
AHAWHAWHAWHAW!
FOUND BETTER'N HIM UP A BILLY-GOAT'S CRACK!
P-PLEASE, SIR, AH DON'T WANT TO GO TO THE BATHROOM...
AH GOT 'NUFF WANT FOR BOTH OF US, HONEY, DON'T YOU WORRY NONE! GODDAMN, I SHORE HOPE YORE THIRSTY--
KACHAK
WHAT NOW?

OLD FAMILIAR FACES

GARTH ENNIS - Writer   STEVE DILLON - Artist

MATT HOLLINGSWORTH - Colorist

CLEM ROBINS - Letterer   AXEL ALONSO - Editor

PREACHER created by GARTH ENNIS and STEVE DILLON

ISN'T THIS FUCKIN' MENTAL, WHEN YEH THINK ABOUT IT?

I MEAN HERE YEH ARE, YEH'VE GOT THE BODILESS OFFSPRING OF A DEMON AN' ANGEL STUCK IN YER HEAD, AN' YER TRYNNA REMEMBER *ITS* MEMORIES SO YEH CAN GO AN' CONFRONT GOD --DO YEH NEVER STOP AN' THINK, JAYSIS, THIS IS MAYBE A WEE BIT WEIRD?

YEAH, BUT ANYTIME I DO, I JUST THINK HOW THE GUY SITTIN' NEXT TO ME CAN BENCH A DAMN STATION WAGON. WE'RE WAY PAST THE WEIRDNESS THING, CASS.

HEH.

OR TO PUT IT ANOTHER WAY...

CAN I HAVE MY COFFEE BACK, PLEASE?

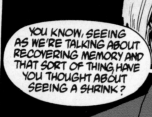

YOU KNOW, SEEING AS WE'RE TALKING ABOUT RECOVERING MEMORY AND THAT SORT OF THING, HAVE YOU THOUGHT ABOUT SEEING A SHRINK?

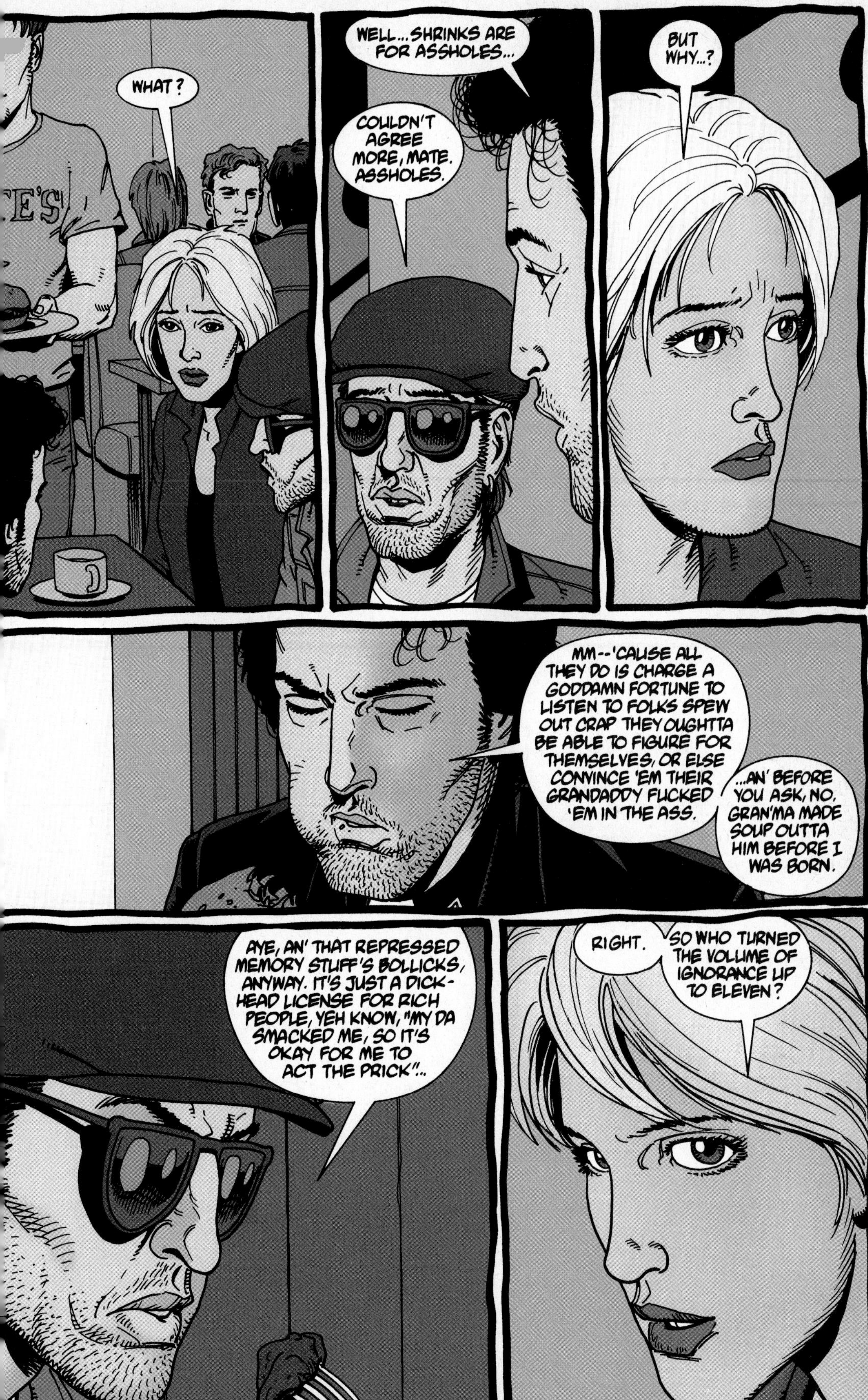
WHAT?
WELL... SHRINKS ARE FOR ASSHOLES...
COULDN'T AGREE MORE, MATE. ASSHOLES.
BUT WHY...?
MM--'CAUSE ALL THEY DO IS CHARGE A GODDAMN FORTUNE TO LISTEN TO FOLKS SPEW OUT CRAP THEY OUGHTTA BE ABLE TO FIGURE FOR THEMSELVES, OR ELSE CONVINCE 'EM THEIR GRANDADDY FUCKED 'EM IN THE ASS.
...AN' BEFORE YOU ASK, NO, GRAN'MA MADE SOUP OUTTA HIM BEFORE I WAS BORN.
AYE, AN' THAT REPRESSED MEMORY STUFF'S BOLLICKS, ANYWAY. IT'S JUST A DICK-HEAD LICENSE FOR RICH PEOPLE, YEH KNOW, "MY DA SMACKED ME, SO IT'S OKAY FOR ME TO ACT THE PRICK"...
RIGHT.
SO WHO TURNED THE VOLUME OF IGNORANCE UP TO ELEVEN?

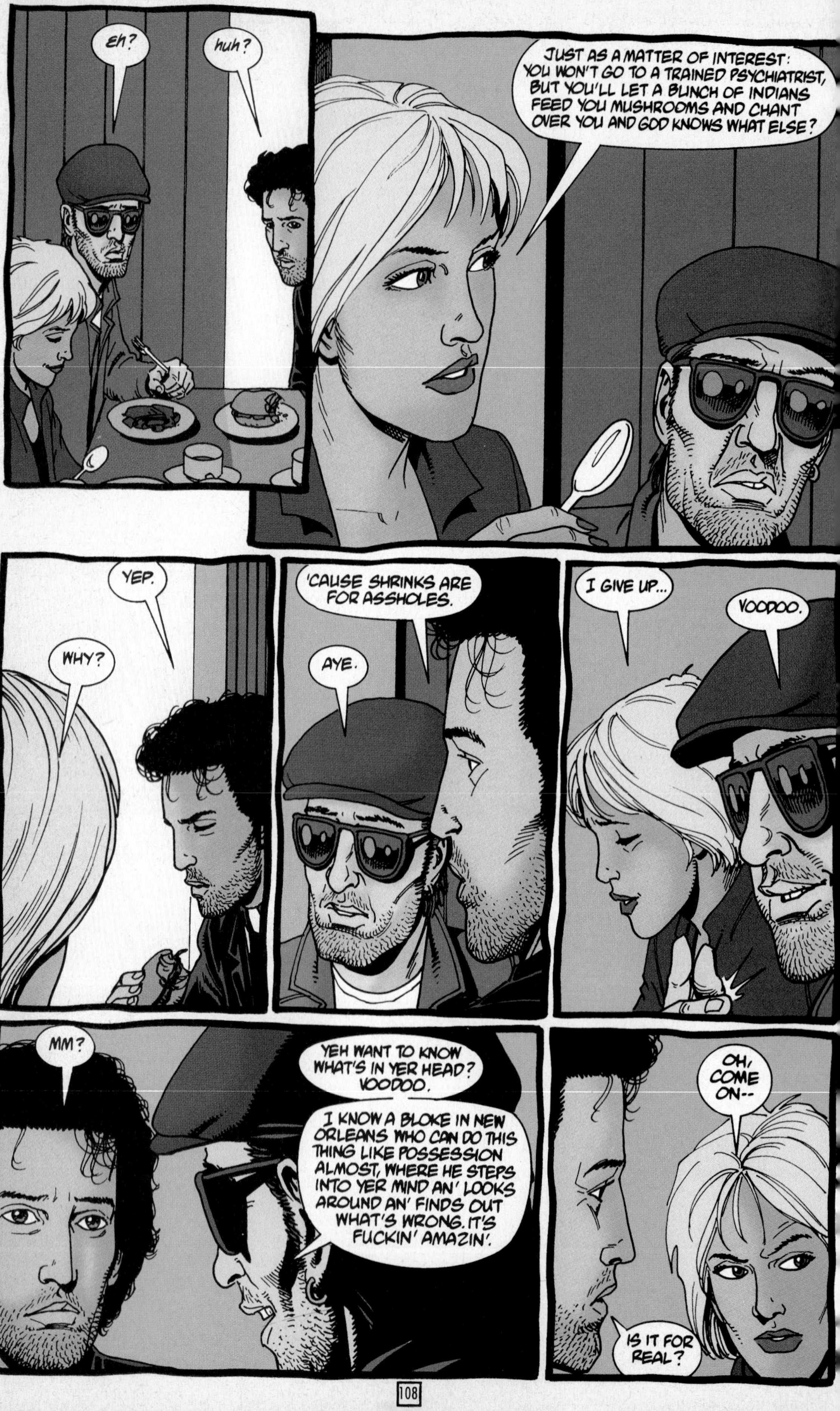
Eh?
huh?
JUST AS A MATTER OF INTEREST: YOU WON'T GO TO A TRAINED PSYCHIATRIST, BUT YOU'LL LET A BUNCH OF INDIANS FEED YOU MUSHROOMS AND CHANT OVER YOU AND GOD KNOWS WHAT ELSE?
YEP.
WHY?
'CAUSE SHRINKS ARE FOR ASSHOLES.
AYE.
I GIVE UP...
VOODOO.
MM?
YEH WANT TO KNOW WHAT'S IN YER HEAD? VOODOO.
I KNOW A BLOKE IN NEW ORLEANS WHO CAN DO THIS THING LIKE POSSESSION ALMOST, WHERE HE STEPS INTO YER MIND AN' LOOKS AROUND AN' FINDS OUT WHAT'S WRONG. IT'S FUCKIN' AMAZIN'.
OH, COME ON--
IS IT FOR REAL?

JAYSIS, WHO CARES? IT DOESN'T MATTER IF IT'S THE POWER'VE THE OCCULT OR JUST SOME SORT'VE HYPNOSIS--THE POINT IS IT *WORKS.*

OH FUCK AYE, I'VE SEEN IT MESELF.

HE PUTS YEH INTO A TRANCE AN' TAKES YEH OVER, AN' WHEN YEH COME OUT'VE IT YEH KNOW YER PROBLEM: LIKE YEH'VE A CURSE ON YEH, OR YEH SHOULDN'T'VE DONE X, Y AN' Z TEN YEARS AGO. THAT'S WHY YEH CAN'T GET A HARD-ON.

THAT'S JUST AN EXAMPLE, LIKE, BUT YEH KNOW WHAT I MEAN.

I DON'T KNOW ABOUT THIS...

REALLY?

I GOTTA ADMIT, NEW ORLEANS IS A HELL OF A LOT MORE APPEALIN' THAN GODDAMN ARIZONA. NEARER, TOO.

ARE YOU SERIOUS?

DIFFERENT METHOD, SAME RESULT.

IS HE ANYTHING LIKE YOUR OTHER *MATE,* THE ONE WHO TURNED OUT TO BE A SERIAL KILLER AND ALMOST MURDERED US ALL?

WELL, NOBODY'S *PERFECT...*

I'M TELLIN' YEH, TULIP, IT WORKS EVERY TIME. THIS MATE'VE MINE'S FANTASTIC...

NO.

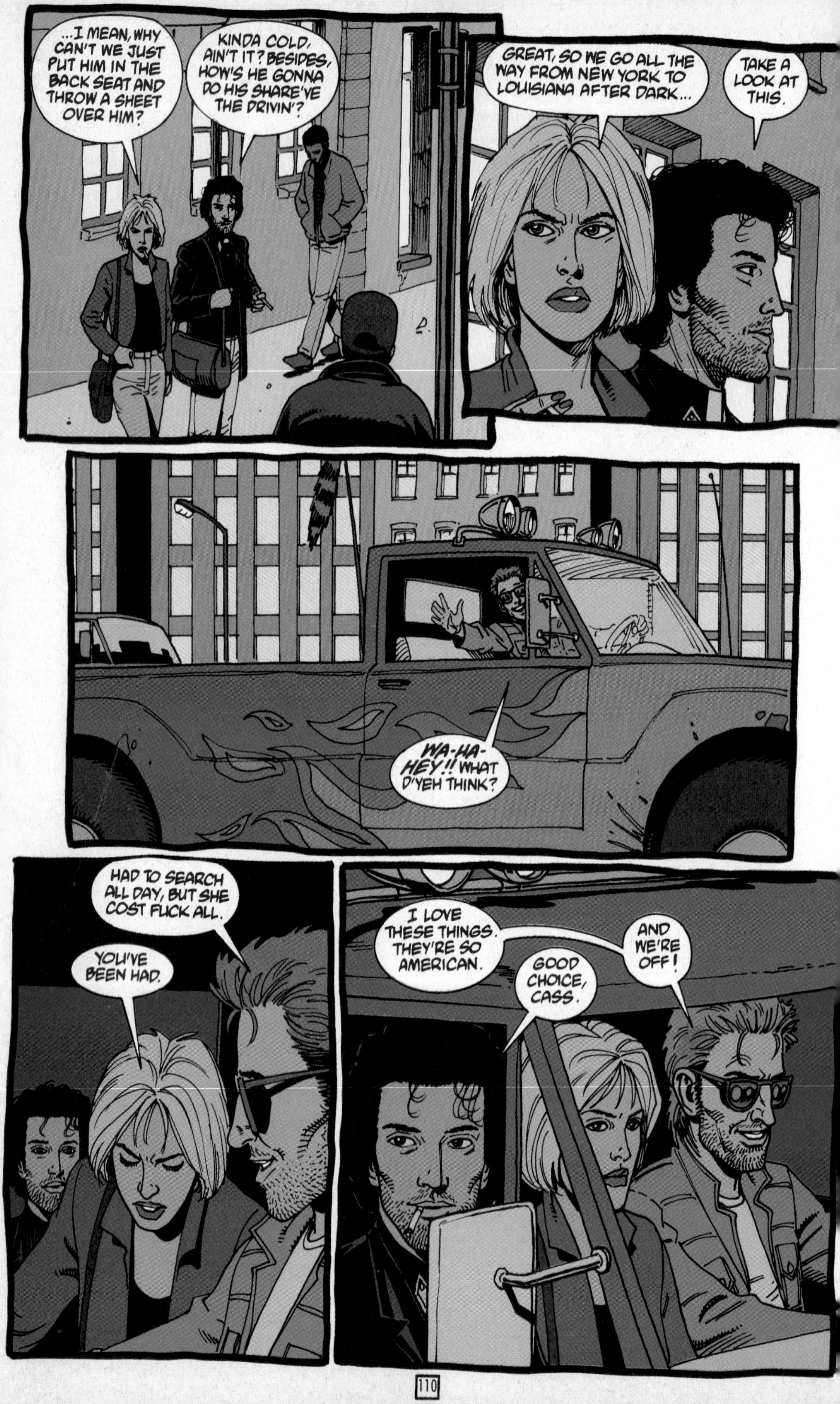
...I MEAN, WHY CAN'T WE JUST PUT HIM IN THE BACK SEAT AND THROW A SHEET OVER HIM?
KINDA COLD, AIN'T IT? BESIDES, HOW'S HE GONNA DO HIS SHARE'VE THE DRIVIN'?
GREAT, SO WE GO ALL THE WAY FROM NEW YORK TO LOUISIANA AFTER DARK...
TAKE A LOOK AT THIS.
WA-HA-HEY!! WHAT D'YEH THINK?
HAD TO SEARCH ALL DAY, BUT SHE COST FUCK ALL.
YOU'VE BEEN HAD.
I LOVE THESE THINGS. THEY'RE SO AMERICAN.
GOOD CHOICE, CASS.
AND WE'RE OFF!

...SUHRUNNKUHH UHHNUHH, UH TRUHHMUHV UHMUH FUHBLUHFF HUBB- MUHA SUHH UHUH UHMUH 'HUHH, UH UHRUHZUHVA BUHVA BUHH SUH MUH- MUMUHDUH CUVRAH HUBFUH!*

*SO IRONICALLY [EN]OUGH, THE TRAUMA [OF] HAVING MY FACE [BL]OWN OFF HELPED ME [TO] SEE THE ERROR OF [MY] WAYS, AND I RESOLVED [TO] BE THE BEST SON MY [M]OM AND DAD COULD [EV]ER HAVE HOPED FOR!

UHFUHYUHHNY, MUHLUV NUHLUHHAVAH THUH...*

IS THAT A FACT?

*UNFORTUNATELY, MOM LEFT NOT LONG AFTER THAT...

MM!

JUST CURIOUS, BUT IS THIS STORY OF YOURS ANYWHERE NEAR DONE?

JUHH GUH SUHHH!*

#JUST GETTING STARTED!

SWELL.

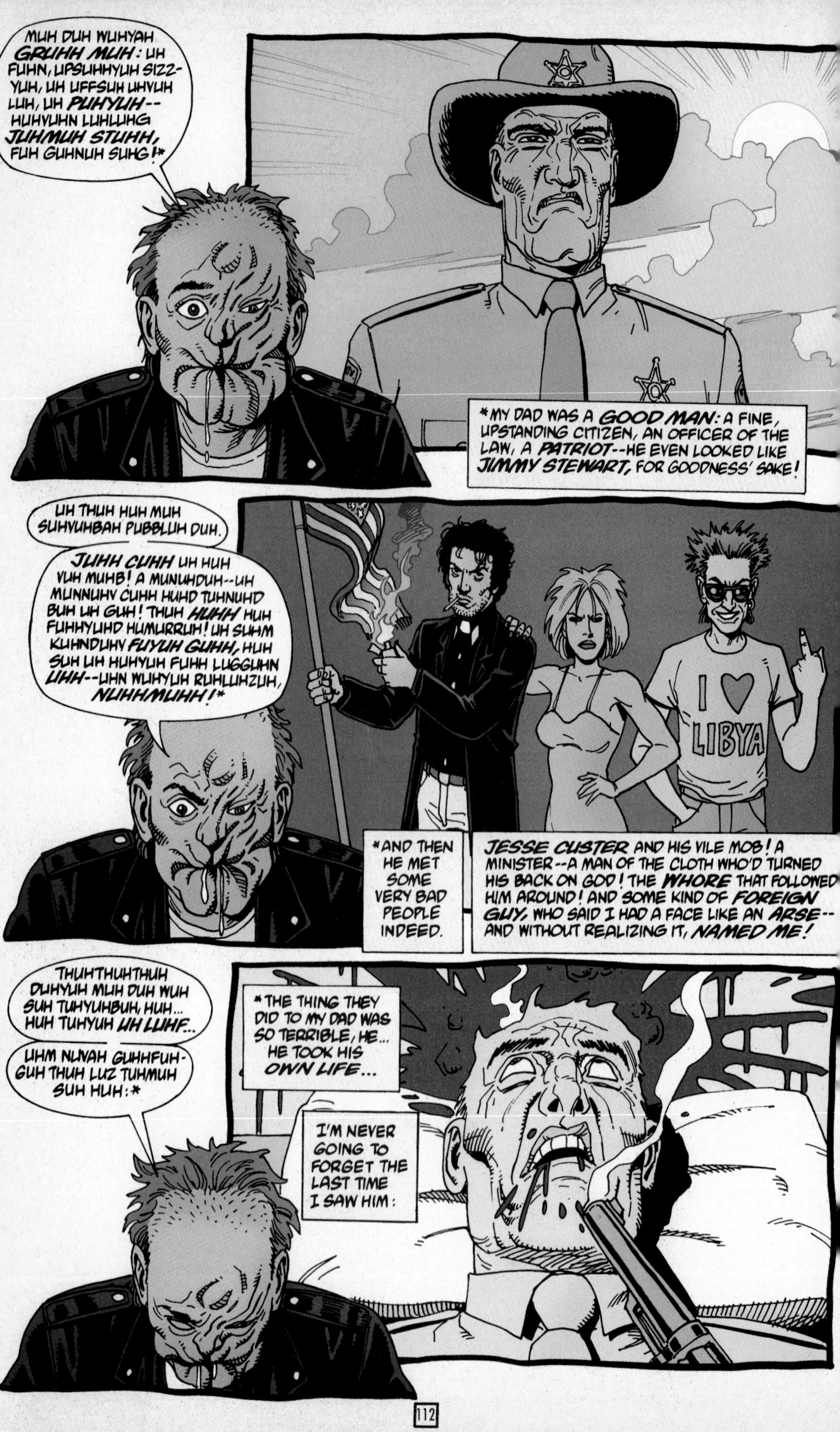
MUH DUH WUHYAH GRUHH MUH: UH FUHN, UPSUHHYUH SIZZ-YUH, UH UFFSUH UHVUH LUH, UH PUHYUH-- HUHYUHN LUHLUHG JUHMUH STUHH, FUH GUHNUH SUHG!*
*MY DAD WAS A GOOD MAN: A FINE, UPSTANDING CITIZEN, AN OFFICER OF THE LAW, A PATRIOT--HE EVEN LOOKED LIKE JIMMY STEWART, FOR GOODNESS' SAKE!
UH THUH HUH MUH SUHVUHBAH PUBBLUH DUH.
JUHH CUHH UH HUH VUH MUHB! A MUNUHDUH--UH MUNNUHV CUHH HUHD TUHNUHD BUH UH GUH! THUH HUHH HUH FUHHYUHD HUMURRUH! UH SUHM KUHNDUHV FUYUH GUHH, HUH SUH UH HUHYUH FUHH LUGGUHN UHH--UHN WUHYUH RUHLUHZUH, NUHHMUHH!*
*AND THEN HE MET SOME VERY BAD PEOPLE INDEED.
JESSE CUSTER AND HIS VILE MOB! A MINISTER--A MAN OF THE CLOTH WHO'D TURNED HIS BACK ON GOD! THE WHORE THAT FOLLOWED HIM AROUND! AND SOME KIND OF FOREIGN GUY, WHO SAID I HAD A FACE LIKE AN ARSE--AND WITHOUT REALIZING IT, NAMED ME!
I ♥ LIBYA
THUHTHUHTHUH DUHYUH MUH DUH WUH SUH TUHYUHBUH, HUH... HUH TUHYUH UH LUHF...
UHM NUVAH GUHHFUH-GUH THUH LUZ TUHMUH SUH HUH:*
*THE THING THEY DID TO MY DAD WAS SO TERRIBLE, HE... HE TOOK HIS OWN LIFE...
I'M NEVER GOING TO FORGET THE LAST TIME I SAW HIM:

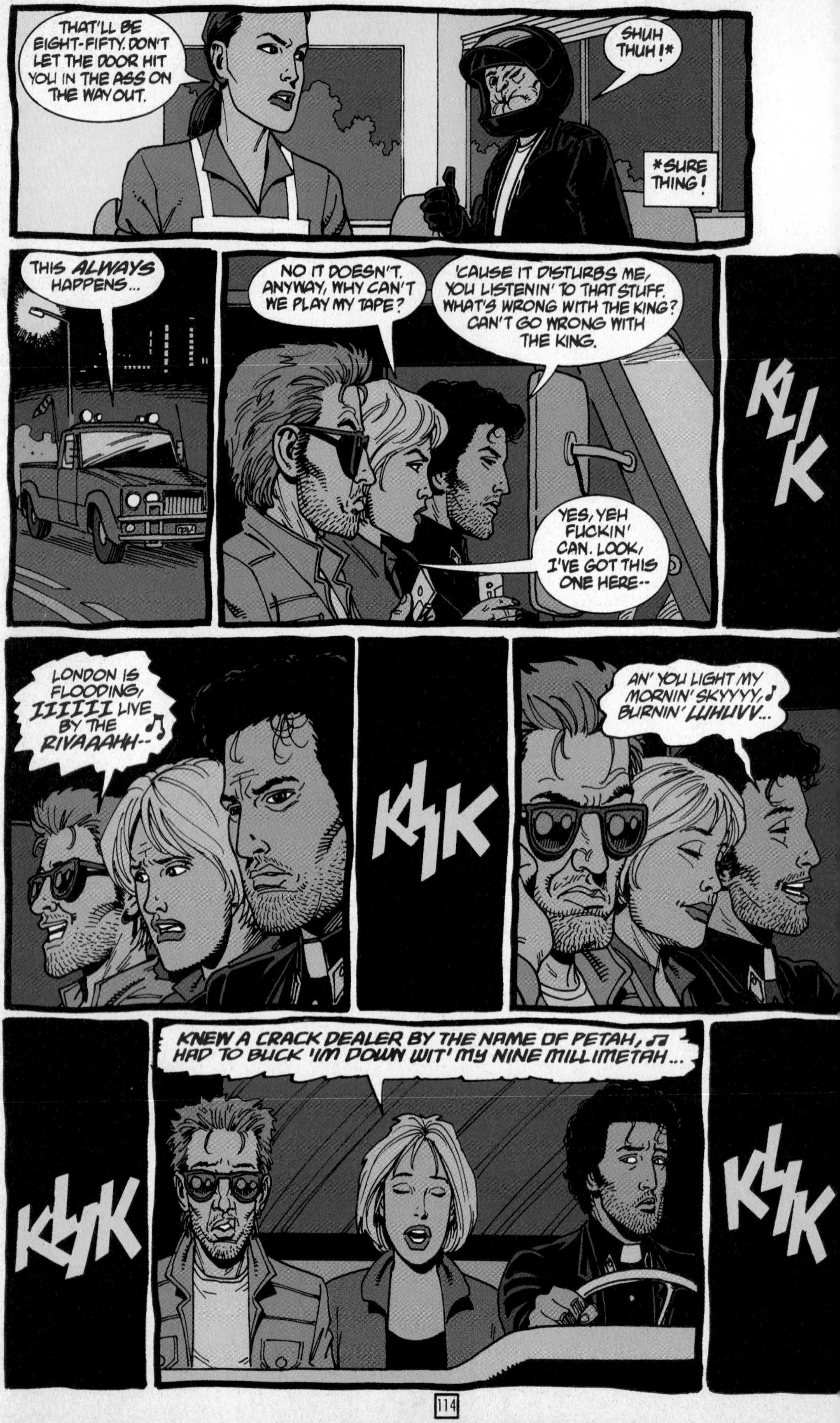
THAT'LL BE EIGHT-FIFTY. DON'T LET THE DOOR HIT YOU IN THE ASS ON THE WAY OUT.
SHUH THUH!*
*SURE THING!
THIS ALWAYS HAPPENS...
NO IT DOESN'T. ANYWAY, WHY CAN'T WE PLAY MY TAPE?
'CAUSE IT DISTURBS ME, YOU LISTENIN' TO THAT STUFF. WHAT'S WRONG WITH THE KING? CAN'T GO WRONG WITH THE KING.
YES, YEH FUCKIN' CAN. LOOK, I'VE GOT THIS ONE HERE--
KLIK
LONDON IS FLOODING, IIIIII LIVE BY THE RIVAAAHH--
KLIK
AN' YOU LIGHT MY MORNIN' SKYYYY, BURNIN' LUHUVV...
KNEW A CRACK DEALER BY THE NAME OF PETAH, HAD TO BUCK 'IM DOWN WIT' MY NINE MILLIMETAH...
KLIK
KLIK

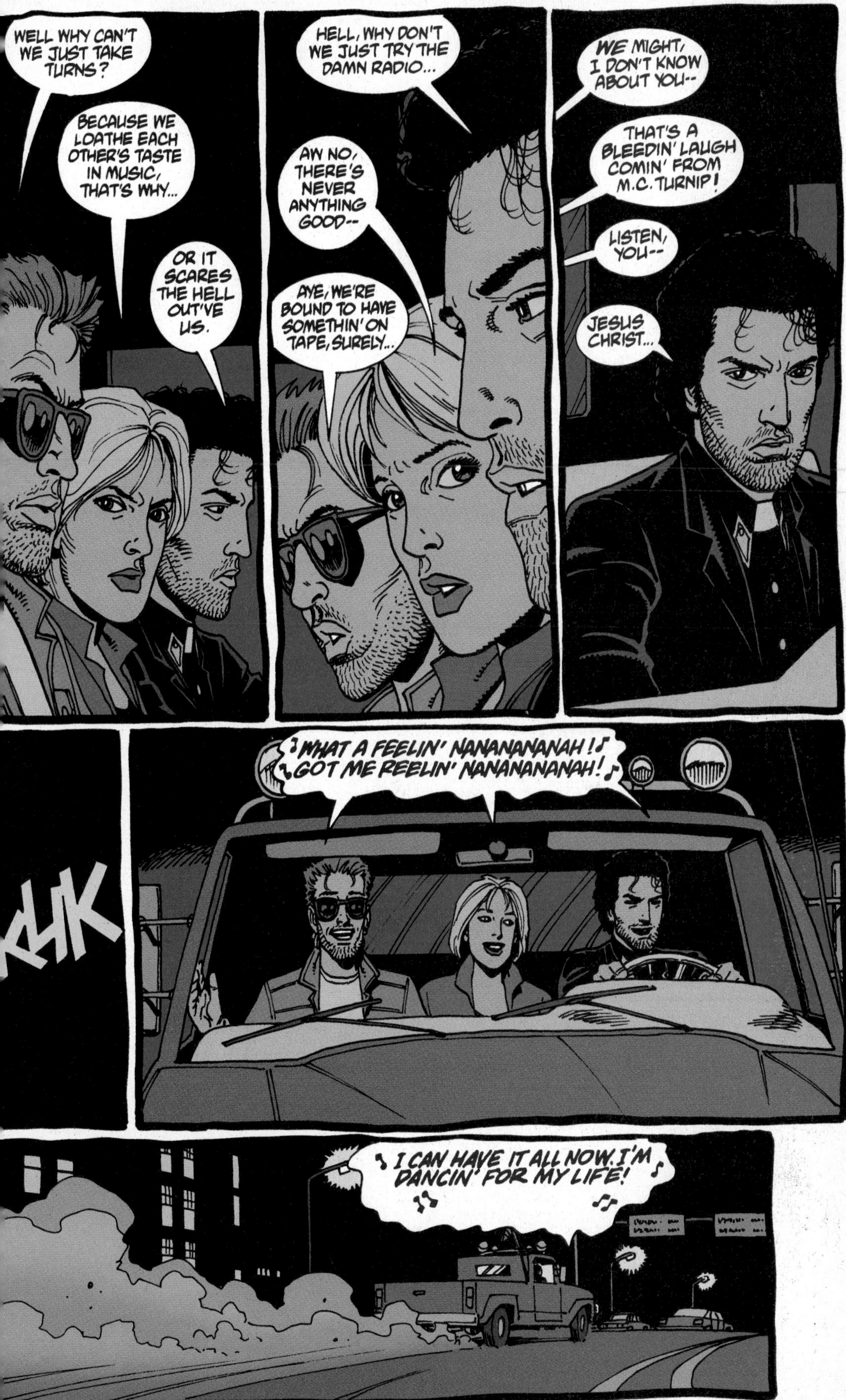
WELL WHY CAN'T WE JUST TAKE TURNS?
BECAUSE WE LOATHE EACH OTHER'S TASTE IN MUSIC, THAT'S WHY...
OR IT SCARES THE HELL OUT'VE US.
HELL, WHY DON'T WE JUST TRY THE DAMN RADIO...
AW NO, THERE'S NEVER ANYTHING GOOD--
AYE, WE'RE BOUND TO HAVE SOMETHIN' ON TAPE, SURELY...
WE MIGHT, I DON'T KNOW ABOUT YOU--
THAT'S A BLEEDIN' LAUGH COMIN' FROM M.C. TURNIP!
LISTEN, YOU--
JESUS CHRIST...
KLIK
WHAT A FEELIN' NANANANANAH! GOT ME REELIN' NANANANANAH!
I CAN HAVE IT ALL NOW. I'M DANCIN' FOR MY LIFE!

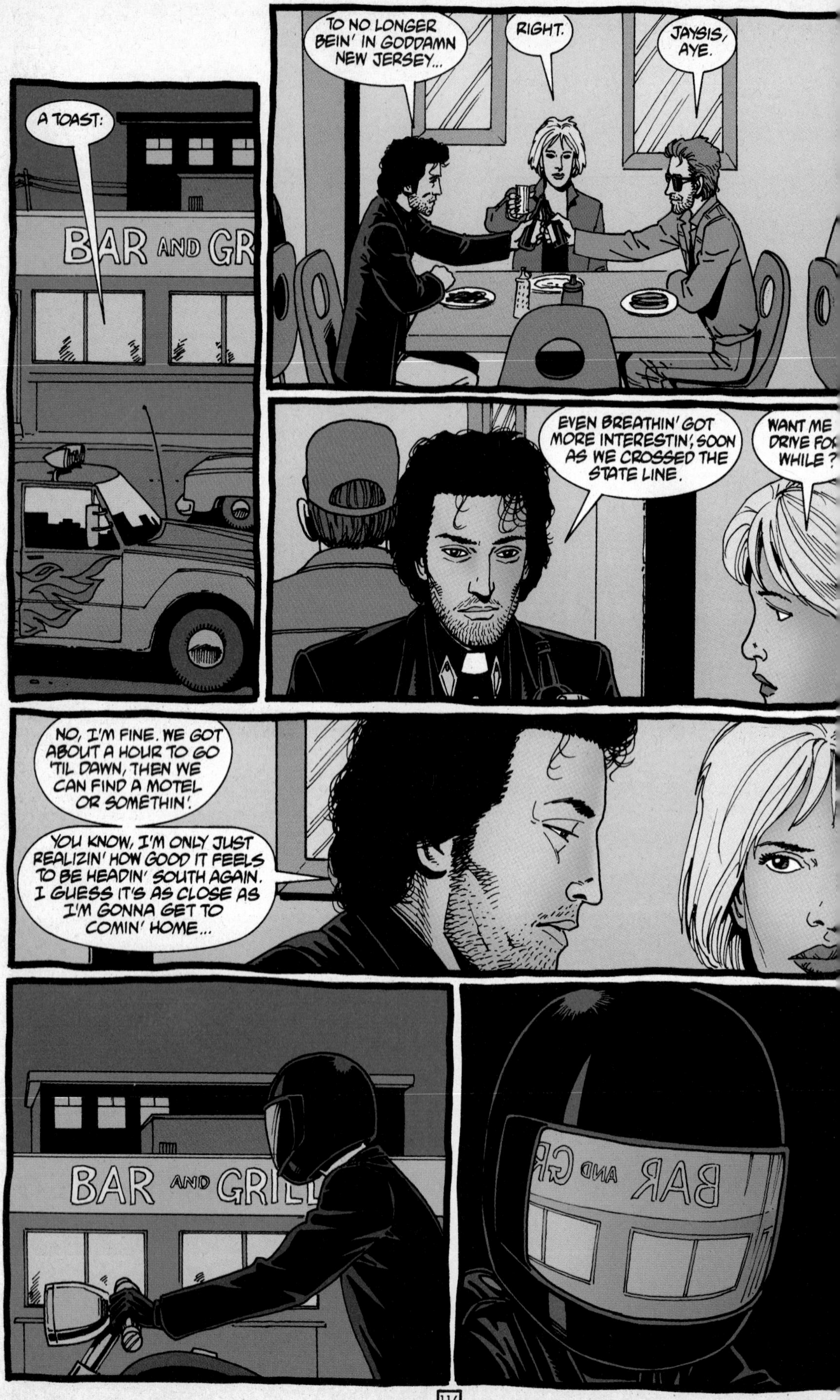
A TOAST:
TO NO LONGER BEIN' IN GODDAMN NEW JERSEY...
RIGHT.
JAYSIS, AYE.
BAR AND GR
EVEN BREATHIN' GOT MORE INTERESTIN', SOON AS WE CROSSED THE STATE LINE.
WANT ME DRIVE FO WHILE?
NO, I'M FINE. WE GOT ABOUT A HOUR TO GO 'TIL DAWN, THEN WE CAN FIND A MOTEL OR SOMETHIN'.
YOU KNOW, I'M ONLY JUST REALIZIN' HOW GOOD IT FEELS TO BE HEADIN' SOUTH AGAIN. I GUESS IT'S AS CLOSE AS I'M GONNA GET TO COMIN' HOME...
BAR AND GRILL

JUST DON'T SEE
OW YOU CAN BE SO
NTIMENTAL ABOUT
E SOUTH, WHEN
UR CHILDHOOD
S SUCH A TOTAL
IGHTMARE...

AYE, AN' WHAT ABOUT
YER FIVE YEARS IN
ANNVILLE? IF I'D HAD
TO FACE THAT PACK'VE
GOAT-RAPISTS EVERY
SUNDAY, I'D'VE PUT
A BLEEDIN' GUN IN
ME MOUTH...

OH?

OKAY, YOU
AIN'T. LIFE
COULDA BEEN
SWEETER.

LIQUOR
STORE SOLD A
LESS DRASTIC
ALTERNATIVE.
BESIDES, YOU'RE
EXAGGERATIN',
BOTHA YOU.

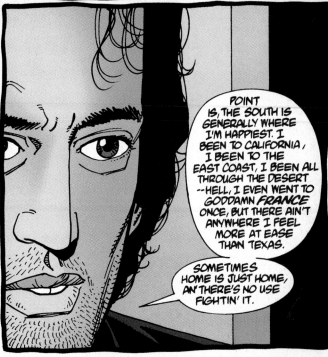

POINT
IS, THE SOUTH IS
GENERALLY WHERE
I'M HAPPIEST. I
BEEN TO CALIFORNIA,
I BEEN TO THE
EAST COAST, I BEEN ALL
THROUGH THE DESERT
--HELL, I EVEN WENT TO
GODDAMN *FRANCE*
ONCE, BUT THERE AIN'T
ANYWHERE I FEEL
MORE AT EASE
THAN TEXAS.

SOMETIMES
HOME IS JUST HOME,
AN' THERE'S NO USE
FIGHTIN' IT.

I DUNNO. I'VE
SUCCESSFULLY
FOUGHT MINE
ALL ME LIFE.

WHAT'S SO
GREAT ABOUT
MARLBORO COUNTRY,
THEN?

THE FOOD. THE
HISTORY.

THE
SKY.

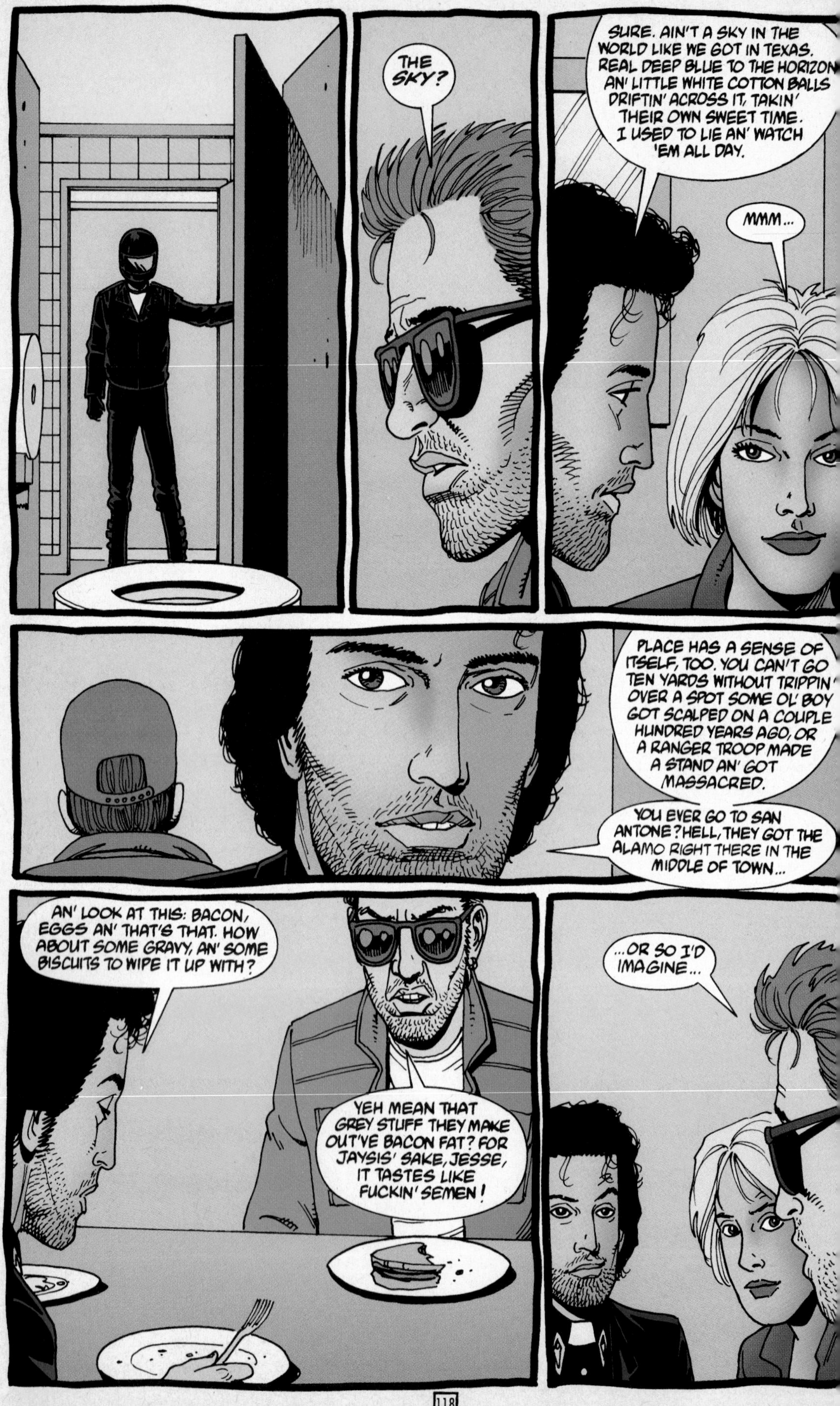
THE SKY?
SURE. AIN'T A SKY IN THE WORLD LIKE WE GOT IN TEXAS. REAL DEEP BLUE TO THE HORIZON AN' LITTLE WHITE COTTON BALLS DRIFTIN' ACROSS IT, TAKIN' THEIR OWN SWEET TIME. I USED TO LIE AN' WATCH 'EM ALL DAY.
MMM...
PLACE HAS A SENSE OF ITSELF, TOO. YOU CAN'T GO TEN YARDS WITHOUT TRIPPIN' OVER A SPOT SOME OL' BOY GOT SCALPED ON A COUPLE HUNDRED YEARS AGO, OR A RANGER TROOP MADE A STAND AN' GOT MASSACRED.
YOU EVER GO TO SAN ANTONE? HELL, THEY GOT THE ALAMO RIGHT THERE IN THE MIDDLE OF TOWN...
AN' LOOK AT THIS: BACON, EGGS AN' THAT'S THAT. HOW ABOUT SOME GRAVY, AN' SOME BISCUITS TO WIPE IT UP WITH?
YEH MEAN THAT GREY STUFF THEY MAKE OUT'VE BACON FAT? FOR JAYSIS' SAKE, JESSE, IT TASTES LIKE FUCKIN' SEMEN!
...OR SO I'D IMAGINE...

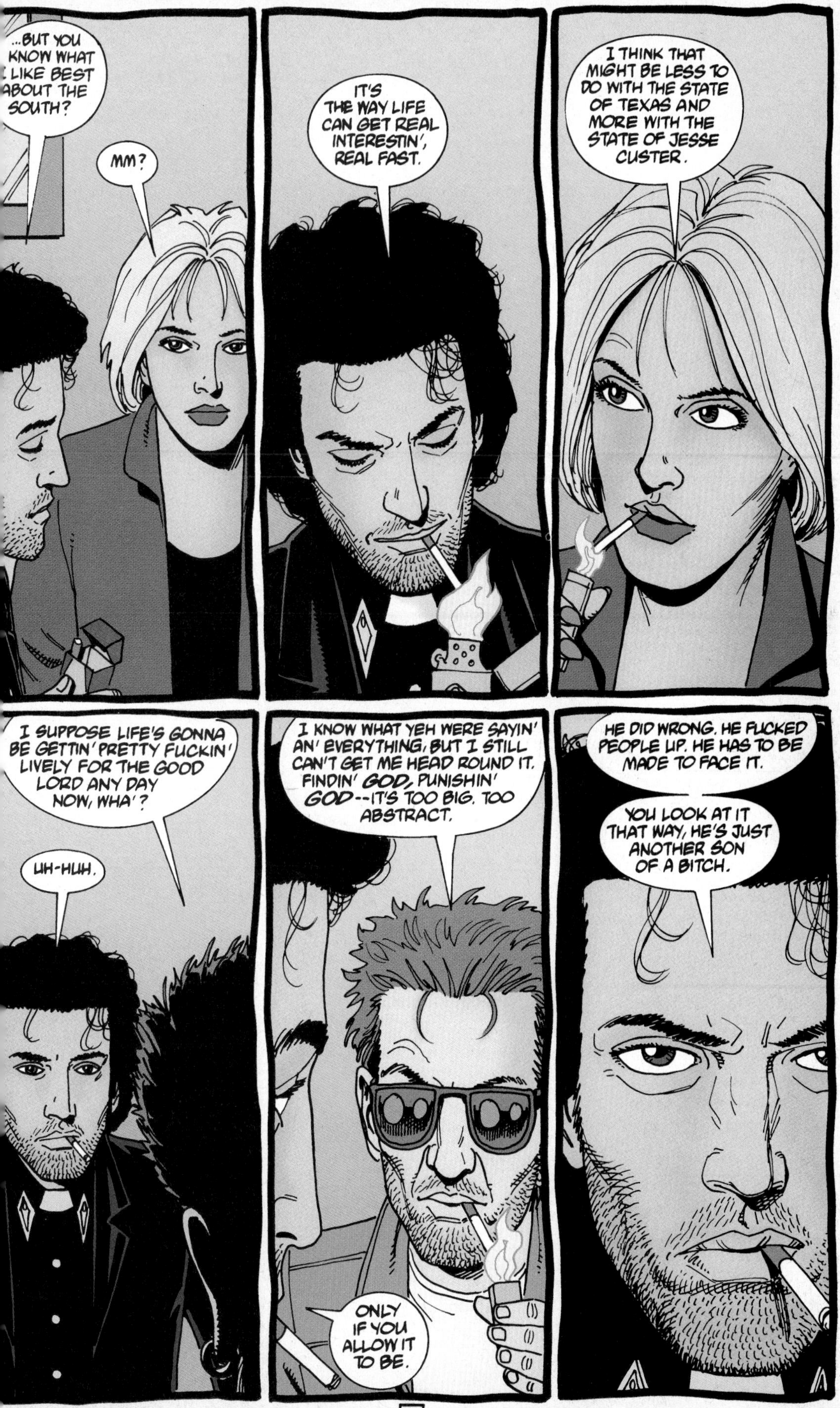
...BUT YOU KNOW WHAT I LIKE BEST ABOUT THE SOUTH?
MM?
IT'S THE WAY LIFE CAN GET REAL INTERESTIN', REAL FAST.
I THINK THAT MIGHT BE LESS TO DO WITH THE STATE OF TEXAS AND MORE WITH THE STATE OF JESSE CUSTER.
I SUPPOSE LIFE'S GONNA BE GETTIN' PRETTY FUCKIN' LIVELY FOR THE GOOD LORD ANY DAY NOW, WHA'?
UH-HUH.
I KNOW WHAT YEH WERE SAYIN' AN' EVERYTHING, BUT I STILL CAN'T GET ME HEAD ROUND IT. FINDIN' GOD, PUNISHIN' GOD--IT'S TOO BIG. TOO ABSTRACT.
ONLY IF YOU ALLOW IT TO BE.
HE DID WRONG. HE FUCKED PEOPLE UP. HE HAS TO BE MADE TO FACE IT.
YOU LOOK AT IT THAT WAY, HE'S JUST ANOTHER SON OF A BITCH.

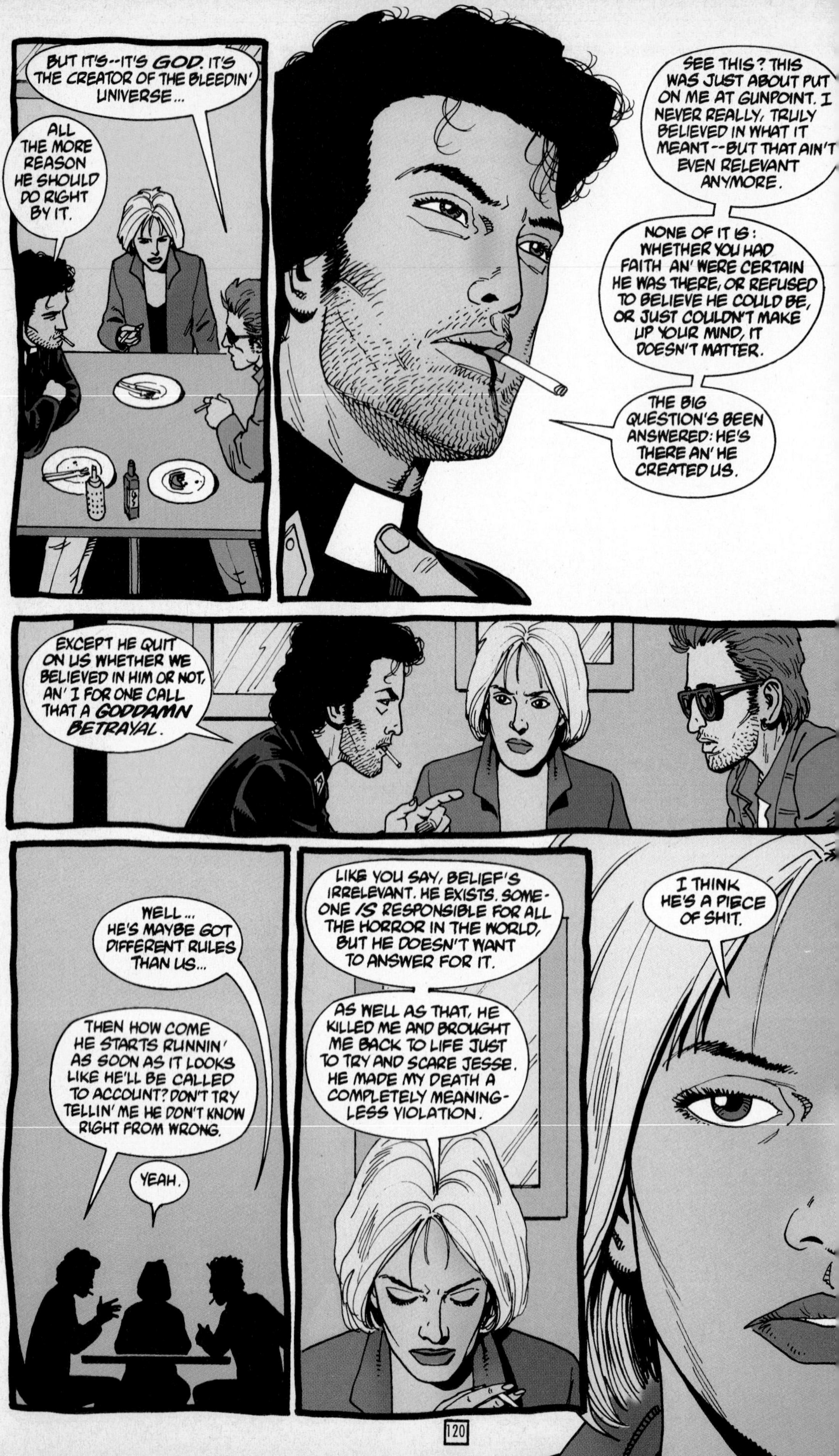
BUT IT'S--IT'S GOD. IT'S THE CREATOR OF THE BLEEDIN' UNIVERSE...
ALL THE MORE REASON HE SHOULD DO RIGHT BY IT.
SEE THIS? THIS WAS JUST ABOUT PUT ON ME AT GUNPOINT. I NEVER REALLY, TRULY BELIEVED IN WHAT IT MEANT--BUT THAT AIN'T EVEN RELEVANT ANYMORE.
NONE OF IT IS: WHETHER YOU HAD FAITH AN' WERE CERTAIN HE WAS THERE, OR REFUSED TO BELIEVE HE COULD BE, OR JUST COULDN'T MAKE UP YOUR MIND, IT DOESN'T MATTER.
THE BIG QUESTION'S BEEN ANSWERED: HE'S THERE AN' HE CREATED US.
EXCEPT HE QUIT ON US WHETHER WE BELIEVED IN HIM OR NOT, AN' I FOR ONE CALL THAT A GODDAMN BETRAYAL.
WELL... HE'S MAYBE GOT DIFFERENT RULES THAN US...
THEN HOW COME HE STARTS RUNNIN' AS SOON AS IT LOOKS LIKE HE'LL BE CALLED TO ACCOUNT? DON'T TRY TELLIN' ME HE DON'T KNOW RIGHT FROM WRONG.
YEAH.
LIKE YOU SAY, BELIEF'S IRRELEVANT. HE EXISTS. SOMEONE IS RESPONSIBLE FOR ALL THE HORROR IN THE WORLD, BUT HE DOESN'T WANT TO ANSWER FOR IT.
AS WELL AS THAT, HE KILLED ME AND BROUGHT ME BACK TO LIFE JUST TO TRY AND SCARE JESSE. HE MADE MY DEATH A COMPLETELY MEANINGLESS VIOLATION.
I THINK HE'S A PIECE OF SHIT.

WELL, WHATEVER. SURE IF YEH WANNA HUNT BILLY-RAY CYRUS TO THE ENDS'VE THE EARTH, YEH KNOW I'LL BE ALONG FOR THE RIDE.

BILLY-RAY'S RIGHT AFTER MICHAEL JACKSON.

I'M AWAY TO GET GAS.

YOU WANT CIGARETTES?

YEAH, COULD YOU? I GOTTA USE THE MEN'S ROOM.

VERY NICE...

"THIS ONE'S FOR THE KIDS," SAYS CUSTER. NOW SPORT...

GODDAMMIT...

SOME THINGS NEVER CHANGE.

HEY.

SIR'S CANCER.

THERE'S VITAMINS IN 'EM. WELL-KNOWN FACT.

I WAS JUST THINKING ABOUT YOUR IRRATIONAL FEAR OF PSYCHIATRISTS...

OH YEAH?

YEAH. ARE YOU SURE YOU'RE NOT JUST...DARE I SAY THE WORD...

INSECURE?

DID IT EVER OCCUR TO YOU THAT WHAT YOU CALL INSECURE, I CALL NOT TAKIN' ANY SHIT...?

RELAX, REVEREND. I'VE HEARD THIS RANT.

JAYSIS FUCK

HUH?

YUH CUH RUH, BUH YUH CUH HUHH, CUHH !*

*YOU CAN RUN, BUT YOU CAN'T HIDE, CUSTER !

UH TUMUHFUHYUH VUHYUHUH UHFUH !*

BA

*IT'S TIME TO FAC
THE VENGEANCE
OF ARSEFACE

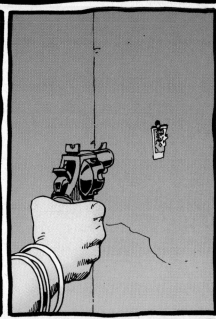

TO BE CONTINUED

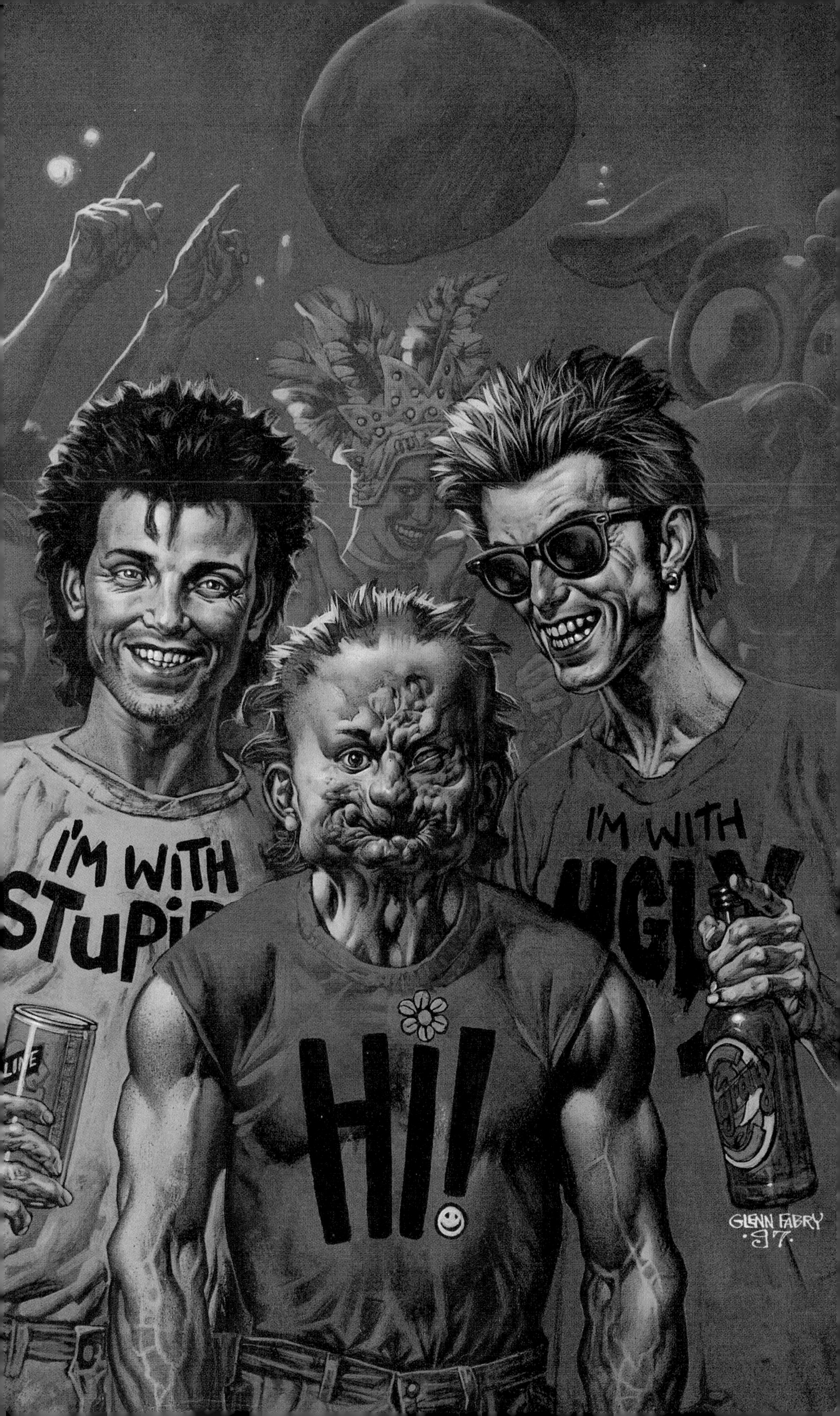
I'M WITH
HI!
I'M WITH
GLENN FABRY ·97·

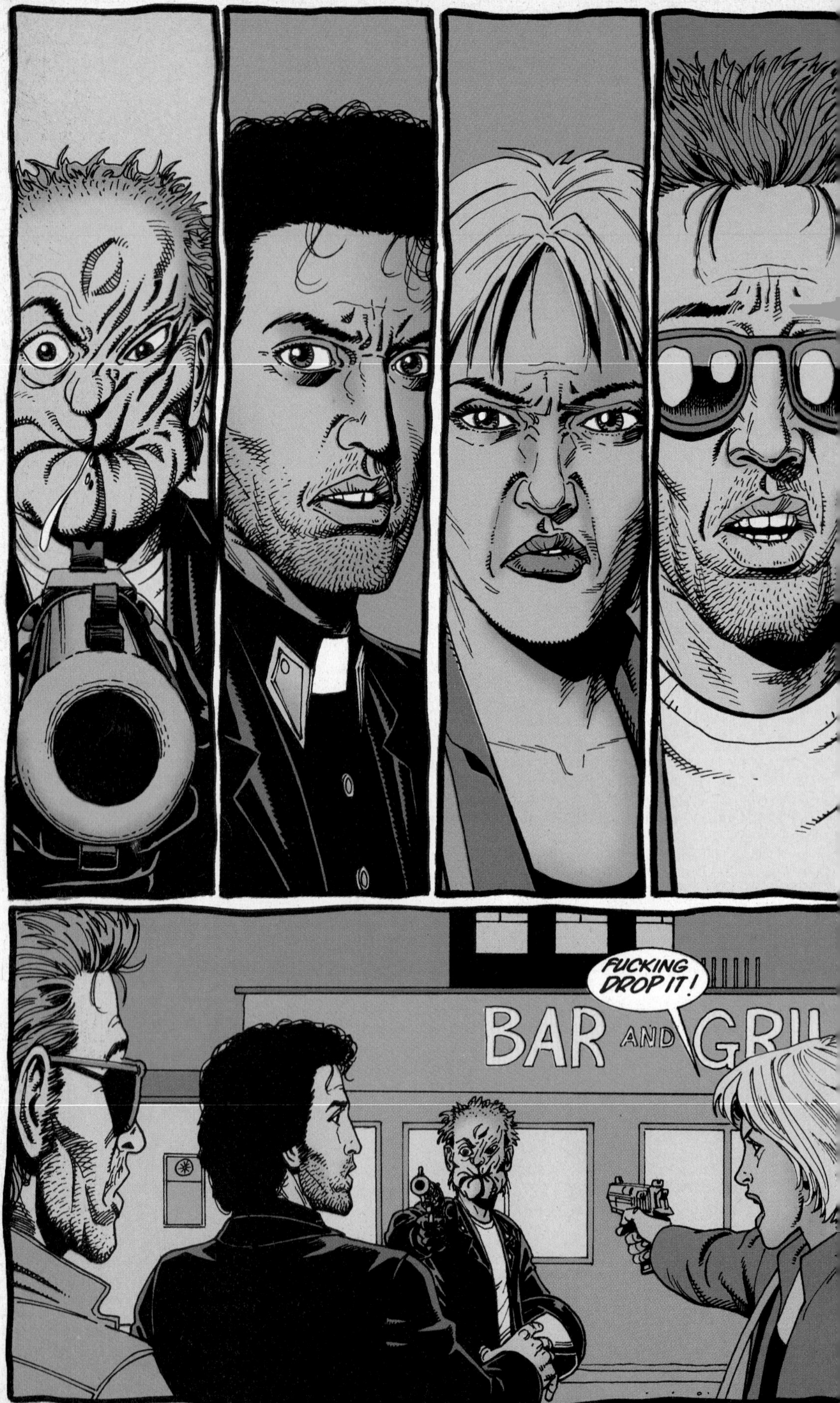
FUCKING DROP IT!
BAR AND GRI

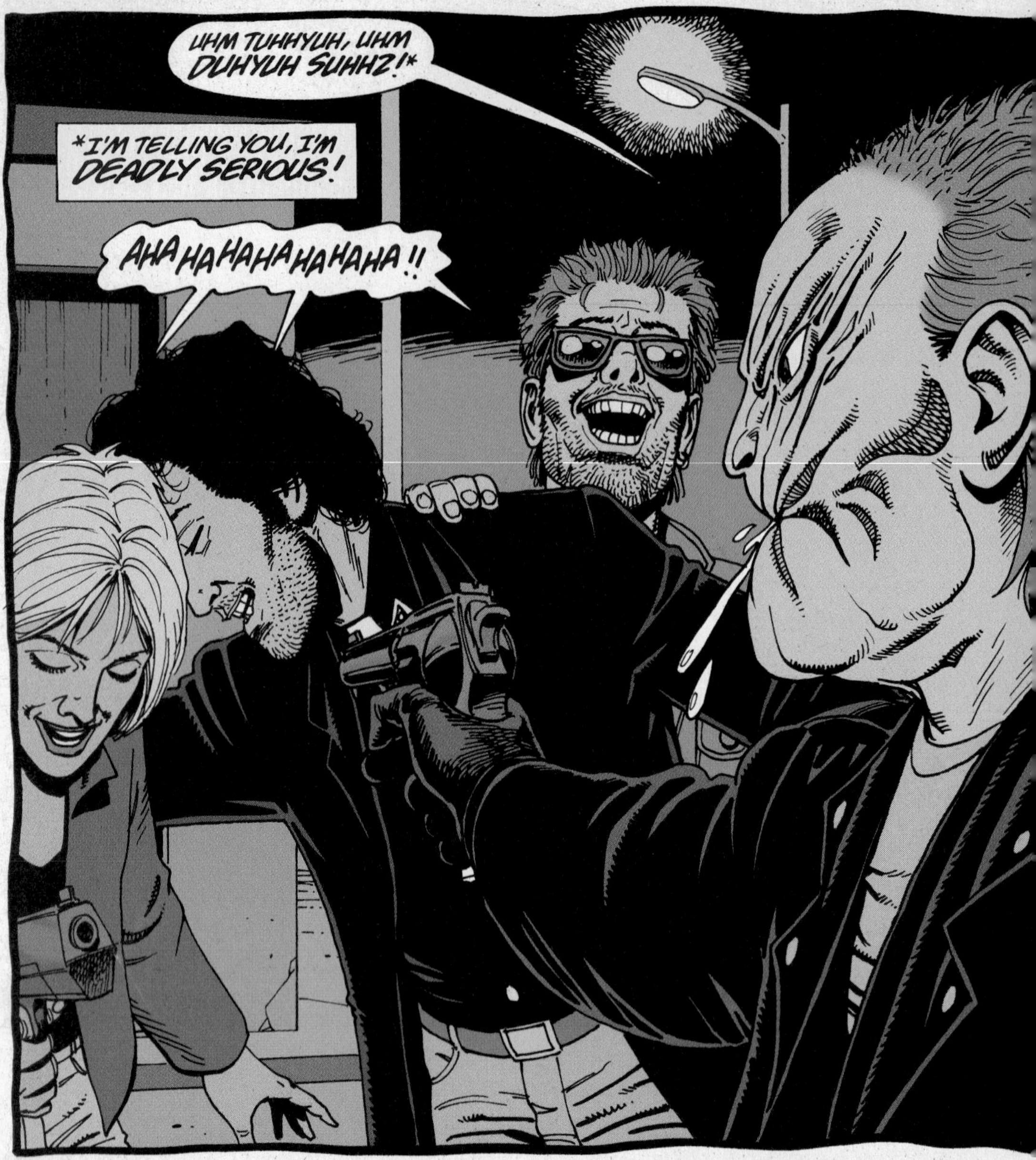
UHM TUHHYUH, UHM DUHYUH SUHHZ!*
*I'M TELLING YOU, I'M DEADLY SERIOUS!
AHA HA HAHA HA HAHA HA!!

GOOD TIMES ROLLING

GARTH ENNIS - Writer STEVE DILLON - Artist
PAMELA RAMBO and JAMES SINCLAIR - Colorists
CLEM ROBINS - Letterer AXEL ALONSO - Editor

PREACHER created by GARTH ENNIS and STEVE DILLON

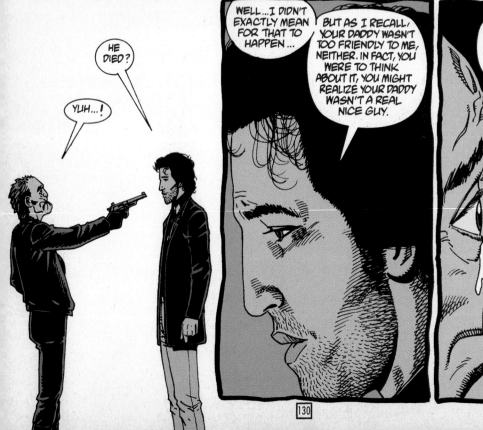

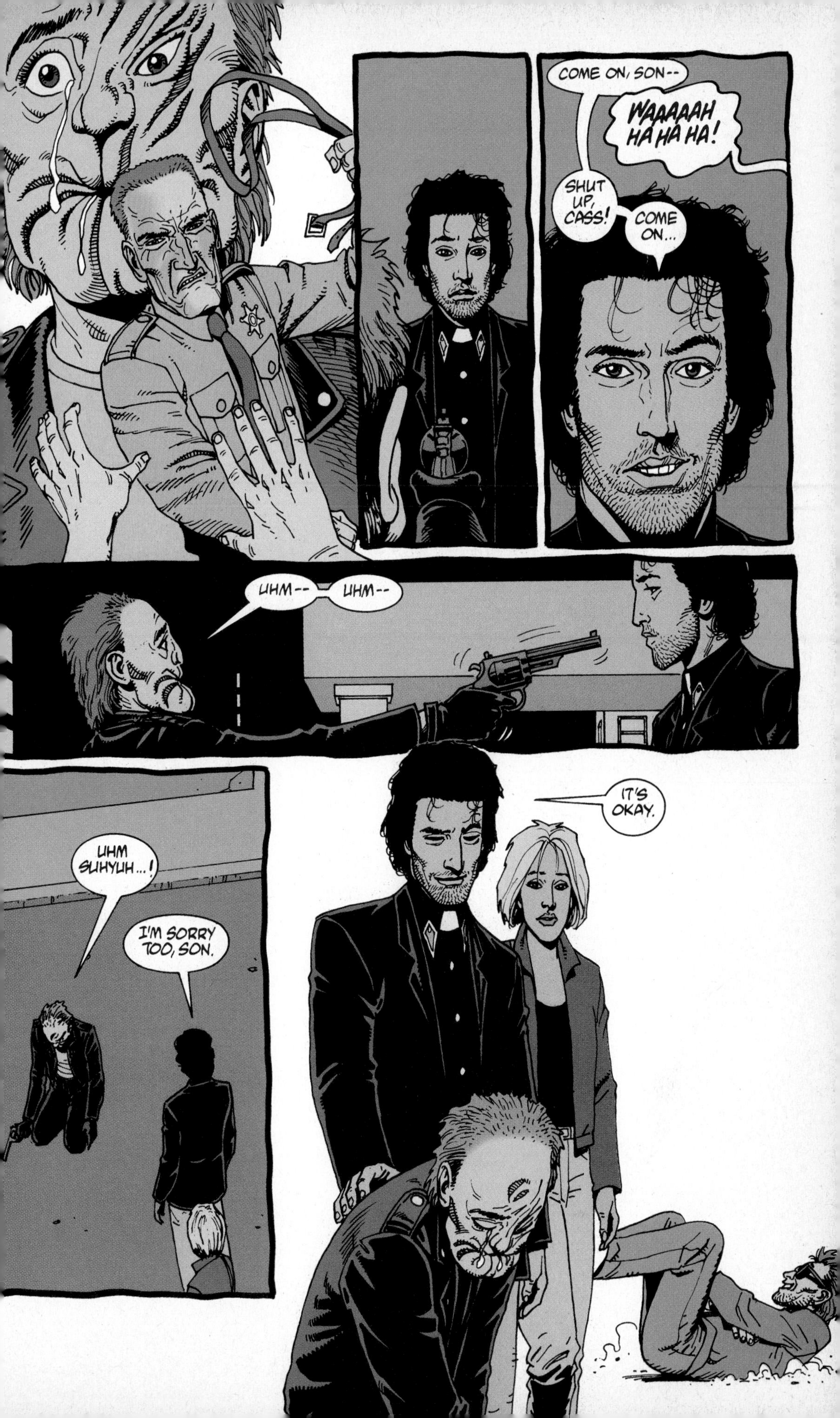
COME ON, SON--
WAAAAAH HA HA HA!
SHUT UP, CASS!
COME ON...
UHM--
UHM--
UHM SUHYUH...!
I'M SORRY TOO, SON.
IT'S OKAY.

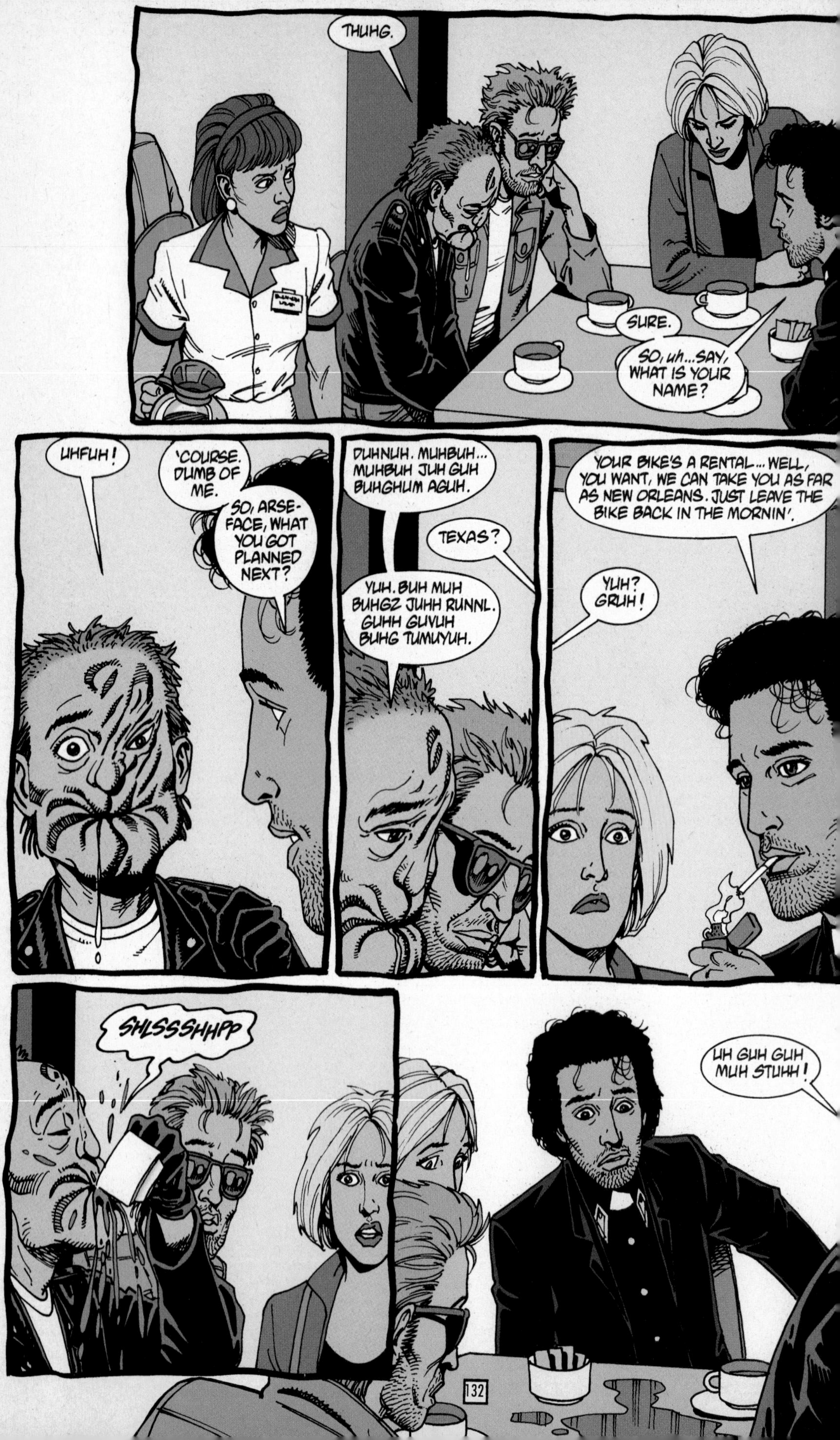
THUHG.
SURE.
SO, uh... SAY, WHAT IS YOUR NAME?
UHFUH!
'COURSE. DUMB OF ME.
SO, ARSE-FACE, WHAT YOU GOT PLANNED NEXT?
DUHNUH. MUHBUH... MUHBUH JUH GUH BUHGHUM AGUH.
TEXAS?
YUH. BUH MUH BUHGZ JUHH RUNNL. GUHH GUVUH BUHG TUMUYUH.
YOUR BIKE'S A RENTAL... WELL, YOU WANT, WE CAN TAKE YOU AS FAR AS NEW ORLEANS. JUST LEAVE THE BIKE BACK IN THE MORNIN'.
YUH? GRUH!
SHLSSSHHPP
UH GUH GUH MUH STUHH!

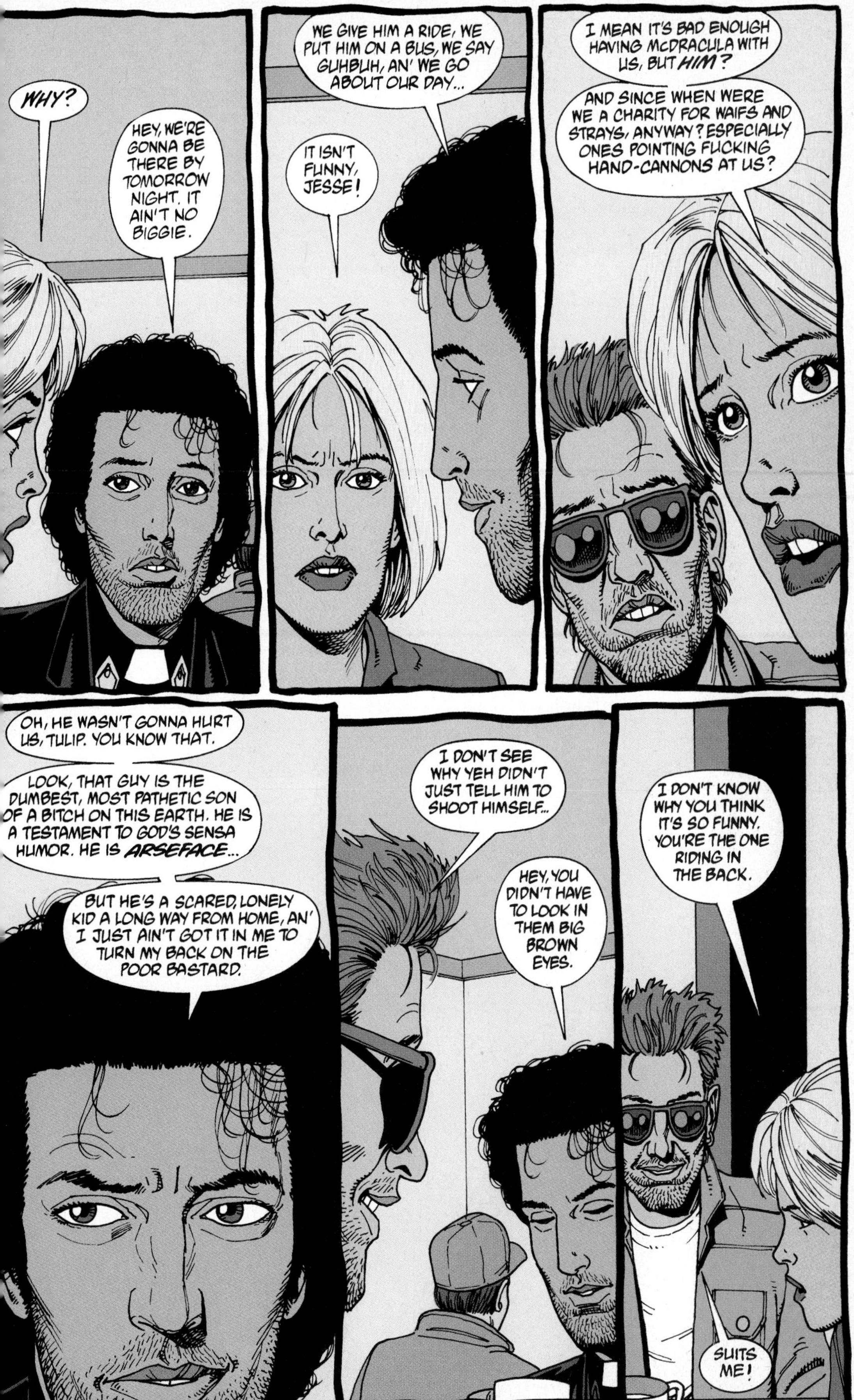
WHY?
HEY, WE'RE GONNA BE THERE BY TOMORROW NIGHT. IT AIN'T NO BIGGIE.
WE GIVE HIM A RIDE, WE PUT HIM ON A BUS, WE SAY GUHBUH, AN' WE GO ABOUT OUR DAY...
IT ISN'T FUNNY, JESSE!
I MEAN IT'S BAD ENOUGH HAVING McDRACULA WITH US, BUT HIM?
AND SINCE WHEN WERE WE A CHARITY FOR WAIFS AND STRAYS, ANYWAY? ESPECIALLY ONES POINTING FUCKING HAND-CANNONS AT US?
OH, HE WASN'T GONNA HURT US, TULIP. YOU KNOW THAT.
LOOK, THAT GUY IS THE DUMBEST, MOST PATHETIC SON OF A BITCH ON THIS EARTH. HE IS A TESTAMENT TO GOD'S SENSA HUMOR. HE IS ARSEFACE...
BUT HE'S A SCARED, LONELY KID A LONG WAY FROM HOME, AN' I JUST AIN'T GOT IT IN ME TO TURN MY BACK ON THE POOR BASTARD.
I DON'T SEE WHY YEH DIDN'T JUST TELL HIM TO SHOOT HIMSELF...
HEY, YOU DIDN'T HAVE TO LOOK IN THEM BIG BROWN EYES.
I DON'T KNOW WHY YOU THINK IT'S SO FUNNY. YOU'RE THE ONE RIDING IN THE BACK.
SUITS ME!

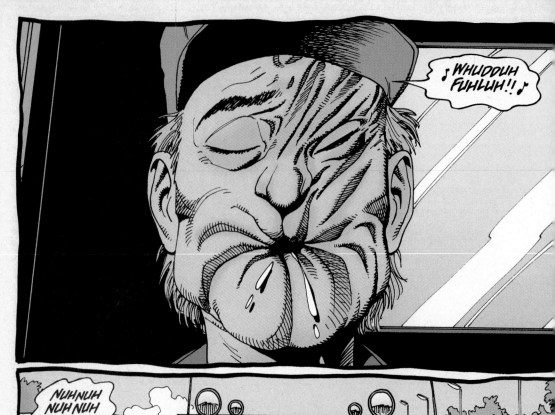

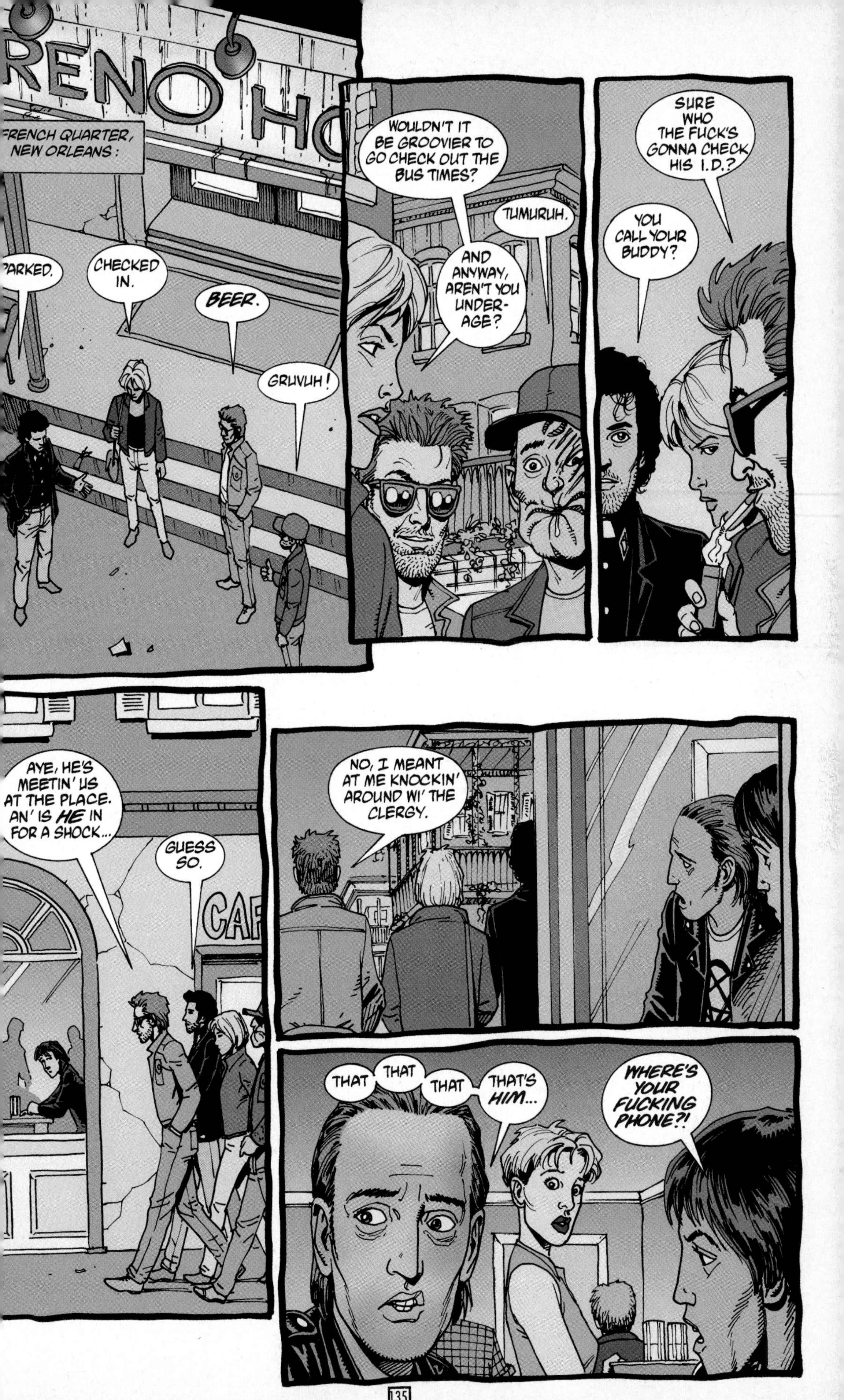
RENO HO
FRENCH QUARTER, NEW ORLEANS:
PARKED.
CHECKED IN.
BEER.
GRUVUH!
WOULDN'T IT BE GROOVIER TO GO CHECK OUT THE BUS TIMES?
TUMURUH.
AND ANYWAY, AREN'T YOU UNDER-AGE?
SURE WHO THE FUCK'S GONNA CHECK HIS I.D.?
YOU CALL YOUR BUDDY?
AYE, HE'S MEETIN' US AT THE PLACE. AN' IS HE IN FOR A SHOCK...
GUESS SO.
CAF
NO, I MEANT AT ME KNOCKIN' AROUND WI' THE CLERGY.
THAT
THAT
THAT
THAT'S HIM...
WHERE'S YOUR FUCKING PHONE?!

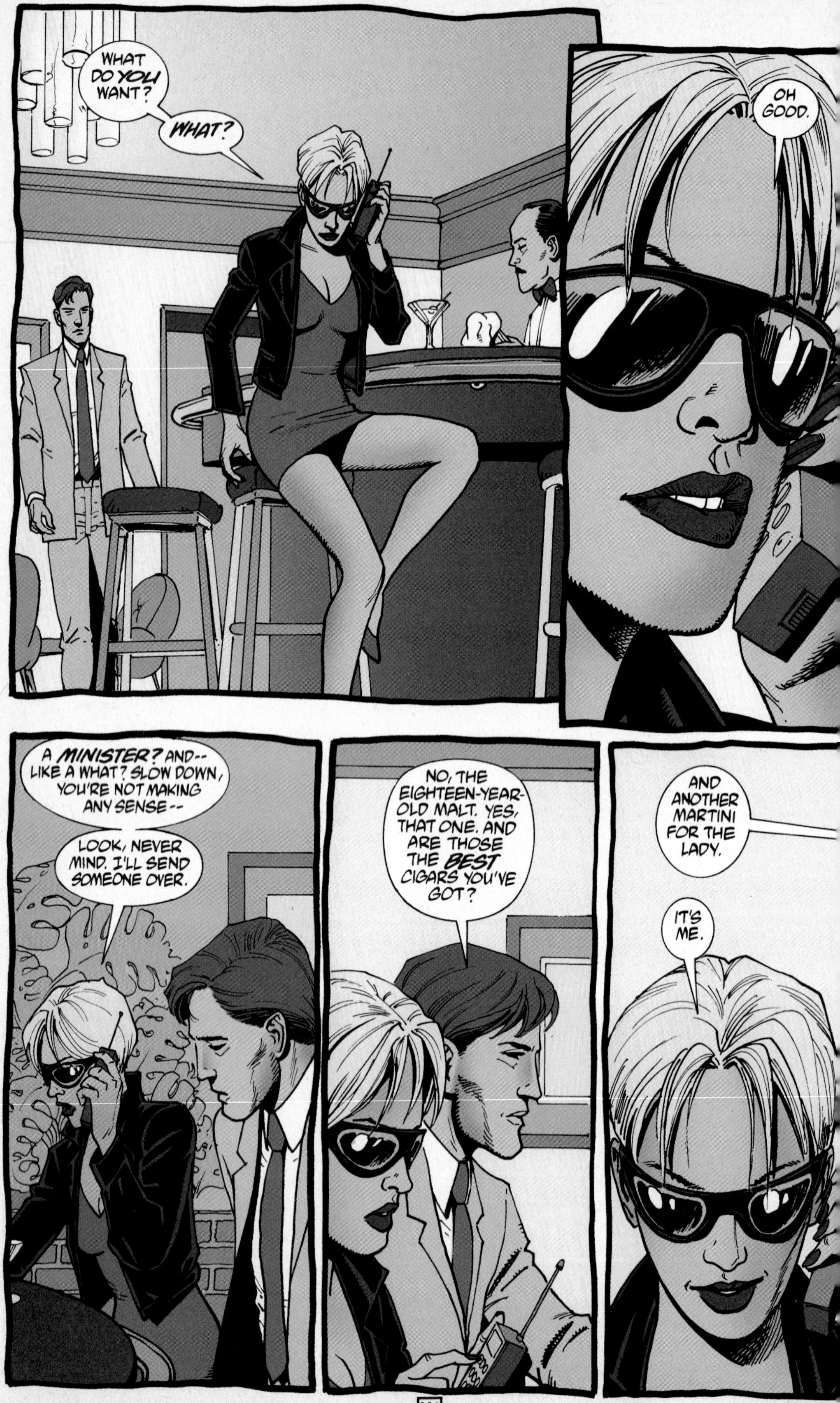
WHAT DO YOU WANT?
WHAT?
OH GOOD.
A MINISTER? AND-- LIKE A WHAT? SLOW DOWN, YOU'RE NOT MAKING ANY SENSE--
LOOK, NEVER MIND. I'LL SEND SOMEONE OVER.
NO, THE EIGHTEEN-YEAR-OLD MALT. YES, THAT ONE. AND ARE THOSE THE BEST CIGARS YOU'VE GOT?
AND ANOTHER MARTINI FOR THE LADY.
IT'S ME.

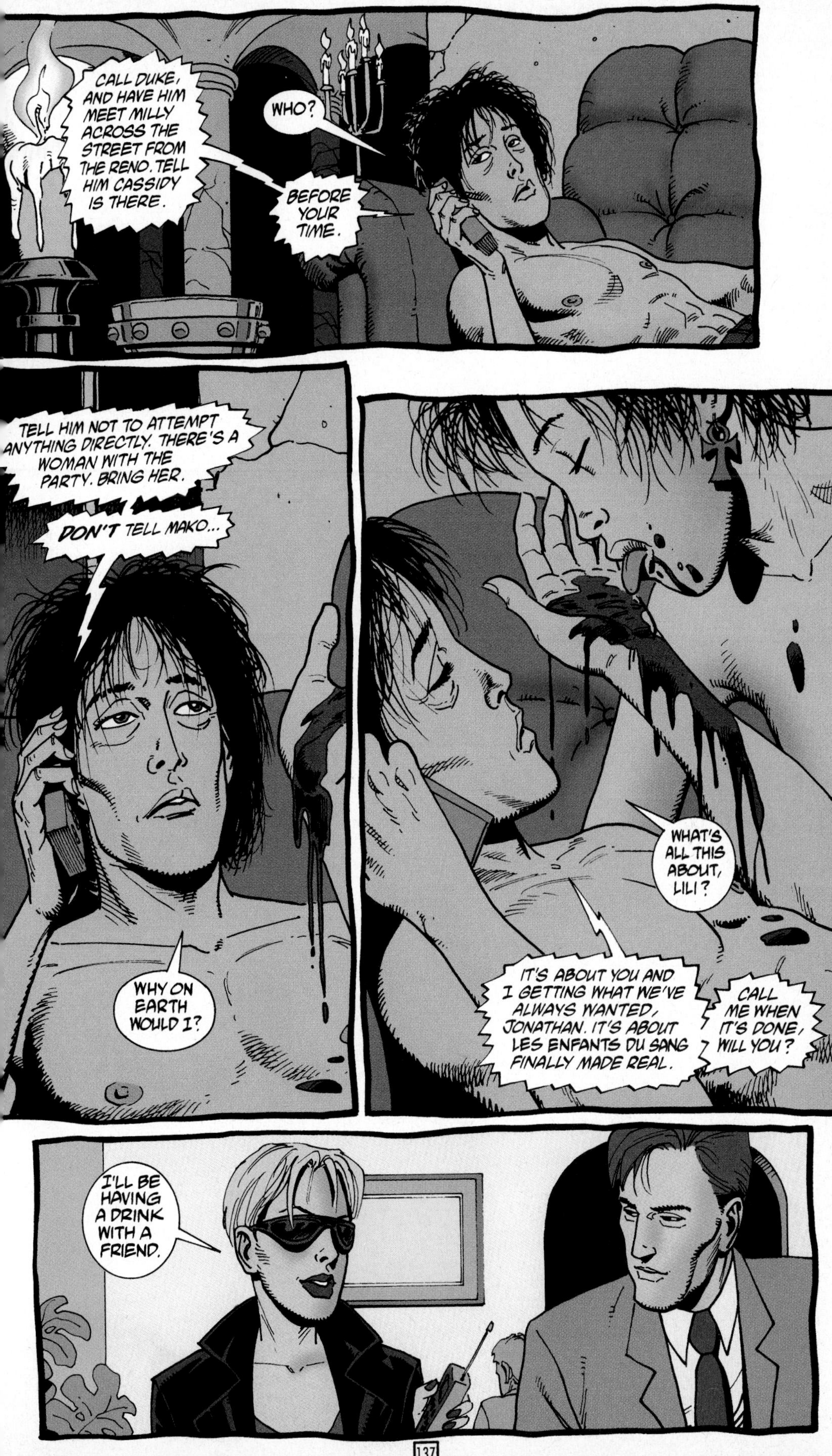
CALL DUKE, AND HAVE HIM MEET MILLY ACROSS THE STREET FROM THE RENO. TELL HIM CASSIDY IS THERE.
WHO?
BEFORE YOUR TIME.
TELL HIM NOT TO ATTEMPT ANYTHING DIRECTLY. THERE'S A WOMAN WITH THE PARTY. BRING HER.
DON'T TELL MAKO...
WHY ON EARTH WOULD I?
WHAT'S ALL THIS ABOUT, LILI?
IT'S ABOUT YOU AND I GETTING WHAT WE'VE ALWAYS WANTED, JONATHAN. IT'S ABOUT LES ENFANTS DU SANG FINALLY MADE REAL.
CALL ME WHEN IT'S DONE, WILL YOU?
I'LL BE HAVING A DRINK WITH A FRIEND.

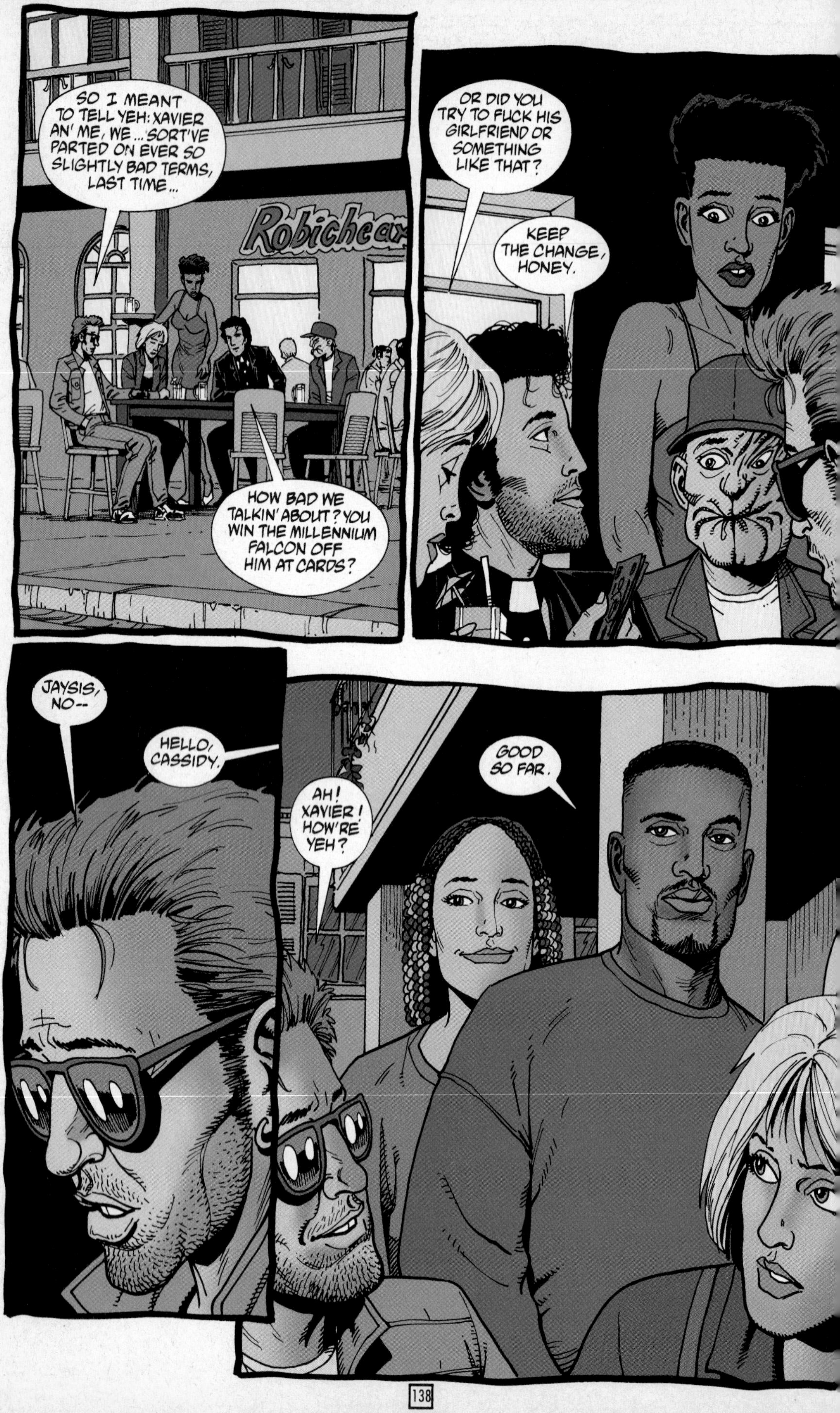
SO I MEANT TO TELL YEH: XAVIER AN' ME, WE... SORT'VE PARTED ON EVER SO SLIGHTLY BAD TERMS, LAST TIME...
Robicheaux
HOW BAD WE TALKIN' ABOUT? YOU WIN THE MILLENNIUM FALCON OFF HIM AT CARDS?
OR DID YOU TRY TO FUCK HIS GIRLFRIEND OR SOMETHING LIKE THAT?
KEEP THE CHANGE, HONEY.
JAYSIS, NO--
HELLO, CASSIDY.
AH! XAVIER! HOW'RE YEH?
GOOD SO FAR.

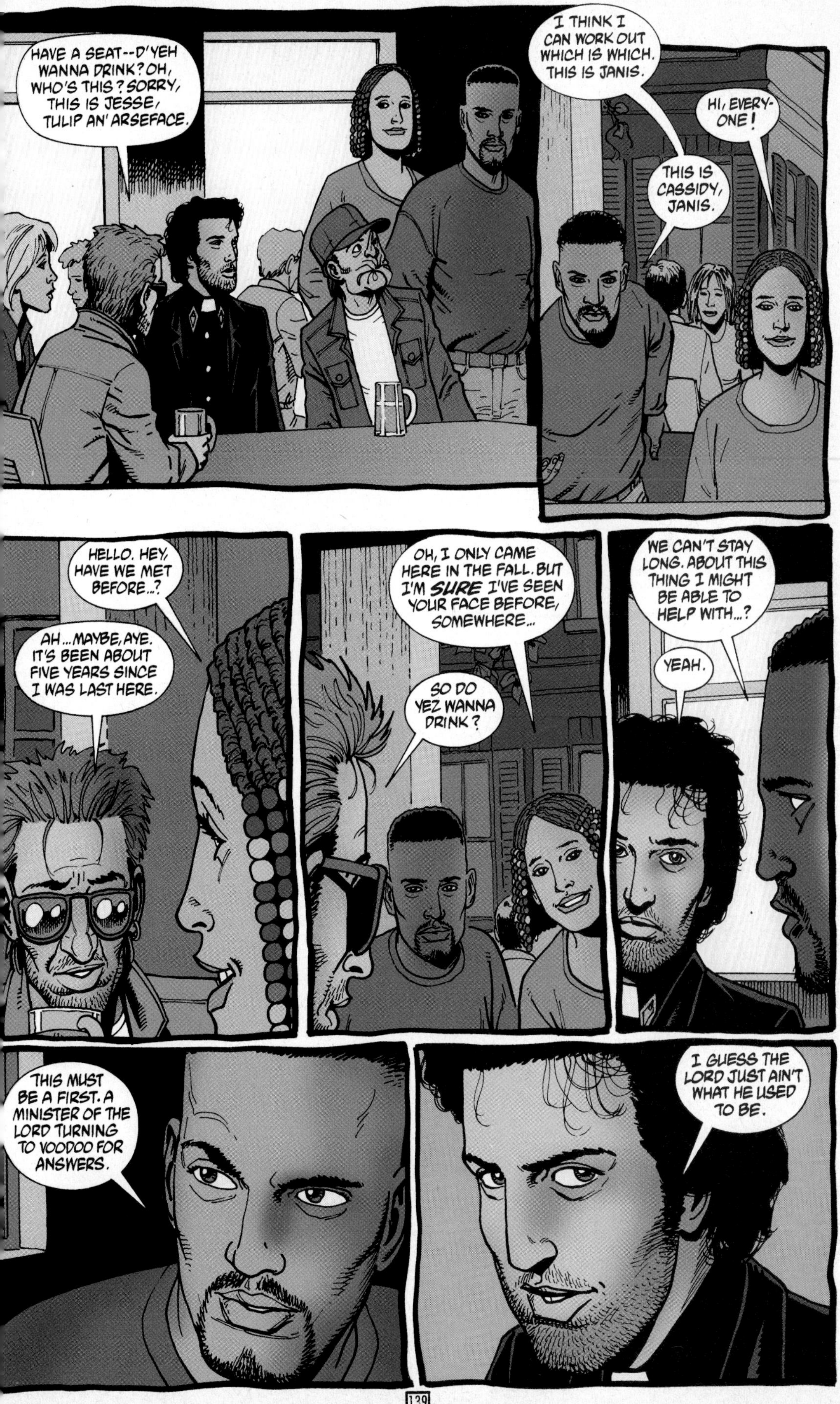
HAVE A SEAT--D'YEH WANNA DRINK? OH, WHO'S THIS? SORRY, THIS IS JESSE, TULIP AN' ARSEFACE.
I THINK I CAN WORK OUT WHICH IS WHICH. THIS IS JANIS.
HI, EVERY-ONE!
THIS IS CASSIDY, JANIS.
HELLO. HEY, HAVE WE MET BEFORE...?
AH...MAYBE, AYE. IT'S BEEN ABOUT FIVE YEARS SINCE I WAS LAST HERE.
OH, I ONLY CAME HERE IN THE FALL. BUT I'M *SURE* I'VE SEEN YOUR FACE BEFORE, SOMEWHERE...
SO DO YEZ WANNA DRINK?
WE CAN'T STAY LONG. ABOUT THIS THING I MIGHT BE ABLE TO HELP WITH...?
YEAH.
THIS MUST BE A FIRST. A MINISTER OF THE LORD TURNING TO VOODOO FOR ANSWERS.
I GUESS THE LORD JUST AIN'T WHAT HE USED TO BE.

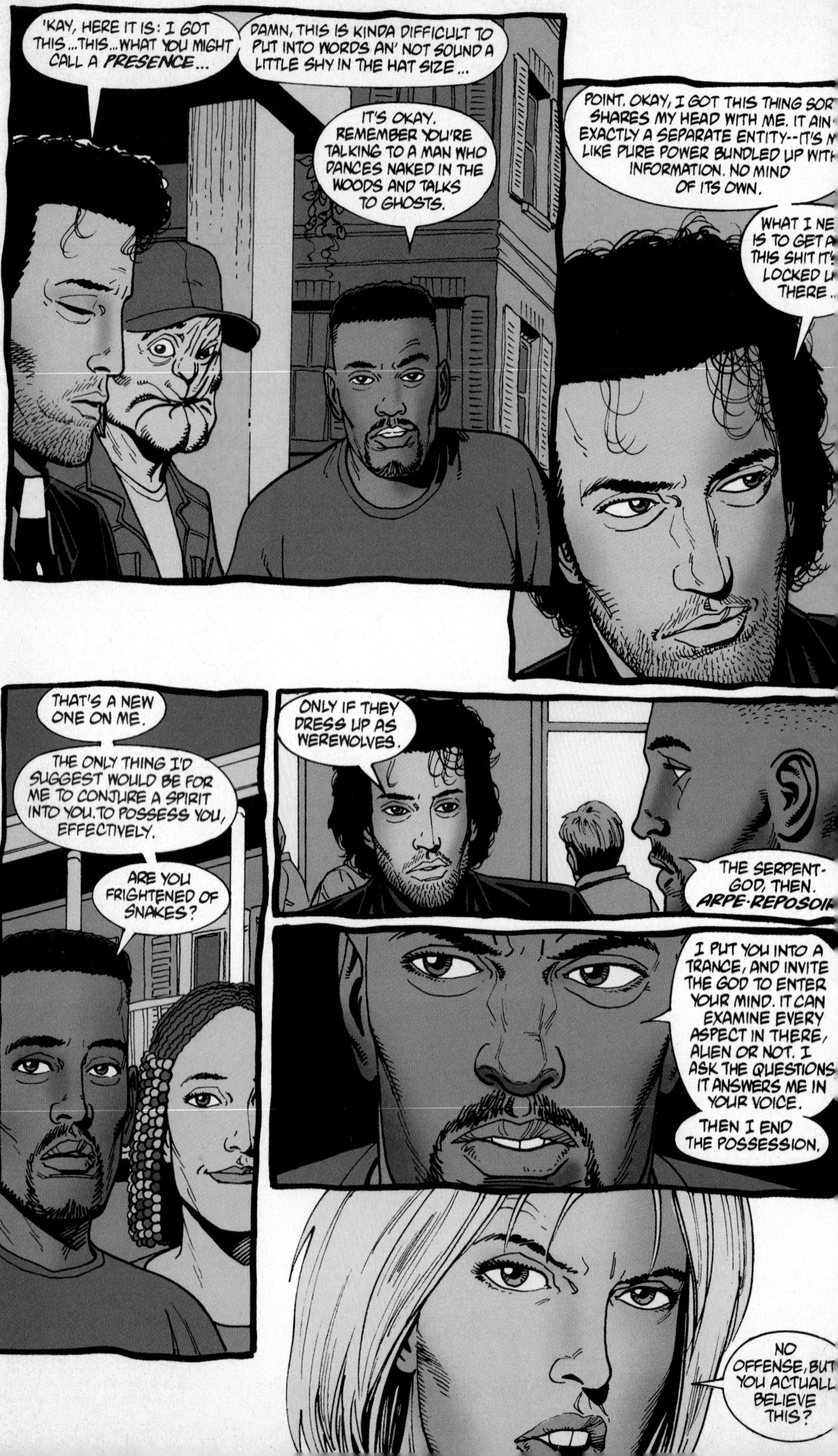

'KAY, HERE IT IS: I GOT THIS...THIS...WHAT YOU MIGHT CALL A *PRESENCE*...
DAMN, THIS IS KINDA DIFFICULT TO PUT INTO WORDS AN' NOT SOUND A LITTLE SHY IN THE HAT SIZE...
IT'S OKAY. REMEMBER YOU'RE TALKING TO A MAN WHO DANCES NAKED IN THE WOODS AND TALKS TO GHOSTS.
POINT. OKAY, I GOT THIS THING SOR SHARES MY HEAD WITH ME. IT AIN EXACTLY A SEPARATE ENTITY--IT'S LIKE PURE POWER BUNDLED UP WITH INFORMATION. NO MIND OF ITS OWN.
WHAT I NE IS TO GET A THIS SHIT IT' LOCKED U THERE...
THAT'S A NEW ONE ON ME.
THE ONLY THING I'D SUGGEST WOULD BE FOR ME TO CONJURE A SPIRIT INTO YOU. TO POSSESS YOU, EFFECTIVELY.
ARE YOU FRIGHTENED OF SNAKES?
ONLY IF THEY DRESS UP AS WEREWOLVES.
THE SERPENT-GOD, THEN. *ARPE-REPOSOIR*
I PUT YOU INTO A TRANCE, AND INVITE THE GOD TO ENTER YOUR MIND. IT CAN EXAMINE EVERY ASPECT IN THERE, ALIEN OR NOT. I ASK THE QUESTIONS IT ANSWERS ME IN YOUR VOICE.
THEN I END THE POSSESSION.
NO OFFENSE, BUT YOU ACTUALL BELIEVE THIS?

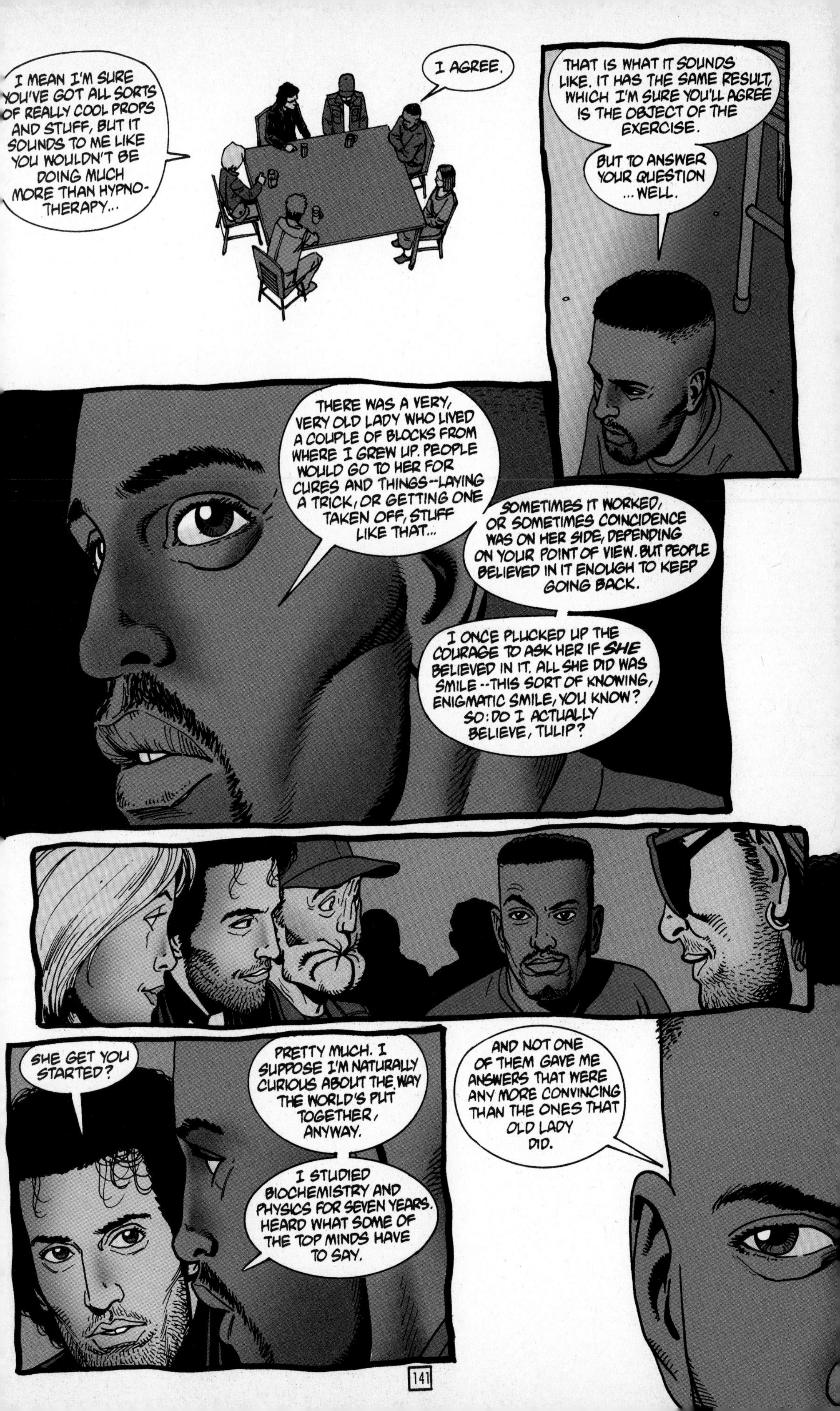

I MEAN I'M SURE YOU'VE GOT ALL SORTS OF REALLY COOL PROPS AND STUFF, BUT IT SOUNDS TO ME LIKE YOU WOULDN'T BE DOING MUCH MORE THAN HYPNO-THERAPY...

I AGREE.

THAT IS WHAT IT SOUNDS LIKE. IT HAS THE SAME RESULT, WHICH I'M SURE YOU'LL AGREE IS THE OBJECT OF THE EXERCISE.

BUT TO ANSWER YOUR QUESTION ...WELL.

THERE WAS A VERY, VERY OLD LADY WHO LIVED A COUPLE OF BLOCKS FROM WHERE I GREW UP. PEOPLE WOULD GO TO HER FOR CURES AND THINGS--LAYING A TRICK, OR GETTING ONE TAKEN OFF, STUFF LIKE THAT...

SOMETIMES IT WORKED, OR SOMETIMES COINCIDENCE WAS ON HER SIDE, DEPENDING ON YOUR POINT OF VIEW. BUT PEOPLE BELIEVED IN IT ENOUGH TO KEEP GOING BACK.

I ONCE PLUCKED UP THE COURAGE TO ASK HER IF *SHE* BELIEVED IN IT. ALL SHE DID WAS SMILE --THIS SORT OF KNOWING, ENIGMATIC SMILE, YOU KNOW? SO: DO I ACTUALLY BELIEVE, TULIP?

SHE GET YOU STARTED?

PRETTY MUCH. I SUPPOSE I'M NATURALLY CURIOUS ABOUT THE WAY THE WORLD'S PUT TOGETHER, ANYWAY.

I STUDIED BIOCHEMISTRY AND PHYSICS FOR SEVEN YEARS. HEARD WHAT SOME OF THE TOP MINDS HAVE TO SAY.

AND NOT ONE OF THEM GAVE ME ANSWERS THAT WERE ANY MORE CONVINCING THAN THE ONES THAT OLD LADY DID.

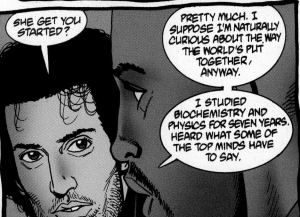

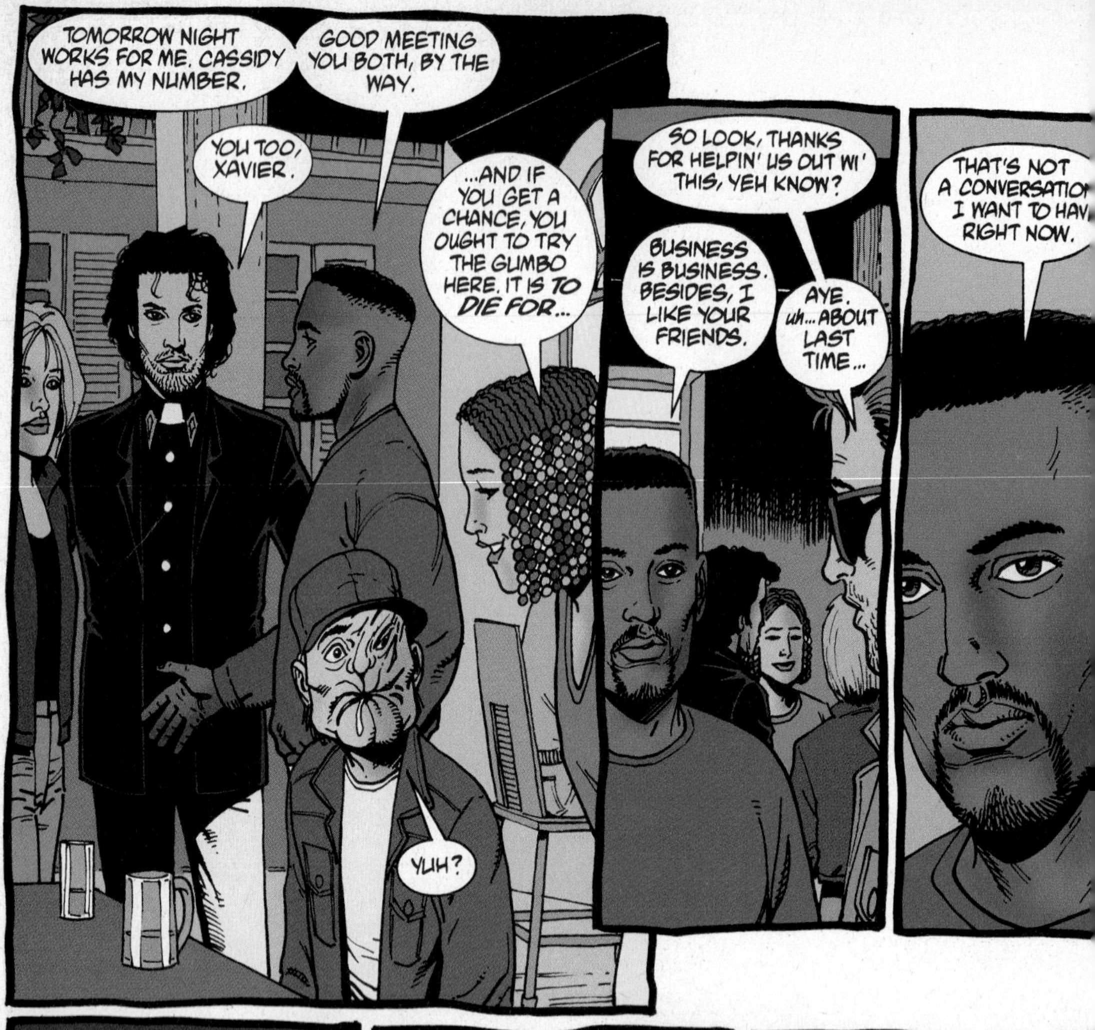

TOMORROW NIGHT WORKS FOR ME. CASSIDY HAS MY NUMBER.
GOOD MEETING YOU BOTH, BY THE WAY.
YOU TOO, XAVIER.
...AND IF YOU GET A CHANCE, YOU OUGHT TO TRY THE GUMBO HERE. IT IS TO DIE FOR...
YUH?
SO LOOK, THANKS FOR HELPIN' US OUT WI' THIS, YEH KNOW?
BUSINESS IS BUSINESS. BESIDES, I LIKE YOUR FRIENDS.
AYE. uh...ABOUT LAST TIME...
THAT'S NOT A CONVERSATION I WANT TO HAVE RIGHT NOW.
GOOD GUY.
YEAH, I LIKED HIM. STILL CAN'T BELIEVE YOU'RE GOING THROUGH WITH THIS CRAP.
YEAH, OKAY, AGENT SCULLY. 'NOTHER DRINK?
NO, I THINK I'M GOING TO TURN IN.
HELL, REALLY?
YOU GUYS LOOK READY TO MAKE A NIGHT OF IT. I'M OKAY, I'VE GOT MY BOOK.
BESIDES, I AM NOT GOING TO SIT HERE AND WATCH HIM EAT GUMBO.
MENU

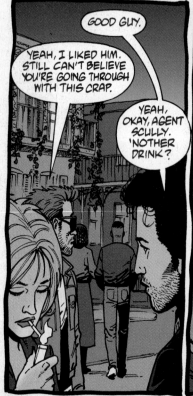

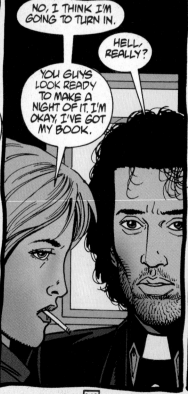

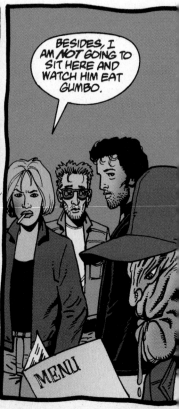

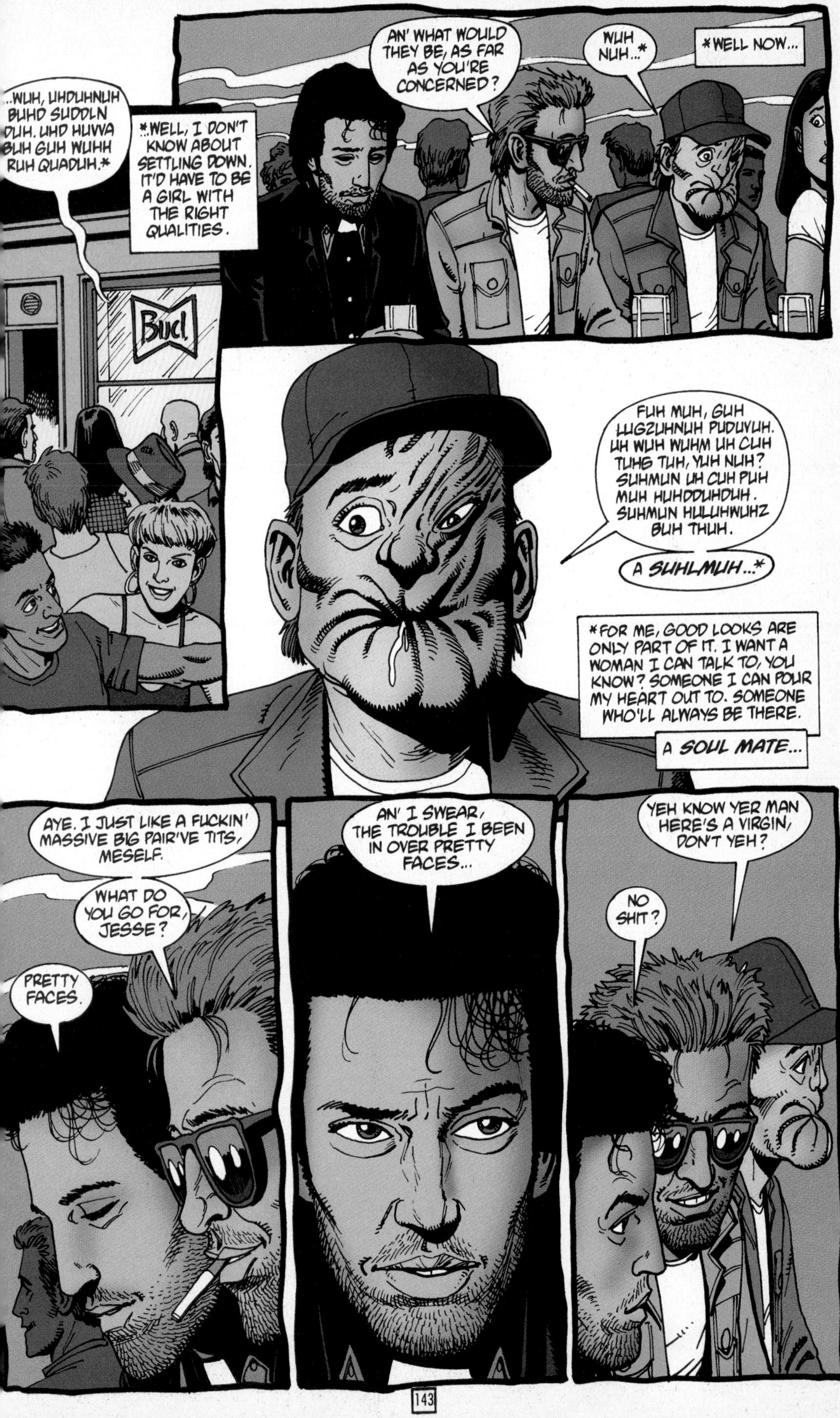

..WUH, UHDUHNUH BUHD SUDDLN DUH. UHD HUVVA BUH GUH WUHH RUH QUADUH.*
*..WELL, I DON'T KNOW ABOUT SETTLING DOWN. IT'D HAVE TO BE A GIRL WITH THE RIGHT QUALITIES.
AN' WHAT WOULD THEY BE, AS FAR AS YOU'RE CONCERNED?
WUH NUH...*
*WELL NOW...
Bud
FUH MUH, GUH LUGZUHNUH PUDUVUH. UH WUH WUHM UH CUH TUHG TUH, YUH NUH? SUHMUN UH CUH PUH MUH HUHDDUHDUH. SUHMUN HULUHWUHZ BUH THUH.
A SUHLMUH...*
*FOR ME, GOOD LOOKS ARE ONLY PART OF IT. I WANT A WOMAN I CAN TALK TO, YOU KNOW? SOMEONE I CAN POUR MY HEART OUT TO. SOMEONE WHO'LL ALWAYS BE THERE.
A SOUL MATE...
AYE. I JUST LIKE A FUCKIN' MASSIVE BIG PAIR'VE TITS, MESELF.
WHAT DO YOU GO FOR, JESSE?
PRETTY FACES.
AN' I SWEAR, THE TROUBLE I BEEN IN OVER PRETTY FACES...
YEH KNOW YER MAN HERE'S A VIRGIN, DON'T YEH?
NO SHIT?

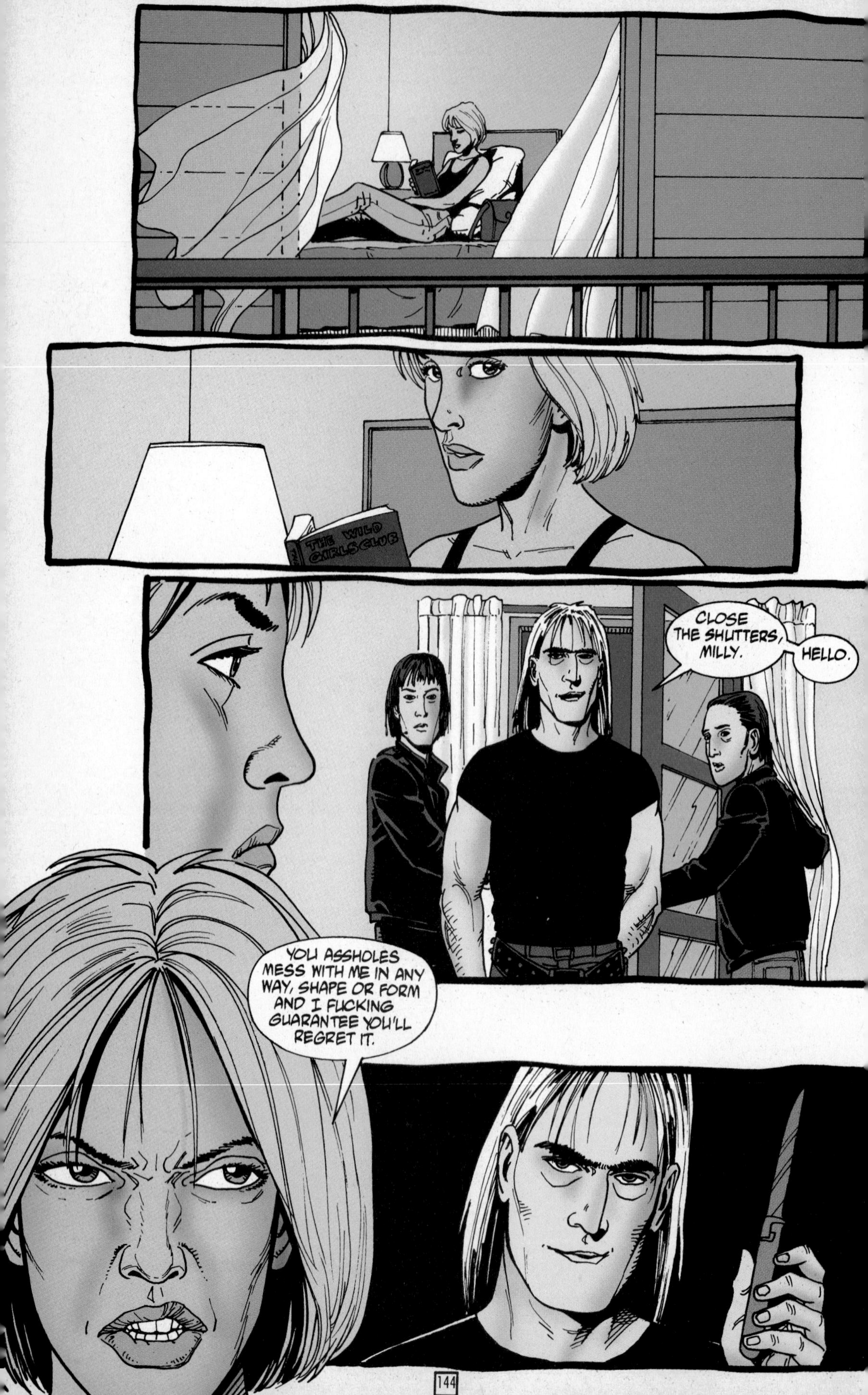
THE WILD GIRLSCLUB
CLOSE THE SHUTTERS, MILLY.
HELLO.
YOU ASSHOLES MESS WITH ME IN ANY WAY, SHAPE OR FORM AND I FUCKING GUARANTEE YOU'LL REGRET IT.

WHAT CAN'T YOU TELL ME?

WE'RE MEANT TO-- BRING YOU TO-- JONATHAN--

ONE OF LES ENFANTS DU SANG--JESUS, I'M GONNA PISS MYSELF HERE!

WHO IS?

NOT IN MY ROOM YOU'RE NOT.

LES ENFANTS... WHAT'S THAT, IS THAT CHILDREN OF BLOOD?

uh...OF THE BLOOD...

PARDON MOI. WHO THE FUCK ARE THEY SUPPOSED TO BE?

IT--IT'S A LITTLE DIFFICULT TO--

IT HAS TO DO WITH YOUR FRIEND-- CASSIDY--

OH JESUS, PLEASE DON'T SHOOT ME. I JUST PISSED MYSELF AFTER ALL.

IT WAS THE GUN...

ALL RIGHT, NEVER MIND. MILLY, ISN'T THAT WHAT HE CALLED YOU?

I'M KIND OF AT A LOOSE END TONIGHT, MILLY.

YOU'RE TAKING ME TO LES ENFANTS DU SANG AFTER ALL.

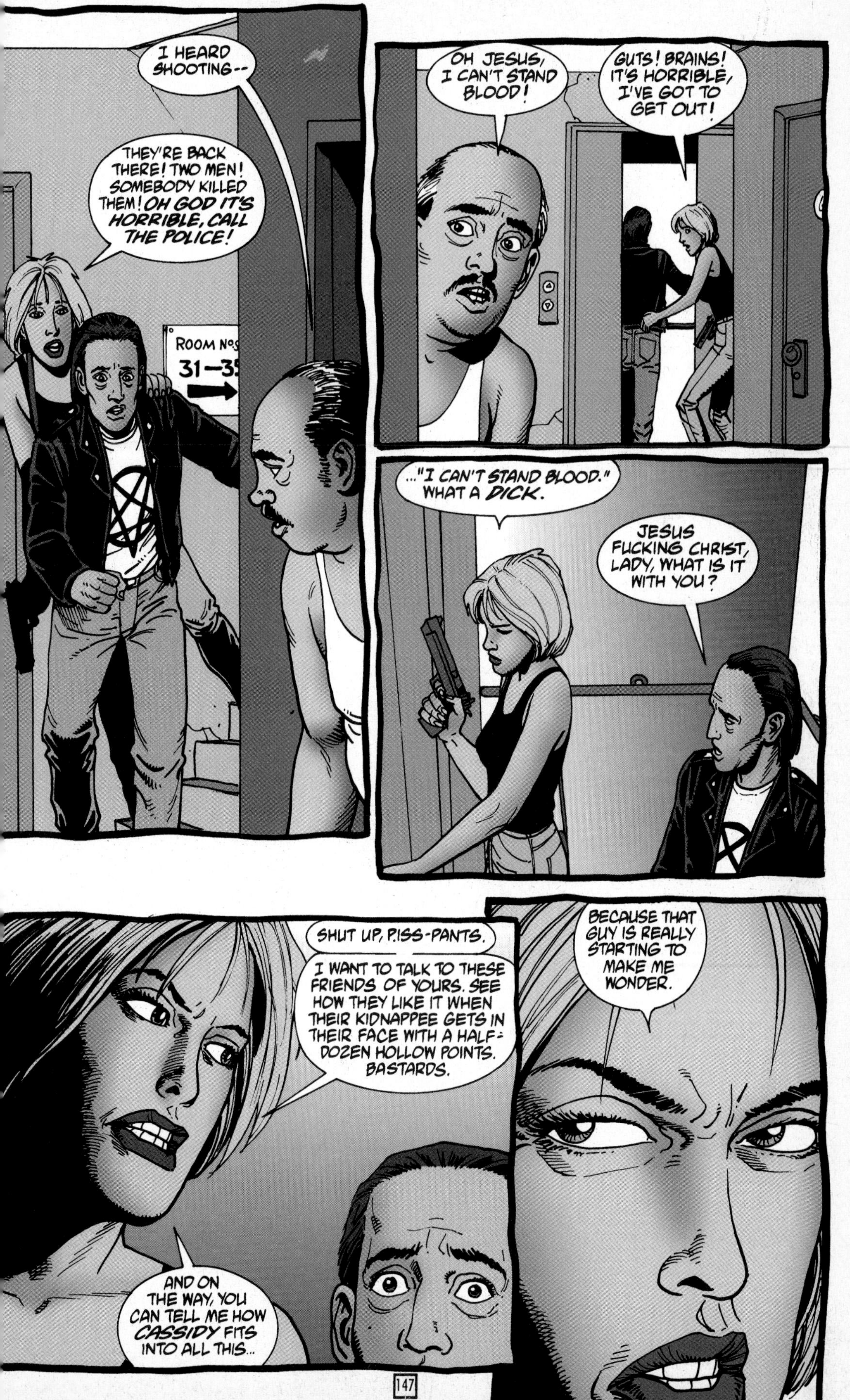
I HEARD SHOOTING--
THEY'RE BACK THERE! TWO MEN! SOMEBODY KILLED THEM! *OH GOD IT'S HORRIBLE, CALL THE POLICE!*
ROOM No.
31—3
OH JESUS, I CAN'T STAND BLOOD!
GUTS! BRAINS! IT'S HORRIBLE, I'VE GOT TO GET OUT!
..."I CAN'T STAND BLOOD." WHAT A *DICK*.
JESUS FUCKING CHRIST, LADY, WHAT IS IT WITH YOU?
SHUT UP, P.ISS-PANTS.
I WANT TO TALK TO THESE FRIENDS OF YOURS. SEE HOW THEY LIKE IT WHEN THEIR KIDNAPPEE GETS IN THEIR FACE WITH A HALF-DOZEN HOLLOW POINTS. BASTARDS.
BECAUSE THAT GUY IS REALLY STARTING TO MAKE ME WONDER.
AND ON THE WAY, YOU CAN TELL ME HOW *CASSIDY* FITS INTO ALL THIS...

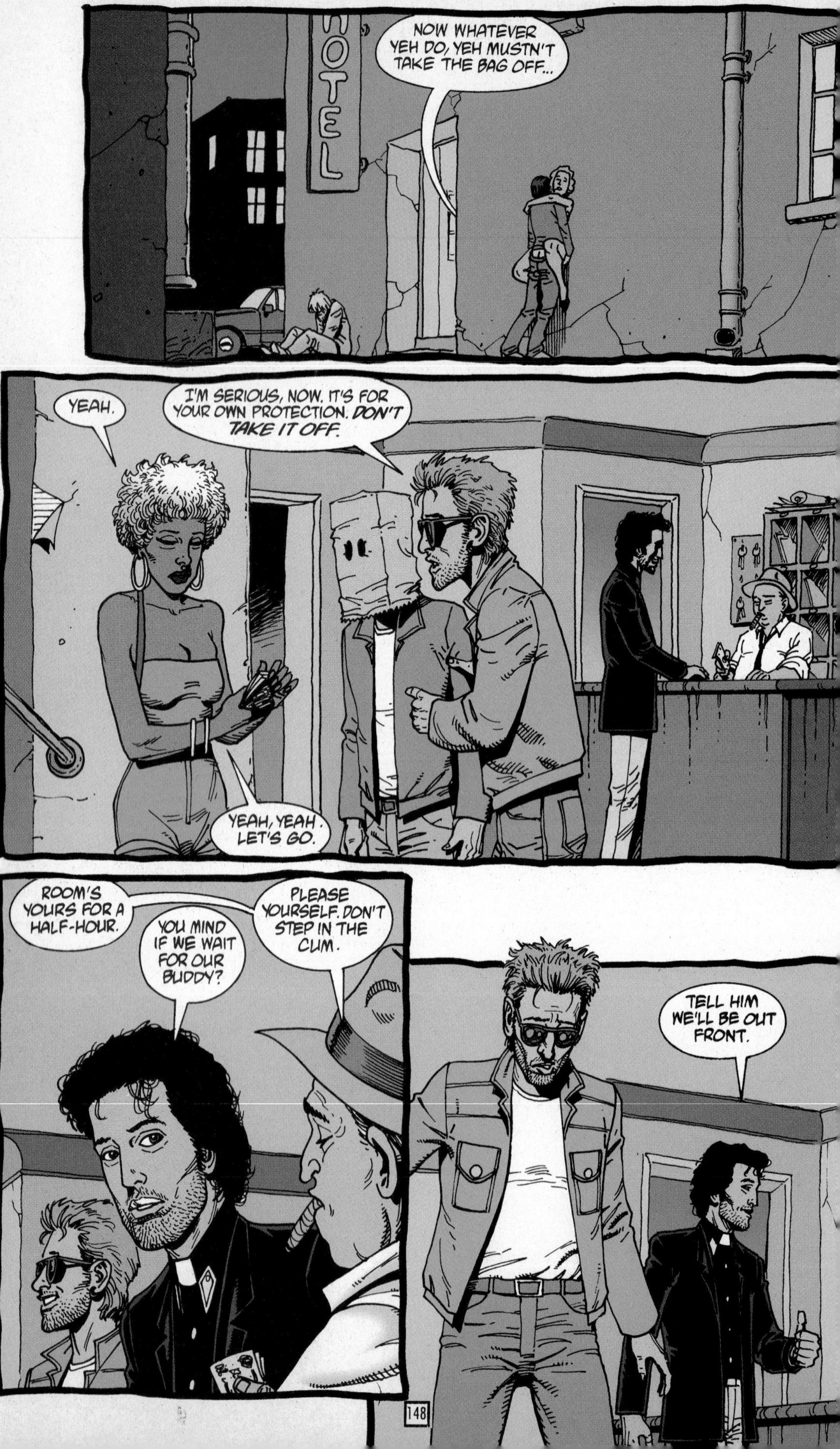
HOTEL
NOW WHATEVER YEH DO, YEH MUSTN'T TAKE THE BAG OFF...
YEAH.
I'M SERIOUS, NOW. IT'S FOR YOUR OWN PROTECTION. *DON'T TAKE IT OFF.*
YEAH, YEAH. LET'S GO.
ROOM'S YOURS FOR A HALF-HOUR.
YOU MIND IF WE WAIT FOR OUR BUDDY?
PLEASE YOURSELF. DON'T STEP IN THE CUM.
TELL HIM WE'LL BE OUT FRONT.

TO BE
CONTINUED

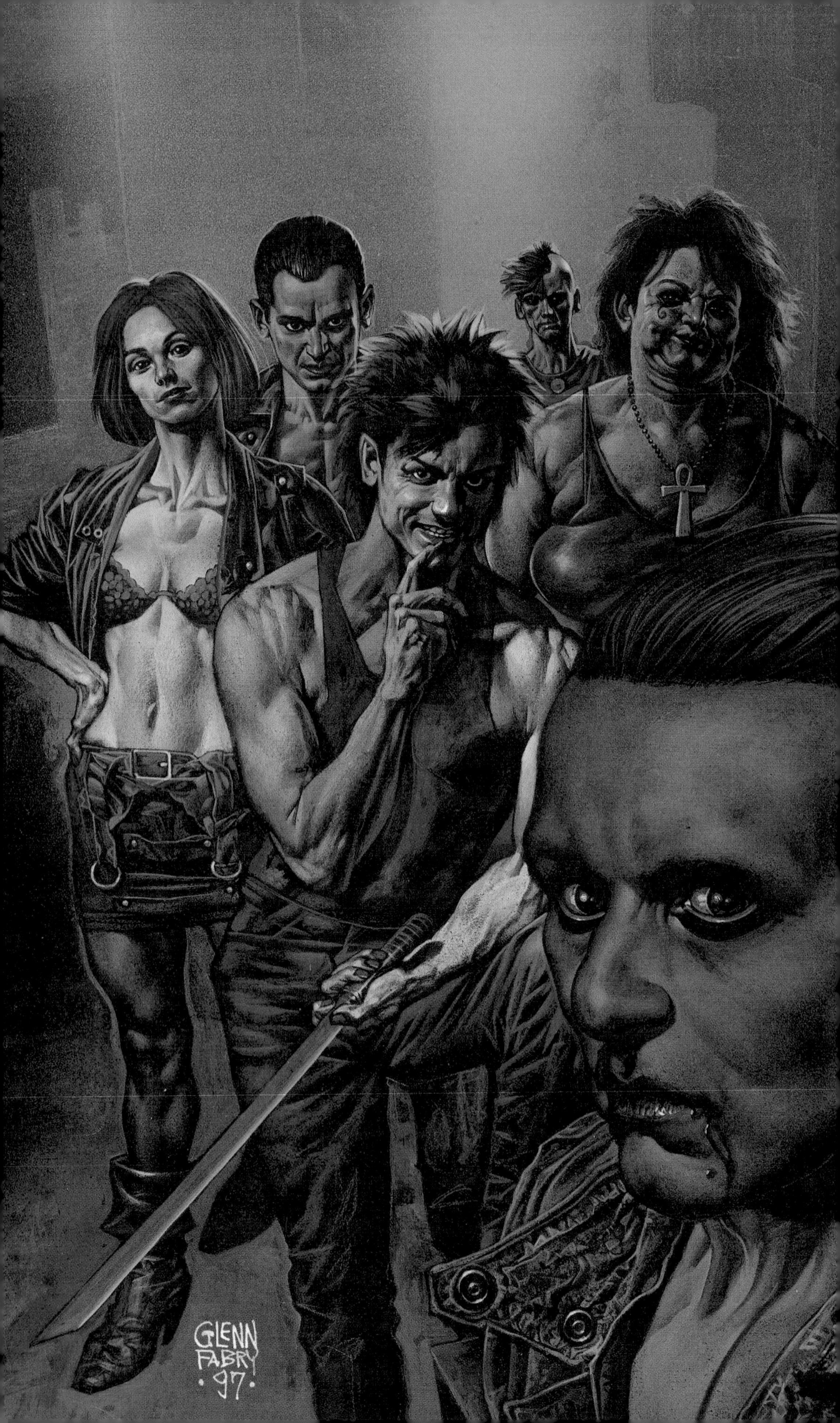
GLENN
FABRY
·97·

UNDERWORLD

GARTH ENNIS - Writer STEVE DILLON - Artist
PAMELA RAMBO - Colorist
CLEM ROBINS - Letterer AXEL ALONSO - Editor

PREACHER created by GARTH ENNIS and STEVE DILLON

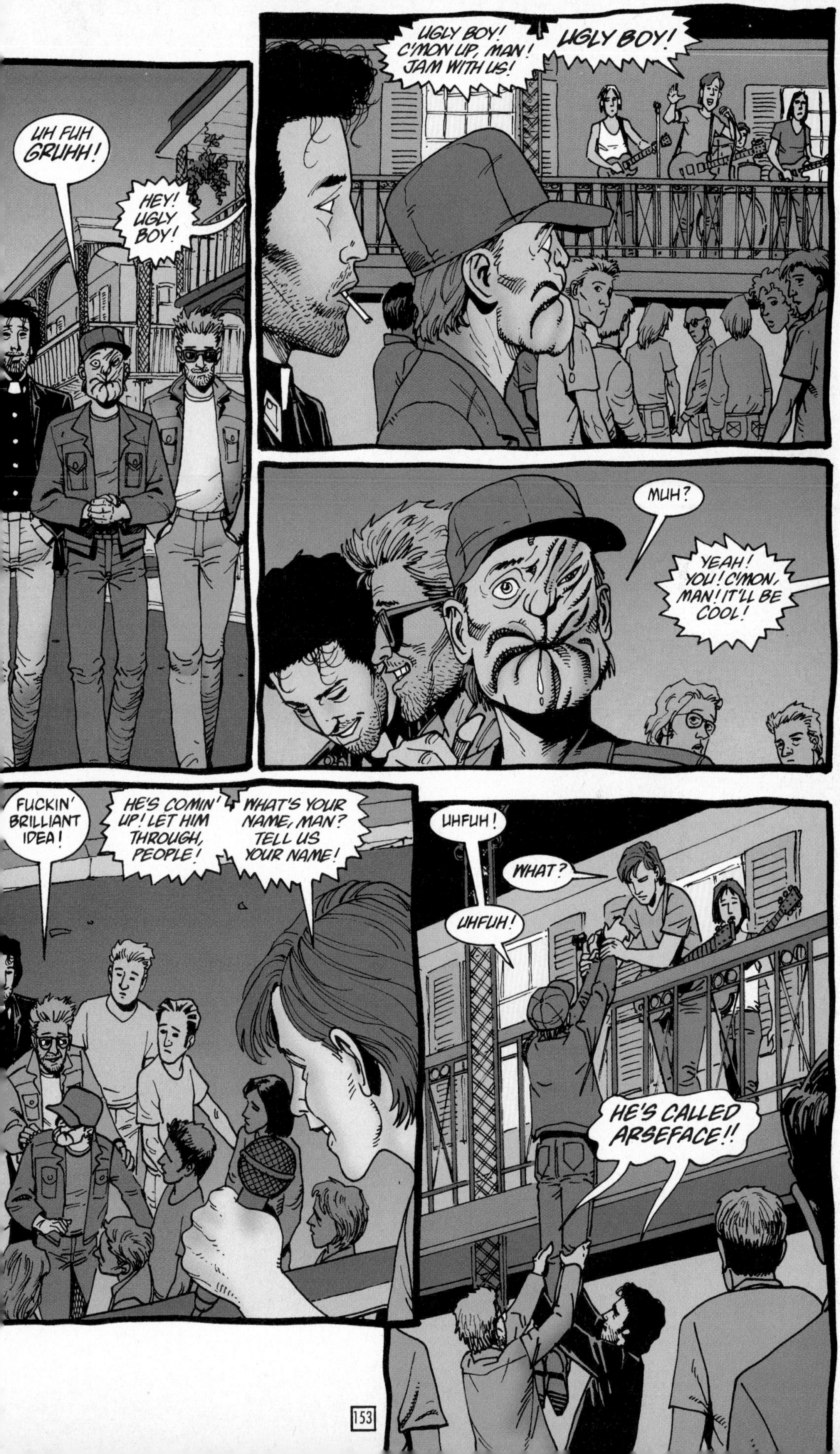
UH FUH GRUHH!
HEY! UGLY BOY!
UGLY BOY! C'MON UP, MAN! JAM WITH US!
UGLY BOY!
MUH?
YEAH! YOU! C'MON, MAN! IT'LL BE COOL!
FUCKIN' BRILLIANT IDEA!
HE'S COMIN' UP! LET HIM THROUGH, PEOPLE!
WHAT'S YOUR NAME, MAN? TELL US YOUR NAME!
UHFUH!
WHAT?
UHFUH!
HE'S CALLED ARSEFACE!!

CHECK IT OUT, WE GOT *ARSEFACE* IN THE HOUSE!

WHAT YOU GONNA SING, MAN?

UH...YUH LUHG OHWAZUH?

YOU START, OKAY? WE'LL JOIN IN.

I CAN'T UNDERSTAND A FUCKIN' WORD HE'S SAYIN'...

WHO GIVES A SHIT, MAN? CHECK OUT THE *CROWD!*

HUH?

♪ TUHDUH, UH GUHYUH BUHYUH DUH THUH THUH GUHYUH THUHYUH BUHGUH YUH...

SUHMUH, YUH SHUYUH BUH NUH RULLUH WHUH YUH GUHYUH DUH... ♪

UH CUH BUHLUV UH LIYUHBUHYUH, FUH UH WUHYUH DUH ABUH ♪ YUH NUH...

A STAR IS BORN.

uh-huh.

SO WHAT DO YOU ASSHOLES WANT WITH CASSIDY?

UH, JONATHAN, SHE--

QUIET, MILLY.

WE WANT HIS POWER.

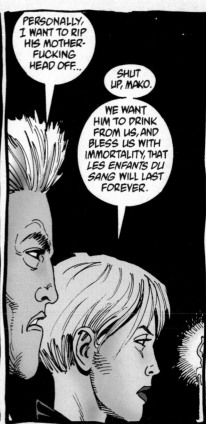

PERSONALLY, I WANT TO RIP HIS MOTHER-FUCKING HEAD OFF...

SHUT UP, MAKO.

WE WANT HIM TO DRINK FROM US, AND BLESS US WITH IMMORTALITY, THAT LES ENFANTS DU SANG WILL LAST FOREVER.

WHAT IS THIS LES ENFANTS SHIT?

LOOK, REALLY, SHE'S GOT--

MILLY.

WE ARE CHILDREN OF BLOOD, AND OF SHADOW, AND OF NIGHT. WE DRINK FROM VEINS AND ARTERY. OURS IS A PALE AND LANGUID PARADISE, AND IN OUR DREAMS WE WALK AS WOLVES AND FLY AS BATS.

AND PREY AT WILL UPON THE HUMAN HERD.

SOUNDS LIKE ONE BIG CIRCLE-JERK TO ME.

ARE YOU CASSIDY'S SOW?

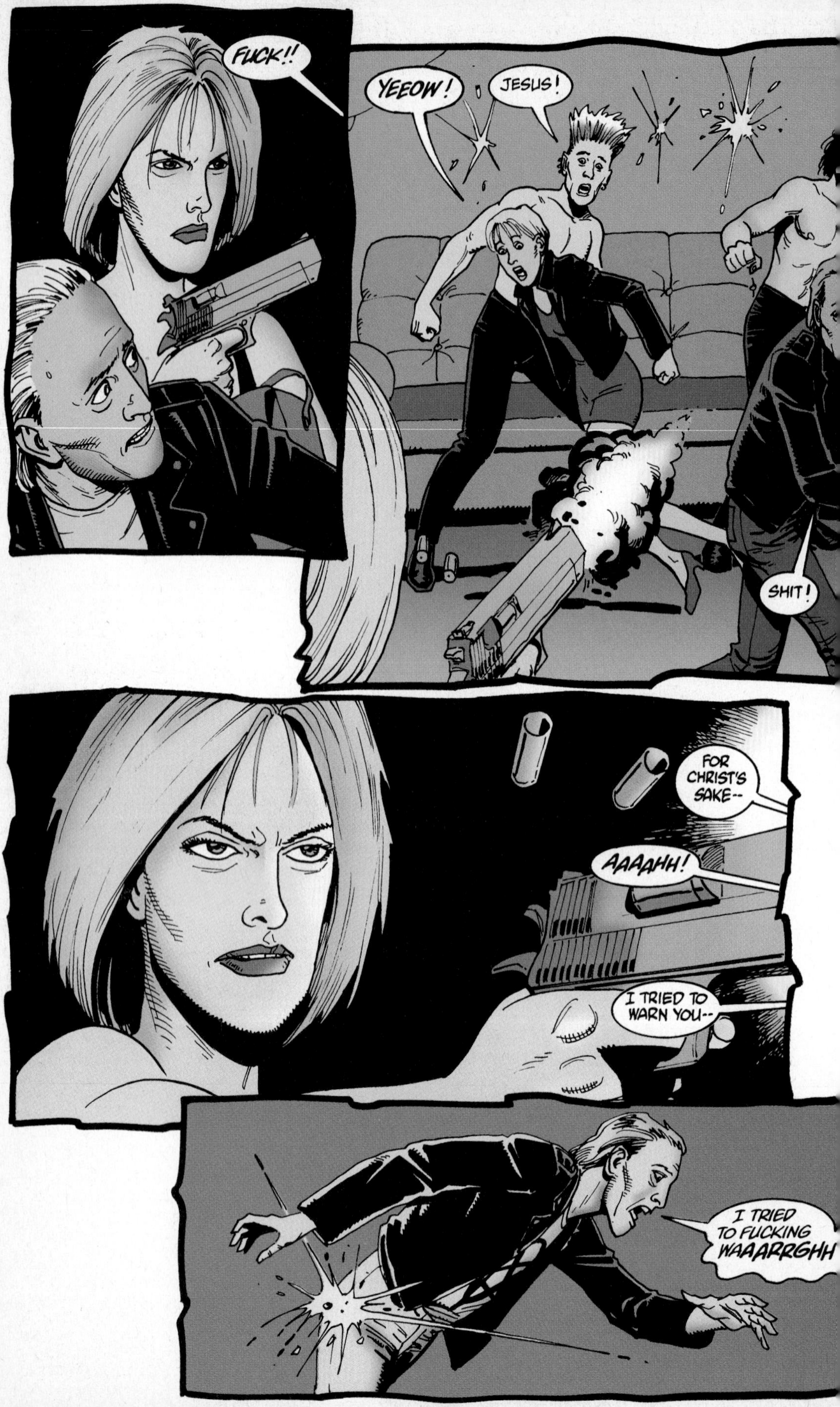
FUCK!!
YEEOW!
JESUS!
SHIT!
FOR CHRIST'S SAKE--
AAAAHH!
I TRIED TO WARN YOU--
I TRIED TO FUCKING WAAARRGHH

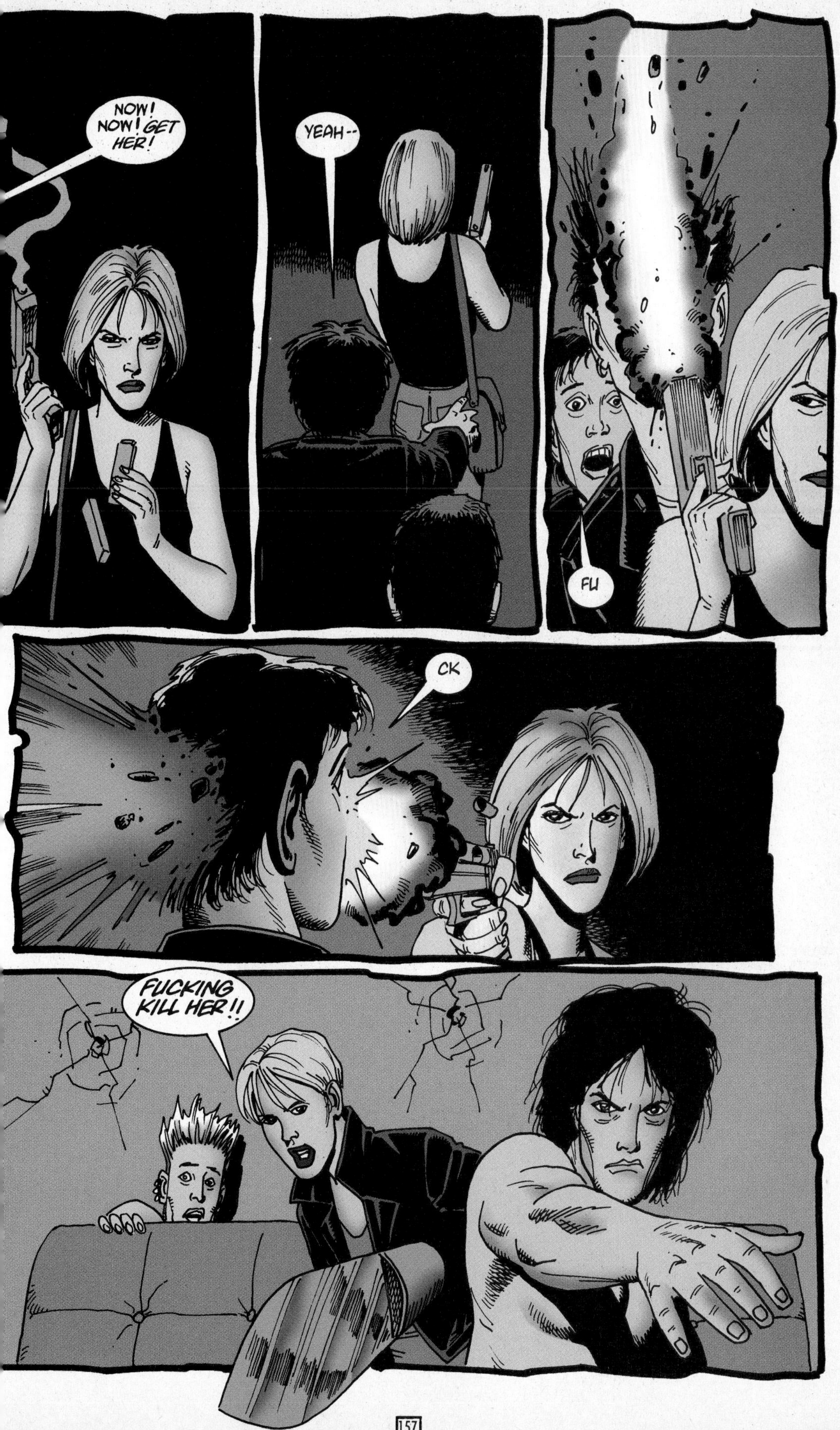
NOW! NOW! GET HER!
YEAH--
FU
CK
FUCKING KILL HER!!

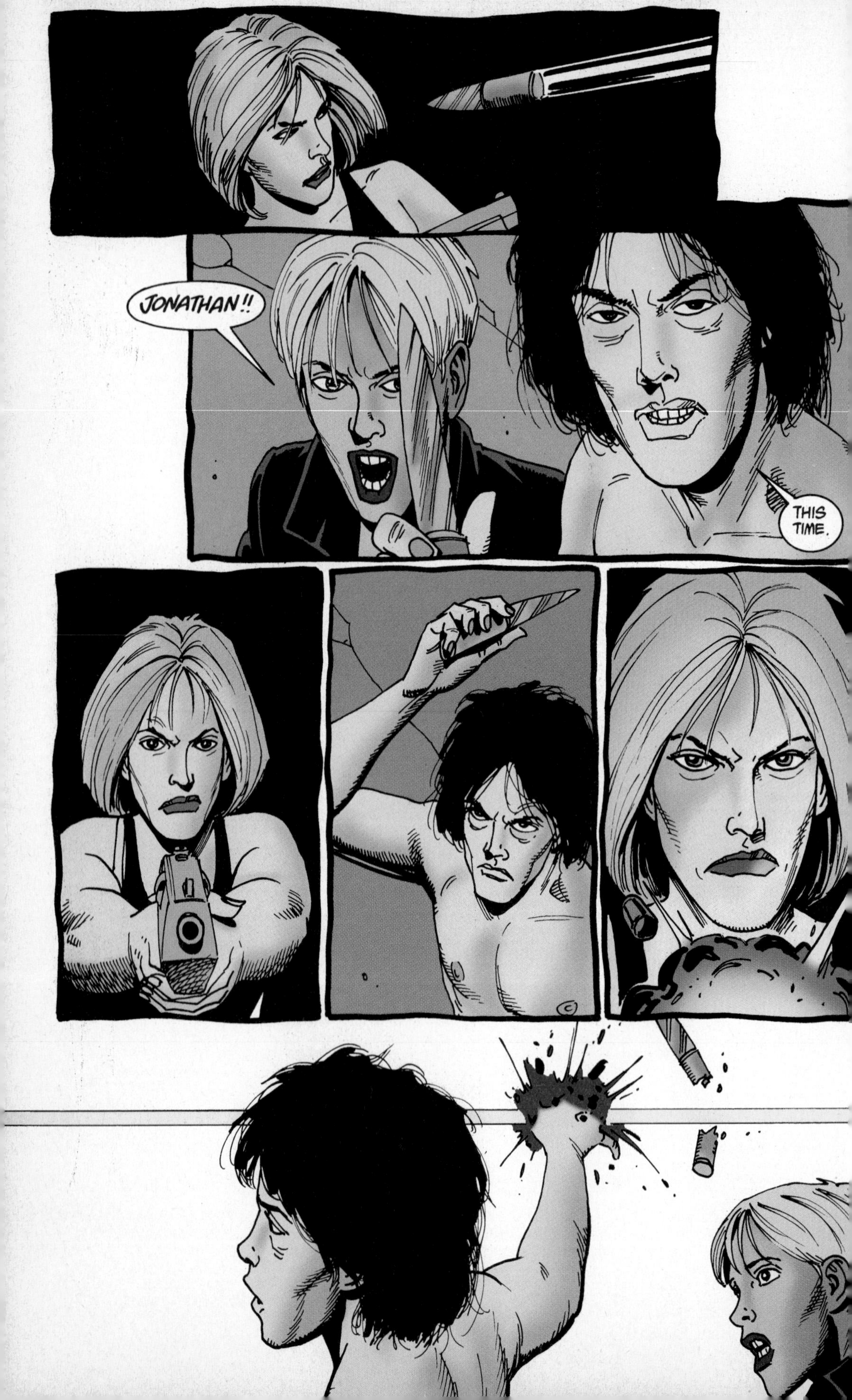
JONATHAN!!
THIS TIME.

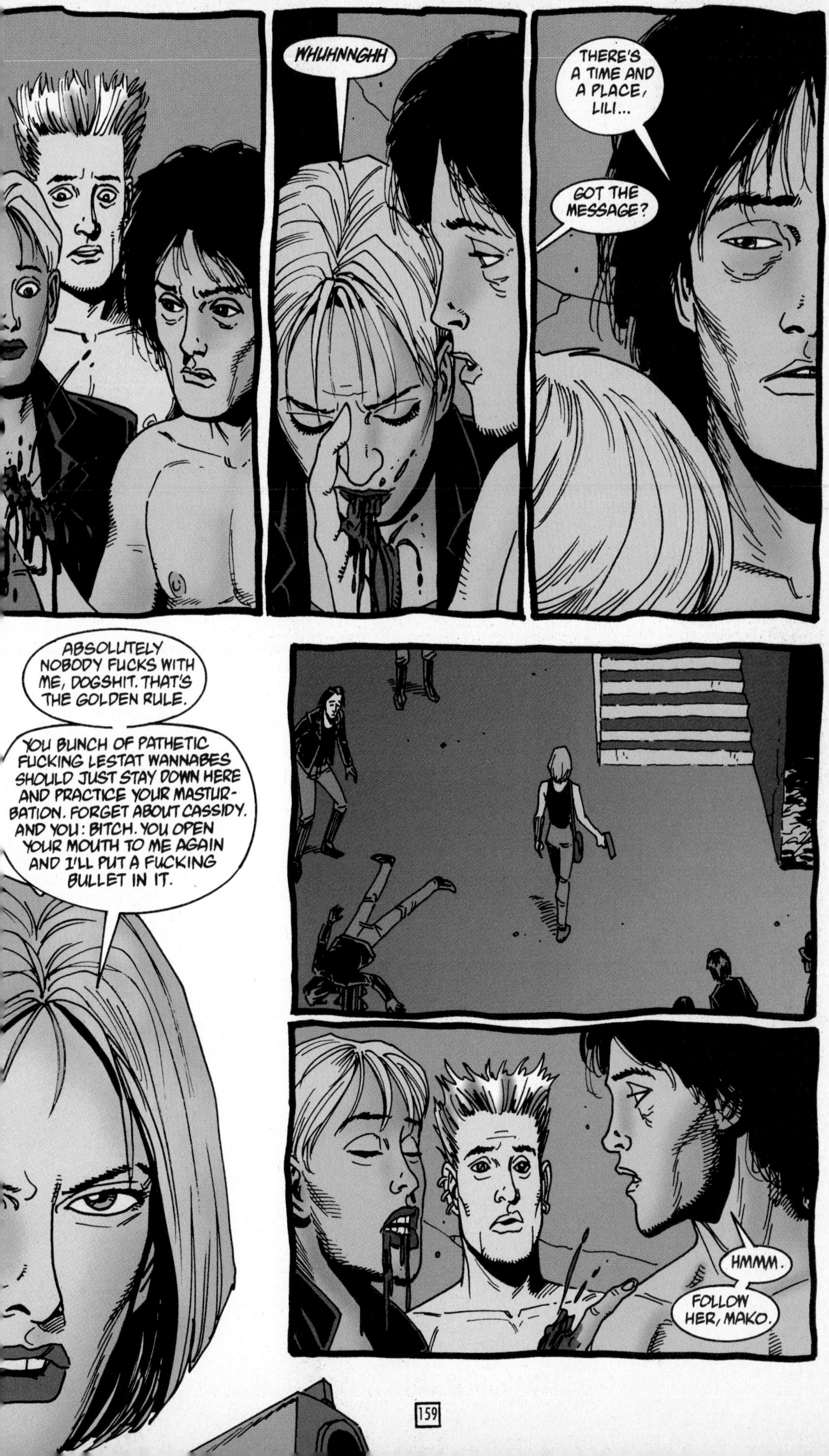
WHUHNNGHH
THERE'S A TIME AND A PLACE, LILI...
GOT THE MESSAGE?
ABSOLUTELY NOBODY FUCKS WITH ME, DOGSHIT. THAT'S THE GOLDEN RULE.
YOU BUNCH OF PATHETIC FUCKING LESTAT WANNABES SHOULD JUST STAY DOWN HERE AND PRACTICE YOUR MASTUR-BATION. FORGET ABOUT CASSIDY. AND YOU: BITCH. YOU OPEN YOUR MOUTH TO ME AGAIN AND I'LL PUT A FUCKING BULLET IN IT.
HMMM.
FOLLOW HER, MAKO.

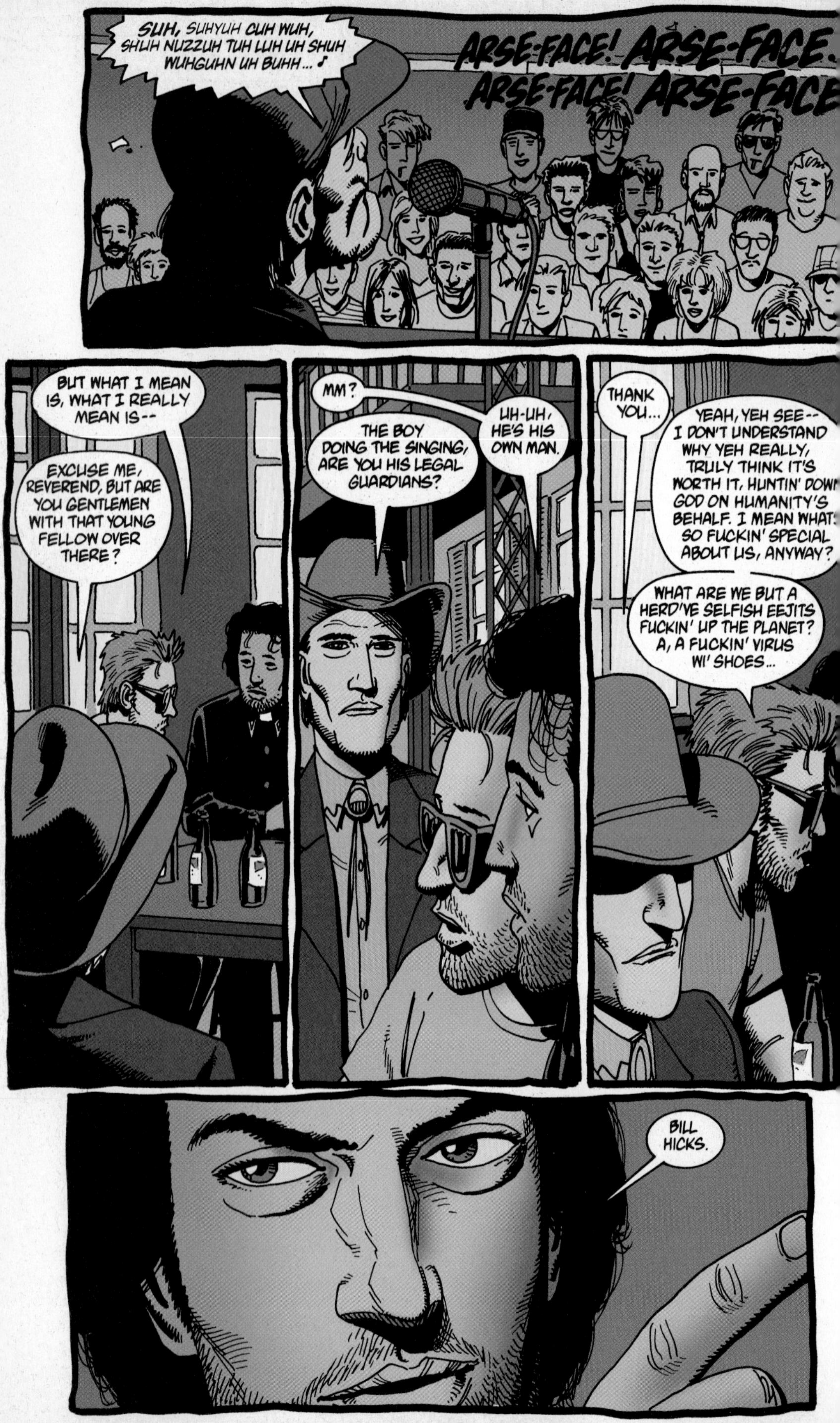
SUH, SUHYUH CUH WUH, SHUH NUZZUH TUH LUH UH SHUH WUHGUHN UH BUHH...
ARSE-FACE! ARSE-FACE
ARSE-FACE! ARSE-FACE
BUT WHAT I MEAN IS, WHAT I REALLY MEAN IS--
EXCUSE ME, REVEREND, BUT ARE YOU GENTLEMEN WITH THAT YOUNG FELLOW OVER THERE?
MM?
THE BOY DOING THE SINGING, ARE YOU HIS LEGAL GUARDIANS?
UH-UH, HE'S HIS OWN MAN.
THANK YOU...
YEAH, YEH SEE-- I DON'T UNDERSTAND WHY YEH REALLY, TRULY THINK IT'S WORTH IT, HUNTIN' DOWN GOD ON HUMANITY'S BEHALF. I MEAN WHAT'S SO FUCKIN' SPECIAL ABOUT US, ANYWAY?
WHAT ARE WE BUT A HERD'VE SELFISH EEJITS FUCKIN' UP THE PLANET? A, A FUCKIN' VIRUS WI' SHOES...
BILL HICKS.

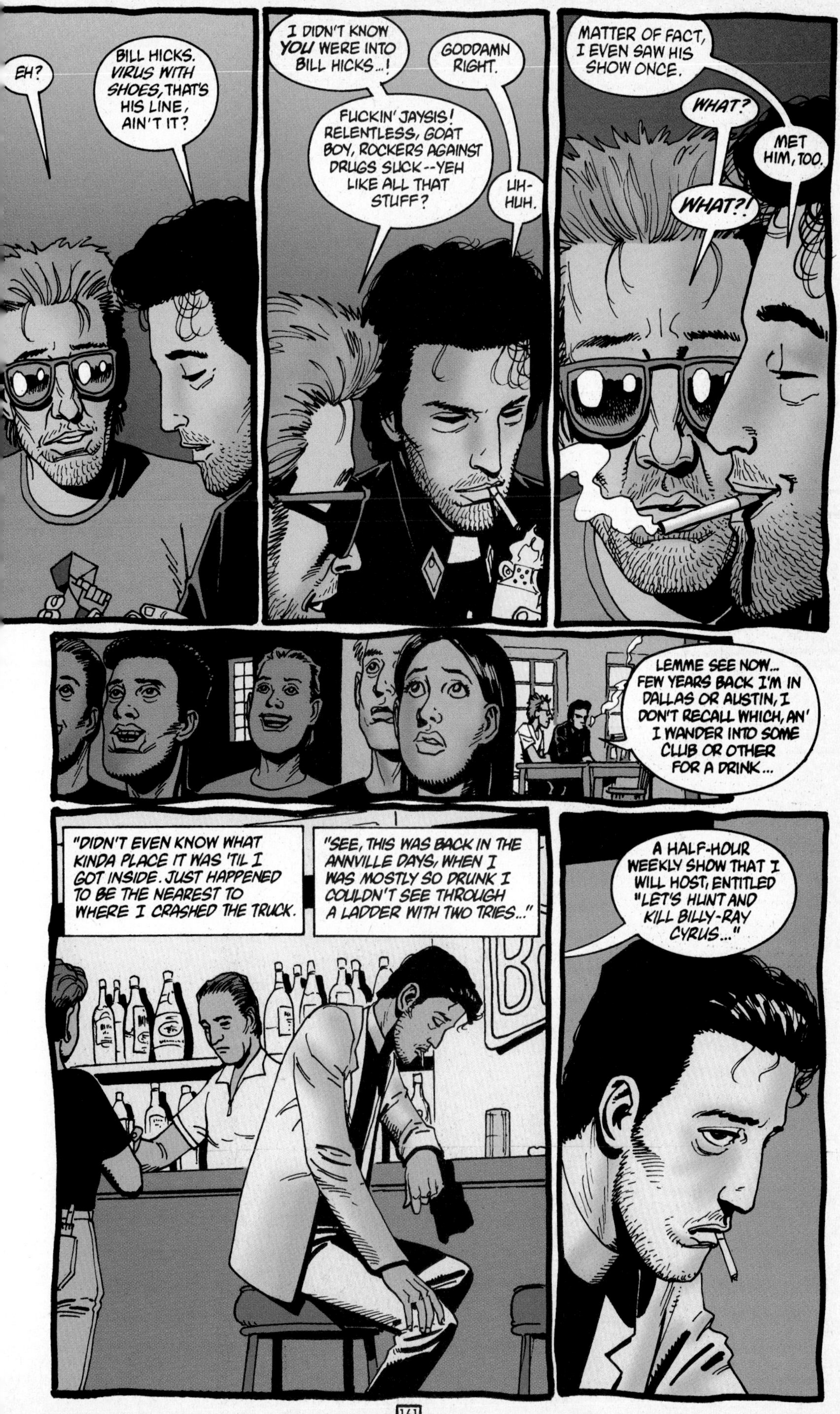

EH?
BILL HICKS. VIRUS WITH SHOES, THAT'S HIS LINE, AIN'T IT?
I DIDN'T KNOW YOU WERE INTO BILL HICKS...!
GODDAMN RIGHT.
FUCKIN' JAYSIS! RELENTLESS, GOAT BOY, ROCKERS AGAINST DRUGS SUCK--YEH LIKE ALL THAT STUFF?
UH-HUH.
MATTER OF FACT, I EVEN SAW HIS SHOW ONCE.
WHAT?
MET HIM, TOO.
WHAT?!
LEMME SEE NOW... FEW YEARS BACK I'M IN DALLAS OR AUSTIN, I DON'T RECALL WHICH, AN' I WANDER INTO SOME CLUB OR OTHER FOR A DRINK...
"DIDN'T EVEN KNOW WHAT KINDA PLACE IT WAS 'TIL I GOT INSIDE. JUST HAPPENED TO BE THE NEAREST TO WHERE I CRASHED THE TRUCK.
"SEE, THIS WAS BACK IN THE ANNVILLE DAYS, WHEN I WAS MOSTLY SO DRUNK I COULDN'T SEE THROUGH A LADDER WITH TWO TRIES..."
A HALF-HOUR WEEKLY SHOW THAT I WILL HOST, ENTITLED "LET'S HUNT AND KILL BILLY-RAY CYRUS..."

IT'S A FAIRLY SELF-EXPLANATORY PLOT, *uh,* EACH WEEK WE LET THE HOUNDS OF HELL LOOSE AND WE CHASE THAT JARHEAD, NO-TALENT CRACKER ASS-HOLE ALL OVER THE GLOBE 'TIL I FINALLY CATCH THAT FRUITY LITTLE PONYTAIL OF HIS IN THE BACK, PULL HIM TO HIS KNEES, PUT A SHOTGUN IN HIS MOUTH LIKE A BIG BLACK COCK OF DEATH--

BKOOOMM!

AN' WE'LL BE BACK IN NINETY-FIVE WITH "LET'S HUNT AND KILL MICHAEL BOLTON"...

THANK YOU VERY MUCH. I'M JUST TRYING TO RID THE WORLD OF ALL THESE *FEVERED EGOS,* THAT ARE TAINTING OUR COLLECTIVE UNCONSCIOUS--AND MAKING US PAY A HIGHER PSYCHIC PRICE THAN WE IMAGINE.

IN FACT, THAT'S HOW I PITCHED IT TO THE NETWORKS, EXACTLY--

CAN I GET A BLACK COFFEE?

YEH LUCKY FUCKIN' BASTARD. WASN'T HE BRILLIANT, BUT?

HE WAS THE GREATEST GODDAMN COMEDIAN I EVER SAW.

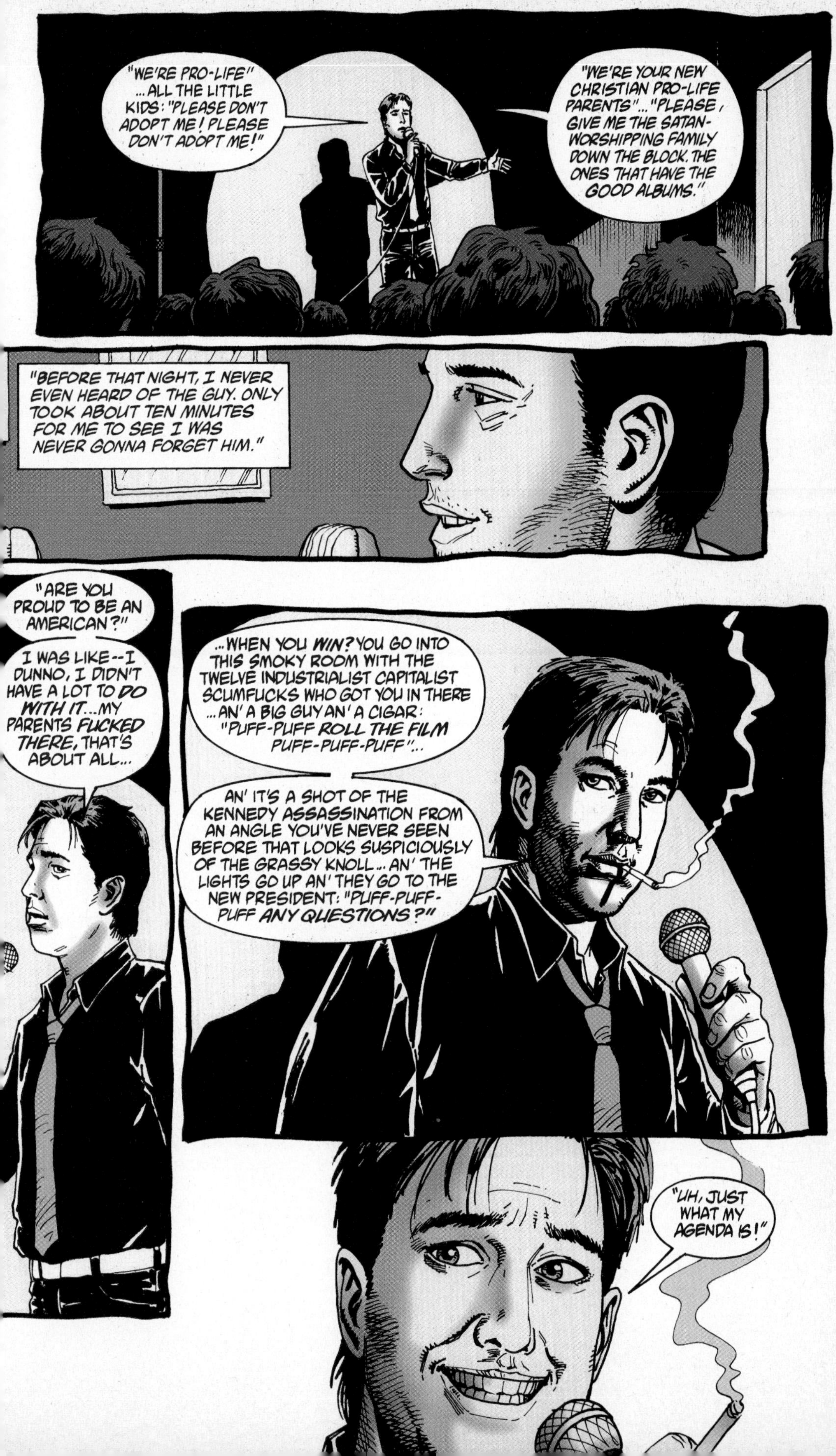
"WE'RE PRO-LIFE" ...ALL THE LITTLE KIDS: "PLEASE DON'T ADOPT ME! PLEASE DON'T ADOPT ME!"
"WE'RE YOUR NEW CHRISTIAN PRO-LIFE PARENTS"..."PLEASE, GIVE ME THE SATAN-WORSHIPPING FAMILY DOWN THE BLOCK. THE ONES THAT HAVE THE GOOD ALBUMS."
"BEFORE THAT NIGHT, I NEVER EVEN HEARD OF THE GUY. ONLY TOOK ABOUT TEN MINUTES FOR ME TO SEE I WAS NEVER GONNA FORGET HIM."
"ARE YOU PROUD TO BE AN AMERICAN?"
I WAS LIKE--I DUNNO, I DIDN'T HAVE A LOT TO DO WITH IT...MY PARENTS FUCKED THERE, THAT'S ABOUT ALL...
...WHEN YOU WIN? YOU GO INTO THIS SMOKY ROOM WITH THE TWELVE INDUSTRIALIST CAPITALIST SCUMFUCKS WHO GOT YOU IN THERE ...AN' A BIG GUY AN' A CIGAR: "PUFF-PUFF ROLL THE FILM PUFF-PUFF-PUFF"...
AN' IT'S A SHOT OF THE KENNEDY ASSASSINATION FROM AN ANGLE YOU'VE NEVER SEEN BEFORE THAT LOOKS SUSPICIOUSLY OF THE GRASSY KNOLL... AN' THE LIGHTS GO UP AN' THEY GO TO THE NEW PRESIDENT: "PUFF-PUFF-PUFF ANY QUESTIONS?"
"UH, JUST WHAT MY AGENDA IS!"

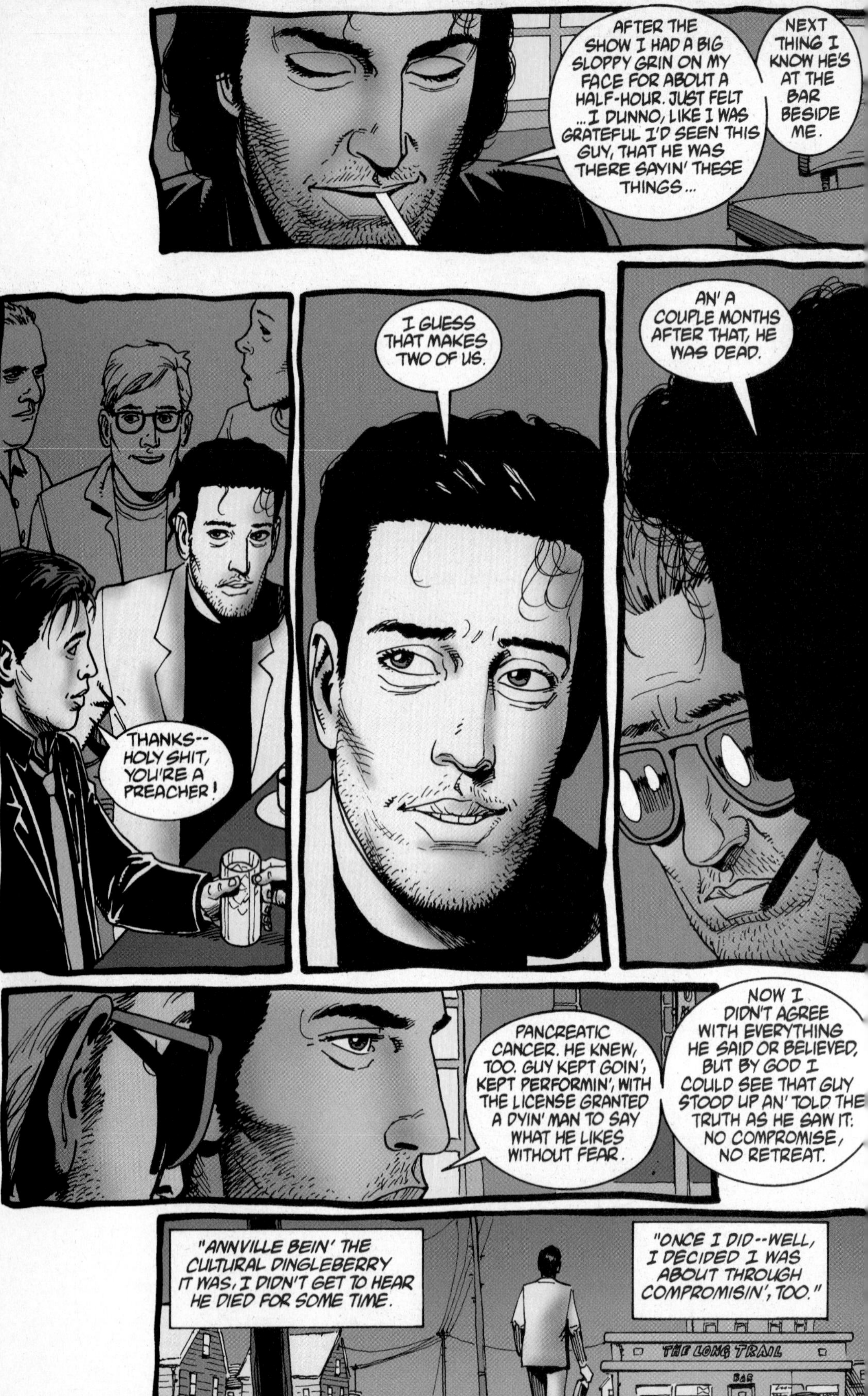
AFTER THE SHOW I HAD A BIG SLOPPY GRIN ON MY FACE FOR ABOUT A HALF-HOUR. JUST FELT ...I DUNNO, LIKE I WAS GRATEFUL I'D SEEN THIS GUY, THAT HE WAS THERE SAYIN' THESE THINGS...
NEXT THING I KNOW HE'S AT THE BAR BESIDE ME.
THANKS-- HOLY SHIT, YOU'RE A PREACHER!
I GUESS THAT MAKES TWO OF US.
AN' A COUPLE MONTHS AFTER THAT, HE WAS DEAD.
PANCREATIC CANCER. HE KNEW, TOO. GUY KEPT GOIN', KEPT PERFORMIN', WITH THE LICENSE GRANTED A DYIN' MAN TO SAY WHAT HE LIKES WITHOUT FEAR.
NOW I DIDN'T AGREE WITH EVERYTHING HE SAID OR BELIEVED, BUT BY GOD I COULD SEE THAT GUY STOOD UP AN' TOLD THE TRUTH AS HE SAW IT: NO COMPROMISE, NO RETREAT.
"ANNVILLE BEIN' THE CULTURAL DINGLEBERRY IT WAS, I DIDN'T GET TO HEAR HE DIED FOR SOME TIME.
"ONCE I DID--WELL, I DECIDED I WAS ABOUT THROUGH COMPROMISIN', TOO."
THE LONG TRAIL
BAR

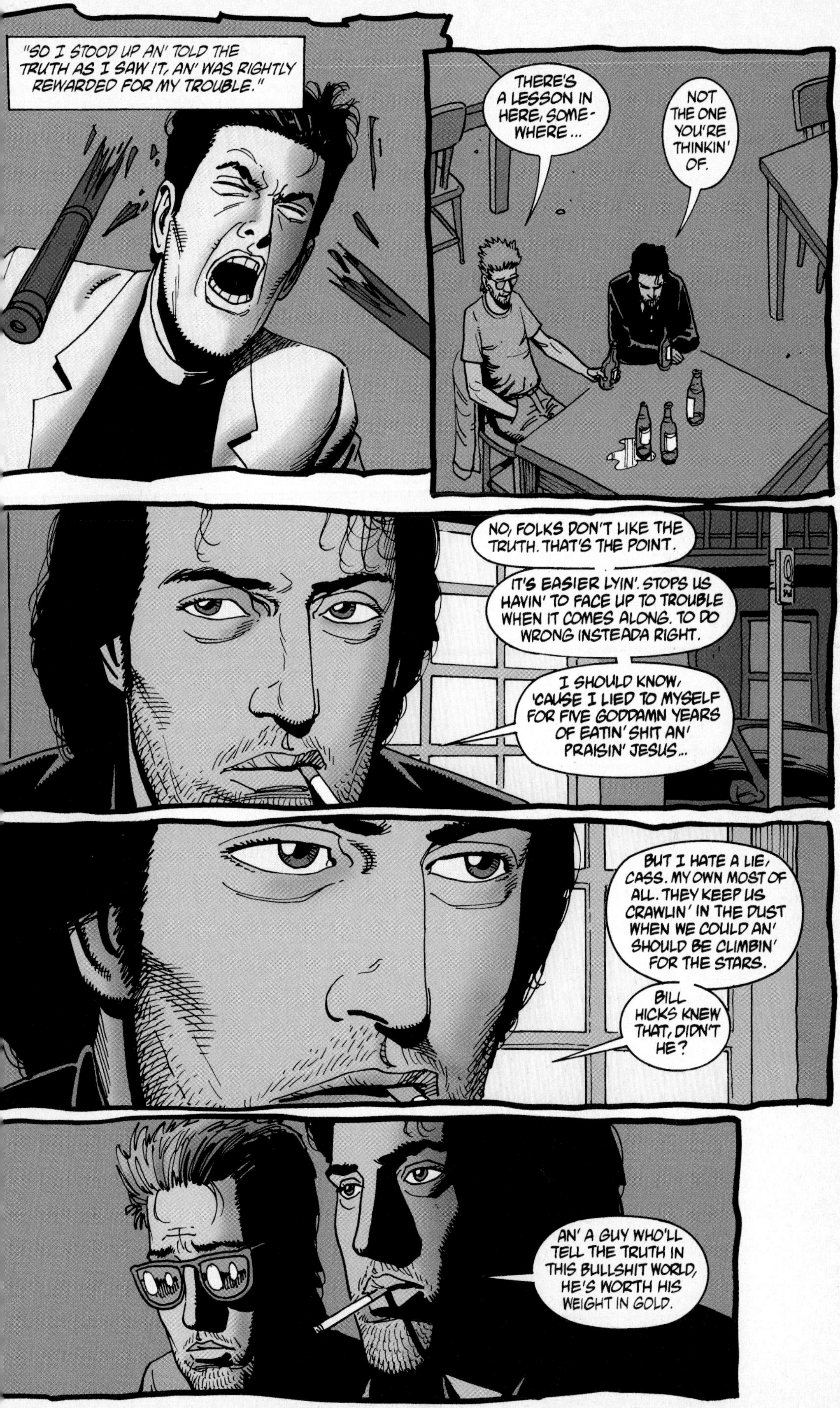
"SO I STOOD UP AN' TOLD THE TRUTH AS I SAW IT, AN' WAS RIGHTLY REWARDED FOR MY TROUBLE."
THERE'S A LESSON IN HERE, SOME-WHERE...
NOT THE ONE YOU'RE THINKIN' OF.
NO, FOLKS DON'T LIKE THE TRUTH. THAT'S THE POINT.
IT'S EASIER LYIN'. STOPS US HAVIN' TO FACE UP TO TROUBLE WHEN IT COMES ALONG. TO DO WRONG INSTEADA RIGHT.
I SHOULD KNOW, 'CAUSE I LIED TO MYSELF FOR FIVE GODDAMN YEARS OF EATIN' SHIT AN' PRAISIN' JESUS...
BUT I HATE A LIE, CASS. MY OWN MOST OF ALL. THEY KEEP US CRAWLIN' IN THE DUST WHEN WE COULD AN' SHOULD BE CLIMBIN' FOR THE STARS.
BILL HICKS KNEW THAT, DIDN'T HE?
AN' A GUY WHO'LL TELL THE TRUTH IN THIS BULLSHIT WORLD, HE'S WORTH HIS WEIGHT IN GOLD.

PSSST!

HEY...!

C'MERE!

BUT--

NO HOTE

WHY AIN'T YOU IN THE ROOM-- WHUP--

C'MERE!

THE ROOM'S A LITTLE BIT HOT RIGHT NOW. I HAD TO SHOOT SOME PEOPLE IN IT.

WHAT?

COPS ARE ALL OVER THE HOTEL. IT HAS TO DO WITH CASSIDY, WHO WE NEED TO HAVE VERY STRONG WORDS WITH RIGHT AWAY.

BUT-- BUT ARE YOU OKAY?

YEAH, FINE. I CHECKED OUT THE BAD GUYS' PLACE AND SHOT THEM UP A LITTLE BIT, YOU KNOW. THERE WERE QUITE A LOT OF THEM, AND ONE GUY NEARLY GOT ME WITH A THROWING KNIFE--

BUT I KNOW YOU'LL BE COOL WITH THAT, BECAUSE YOU KNOW YOU CAN TRUST ME TO HANDLE MYSELF.

LET'S GO.

ARE YOU SURE YOU'RE OKAY? YOU OUGHT TO BE IN SHOCK, AT LEAST.

I'M NOT A VERY SHOCKABLE PERSON, LILI.

WHAT DOES CONCERN ME IS THE GENERAL LEVEL OF SQUEAMISHNESS AMONG LES ENFANTS. YOU NEVER SAW *NOSFERATU* HAVING TO GO HOME BECAUSE "I JUST ABOUT SHIT MY PANTS"...

THEY'LL BE BACK TONIGHT. THEY KNOW THERE'S TOO MUCH AT STAKE.

ACTUALLY, THIS KIND OF REMINDS ME OF *ROGER*...

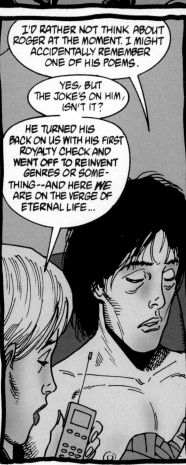

I'D RATHER NOT THINK ABOUT ROGER AT THE MOMENT. I MIGHT ACCIDENTALLY REMEMBER ONE OF HIS POEMS.

YES, BUT THE JOKE'S ON HIM, ISN'T IT?

HE TURNED HIS BACK ON US WITH HIS FIRST ROYALTY CHECK AND WENT OFF TO REINVENT GENRES OR SOMETHING--AND HERE *WE* ARE ON THE VERGE OF ETERNAL LIFE...

IN FACT, THE FIRST THING I'LL DO IS PAY THE LITTLE PRICK A VISIT--

HELLO? MAKO?

IT'S HIM.

IT'S CASSIDY. I FUCKING GOT THE BASTARD.

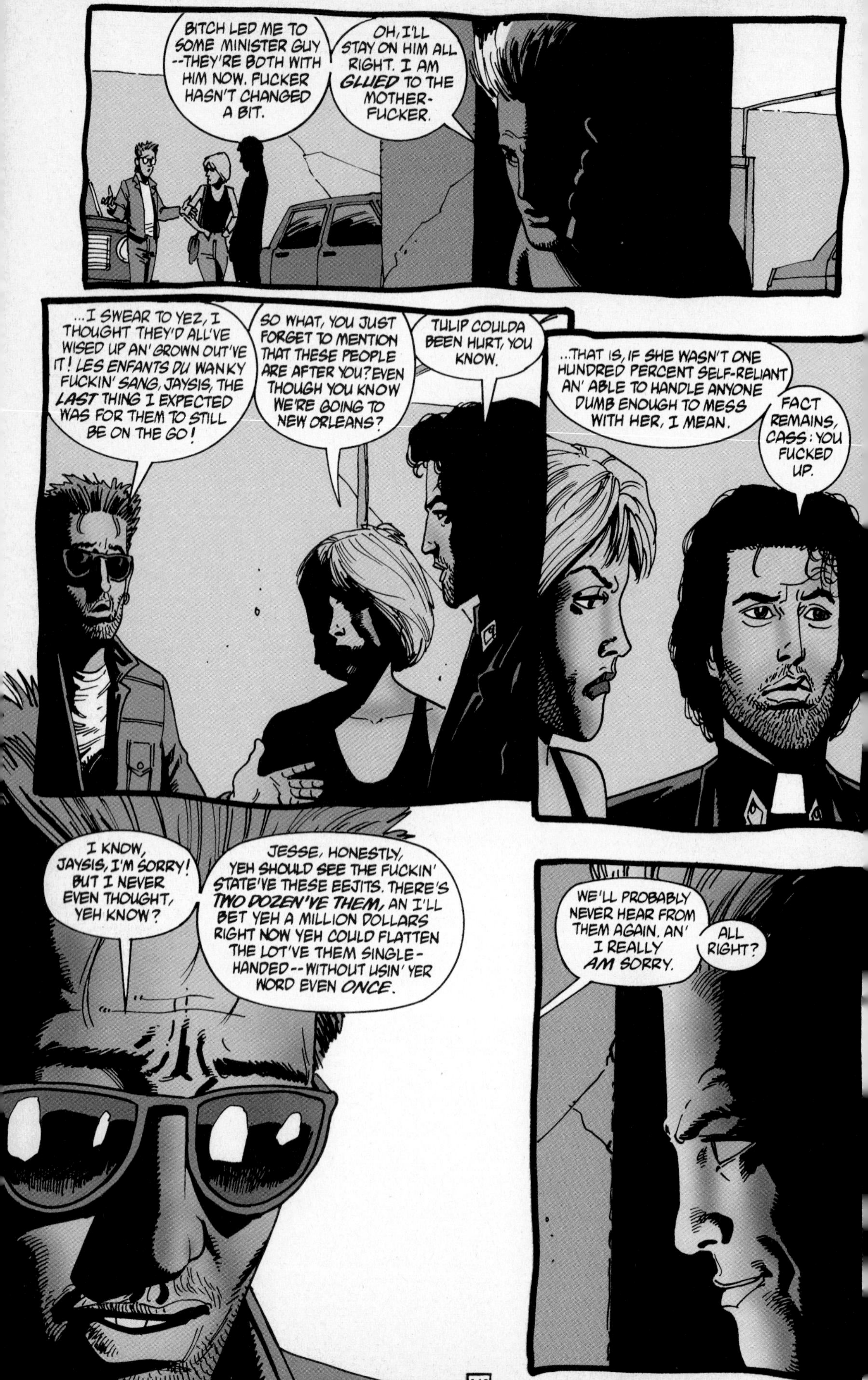
BITCH LED ME TO SOME MINISTER GUY --THEY'RE BOTH WITH HIM NOW. FUCKER HASN'T CHANGED A BIT.
OH, I'LL STAY ON HIM ALL RIGHT. I AM GLUED TO THE MOTHER-FUCKER.
...I SWEAR TO YEZ, I THOUGHT THEY'D ALL'VE WISED UP AN' GROWN OUT'VE IT! LES ENFANTS DU WANKY FUCKIN' SANG, JAYSIS, THE LAST THING I EXPECTED WAS FOR THEM TO STILL BE ON THE GO!
SO WHAT, YOU JUST FORGET TO MENTION THAT THESE PEOPLE ARE AFTER YOU? EVEN THOUGH YOU KNOW WE'RE GOING TO NEW ORLEANS?
TULIP COULDA BEEN HURT, YOU KNOW.
...THAT IS, IF SHE WASN'T ONE HUNDRED PERCENT SELF-RELIANT AN' ABLE TO HANDLE ANYONE DUMB ENOUGH TO MESS WITH HER, I MEAN.
FACT REMAINS, CASS: YOU FUCKED UP.
I KNOW, JAYSIS, I'M SORRY! BUT I NEVER EVEN THOUGHT, YEH KNOW?
JESSE, HONESTLY, YEH SHOULD SEE THE FUCKIN' STATE'VE THESE EEJITS. THERE'S TWO DOZEN'VE THEM, AN I'LL BET YEH A MILLION DOLLARS RIGHT NOW YEH COULD FLATTEN THE LOT'VE THEM SINGLE-HANDED--WITHOUT USIN' YER WORD EVEN ONCE.
WE'LL PROBABLY NEVER HEAR FROM THEM AGAIN. AN' I REALLY AM SORRY.
ALL RIGHT?

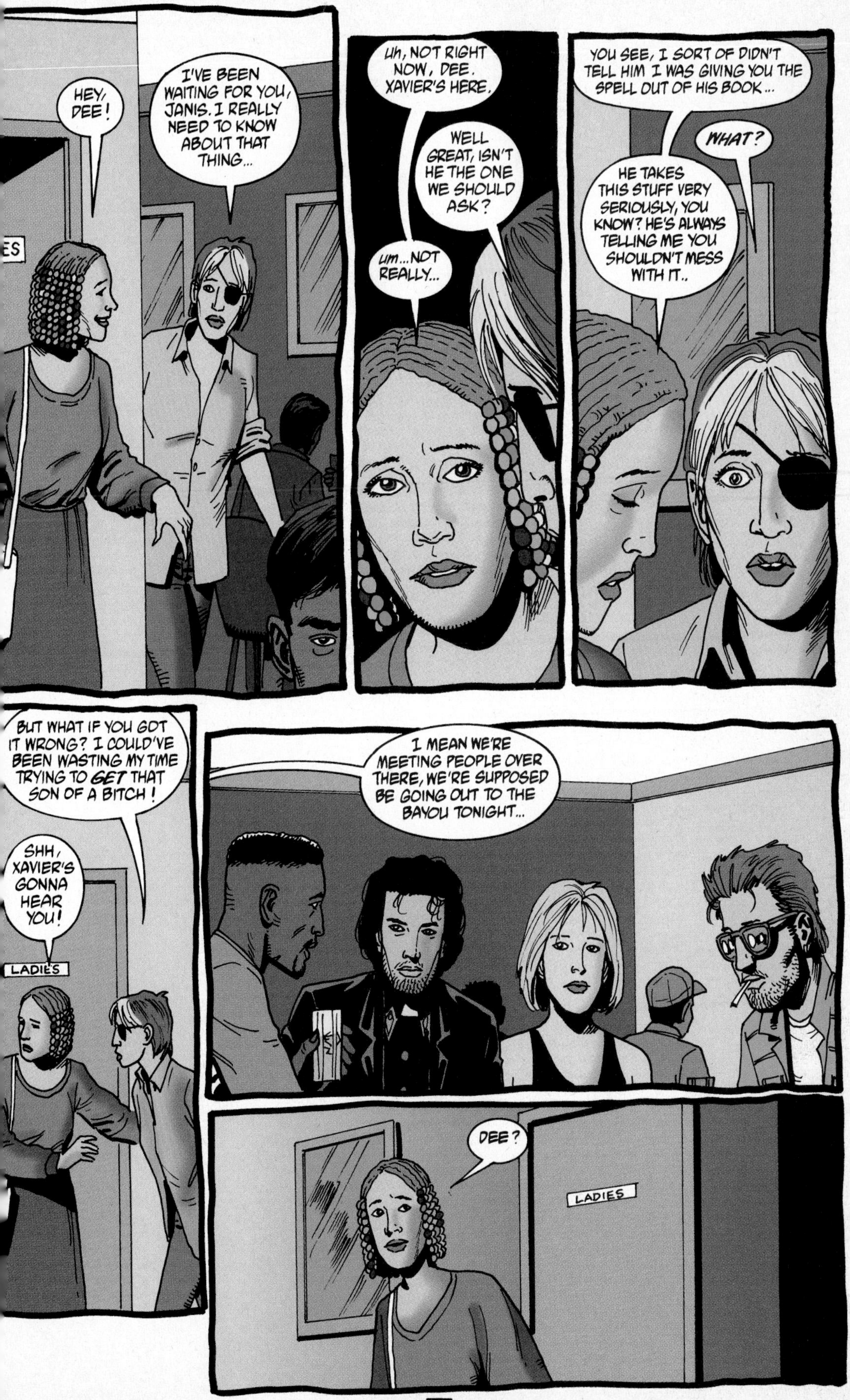
HEY, DEE!
I'VE BEEN WAITING FOR YOU, JANIS. I REALLY NEED TO KNOW ABOUT THAT THING...
ES
UH, NOT RIGHT NOW, DEE. XAVIER'S HERE.
WELL GREAT, ISN'T HE THE ONE WE SHOULD ASK?
UM...NOT REALLY...
YOU SEE, I SORT OF DIDN'T TELL HIM I WAS GIVING YOU THE SPELL OUT OF HIS BOOK...
WHAT?
HE TAKES THIS STUFF VERY SERIOUSLY, YOU KNOW? HE'S ALWAYS TELLING ME YOU SHOULDN'T MESS WITH IT..
BUT WHAT IF YOU GOT IT WRONG? I COULD'VE BEEN WASTING MY TIME TRYING TO GET THAT SON OF A BITCH!
SHH, XAVIER'S GONNA HEAR YOU!
LADIES
I MEAN WE'RE MEETING PEOPLE OVER THERE, WE'RE SUPPOSED BE GOING OUT TO THE BAYOU TONIGHT...
DEE?
LADIES

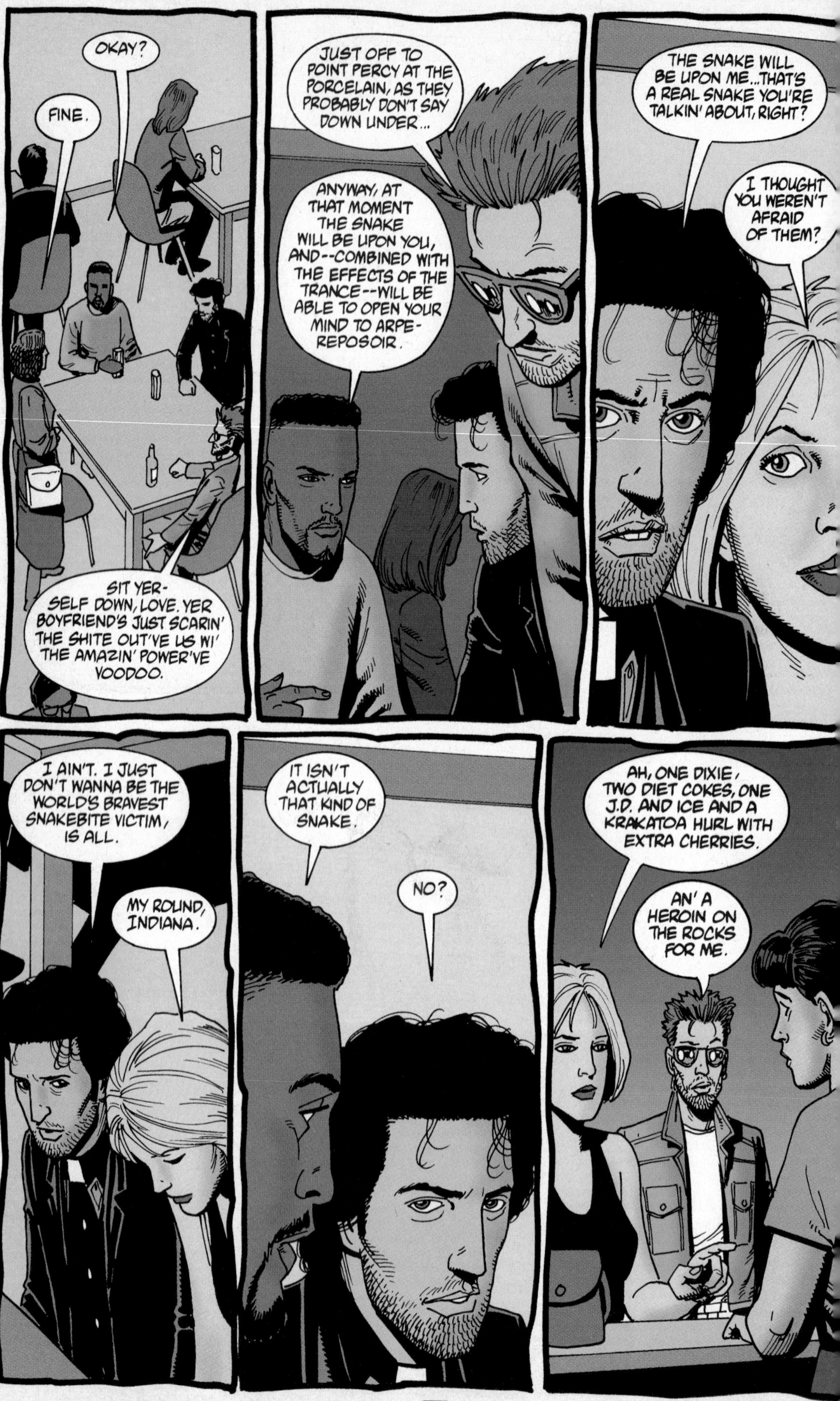
OKAY?
FINE.
SIT YER-SELF DOWN, LOVE. YER BOYFRIEND'S JUST SCARIN' THE SHITE OUT'VE US WI' THE AMAZIN' POWER'VE VOODOO.
JUST OFF TO POINT PERCY AT THE PORCELAIN, AS THEY PROBABLY DON'T SAY DOWN UNDER...
ANYWAY, AT THAT MOMENT THE SNAKE WILL BE UPON YOU, AND--COMBINED WITH THE EFFECTS OF THE TRANCE--WILL BE ABLE TO OPEN YOUR MIND TO ARPE-REPOSOIR.
THE SNAKE WILL BE UPON ME...THAT'S A REAL SNAKE YOU'RE TALKIN' ABOUT, RIGHT?
I THOUGHT YOU WEREN'T AFRAID OF THEM?
I AIN'T. I JUST DON'T WANNA BE THE WORLD'S BRAVEST SNAKEBITE VICTIM, IS ALL.
MY ROUND, INDIANA.
IT ISN'T ACTUALLY THAT KIND OF SNAKE.
NO?
AH, ONE DIXIE, TWO DIET COKES, ONE J.D. AND ICE AND A KRAKATOA HURL WITH EXTRA CHERRIES.
AN' A HEROIN ON THE ROCKS FOR ME.

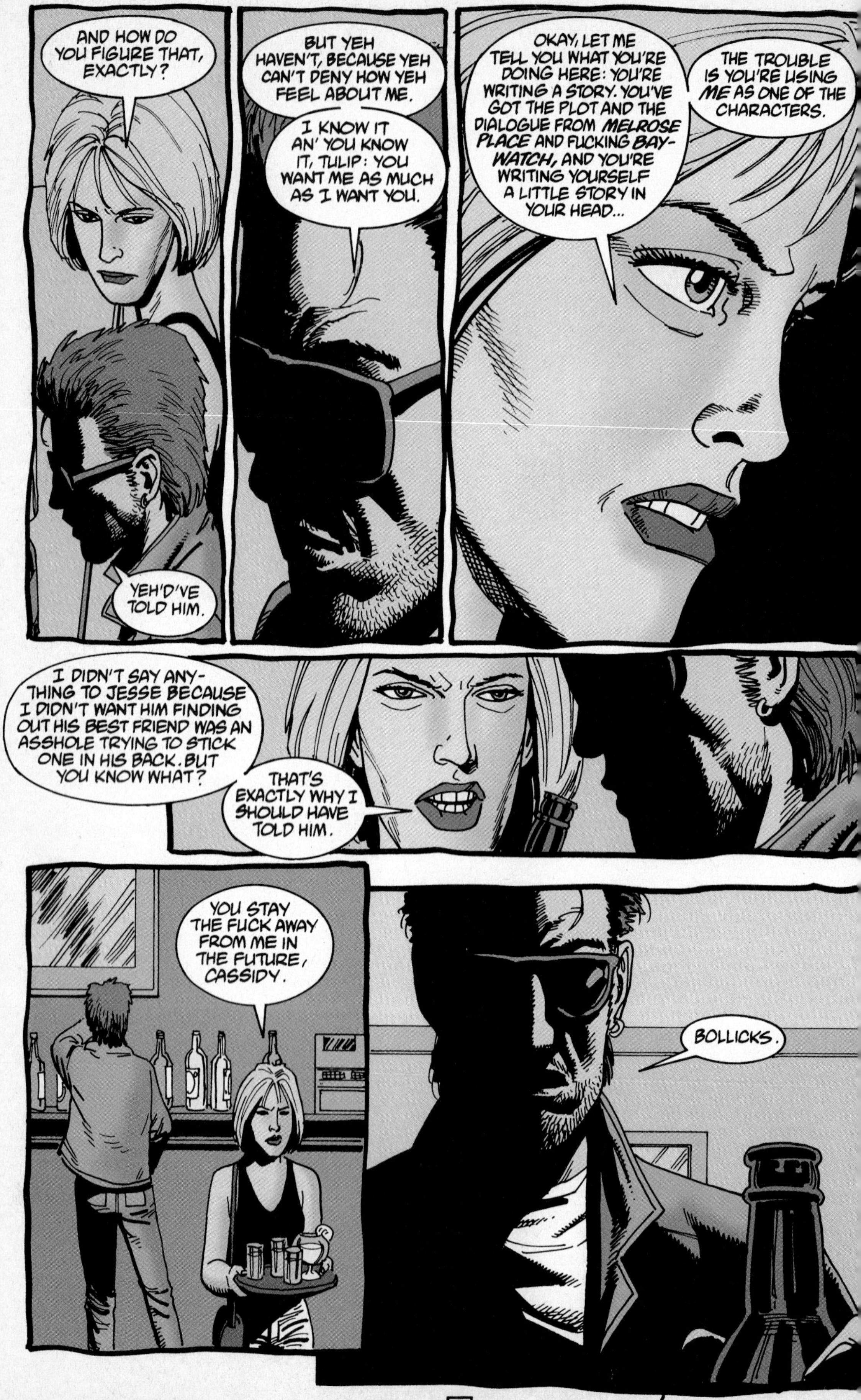
AND HOW DO YOU FIGURE THAT, EXACTLY?
YEH'D'VE TOLD HIM.
BUT YEH HAVEN'T, BECAUSE YEH CAN'T DENY HOW YEH FEEL ABOUT ME.
I KNOW IT AN' YOU KNOW IT, TULIP: YOU WANT ME AS MUCH AS I WANT YOU.
OKAY, LET ME TELL YOU WHAT YOU'RE DOING HERE: YOU'RE WRITING A STORY. YOU'VE GOT THE PLOT AND THE DIALOGUE FROM MELROSE PLACE AND FUCKING BAY-WATCH, AND YOU'RE WRITING YOURSELF A LITTLE STORY IN YOUR HEAD...
THE TROUBLE IS YOU'RE USING ME AS ONE OF THE CHARACTERS.
I DIDN'T SAY ANY-THING TO JESSE BECAUSE I DIDN'T WANT HIM FINDING OUT HIS BEST FRIEND WAS AN ASSHOLE TRYING TO STICK ONE IN HIS BACK. BUT YOU KNOW WHAT?
THAT'S EXACTLY WHY I SHOULD HAVE TOLD HIM.
YOU STAY THE FUCK AWAY FROM ME IN THE FUTURE, CASSIDY.
BOLLICKS.

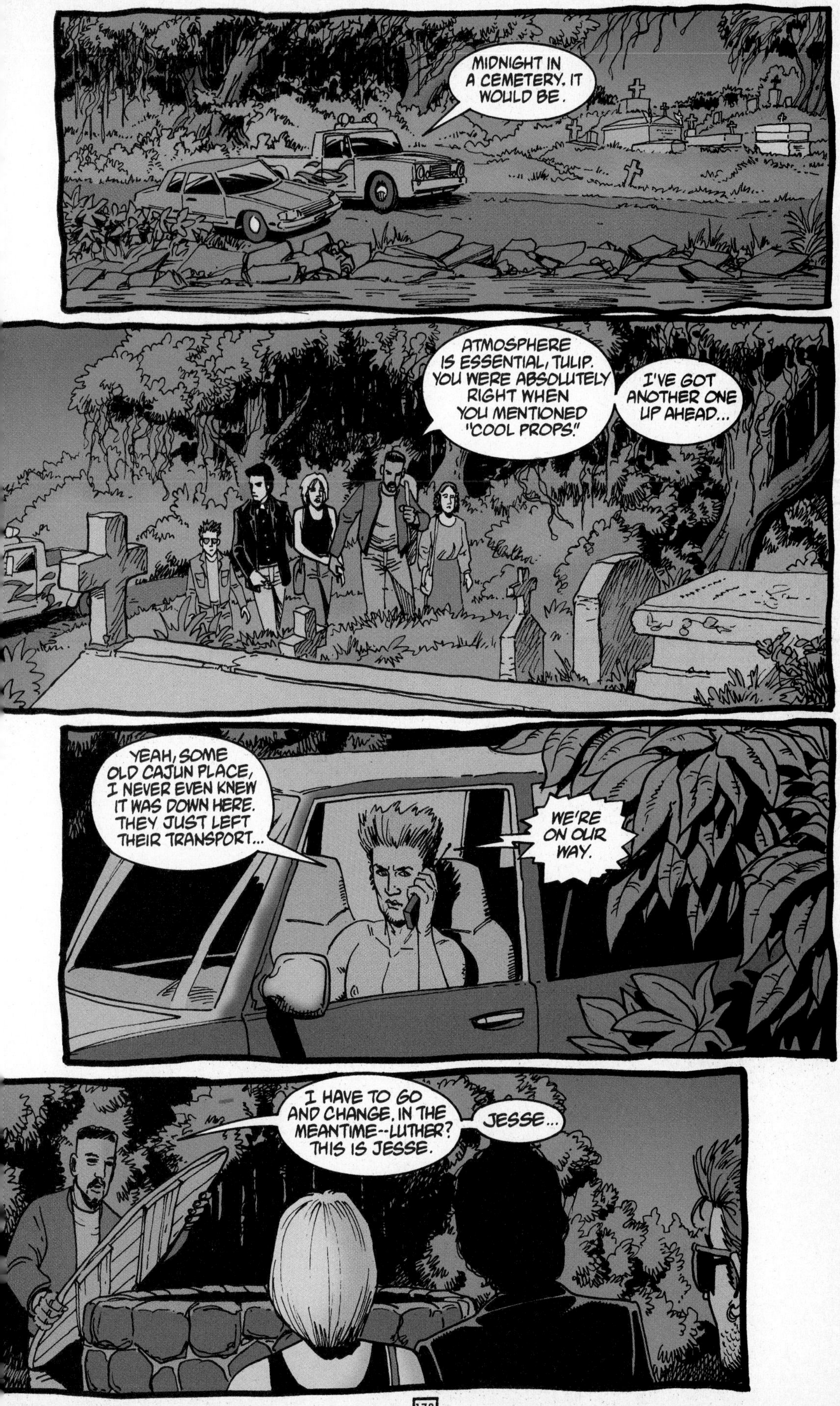
MIDNIGHT IN A CEMETERY. IT WOULD BE.
ATMOSPHERE IS ESSENTIAL, TULIP. YOU WERE ABSOLUTELY RIGHT WHEN YOU MENTIONED "COOL PROPS."
I'VE GOT ANOTHER ONE UP AHEAD...
YEAH, SOME OLD CAJUN PLACE, I NEVER EVEN KNEW IT WAS DOWN HERE. THEY JUST LEFT THEIR TRANSPORT...
WE'RE ON OUR WAY.
I HAVE TO GO AND CHANGE. IN THE MEANTIME--LUTHER? THIS IS JESSE.
JESSE...

TO BE CONTINUED.

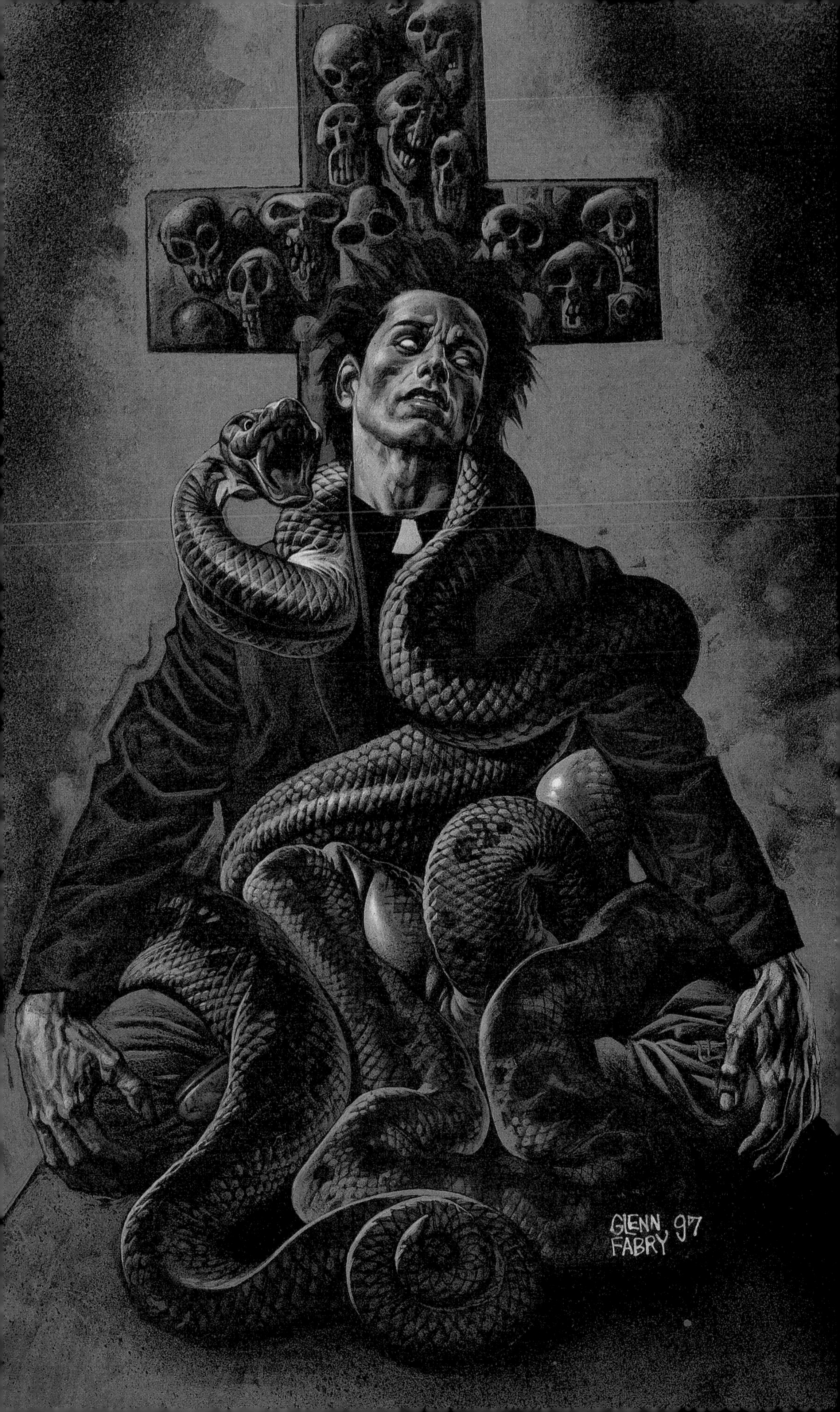
GLENN 97
FABRY

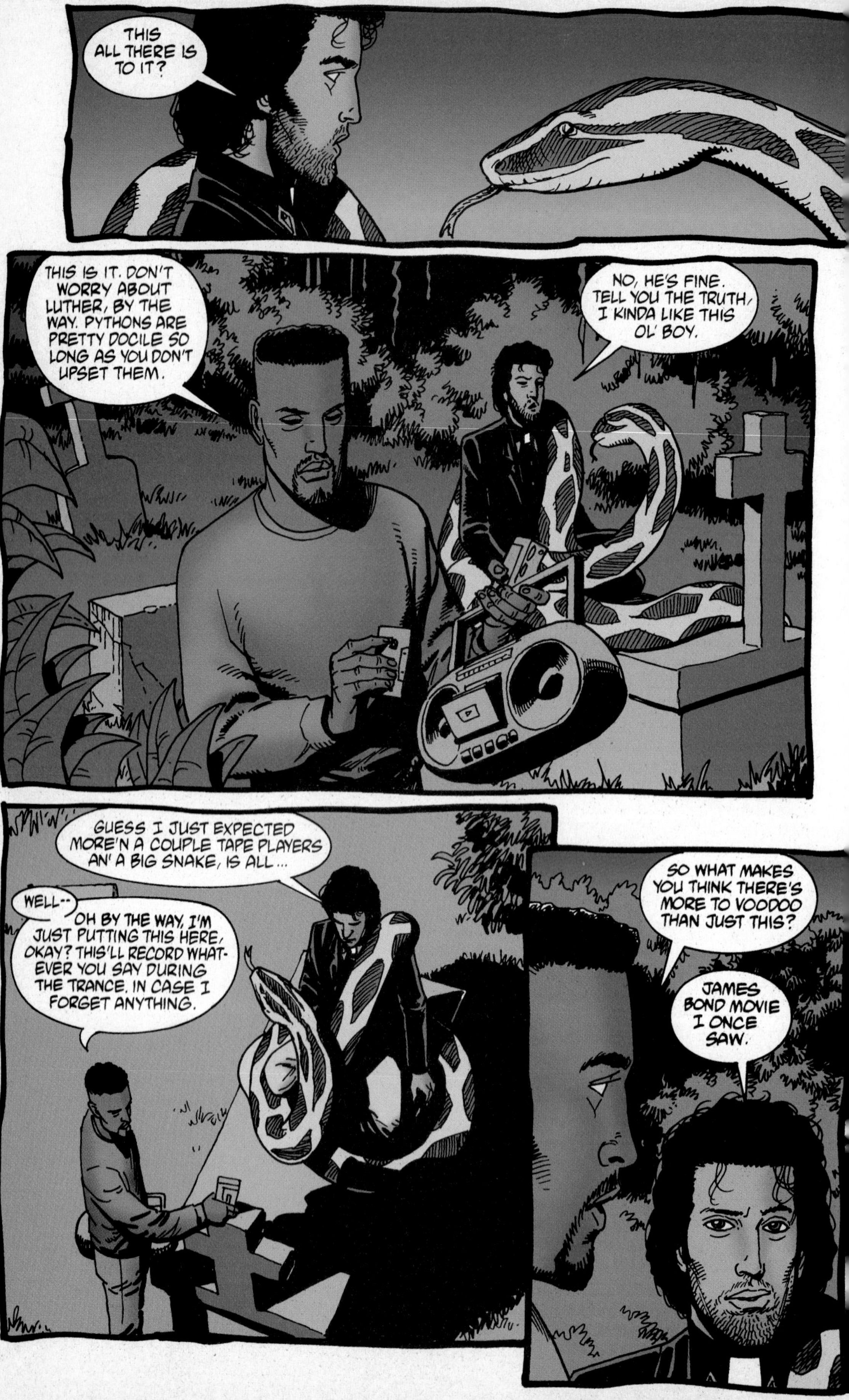
THIS ALL THERE IS TO IT?
THIS IS IT. DON'T WORRY ABOUT LUTHER, BY THE WAY. PYTHONS ARE PRETTY DOCILE SO LONG AS YOU DON'T UPSET THEM.
NO, HE'S FINE. TELL YOU THE TRUTH, I KINDA LIKE THIS OL' BOY.
GUESS I JUST EXPECTED MORE'N A COUPLE TAPE PLAYERS AN' A BIG SNAKE, IS ALL...
WELL--
OH BY THE WAY, I'M JUST PUTTING THIS HERE, OKAY? THIS'LL RECORD WHATEVER YOU SAY DURING THE TRANCE. IN CASE I FORGET ANYTHING.
SO WHAT MAKES YOU THINK THERE'S MORE TO VOODOO THAN JUST THIS?
JAMES BOND MOVIE I ONCE SAW.

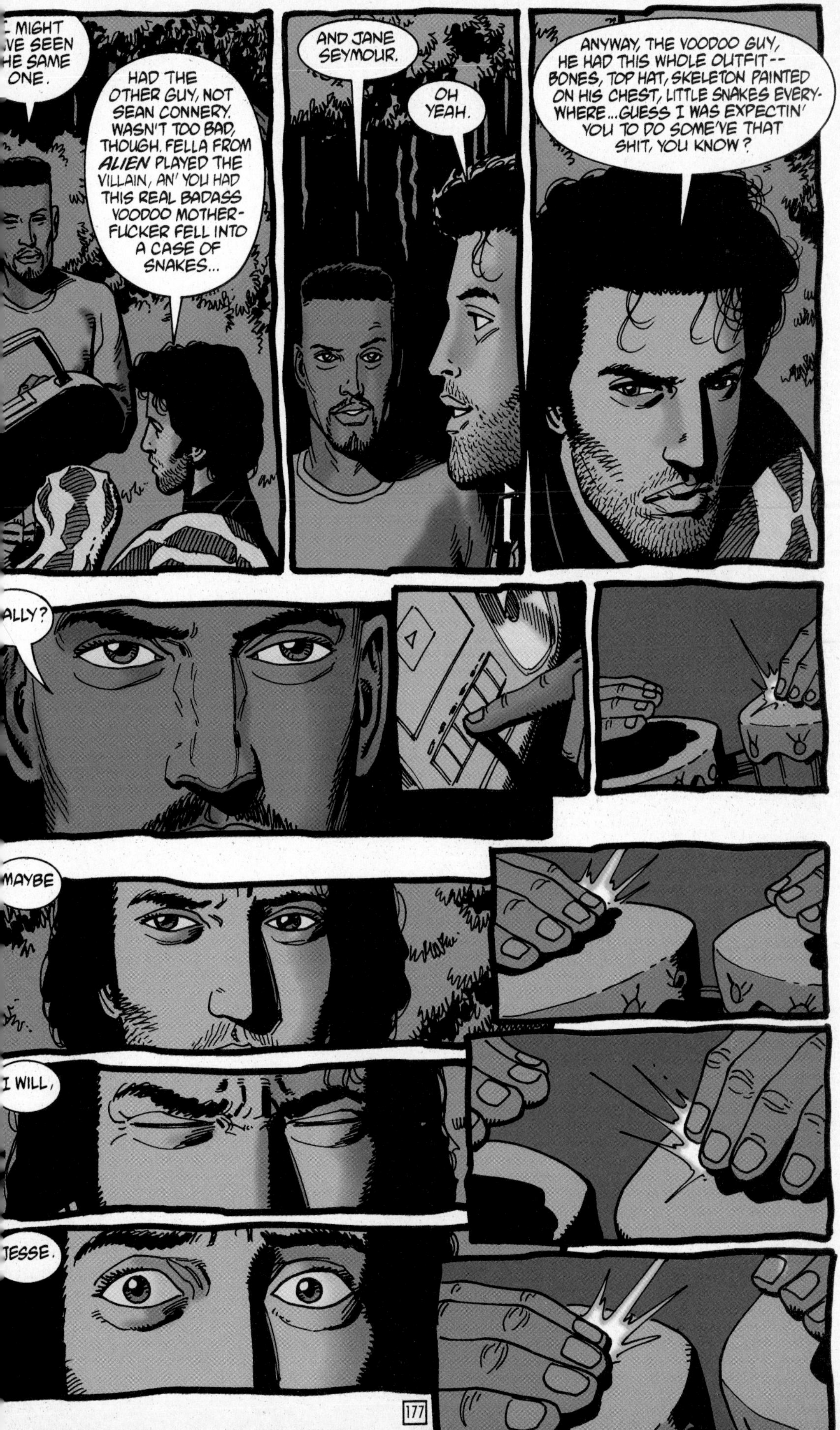

MIGHT
VE SEEN
HE SAME
ONE.
HAD THE OTHER GUY, NOT SEAN CONNERY. WASN'T TOO BAD, THOUGH. FELLA FROM ALIEN PLAYED THE VILLAIN, AN' YOU HAD THIS REAL BADASS VOODOO MOTHER-FUCKER FELL INTO A CASE OF SNAKES...
AND JANE SEYMOUR.
OH YEAH.
ANYWAY, THE VOODOO GUY, HE HAD THIS WHOLE OUTFIT-- BONES, TOP HAT, SKELETON PAINTED ON HIS CHEST, LITTLE SNAKES EVERY-WHERE...GUESS I WAS EXPECTIN' YOU TO DO SOME'VE THAT SHIT, YOU KNOW?
ALLY?
MAYBE
I WILL,
JESSE.

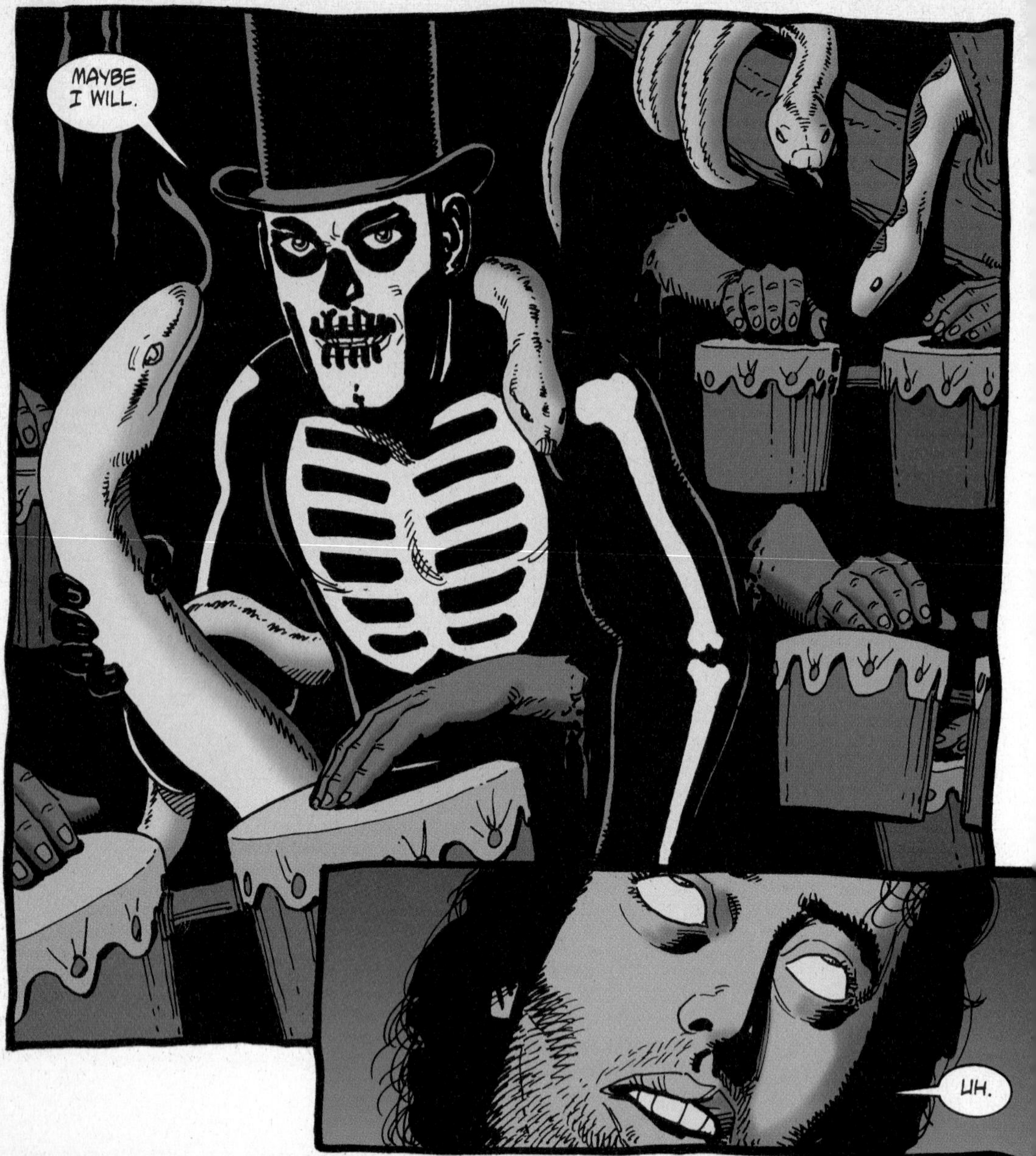
MAYBE I WILL.
UH.

SNAKES IN THE GRASS

GARTH ENNIS - Writer STEVE DILLON - Artist
PAMELA RAMBO - Colorist
CLEM ROBINS - Letterer AXEL ALONSO - Editor

PREACHER created by GARTH ENNIS and STEVE DILLON

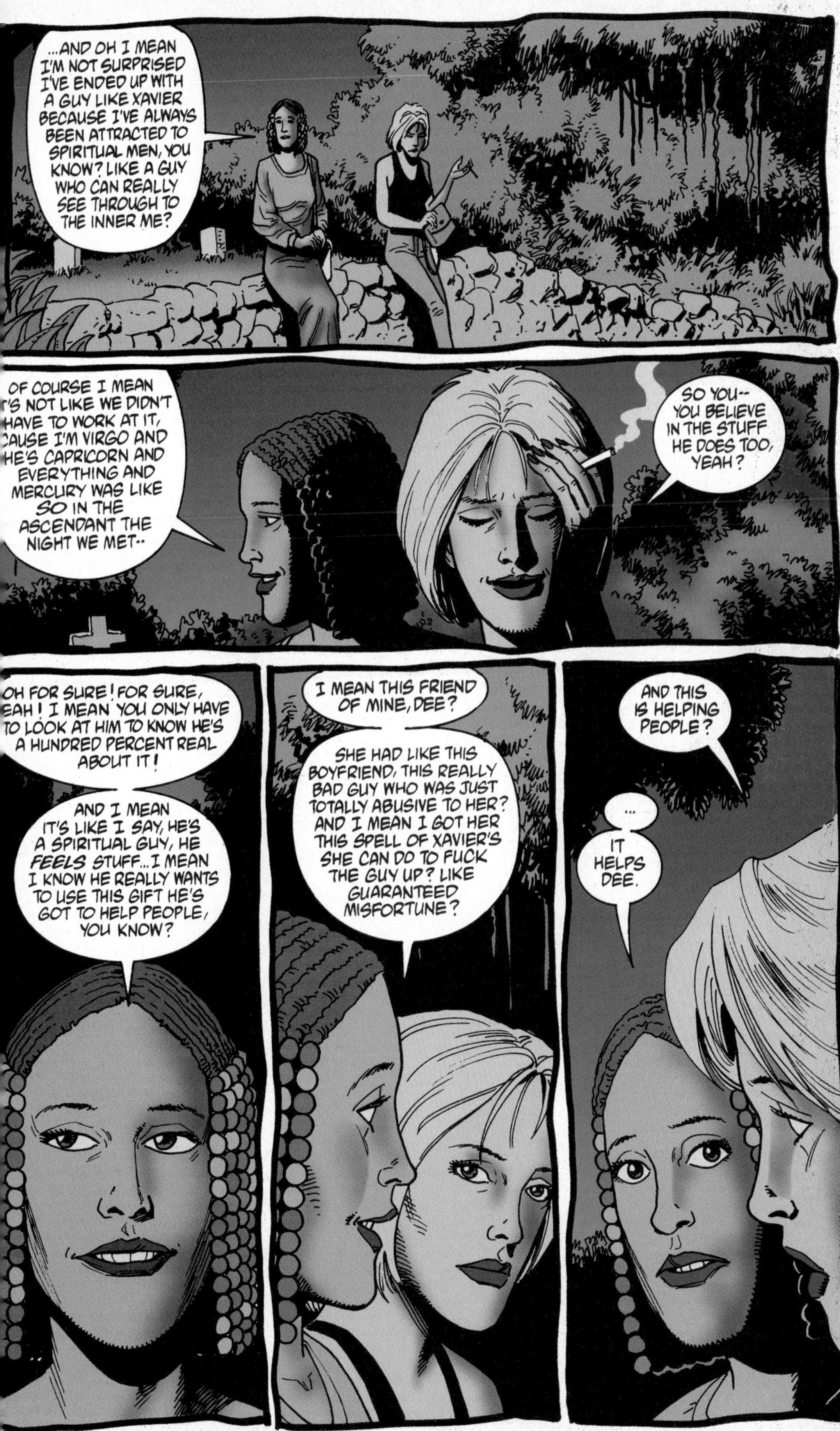
...AND OH I MEAN I'M NOT SURPRISED I'VE ENDED UP WITH A GUY LIKE XAVIER BECAUSE I'VE ALWAYS BEEN ATTRACTED TO SPIRITUAL MEN, YOU KNOW? LIKE A GUY WHO CAN REALLY SEE THROUGH TO THE INNER ME?
OF COURSE I MEAN IT'S NOT LIKE WE DIDN'T HAVE TO WORK AT IT, 'CAUSE I'M VIRGO AND HE'S CAPRICORN AND EVERYTHING AND MERCURY WAS LIKE *SO* IN THE ASCENDANT THE NIGHT WE MET--
SO YOU-- YOU BELIEVE IN THE STUFF HE DOES TOO, YEAH?
OH FOR SURE! FOR SURE, YEAH! I MEAN YOU ONLY HAVE TO LOOK AT HIM TO KNOW HE'S A HUNDRED PERCENT REAL ABOUT IT!
AND I MEAN IT'S LIKE I SAY, HE'S A SPIRITUAL GUY, HE *FEELS* STUFF... I MEAN I KNOW HE REALLY WANTS TO USE THIS GIFT HE'S GOT TO HELP PEOPLE, YOU KNOW?
I MEAN THIS FRIEND OF MINE, DEE?
SHE HAD LIKE THIS BOYFRIEND, THIS REALLY BAD GUY WHO WAS JUST TOTALLY ABUSIVE TO HER? AND I MEAN I GOT HER THIS SPELL OF XAVIER'S SHE CAN DO TO FUCK THE GUY UP? LIKE GUARANTEED MISFORTUNE?
AND THIS IS HELPING PEOPLE?
...
IT HELPS DEE.

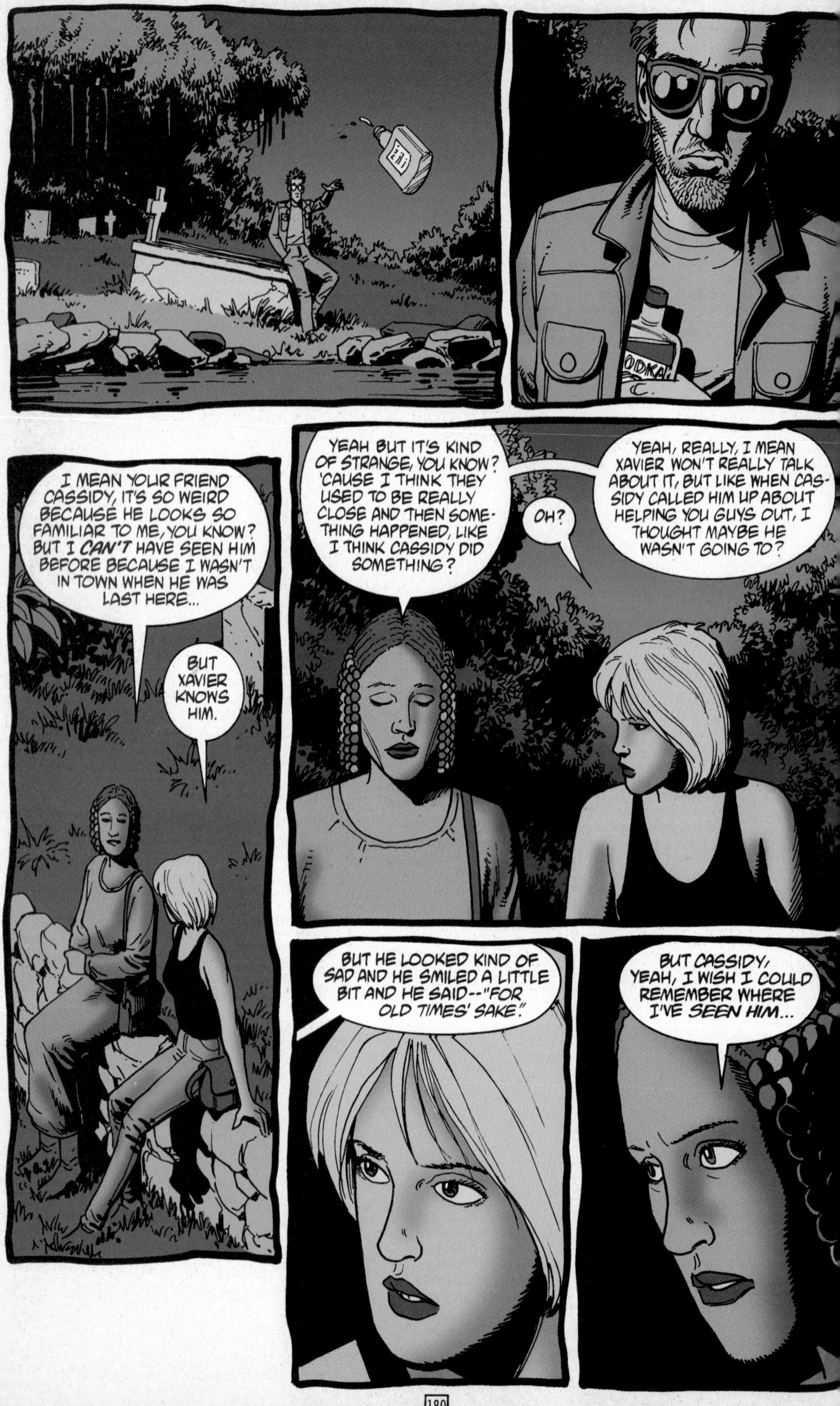

I MEAN YOUR FRIEND CASSIDY, IT'S SO WEIRD BECAUSE HE LOOKS SO FAMILIAR TO ME, YOU KNOW? BUT I *CAN'T* HAVE SEEN HIM BEFORE BECAUSE I WASN'T IN TOWN WHEN HE WAS LAST HERE...
BUT XAVIER KNOWS HIM.
YEAH BUT IT'S KIND OF STRANGE, YOU KNOW? 'CAUSE I THINK THEY USED TO BE REALLY CLOSE AND THEN SOMETHING HAPPENED, LIKE I THINK CASSIDY DID SOMETHING?
OH?
YEAH, REALLY, I MEAN XAVIER WON'T REALLY TALK ABOUT IT, BUT LIKE WHEN CASSIDY CALLED HIM UP ABOUT HELPING YOU GUYS OUT, I THOUGHT MAYBE HE WASN'T GOING TO?
BUT HE LOOKED KIND OF SAD AND HE SMILED A LITTLE BIT AND HE SAID--"FOR OLD TIMES' SAKE."
BUT CASSIDY, YEAH, I WISH I COULD REMEMBER WHERE I'VE *SEEN HIM*...

ARPE-REPOSOIR. YOU ARE ON HIM. UPON HIM. AROUND HIM. *IN* HIM.

SLIDE INTO HIS SPIRIT. UNCOIL THE SECRETS TANGLED THERE.

AND SPEAK TO ME.

VOODOO FEATURES PRESENTS

A MIND'S EYE PRODUCTION

OF A JESSE CUSTER FILM

WAIT. WHERE IS HE?

IN A PLACE HE FEELS AT EASE.

GO ON.

GOD ALMIGHTY

THE SAINT OF KILLERS

THOSE DAMN ANGELS

AND THE DUKE

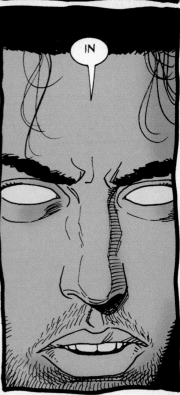

IN

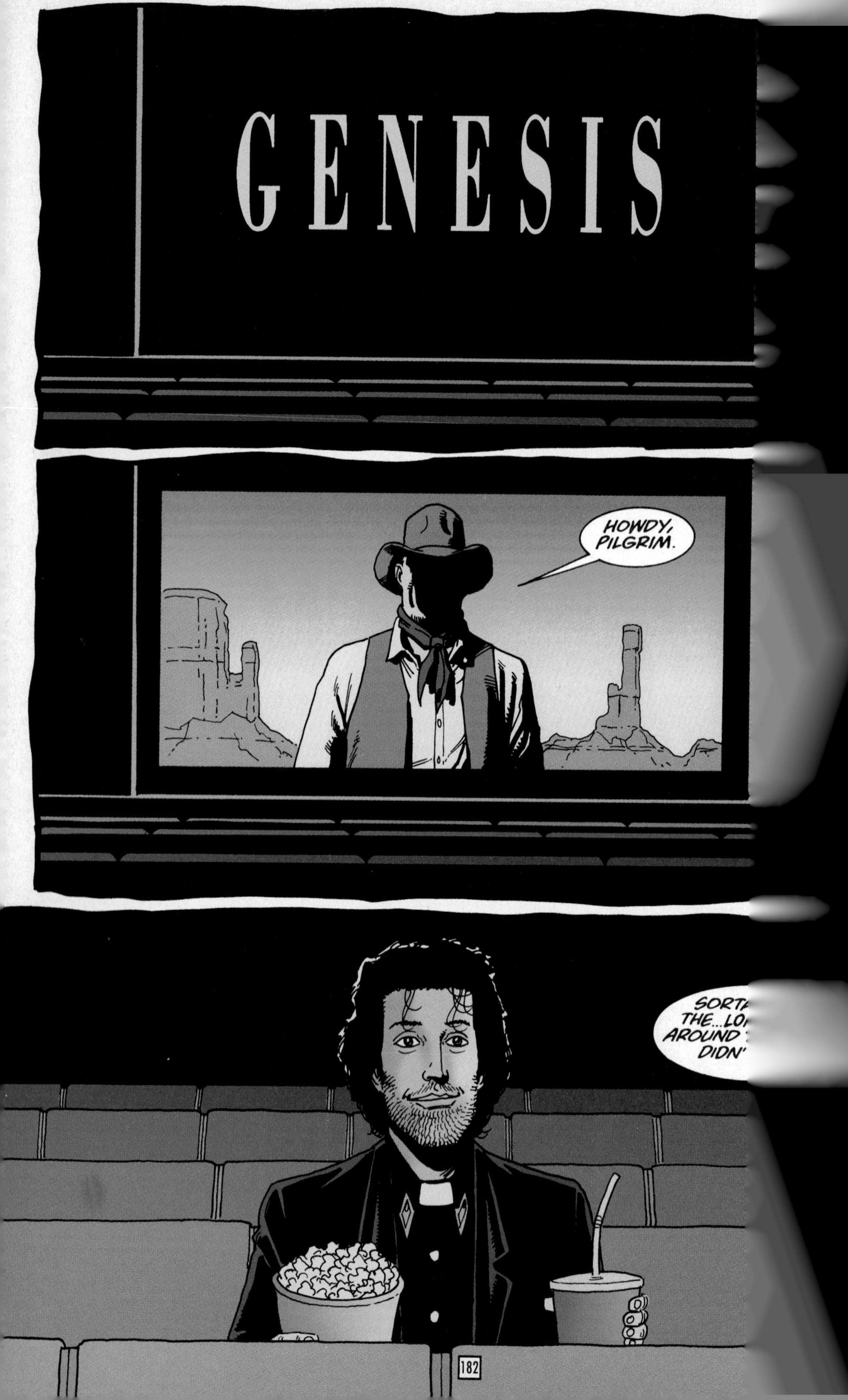
GENESIS
HOWDY, PILGRIM.
SORT THE...LO AROUND DIDN'

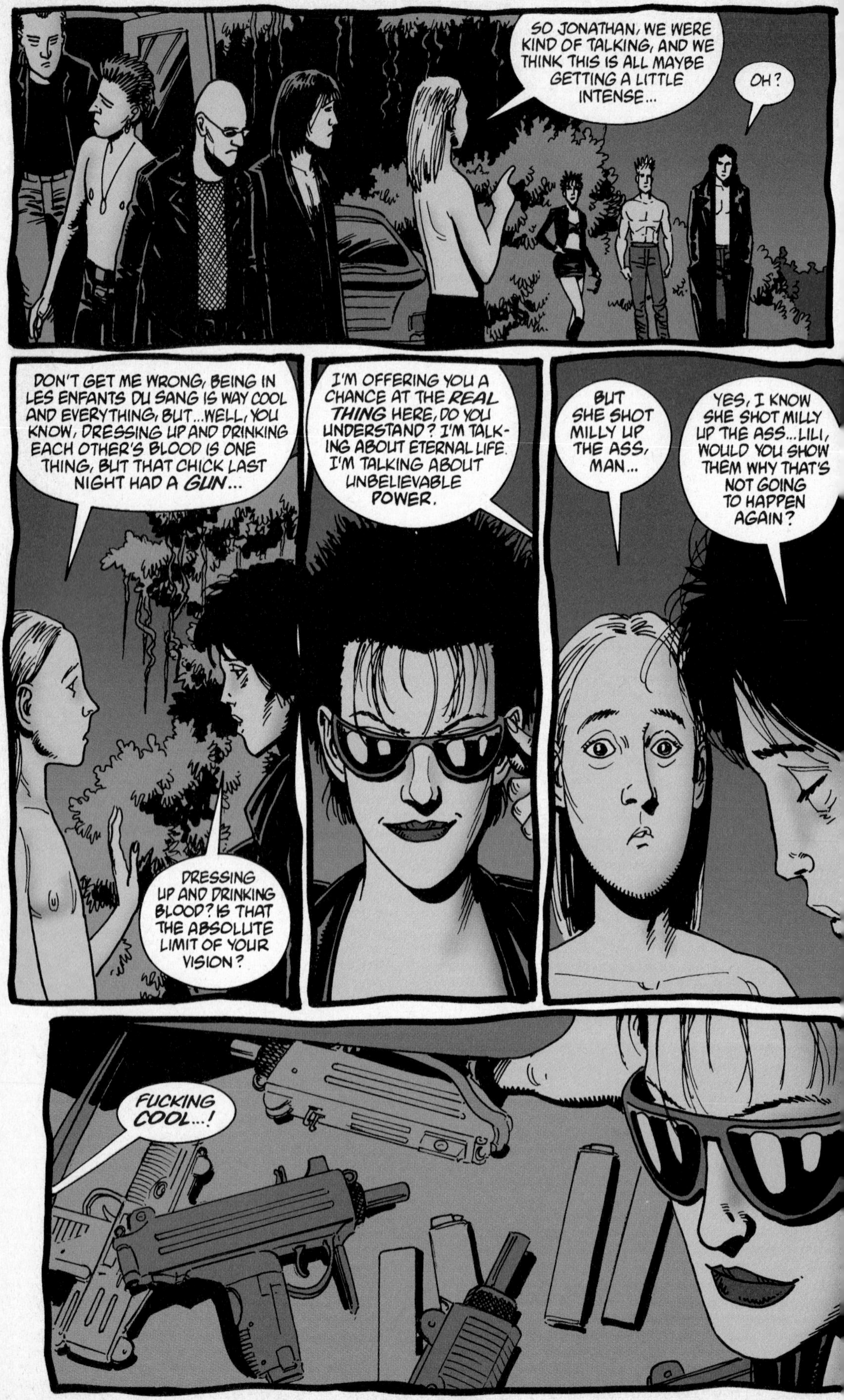
SO JONATHAN, WE WERE KIND OF TALKING, AND WE THINK THIS IS ALL MAYBE GETTING A LITTLE INTENSE...
OH?
DON'T GET ME WRONG, BEING IN LES ENFANTS DU SANG IS WAY COOL AND EVERYTHING, BUT...WELL, YOU KNOW, DRESSING UP AND DRINKING EACH OTHER'S BLOOD IS ONE THING, BUT THAT CHICK LAST NIGHT HAD A GUN...
DRESSING UP AND DRINKING BLOOD? IS THAT THE ABSOLUTE LIMIT OF YOUR VISION?
I'M OFFERING YOU A CHANCE AT THE REAL THING HERE, DO YOU UNDERSTAND? I'M TALKING ABOUT ETERNAL LIFE. I'M TALKING ABOUT UNBELIEVABLE POWER.
BUT SHE SHOT MILLY UP THE ASS, MAN...
YES, I KNOW SHE SHOT MILLY UP THE ASS...LILI, WOULD YOU SHOW THEM WHY THAT'S NOT GOING TO HAPPEN AGAIN?
FUCKING COOL...!

DON'T PLAY WITH THEM. ANYONE DIS-CHARGING A ROUND AND BLOWING OUR COVER IS GOING TO GET THE NEXT ONE IN HIS FACE.

THE THING I DON'T UNDER-STAND IS THIS *MINISTER*... I MEAN WHY WOULD AN UNDEAD GUY HANG WITH SOMEONE LIKE THAT?

DOES IT MATTER? WHAT'S HE GOING TO DO, BEAT US TO DEATH WITH HIS BIBLE?

WELL, FUCK IT. SO LONG AS I GET MY SHOT AT CASSIDY.

WHAT IS IT WITH YOU AND HIM ANY-WAY, MAKO?

A LITTLE MATTER OF SOMEONE ONCE HAVING GOT THE SHIT KICKED OUT OF HIM...

I WASN'T READY.

WHATEVER. ANY SCORES TO BE SETTLED, WAIT 'TIL *AFTER* HE'S GIVEN US WHAT WE WANT.

NOW, THESE PEOPLE ARE AN UN-KNOWN QUANTITY. THE WOMAN IN PARTICULAR IS *VERY GOOD*, WHICH IS WHY THE REST OF LES ENFANTS ARE GOING IN FIRST. UZIS OR NOT, THEY'RE NO USE AS ANYTHING BUT CANNON FODDER.

BUT THEY WILL ALLOW US A CLEAR RUN AT CASSIDY...

YES, BUT HE'S TOTALLY UNKILLABLE -- AND EVEN IF HE WASN'T, WE NEED HIM ALIVE TO DO WHAT WE SAY...

HOW EXACTLY ARE YOU GOING TO TAKE HIM, JONATHAN?

YOU LEAVE THAT TO ME.

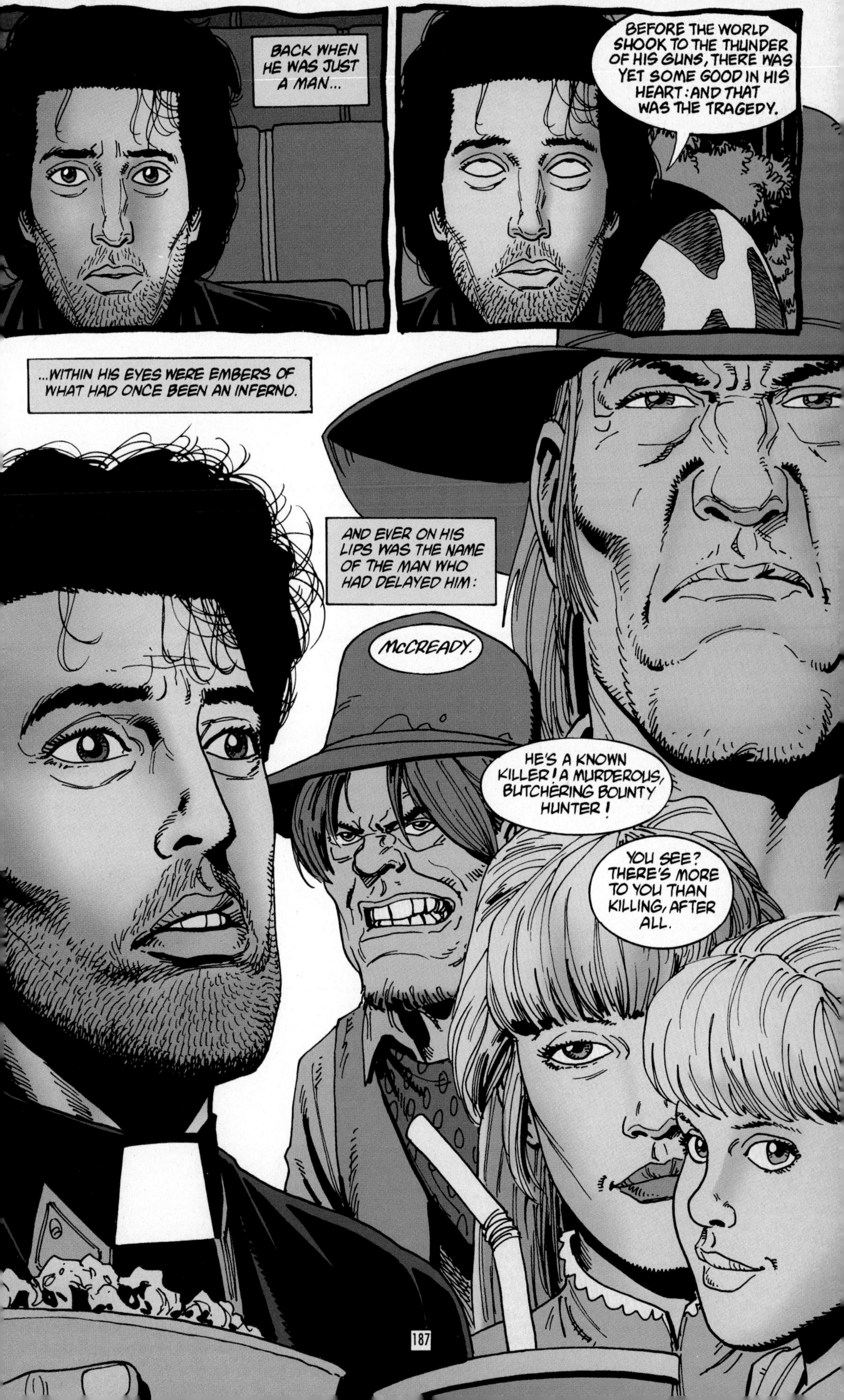
BACK WHEN HE WAS JUST A MAN...
BEFORE THE WORLD SHOOK TO THE THUNDER OF HIS GUNS, THERE WAS YET SOME GOOD IN HIS HEART: AND THAT WAS THE TRAGEDY.
...WITHIN HIS EYES WERE EMBERS OF WHAT HAD ONCE BEEN AN INFERNO.
AND EVER ON HIS LIPS WAS THE NAME OF THE MAN WHO HAD DELAYED HIM:
McCREADY.
HE'S A KNOWN KILLER! A MURDEROUS, BUTCHERING BOUNTY HUNTER!
YOU SEE? THERE'S MORE TO YOU THAN KILLING, AFTER ALL.

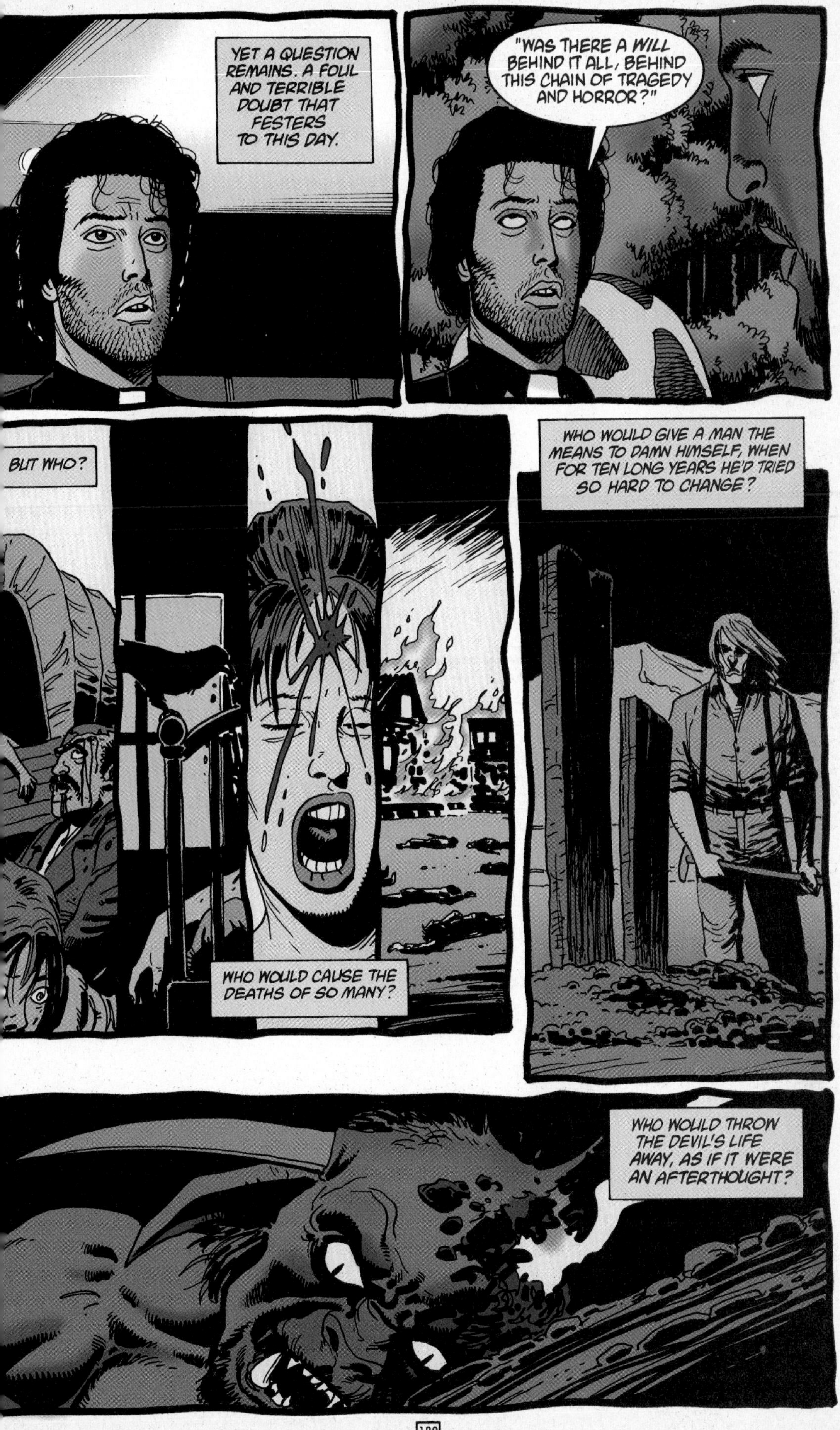
YET A QUESTION REMAINS. A FOUL AND TERRIBLE DOUBT THAT FESTERS TO THIS DAY.
"WAS THERE A WILL BEHIND IT ALL, BEHIND THIS CHAIN OF TRAGEDY AND HORROR?"
BUT WHO?
WHO WOULD CAUSE THE DEATHS OF SO MANY?
WHO WOULD GIVE A MAN THE MEANS TO DAMN HIMSELF, WHEN FOR TEN LONG YEARS HE'D TRIED SO HARD TO CHANGE?
WHO WOULD THROW THE DEVIL'S LIFE AWAY, AS IF IT WERE AN AFTERTHOUGHT?

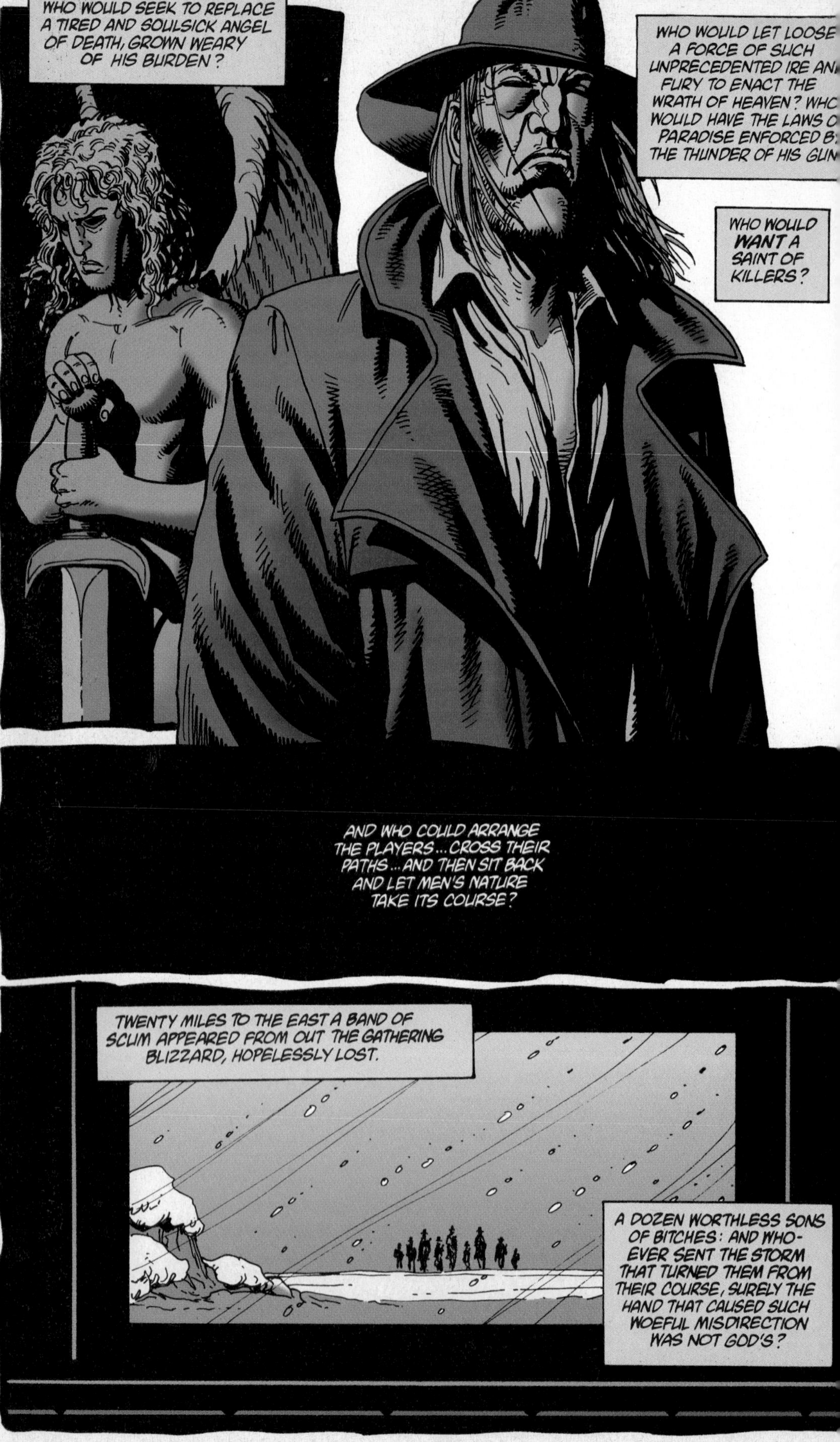
WHO WOULD SEEK TO REPLACE A TIRED AND SOULSICK ANGEL OF DEATH, GROWN WEARY OF HIS BURDEN?
WHO WOULD LET LOOSE A FORCE OF SUCH UNPRECEDENTED IRE AN FURY TO ENACT THE WRATH OF HEAVEN? WH WOULD HAVE THE LAWS PARADISE ENFORCED B THE THUNDER OF HIS GU
WHO WOULD *WANT* A SAINT OF KILLERS?
AND WHO COULD ARRANGE THE PLAYERS... CROSS THEIR PATHS... AND THEN SIT BACK AND LET MEN'S NATURE TAKE ITS COURSE?
TWENTY MILES TO THE EAST A BAND OF SCUM APPEARED FROM OUT THE GATHERING BLIZZARD, HOPELESSLY LOST.
A DOZEN WORTHLESS SONS OF BITCHES: AND WHO-EVER SENT THE STORM THAT TURNED THEM FROM THEIR COURSE, SURELY THE HAND THAT CAUSED SUCH WOEFUL MISDIRECTION WAS NOT GOD'S?

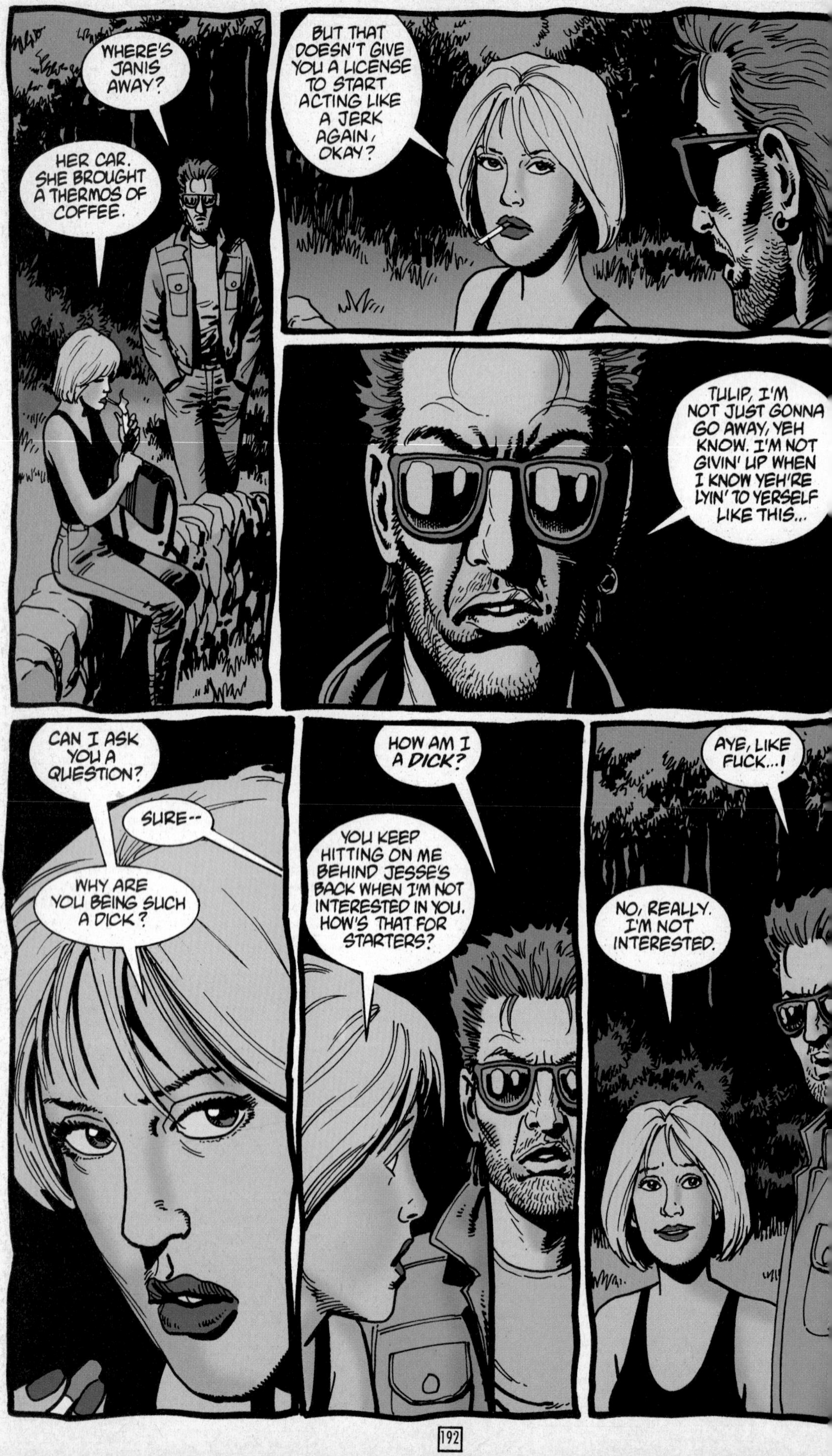

WHERE'S JANIS AWAY?
HER CAR. SHE BROUGHT A THERMOS OF COFFEE.
BUT THAT DOESN'T GIVE YOU A LICENSE TO START ACTING LIKE A JERK AGAIN, OKAY?
TULIP, I'M NOT JUST GONNA GO AWAY, YEH KNOW. I'M NOT GIVIN' UP WHEN I KNOW YEH'RE LYIN' TO YERSELF LIKE THIS...
CAN I ASK YOU A QUESTION?
SURE--
WHY ARE YOU BEING SUCH A DICK?
HOW AM I A DICK?
YOU KEEP HITTING ON ME BEHIND JESSE'S BACK WHEN I'M NOT INTERESTED IN YOU. HOW'S THAT FOR STARTERS?
AYE, LIKE FUCK...!
NO, REALLY. I'M NOT INTERESTED.

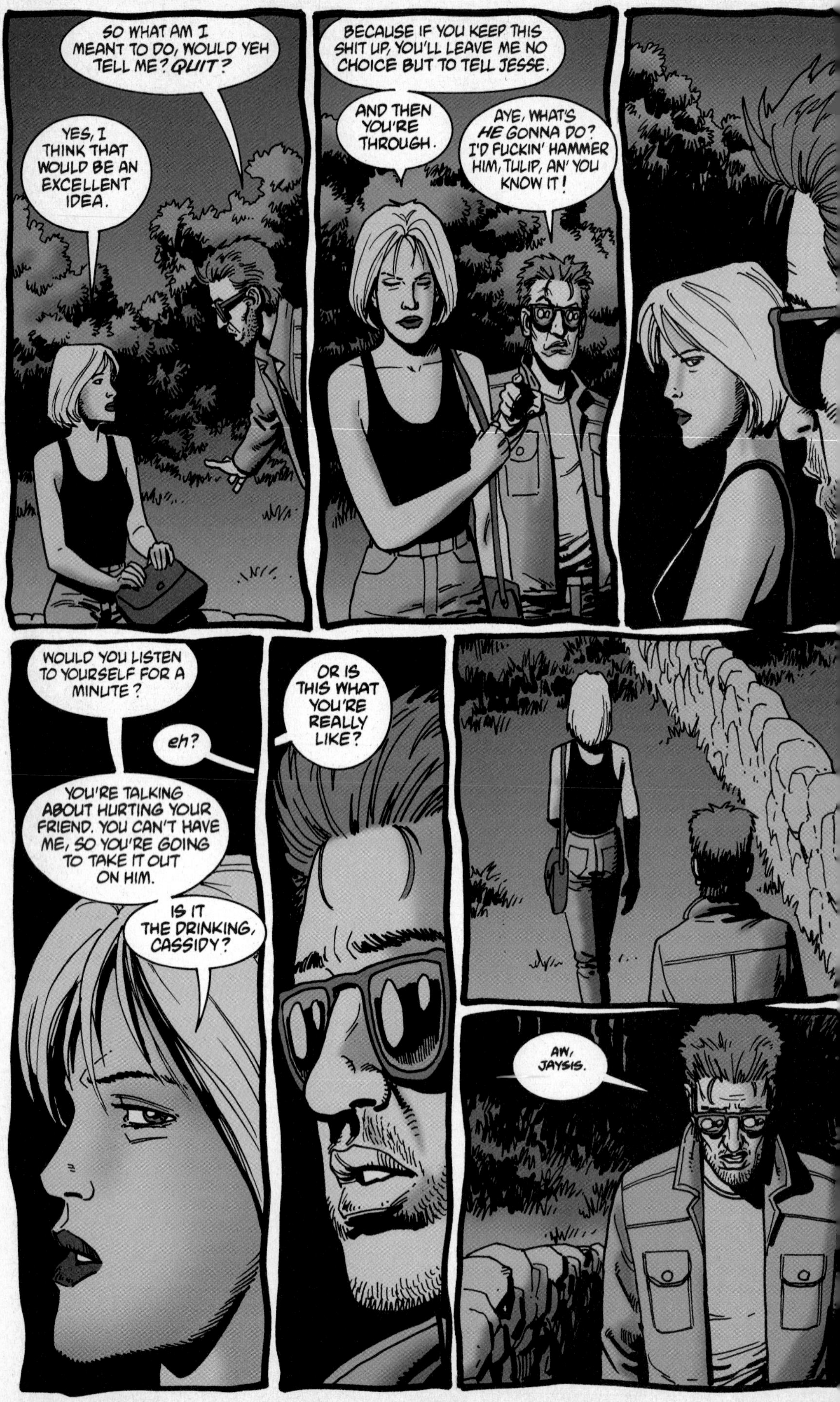
SO WHAT AM I MEANT TO DO, WOULD YEH TELL ME? *QUIT?*
YES, I THINK THAT WOULD BE AN EXCELLENT IDEA.
BECAUSE IF YOU KEEP THIS SHIT UP, YOU'LL LEAVE ME NO CHOICE BUT TO TELL JESSE.
AND THEN YOU'RE THROUGH.
AYE, WHAT'S *HE* GONNA DO? I'D FUCKIN' HAMMER HIM, TULIP, AN' YOU KNOW IT!
WOULD YOU LISTEN TO YOURSELF FOR A MINUTE?
eh?
YOU'RE TALKING ABOUT HURTING YOUR FRIEND. YOU CAN'T HAVE ME, SO YOU'RE GOING TO TAKE IT OUT ON HIM.
IS IT THE DRINKING, CASSIDY?
OR IS THIS WHAT YOU'RE REALLY LIKE?
AW, JAYSIS.

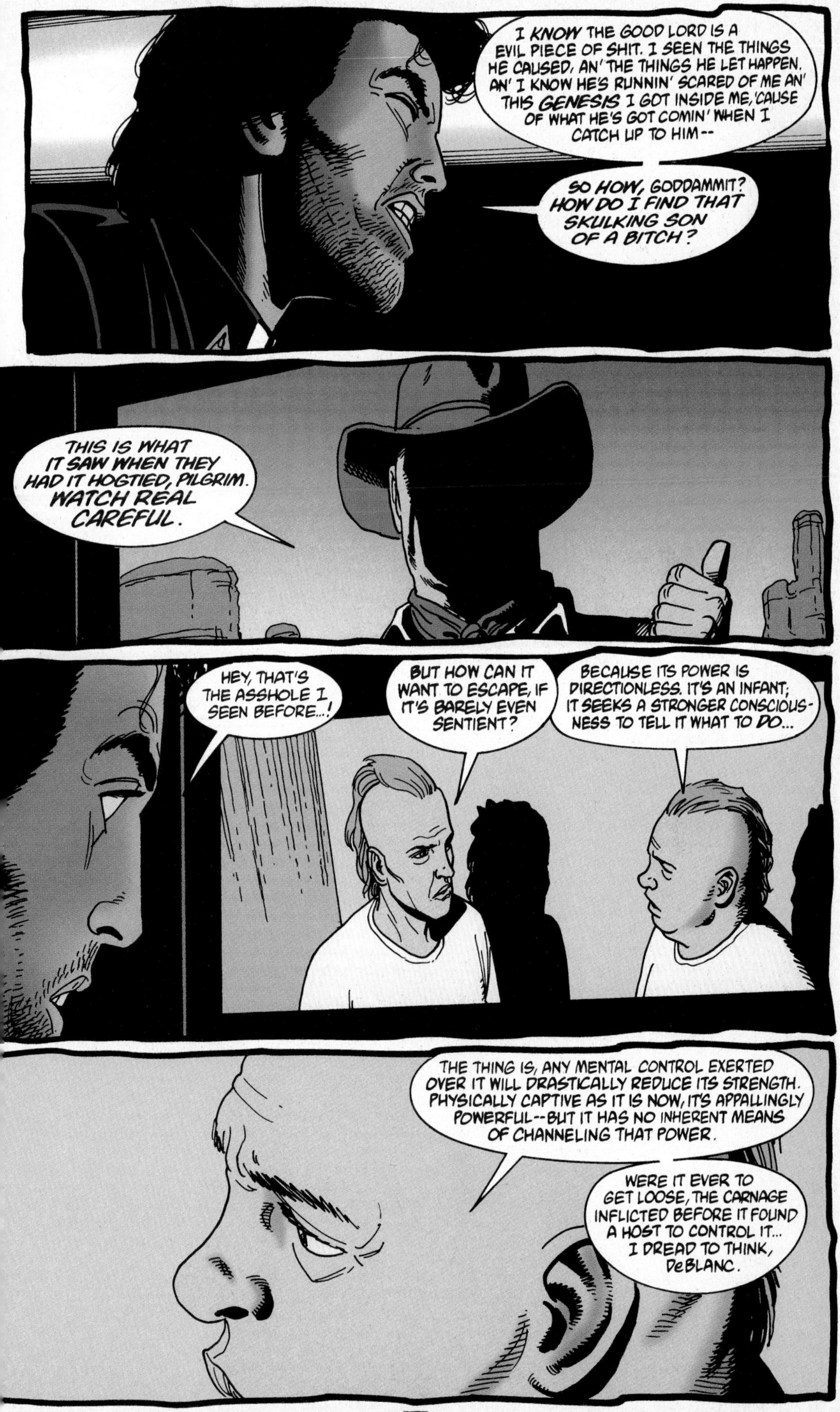
I KNOW THE GOOD LORD IS A EVIL PIECE OF SHIT. I SEEN THE THINGS HE CAUSED, AN' THE THINGS HE LET HAPPEN. AN' I KNOW HE'S RUNNIN' SCARED OF ME AN' THIS GENESIS I GOT INSIDE ME, 'CAUSE OF WHAT HE'S GOT COMIN' WHEN I CATCH UP TO HIM--
SO HOW, GODDAMMIT? HOW DO I FIND THAT SKULKING SON OF A BITCH?
THIS IS WHAT IT SAW WHEN THEY HAD IT HOGTIED, PILGRIM. WATCH REAL CAREFUL.
HEY, THAT'S THE ASSHOLE I SEEN BEFORE...!
BUT HOW CAN IT WANT TO ESCAPE, IF IT'S BARELY EVEN SENTIENT?
BECAUSE ITS POWER IS DIRECTIONLESS. IT'S AN INFANT; IT SEEKS A STRONGER CONSCIOUS-NESS TO TELL IT WHAT TO DO...
THE THING IS, ANY MENTAL CONTROL EXERTED OVER IT WILL DRASTICALLY REDUCE ITS STRENGTH. PHYSICALLY CAPTIVE AS IT IS NOW, IT'S APPALLINGLY POWERFUL--BUT IT HAS NO INHERENT MEANS OF CHANNELING THAT POWER.
WERE IT EVER TO GET LOOSE, THE CARNAGE INFLICTED BEFORE IT FOUND A HOST TO CONTROL IT... I DREAD TO THINK, DeBLANC.

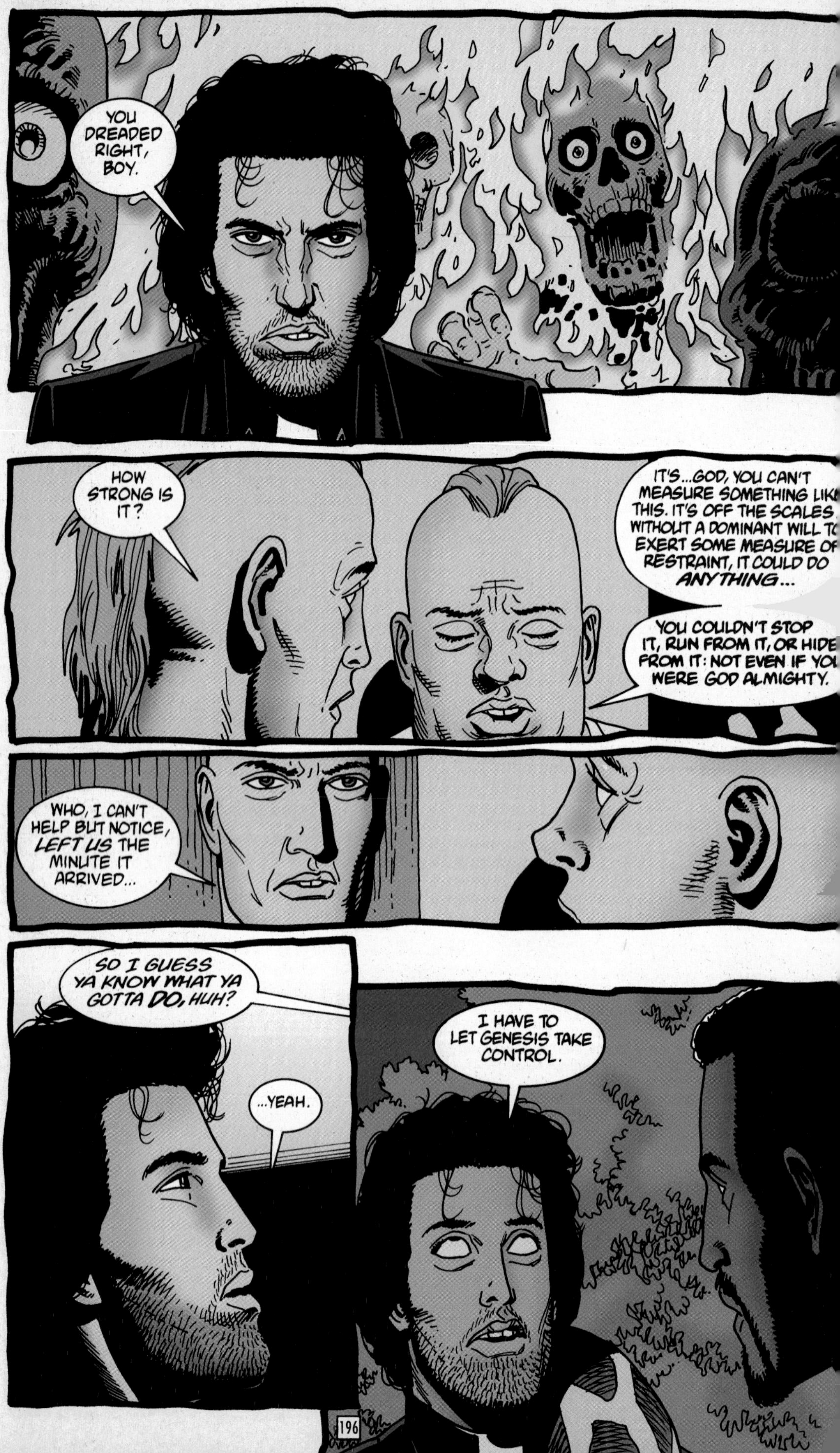
YOU DREADED RIGHT, BOY.
HOW STRONG IS IT?
IT'S...GOD, YOU CAN'T MEASURE SOMETHING LIK THIS. IT'S OFF THE SCALES WITHOUT A DOMINANT WILL T EXERT SOME MEASURE OF RESTRAINT, IT COULD DO ANYTHING...
YOU COULDN'T STOP IT, RUN FROM IT, OR HIDE FROM IT: NOT EVEN IF YO WERE GOD ALMIGHTY.
WHO, I CAN'T HELP BUT NOTICE, LEFT US THE MINUTE IT ARRIVED...
SO I GUESS YA KNOW WHAT YA GOTTA DO, HUH?
...YEAH.
I HAVE TO LET GENESIS TAKE CONTROL.

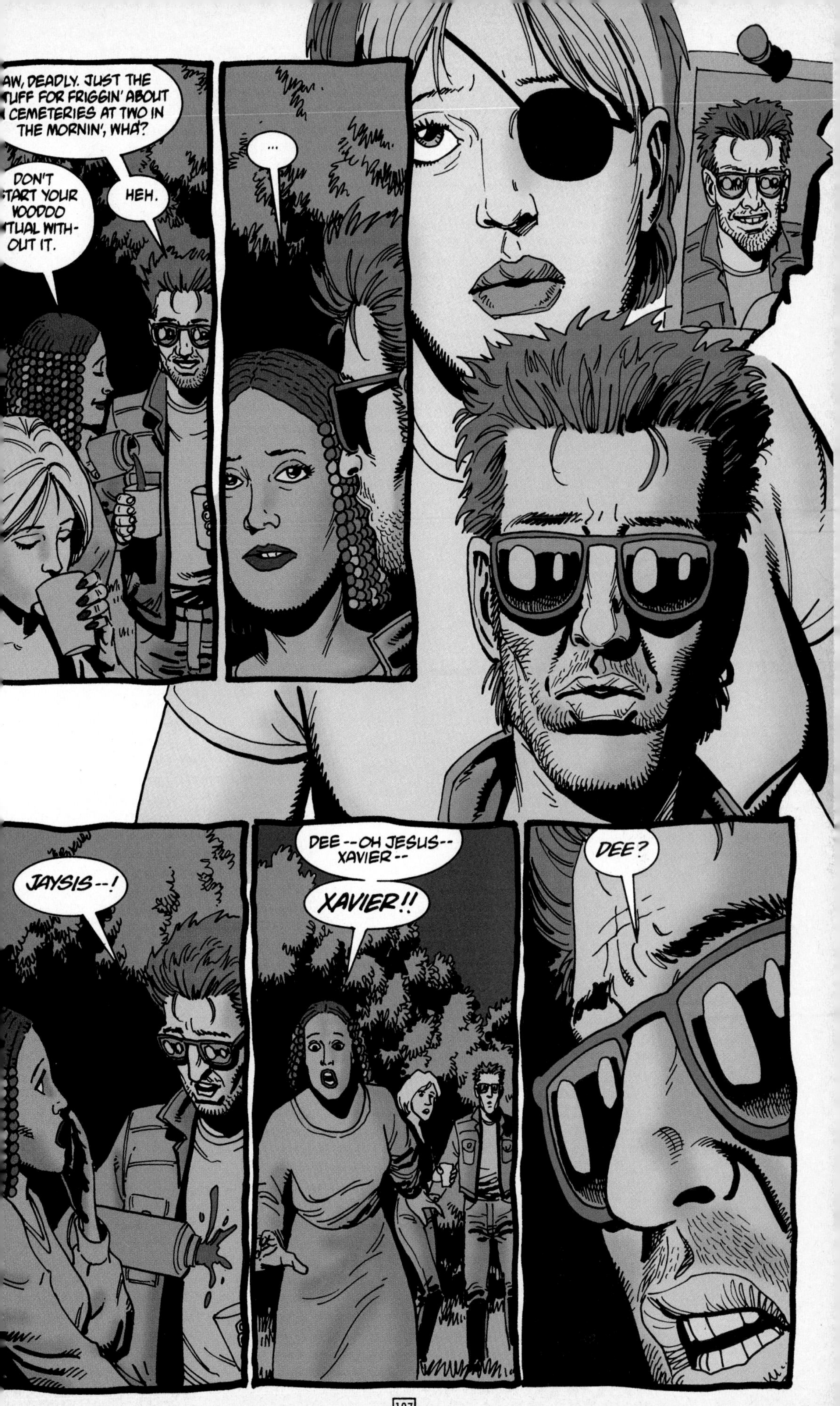
AW, DEADLY. JUST THE
TUFF FOR FRIGGIN' ABOUT
CEMETERIES AT TWO IN
THE MORNIN', WHA'?
HEH.
DON'T
TART YOUR
VOODOO
TUAL WITH-
OUT IT.
...
JAYSIS--!
DEE--OH JESUS--
XAVIER--
XAVIER!!
DEE?

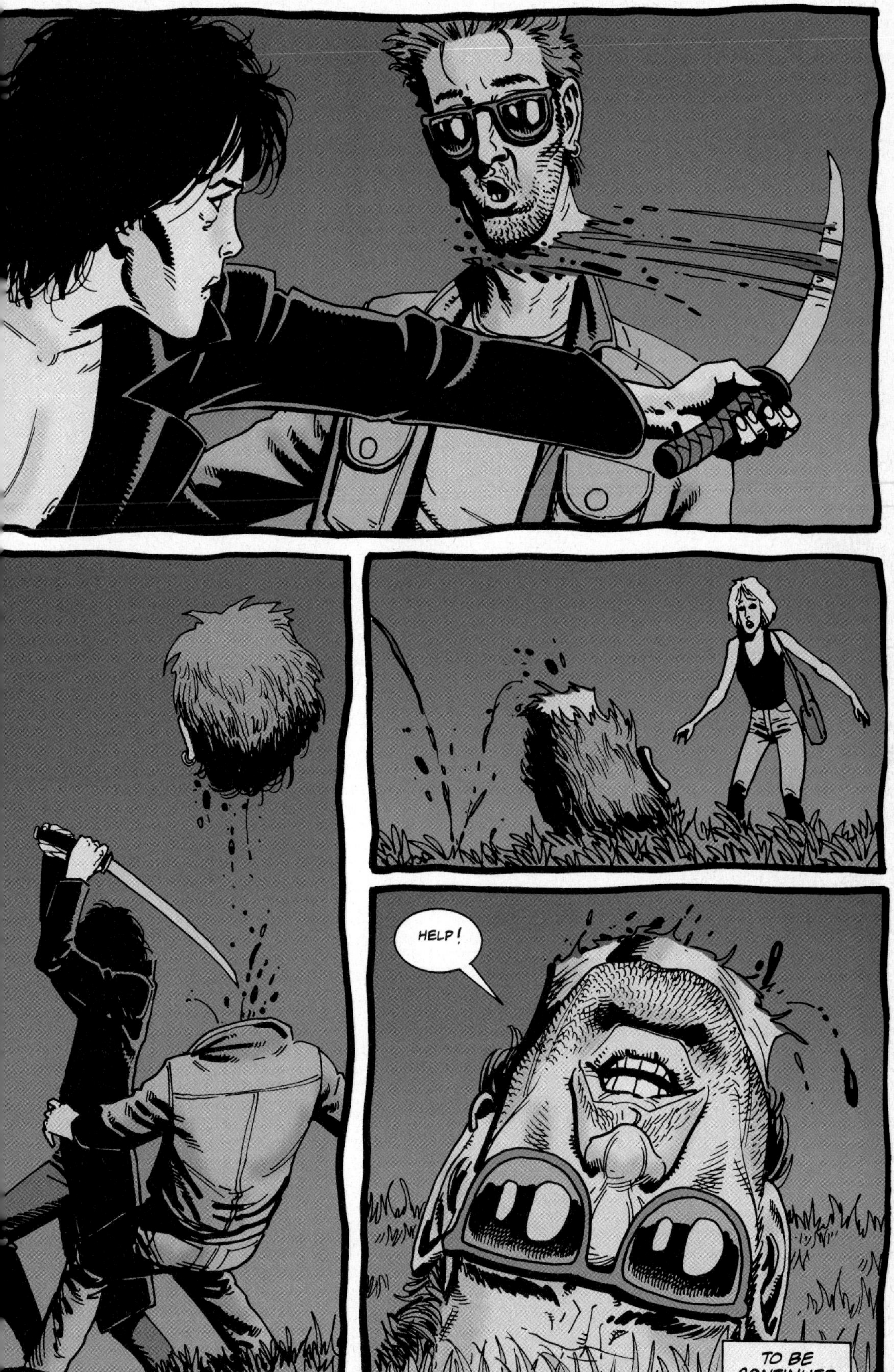
HELP!
TO BE CONTINUED

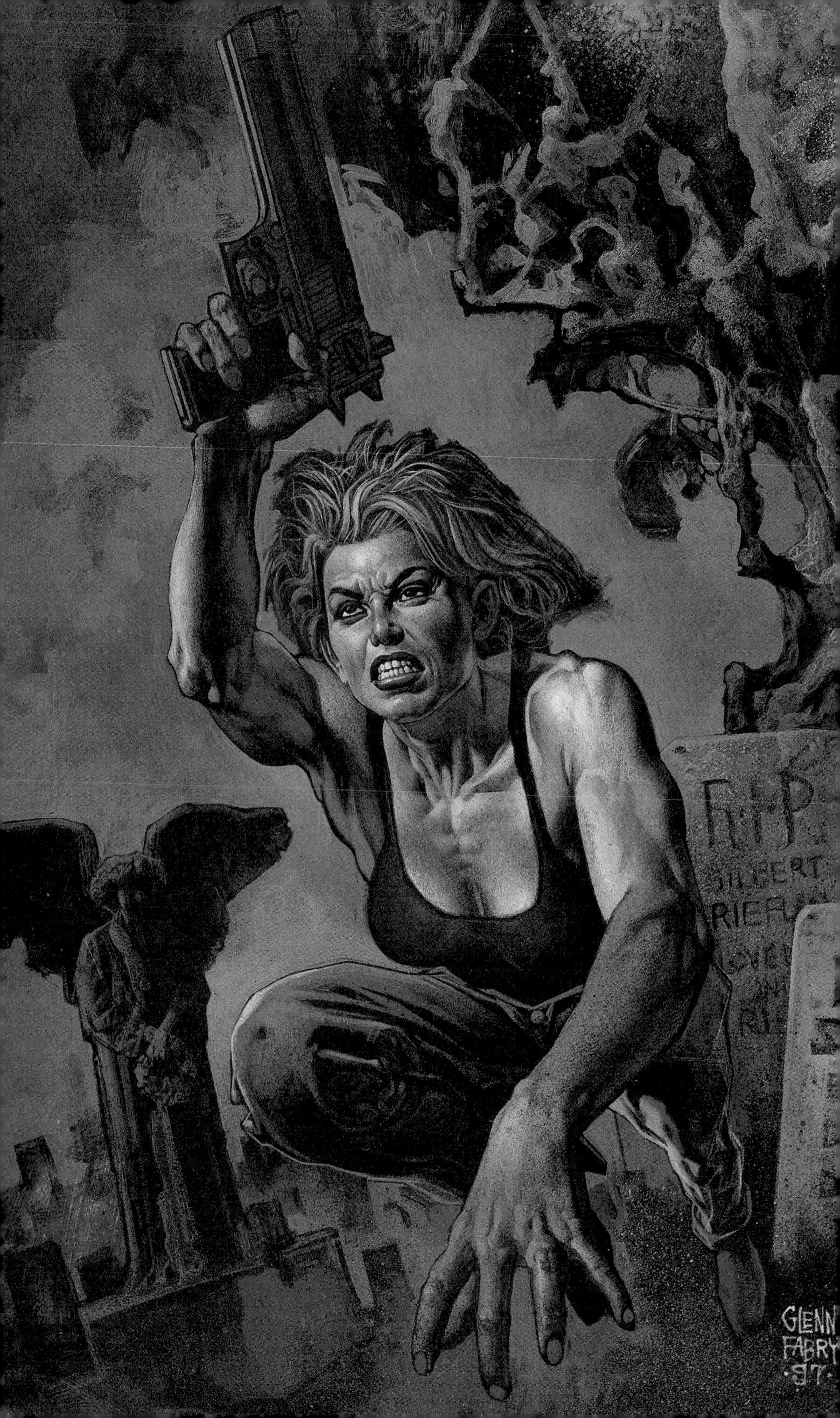
GLENN
FABRY
·97·

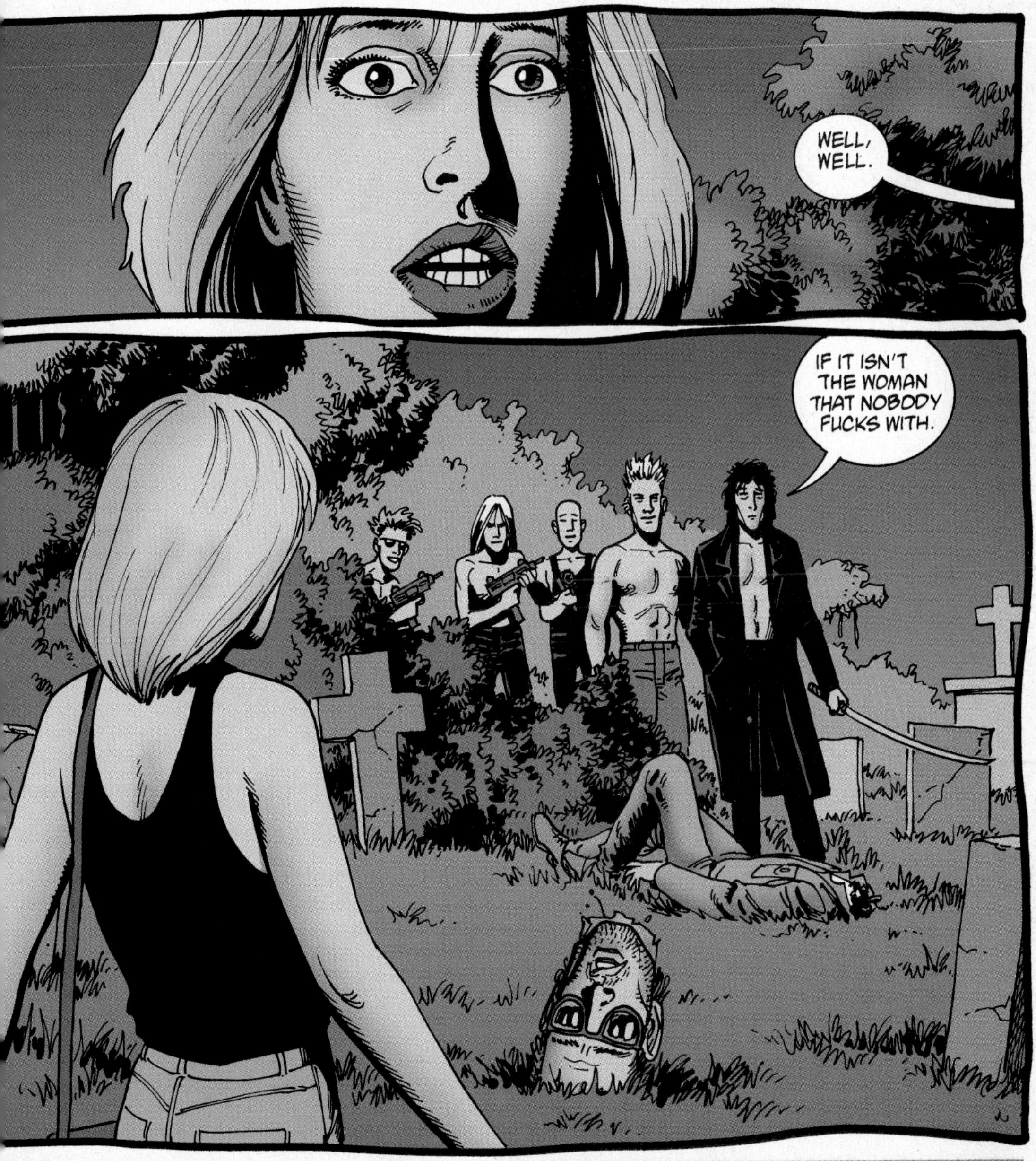
WELL, WELL.
IF IT ISN'T THE WOMAN THAT NOBODY FUCKS WITH.

PRICE OF NIGHT

GARTH ENNIS - Writer STEVE DILLON - Artist
PAMELA RAMBO - Colorist
CLEM ROBINS - Letterer AXEL ALONSO - Editor

PREACHER created by GARTH ENNIS and STEVE DILLON

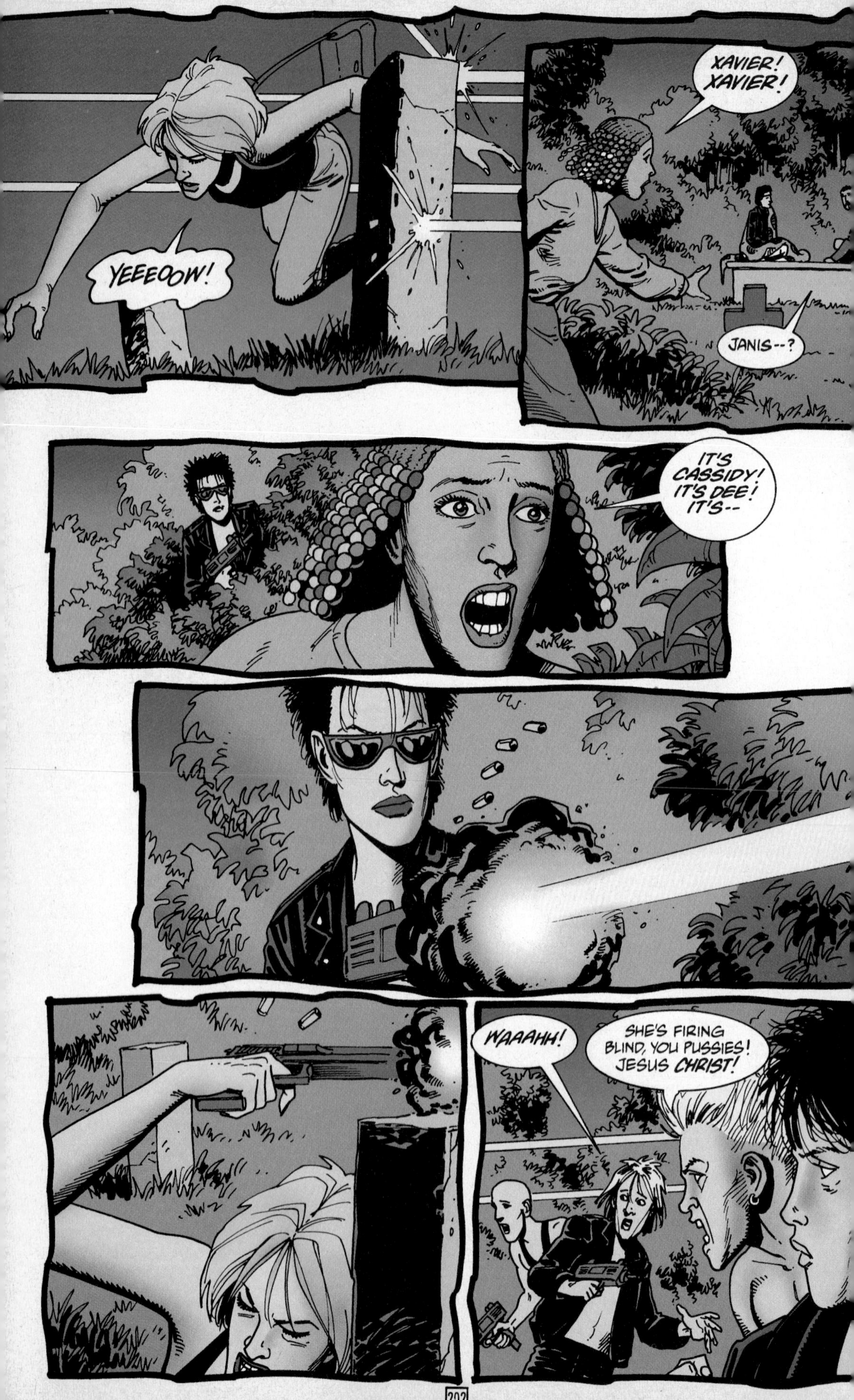
YEEEOOW!
XAVIER! XAVIER!
JANIS--?
IT'S CASSIDY! IT'S DEE! IT'S--
WAAAHH!
SHE'S FIRING BLIND, YOU PUSSIES! JESUS CHRIST!

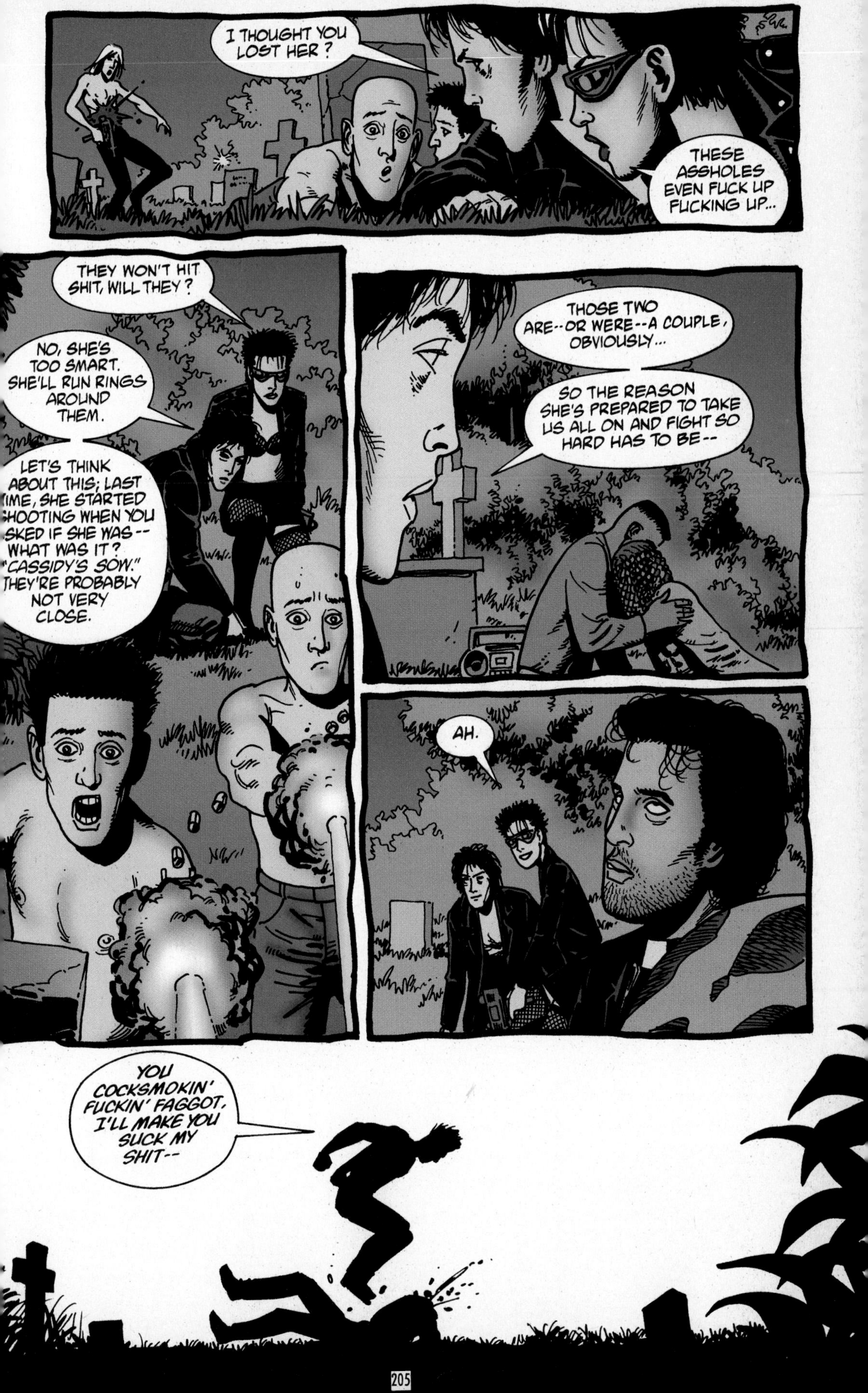
I THOUGHT YOU LOST HER ?
THESE ASSHOLES EVEN FUCK UP FUCKING UP...
THEY WON'T HIT SHIT, WILL THEY ?
NO, SHE'S TOO SMART. SHE'LL RUN RINGS AROUND THEM.
LET'S THINK ABOUT THIS; LAST TIME, SHE STARTED SHOOTING WHEN YOU ASKED IF SHE WAS -- WHAT WAS IT ? "CASSIDY'S SOW." THEY'RE PROBABLY NOT VERY CLOSE.
THOSE TWO ARE--OR WERE--A COUPLE, OBVIOUSLY...
SO THE REASON SHE'S PREPARED TO TAKE US ALL ON AND FIGHT SO HARD HAS TO BE --
AH.
YOU COCKSMOKIN' FUCKIN' FAGGOT, I'LL MAKE YOU SUCK MY SHIT--

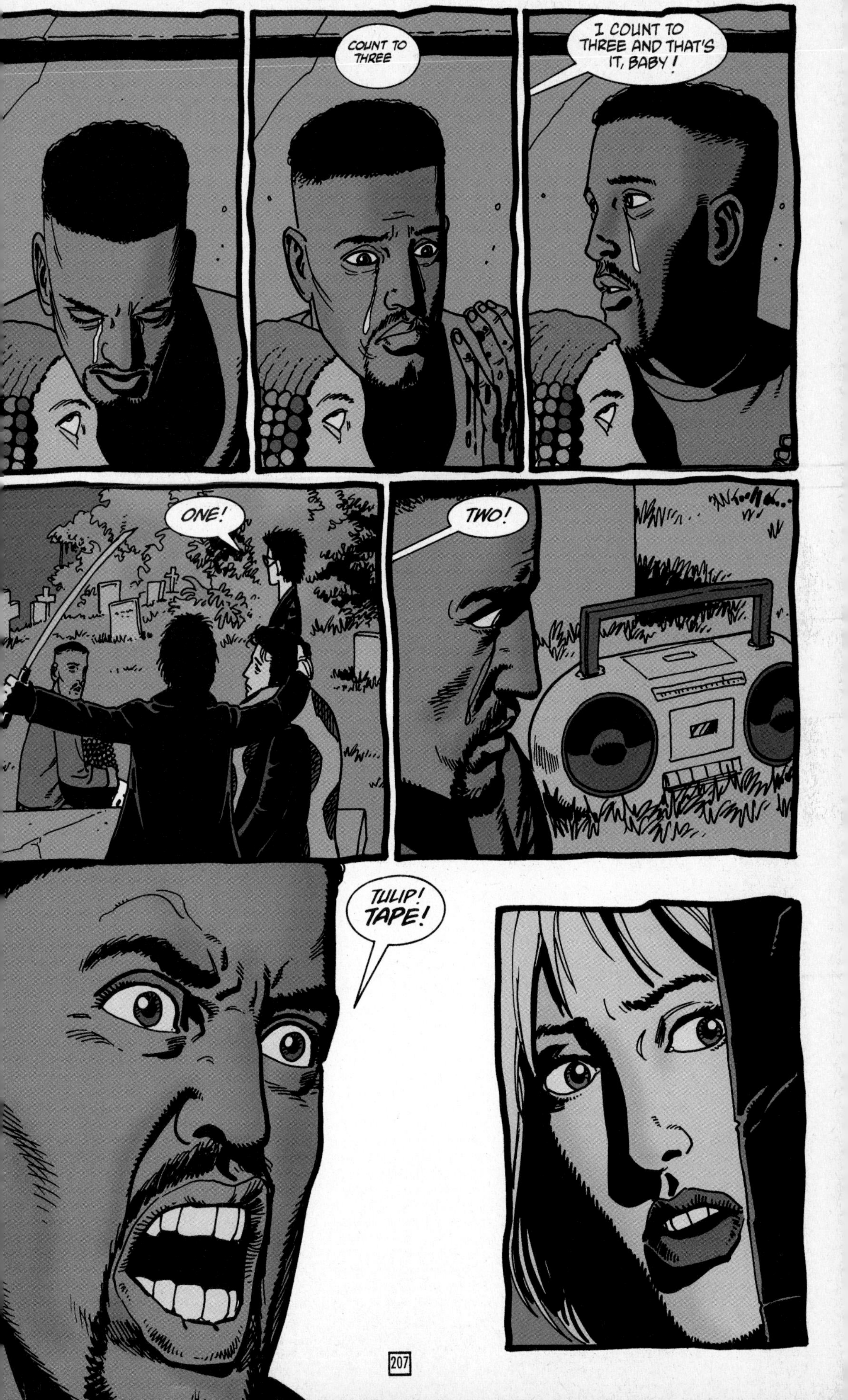
COUNT TO THREE
I COUNT TO THREE AND THAT'S IT, BABY!
ONE!
TWO!
TULIP! TAPE!

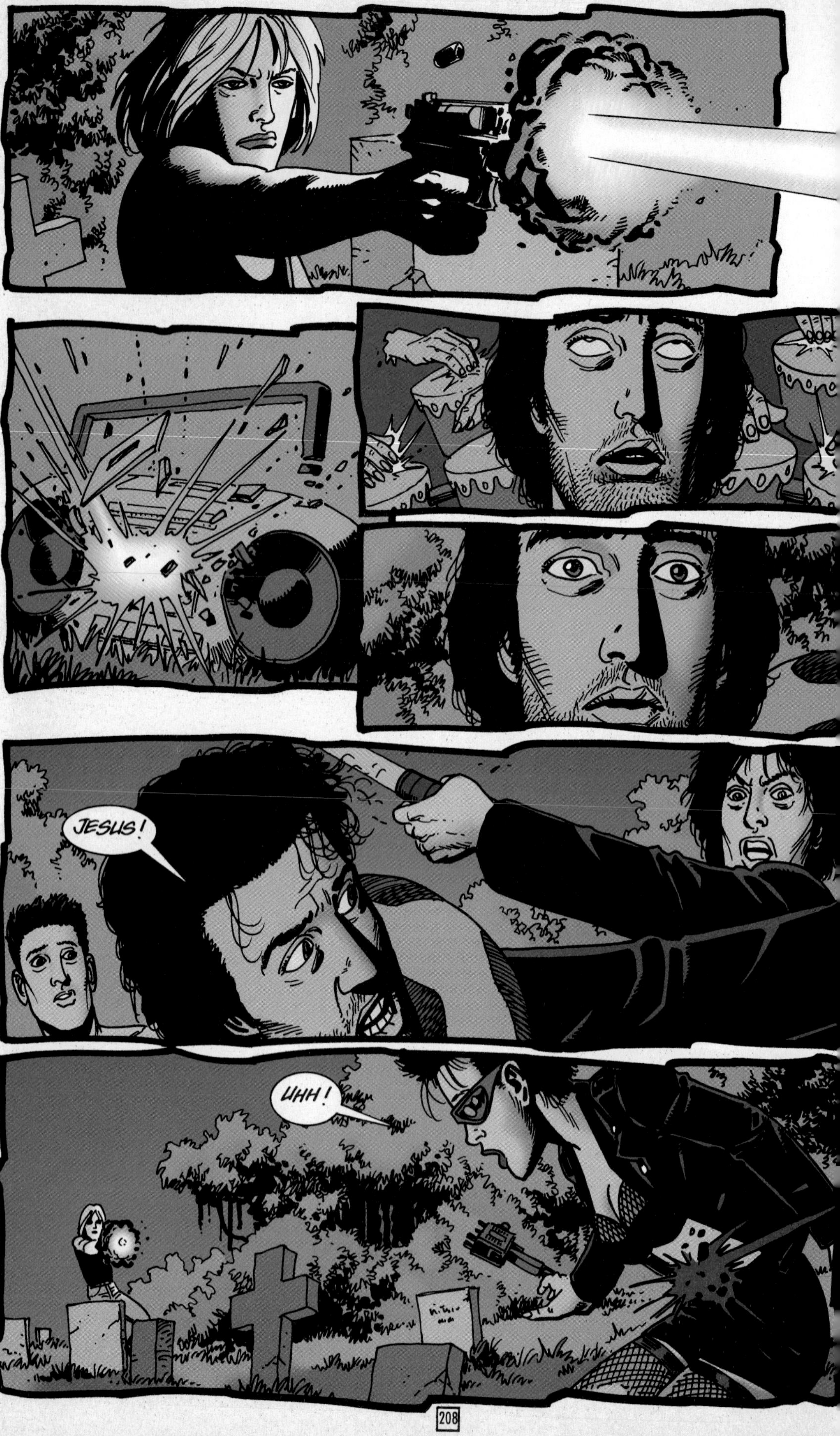
JESUS!
UHH!

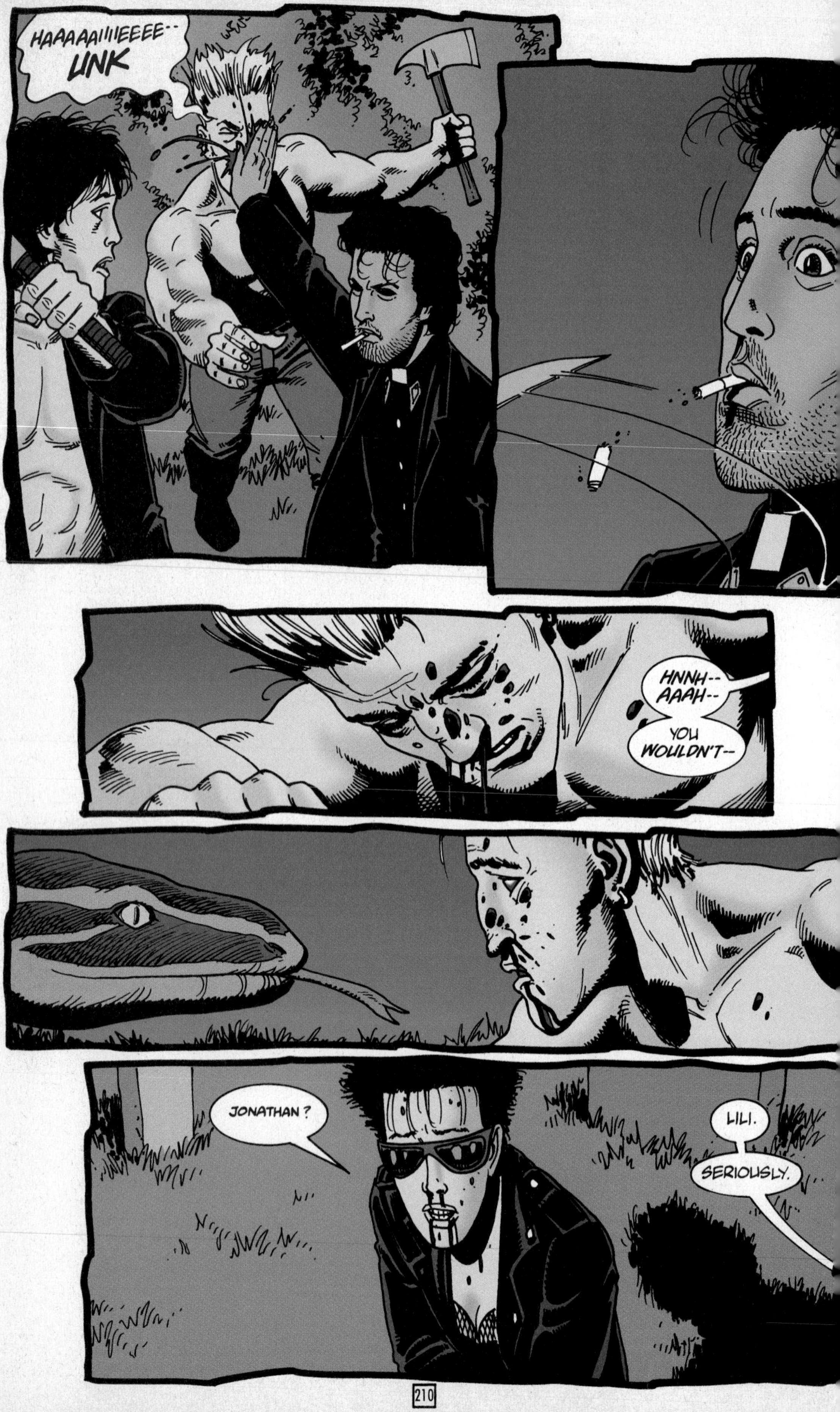
HAAAAAIIIIEEEE--
UNK
HNNH--
AAAH--
YOU WOULDN'T--
JONATHAN?
LILI.
SERIOUSLY.

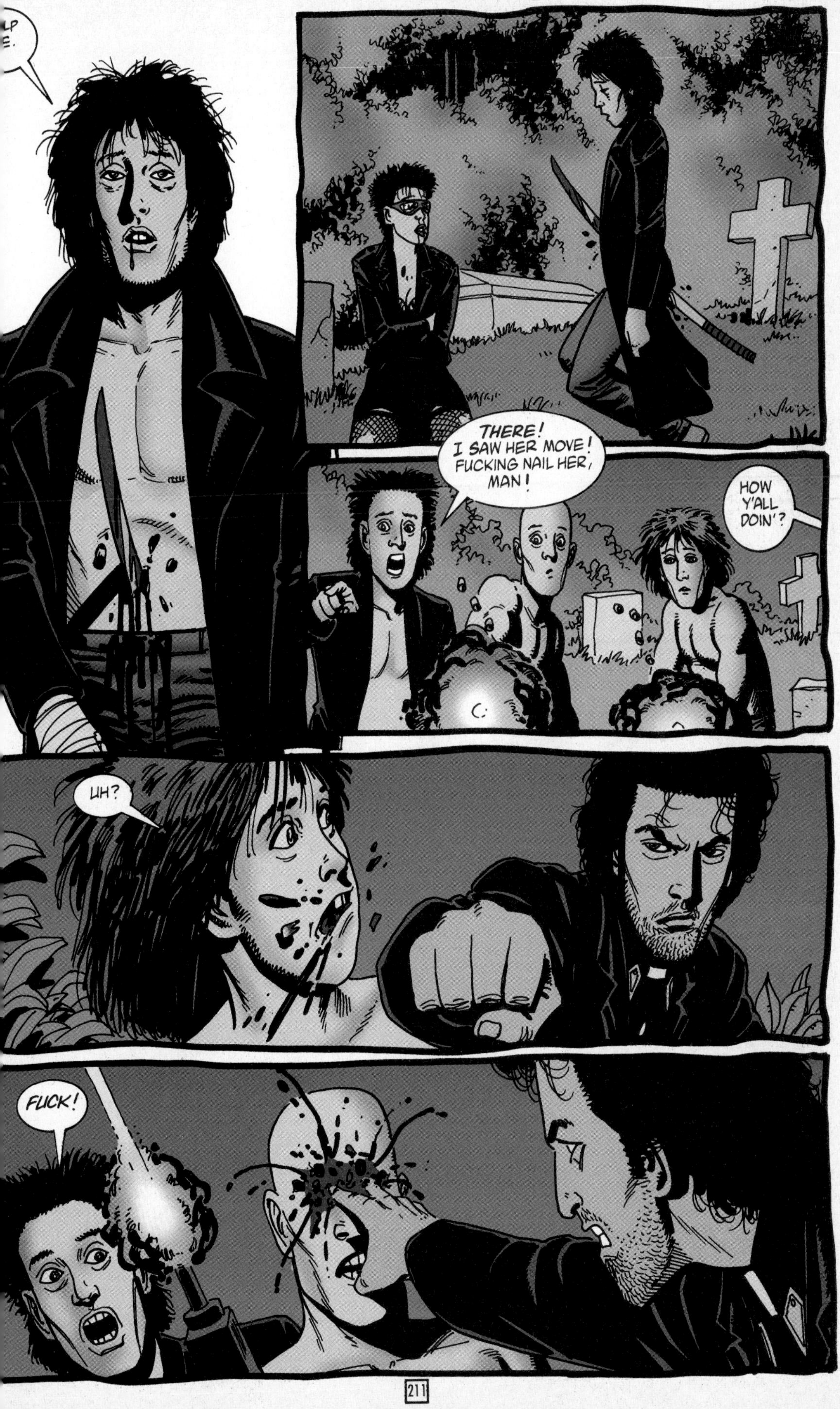
THERE! I SAW HER MOVE! FUCKING NAIL HER, MAN!
HOW Y'ALL DOIN'?
UH?
FUCK!

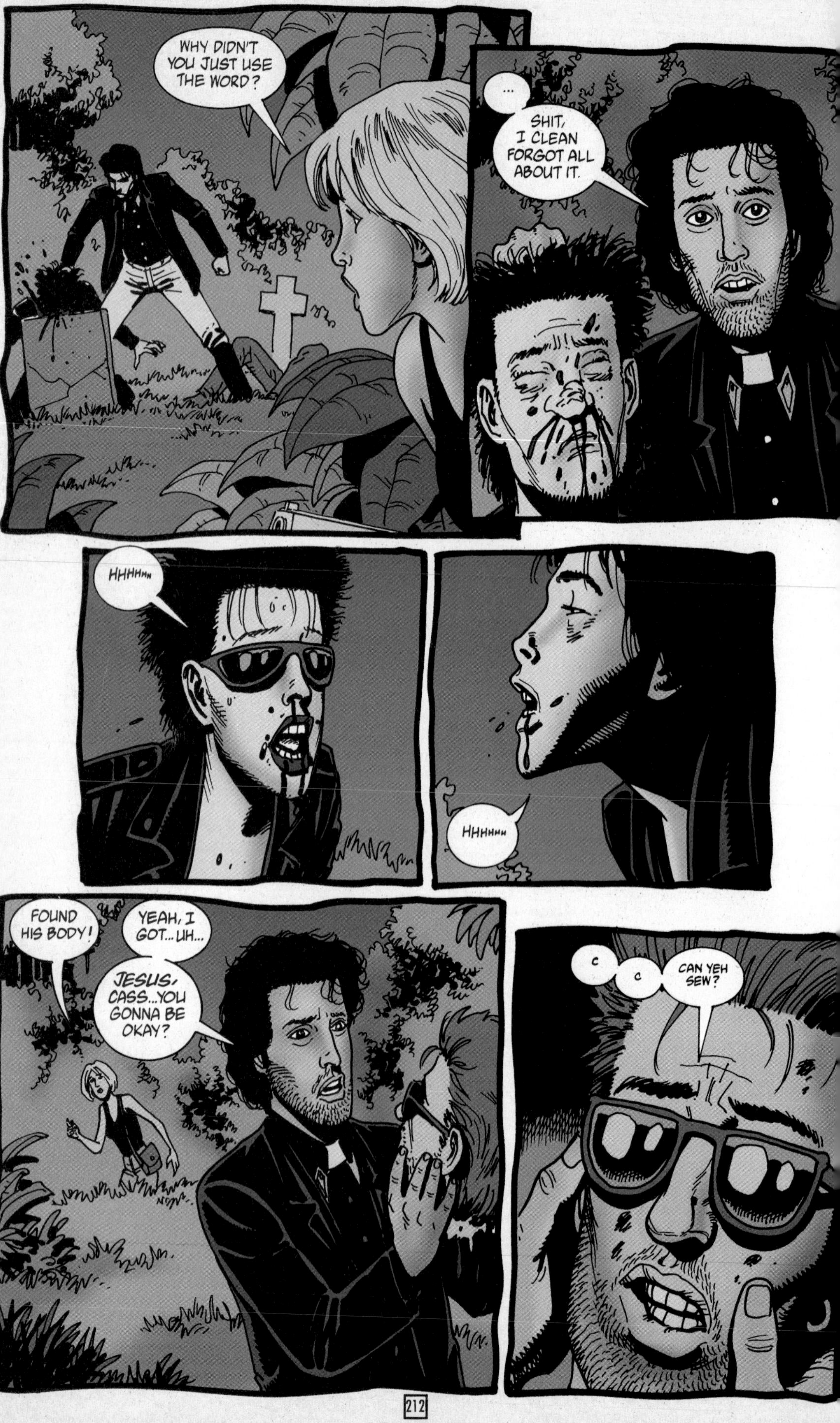

WHY DIDN'T YOU JUST USE THE WORD?
...
SHIT, I CLEAN FORGOT ALL ABOUT IT.
HHHHHH
HHHHHH
FOUND HIS BODY!
YEAH, I GOT... UH...
JESUS, CASS... YOU GONNA BE OKAY?
C
C
CAN YEH SEW?

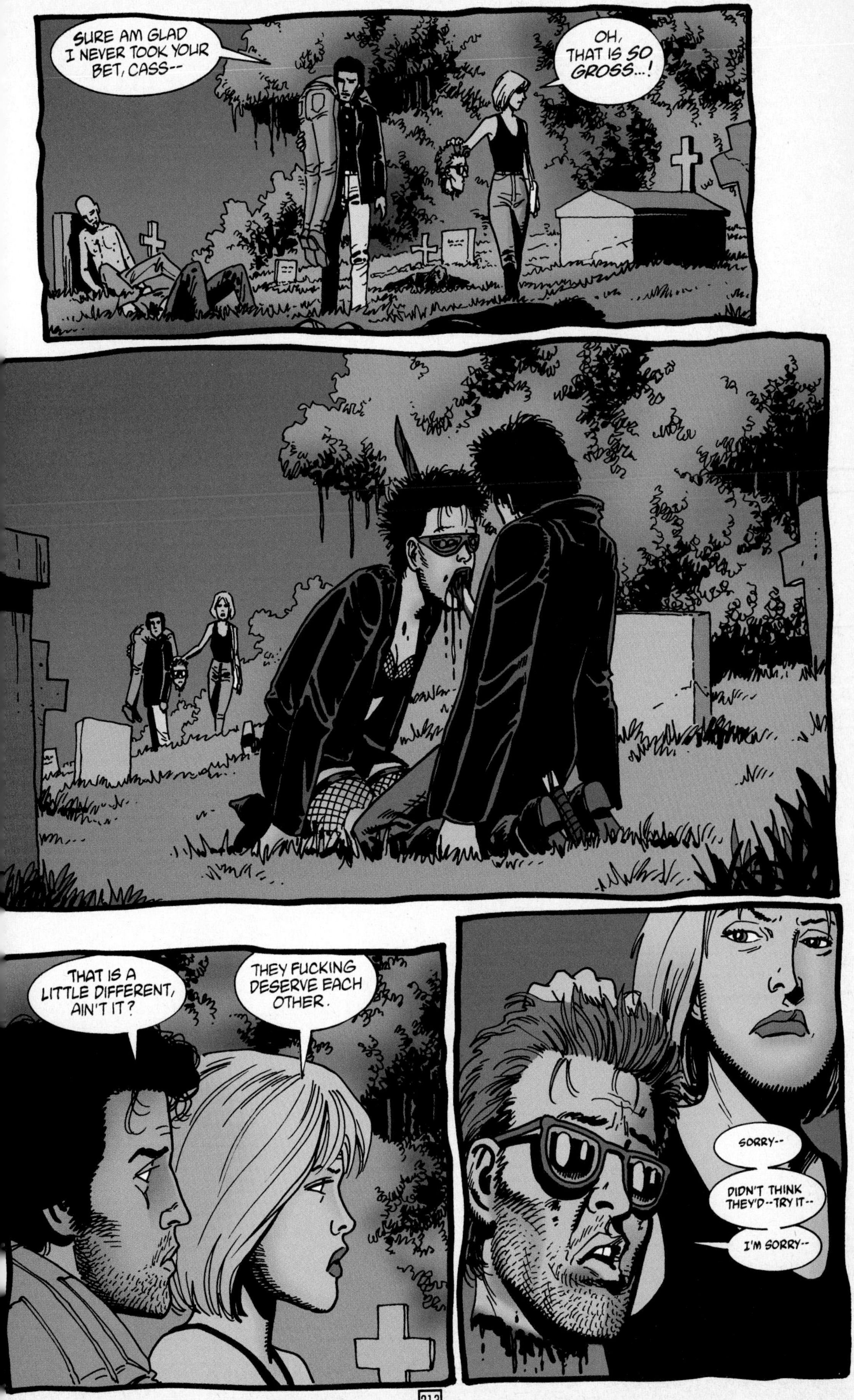
SURE AM GLAD I NEVER TOOK YOUR BET, CASS--
OH, THAT IS SO GROSS...!
THAT IS A LITTLE DIFFERENT, AIN'T IT?
THEY FUCKING DESERVE EACH OTHER.
SORRY--
DIDN'T THINK THEY'D--TRY IT--
I'M SORRY--

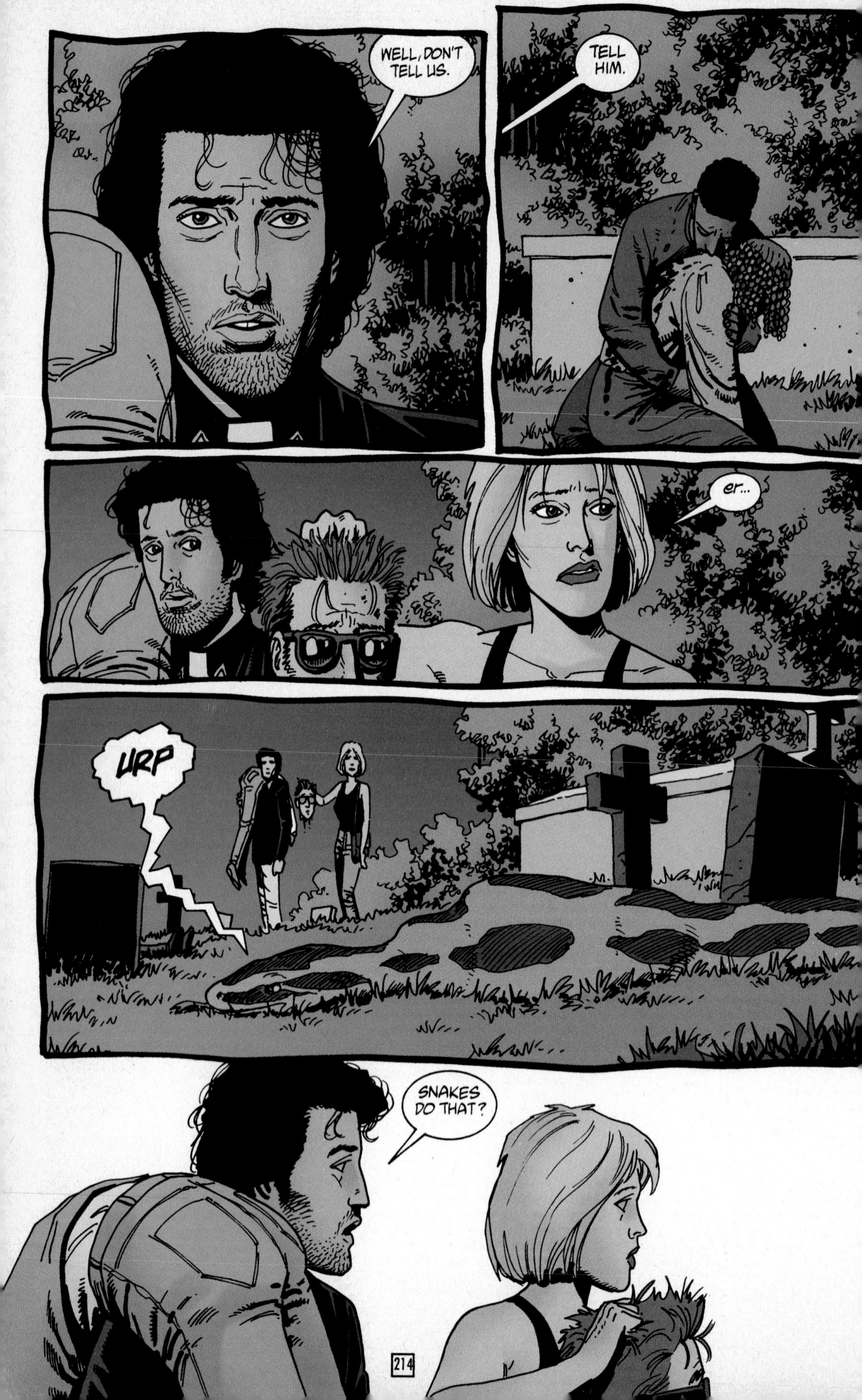
WELL, DON'T TELL US.
TELL HIM.
er...
URP
SNAKES DO THAT?

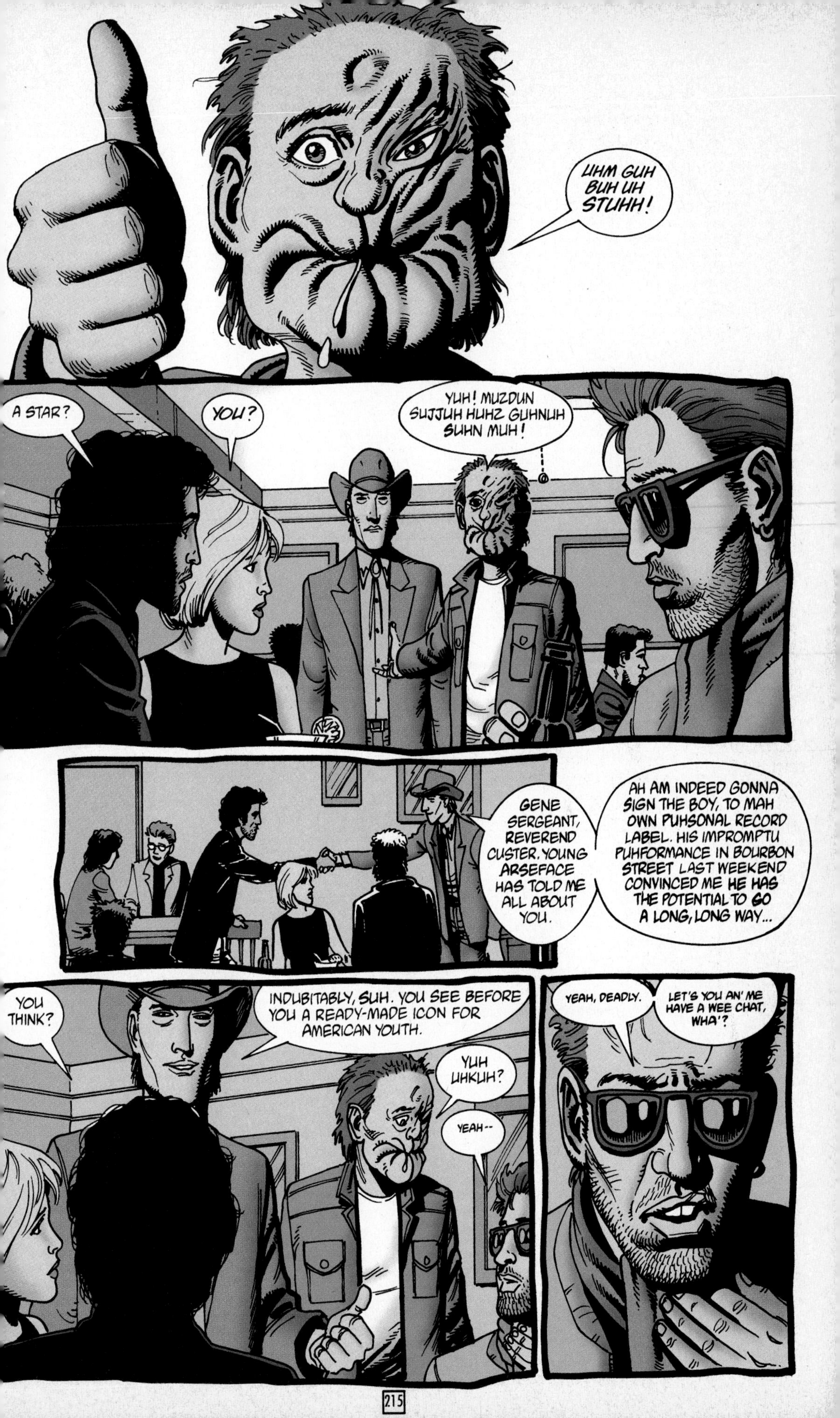
UHM GUH BUH UH STUHH!
A STAR?
YOU?
YUH! MUZDUN SUJJUH HUHZ GUHNUH SUHN MUH!
GENE SERGEANT, REVEREND CUSTER. YOUNG ARSEFACE HAS TOLD ME ALL ABOUT YOU.
AH AM INDEED GONNA SIGN THE BOY, TO MAH OWN PUHSONAL RECORD LABEL. HIS IMPROMPTU PUHFORMANCE IN BOURBON STREET LAST WEEKEND CONVINCED ME HE HAS THE POTENTIAL TO GO A LONG, LONG WAY...
YOU THINK?
INDUBITABLY, SUH. YOU SEE BEFORE YOU A READY-MADE ICON FOR AMERICAN YOUTH.
YUH UHKUH?
YEAH--
YEAH, DEADLY.
LET'S YOU AN' ME HAVE A WEE CHAT, WHA'?

WHAT HAPPENED BETWEEN THE TWO OF YOU, ANYWAY?

A WOMAN.

CASSIDY SEDUCED HER WHILE I WAS OUT OF TOWN.

SEDUCED...THEY WERE DRUNK AND THEY FUCKED. IT WAS HER AS MUCH AS HIM.

THE POINT IS, WE WERE SO CLOSE I TRUSTED HIM IMPLICITLY. I NEVER *IMAGINED* HE WOULD DO A THING LIKE THAT, THAT THE THREAT OF IT COULD COME FROM HIS DIRECTION.

HE'S BRILLIANT AT BEING YOUR BEST FRIEND, TULIP. MEN RESPOND TO THAT ROGUEISH FREE SPIRIT OF HIS ON SOME BASIC MALE LEVEL: A COMRADE, A *GOOD MATE*, AS HE HIMSELF WOULD SAY. I DON'T THINK IT'S CALCULATED, I THINK HE'S REALLY LIKE THAT...

BUT THAT'S WHY I'M HAVING THIS CONVERSATION WITH YOU, AND NOT WITH JESSE.

EVERY TIME HE CAME TO TOWN WAS AN OCCASION. I LOVED HIM SO MUCH I LET HIM CLIMB RIGHT INSIDE OF ME, UNTIL I COULDN'T IMAGINE LIFE WITHOUT HIM.

AND THEN HE LET ME DOWN.

YOU THINK THAT'S HOW IT ALWAYS IS WITH HIM?

IT'S JUST CASSIDY, TULIP.

I THINK HE GOES THROUGH LIFE WITHOUT A SENSE OF CONSEQUENCE.

HE DIDN'T CARE THAT LES ENFANTS MIGHT BE DANGEROUS, THAT THEY'D STILL BE OUT TO GET HIM AFTER WHATEVER HAPPENED BEFORE. IT DIDN'T EVEN OCCUR TO HIM.

TOO BAD FOR JANIS, MM?

SHIT HAPPENS IN HIS WAKE.

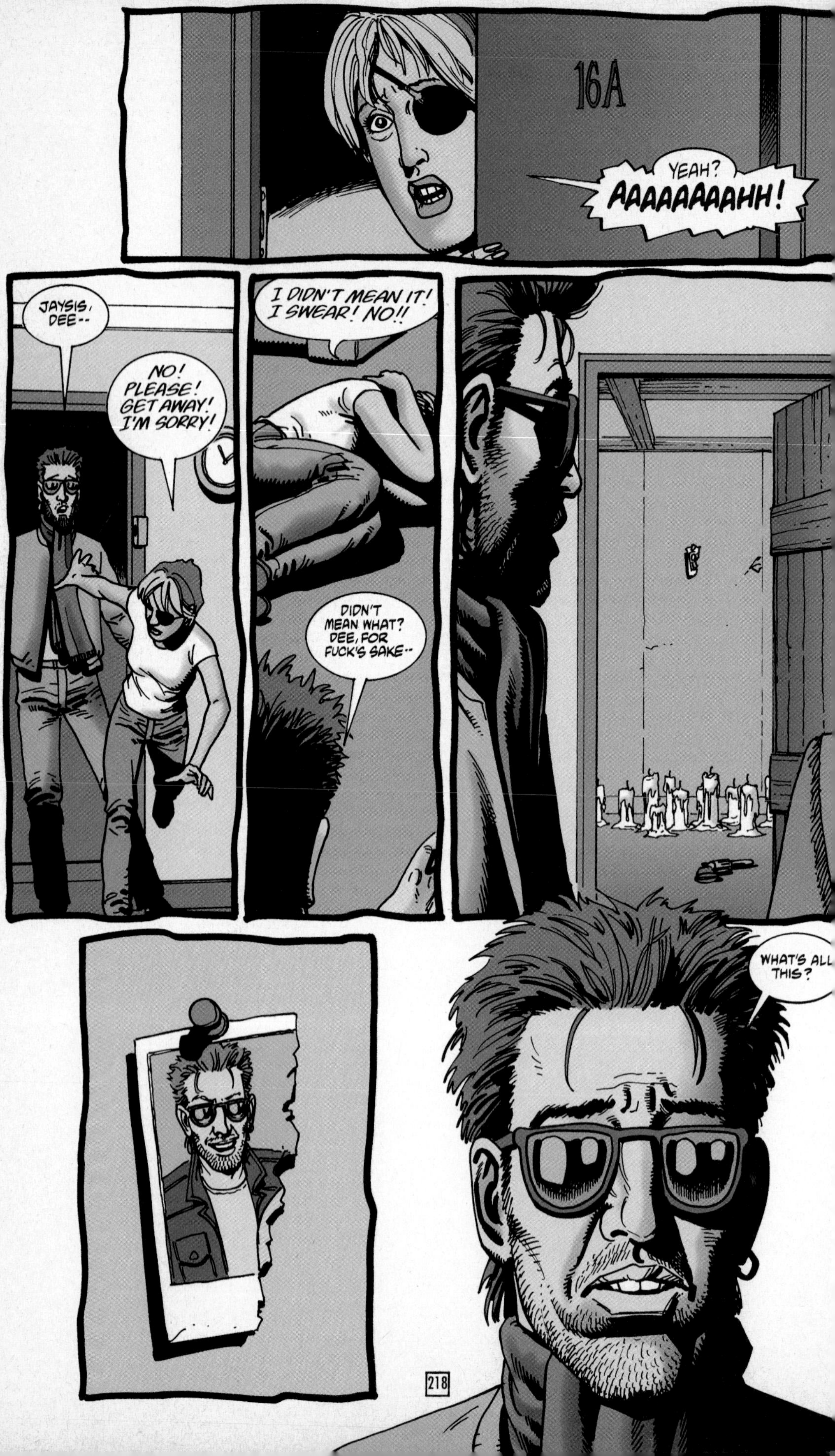

16A
YEAH? AAAAAAAAHH!
JAYSIS, DEE--
NO! PLEASE! GET AWAY! I'M SORRY!
I DIDN'T MEAN IT! I SWEAR! NO!!
DIDN'T MEAN WHAT? DEE, FOR FUCK'S SAKE--
WHAT'S ALL THIS?

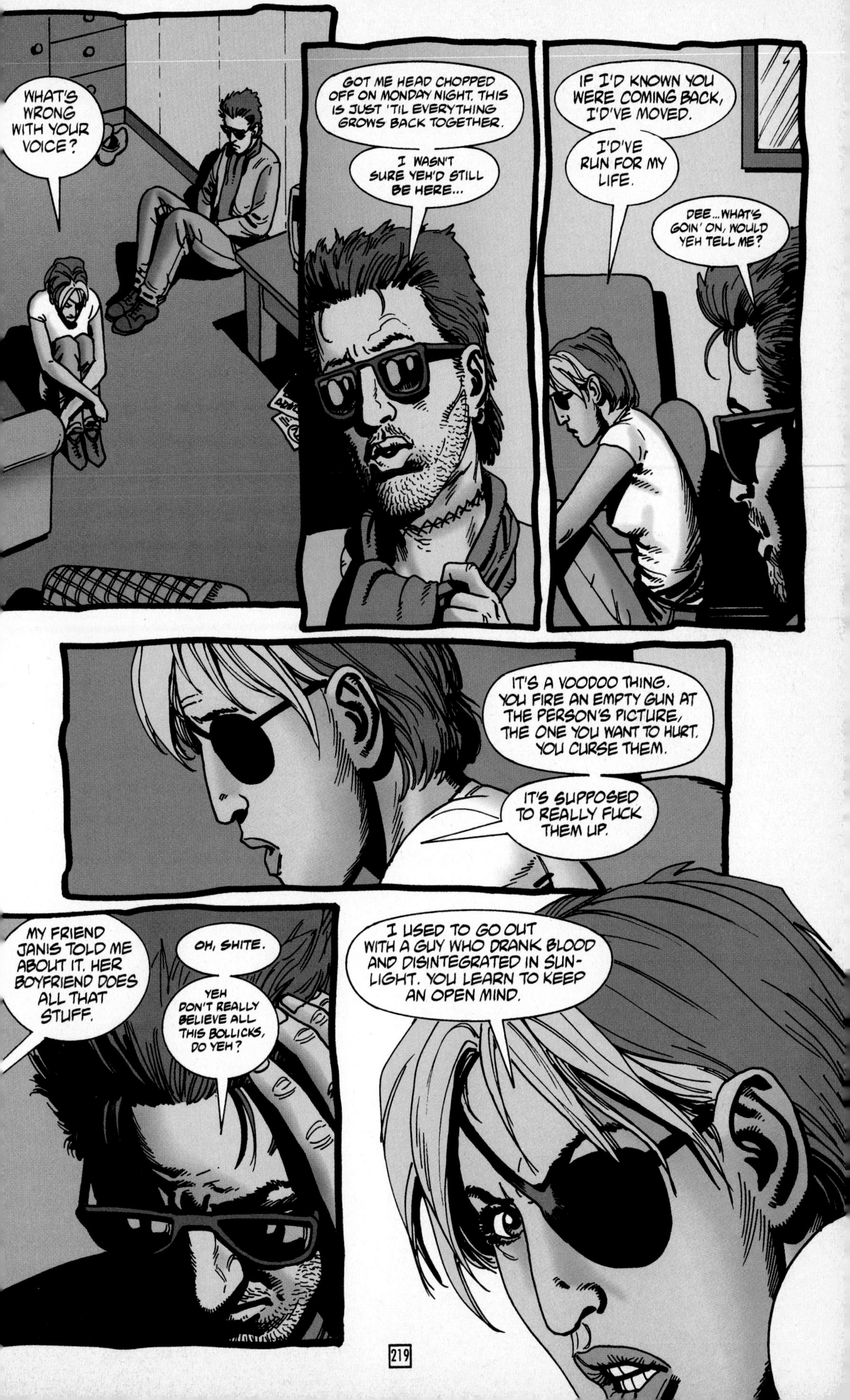

WHAT'S WRONG WITH YOUR VOICE?
GOT ME HEAD CHOPPED OFF ON MONDAY NIGHT. THIS IS JUST 'TIL EVERYTHING GROWS BACK TOGETHER.
I WASN'T SURE YEH'D STILL BE HERE...
IF I'D KNOWN YOU WERE COMING BACK, I'D'VE MOVED.
I'D'VE RUN FOR MY LIFE.
DEE...WHAT'S GOIN' ON, WOULD YEH TELL ME?
IT'S A VOODOO THING. YOU FIRE AN EMPTY GUN AT THE PERSON'S PICTURE, THE ONE YOU WANT TO HURT. YOU CURSE THEM.
IT'S SUPPOSED TO REALLY FUCK THEM UP.
MY FRIEND JANIS TOLD ME ABOUT IT. HER BOYFRIEND DOES ALL THAT STUFF.
OH, SHITE.
YEH DON'T REALLY BELIEVE ALL THIS BOLLICKS, DO YEH?
I USED TO GO OUT WITH A GUY WHO DRANK BLOOD AND DISINTEGRATED IN SUN-LIGHT. YOU LEARN TO KEEP AN OPEN MIND.

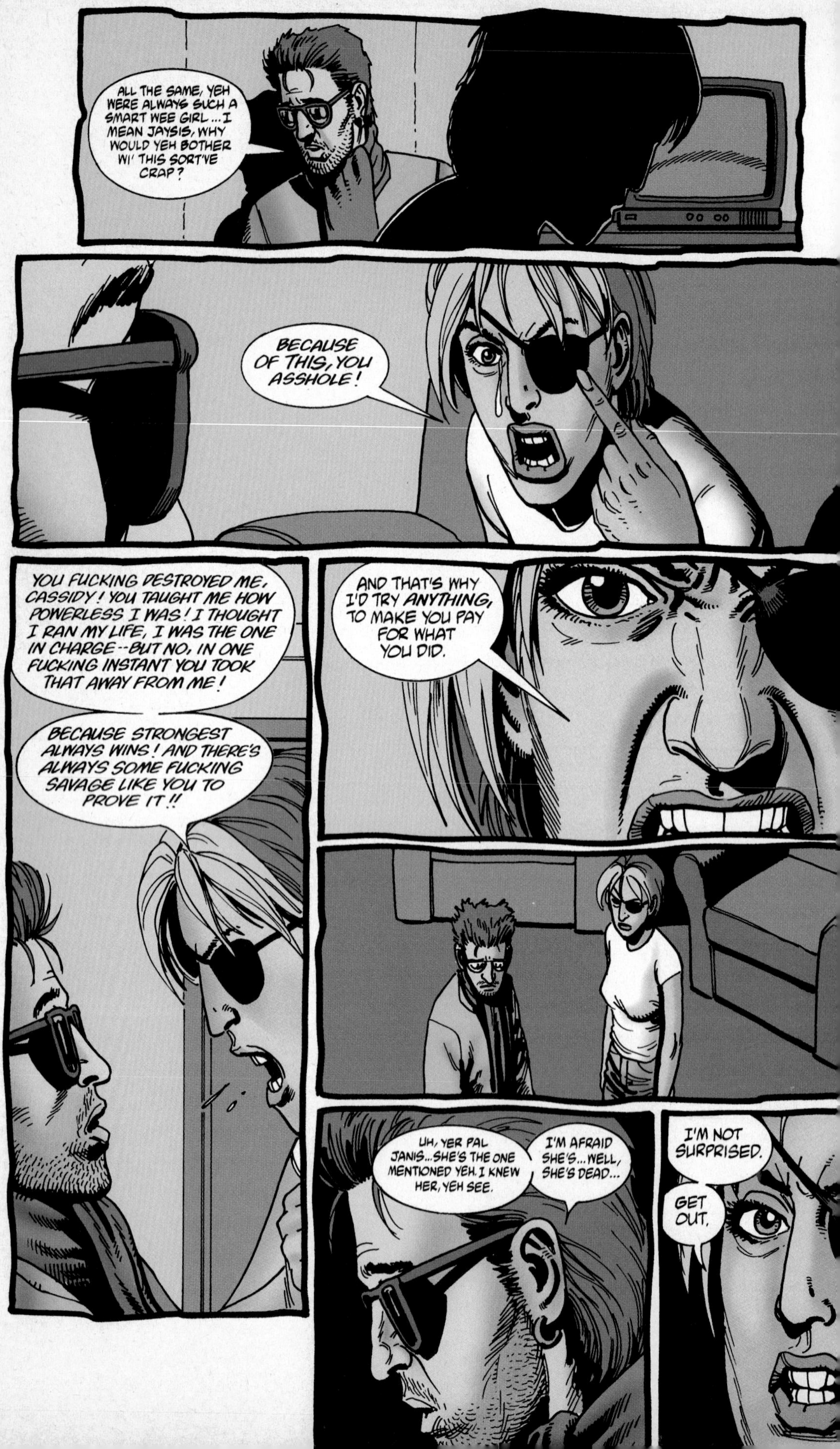
ALL THE SAME, YEH WERE ALWAYS SUCH A SMART WEE GIRL... I MEAN JAYSIS, WHY WOULD YEH BOTHER WI' THIS SORT'VE CRAP?
BECAUSE OF THIS, YOU ASSHOLE!
YOU FUCKING DESTROYED ME, CASSIDY! YOU TAUGHT ME HOW POWERLESS I WAS! I THOUGHT I RAN MY LIFE, I WAS THE ONE IN CHARGE--BUT NO, IN ONE FUCKING INSTANT YOU TOOK THAT AWAY FROM ME!
BECAUSE STRONGEST ALWAYS WINS! AND THERE'S ALWAYS SOME FUCKING SAVAGE LIKE YOU TO PROVE IT!!
AND THAT'S WHY I'D TRY ANYTHING, TO MAKE YOU PAY FOR WHAT YOU DID.
UH, YER PAL JANIS... SHE'S THE ONE MENTIONED YEH. I KNEW HER, YEH SEE.
I'M AFRAID SHE'S... WELL, SHE'S DEAD...
I'M NOT SURPRISED.
GET OUT.

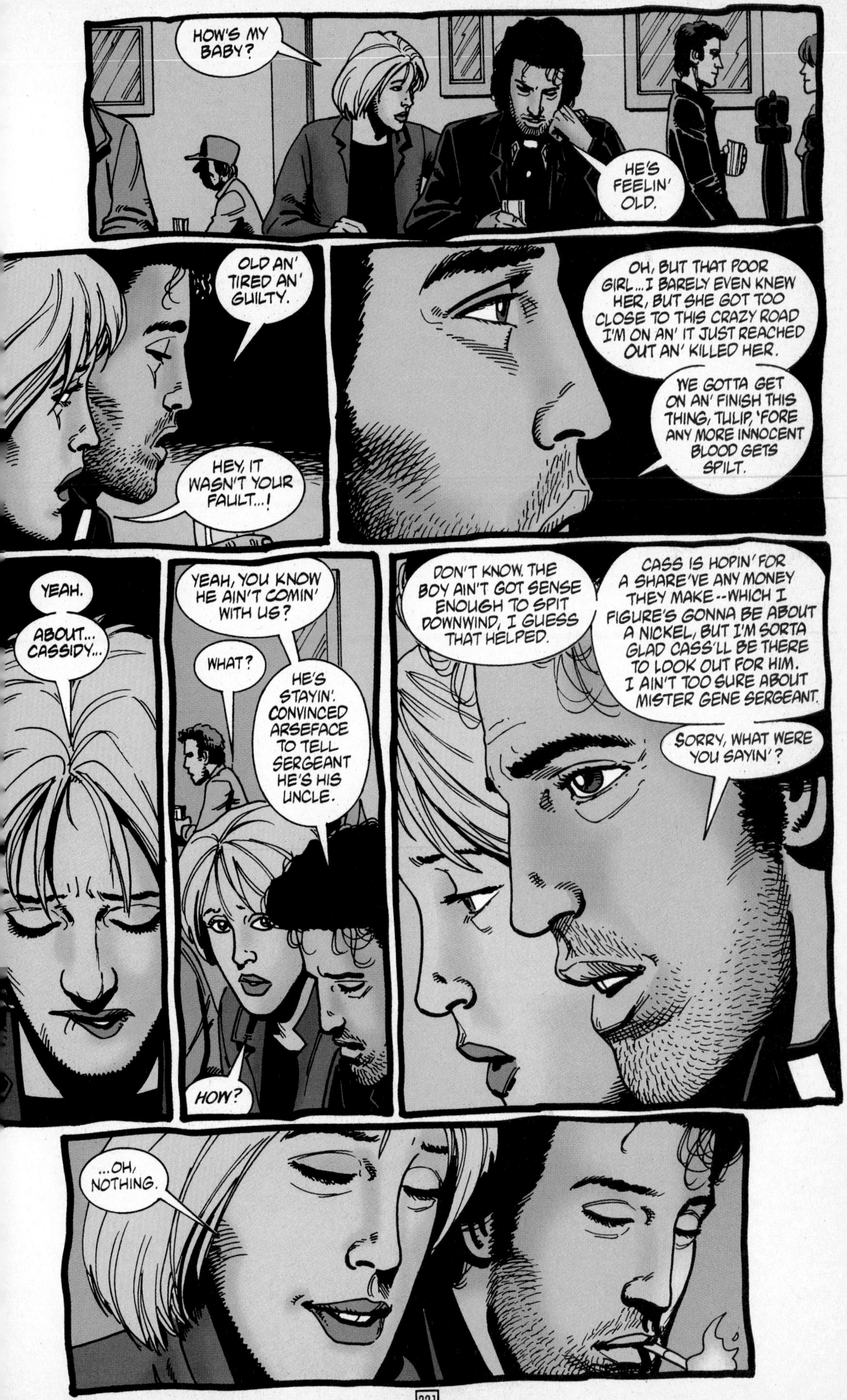
HOW'S MY BABY?
HE'S FEELIN' OLD.
OLD AN' TIRED AN' GUILTY.
HEY, IT WASN'T YOUR FAULT...!
OH, BUT THAT POOR GIRL...I BARELY EVEN KNEW HER, BUT SHE GOT TOO CLOSE TO THIS CRAZY ROAD I'M ON AN' IT JUST REACHED OUT AN' KILLED HER.
WE GOTTA GET ON AN' FINISH THIS THING, TULIP, 'FORE ANY MORE INNOCENT BLOOD GETS SPILT.
YEAH.
ABOUT... CASSIDY...
YEAH, YOU KNOW HE AIN'T COMIN' WITH US?
WHAT?
HE'S STAYIN'. CONVINCED ARSEFACE TO TELL SERGEANT HE'S HIS UNCLE.
HOW?
DON'T KNOW. THE BOY AIN'T GOT SENSE ENOUGH TO SPIT DOWNWIND, I GUESS THAT HELPED.
CASS IS HOPIN' FOR A SHARE'VE ANY MONEY THEY MAKE--WHICH I FIGURE'S GONNA BE ABOUT A NICKEL, BUT I'M SORTA GLAD CASS'LL BE THERE TO LOOK OUT FOR HIM. I AIN'T TOO SURE ABOUT MISTER GENE SERGEANT.
SORRY, WHAT WERE YOU SAYIN'?
...OH, NOTHING.

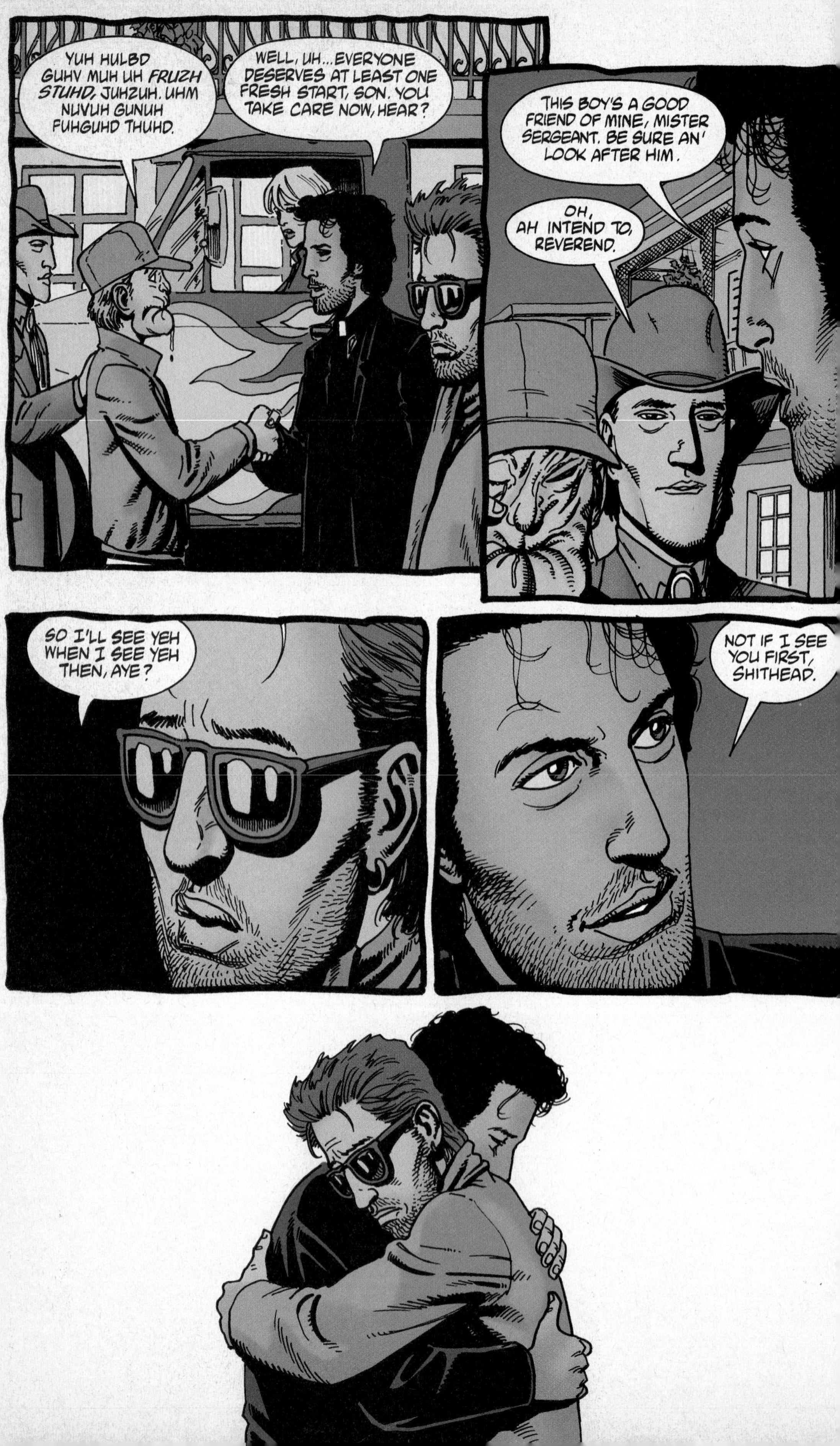
YUH HULBD GUHV MUH UH *FRUZH STUHD*, JUHZUH. UHM NUVUH GUNUH FUHGUHD THUHD.
WELL, UH... EVERYONE DESERVES AT LEAST ONE FRESH START, SON. YOU TAKE CARE NOW, HEAR?
THIS BOY'S A GOOD FRIEND OF MINE, MISTER SERGEANT. BE SURE AN' LOOK AFTER HIM.
OH, AH INTEND TO, REVEREND.
SO I'LL SEE YEH WHEN I SEE YEH THEN, AYE?
NOT IF I SEE YOU FIRST, SHITHEAD.

WHERE TO?

GONNA TAKE THE ANGEL'S ADVICE, TRY AN' ACCESS GENESIS DIRECTLY. I THINK I KNOW EXACTLY WHAT I NEED FROM IT.

GO WEST, YOUNG TULIP.

YOU UPSET ABOUT CASSIDY?

MM?

HE PROMISED YOU HE'D STAY 'TIL IT WAS FINISHED, AS I REMEMBER. SO MUCH FOR HIS WORD.

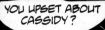

HE JUST GOT DECAPITATED, HONEY. THAT'LL PLUMB RATTLE SOME FELLAS.

FAME AN' FORTUNE BE FUCKED! HAVE YEZ ROOM FOR A BASTARD?